RUSSIA'S THEATRICAL PAST

RUSSIAN MUSIC STUDIES
SIMON A. MORRISON AND PETER SCHMELZ, EDITORS

RUSSIA'S
THEATRICAL PAST

Court Entertainment in the Seventeenth Century

CLAUDIA JENSEN, INGRID MAIER, and
STEPAN SHAMIN, with DANIEL C. WAUGH

INDIANA UNIVERSITY PRESS

This book is a publication of

Indiana University Press
Office of Scholarly Publishing
Herman B Wells Library 350
1320 East 10th Street
Bloomington, Indiana 47405 USA

iupress.org

© 2021 by Indiana University Press

All rights reserved

No part of this book may be reproduced or utilized in any form or by any means, electronic or mechanical, including photocopying and recording, or by any information storage and retrieval system, without permission in writing from the publisher. The paper used in this publication meets the minimum requirements of the American National Standard for Information Sciences—Permanence of Paper for Printed Library Materials, ANSI Z39.48-1992.

*Manufactured in the
United States of America*

First printing 2021

Library of Congress Cataloging-in-Publication Data

Names: Jensen, Claudia Rae, author. | Maier, Ingrid, author. | Shamin, S. M., author. | Waugh, Daniel Clarke, author.
Title: Russia's theatrical past : court entertainment in the seventeenth century / Claudia Jensen, Ingrid Maier, and Stepan Shamin ; with Daniel C. Waugh.
Other titles: Russian music studies.
Description: Bloomington : Indiana University Press, 2021. | Series: Russian music studies | Includes bibliographical references and index.
Identifiers: LCCN 2020043802 (print) | LCCN 2020043803 (ebook) | ISBN 9780253056337 (hardback) | ISBN 9780253056344 (paperback) | ISBN 9780253056351 (ebook)
Subjects: LCSH: Theater—Russia (Federation)—Moscow—History—17th century. | Music—Russia (Federation)—Moscow—17th century—History and criticism.
Classification: LCC PN2726.M6 J46 2021 (print) | LCC PN2726.M6 (ebook) | DDC 782.1/4094709032—dc23
LC record available at https://lccn.loc.gov/2020043802
LC ebook record available at https://lccn.loc.gov/2020043803

CONTENTS

Acknowledgments vii

A Note on Dates, Transliteration, and Translation xi

List of Abbreviations xiii

Introduction: The Comedians Come to Pskov   1

1. Court Music at Home and Abroad   19

2. The Theater of Diplomacy   57

3. Introducing Pickleherring: The Origins of the Russian Court Theater   104

4. The Plays and "Ballets" for the Tsar   141

5. The Play of Tamerlane   188

6. From Tamerlane to Tamerlane and Beyond   235

Bibliography   261

Index   285

ACKNOWLEDGMENTS

IT IS a great pleasure to acknowledge the support we received from the National Endowment for the Humanities for this project through its Collaborative Research Grant (RZ-51635-13). Each member of the research group contributed, gave feedback during all stages of the work, and benefited from the NEH's long-term commitment to this project. The project began through the collaborative work by Ingrid Maier and Claudia Jensen, who wrote an initial series of articles documenting the earliest phase of the Russian court theater. These articles formed the basis for the detailed treatment in the present study. During the course of the project, the authors worked together both in person and via voluminous emails and Dropbox folders, and we shared the results of archival studies that ranged from Moscow to Stockholm to London and beyond. Stepan Shamin did the bulk of the archival investigations in Moscow, and Maier did the same in Copenhagen, Uppsala, and Stockholm. Maier and Daniel Waugh also carried out archival work elsewhere in Europe, and we are grateful that three of the authors (Jensen, Maier, and Waugh) were able to work together in Uppsala during the course of this project; Maier and Shamin worked together in the Moscow archives as well. Our research is presented here in a narrative drafted by Jensen, with extensive input from the other authors, especially Maier.

We also owe thanks to scholars who generously shared their own research and linguistic expertise with us. We name many of them in our notes, but we'd like to include them here, as their contributions allowed us to cover such wide archival and linguistic territory in this book. Heiko Droste

(Stockholm) gave us expert advice on the Riksarkivet in Stockholm, helping us with transcriptions and translations of German-language sources there, and Kaarel Vanamölder (Tallinn/Tartu) investigated the Riga archives for us.

Many Russian scholars supported our work, and we give our thanks especially to Tat'iana Oparina and Egor Gorbatov, who, along with coauthor Shamin, produced (and shared) a series of detailed archival studies we have used extensively in this book. Other Russian scholars have helped us, including Kirill Khudin, Vadim Krys'ko, Aleksandr Lavrent'ev, and Tat'iana Matasovaia, and we thank Vera Chentsova, Dmitrii Liseitsev, and Maksim Moiseev for their input into the project. Our work would not have been possible without the support and expertise of the staff of the Russian State Archives of Ancient Documents (RGADA) in Moscow, to whom we give our thanks. We express our gratitude to Iskra Schwarcz, in Vienna, who consulted on our work on many occasions, and to Olena Jansson, in Uppsala, for help in locating some unpublished theses. We also note the generosity of American scholar Martha Lahana, who introduced us to the Swedish archival materials many years ago.

The music historical work for this project was greatly enhanced by the advice of Hendrik Schulze and Beth and Jon Glixon on the Venetian context, Nicola Usula and Christine Jeanneret for information about the Florentine court, and Michael Brennan, who shared his work on English travel accounts to Florence. We had a great deal of expert advice on the complex translations we present. For the Italian sources, we consulted with Dan Nosell and Nicla Riverso, and our understanding of the Latin sources was greatly enhanced by Bartosz Awianowicz, Hans Helander, Winfried Schumacher, and Marianne Wifstrand Schiebe. We also wish to acknowledge help from Jürgen Beyer during the initial stages of our research.

Two chapters of the present work expand on the English-language articles by Jensen and Maier, which were published during the course of this project in Russian translation as *Pridvornyi teatr v Rossii XVII veka* (2016), a publication that was supported by the *Riksbankens jubileumsfond* (Stockholm; RFP12-0055:1). We are grateful to Vladimir Bolotnikov and Tat'iana Marchenko for their work and skill in producing this Russian translation, and we appreciate the input from the participants at the "Newspapers and Beyond" conference, also sponsored by this fund, held in Uppsala in 2015. Two of our researchers, Shamin and Maier, also participated in the exposition held at the Kolomenskoe Museum-Reserve in Moscow (2018), "The Sovereign Entertainers: Theatrical Culture in Russia in the Seventeenth Century," which featured the relevant archival documents discussed throughout this volume.

We also enjoyed continuing support from the Slavic Languages and Literatures Department at the University of Washington (Seattle) and the university's library (especially from Michael Biggins, the Slavic librarian) and from Uppsala University Library, particularly from librarian Mirka Bialecka. Finally, we wish to acknowledge the helpful advice offered by the two anonymous readers for Indiana University Press, whose informed criticism made this book much stronger. In spite of all the advice and support we have received, we know that some errors inevitably remain, for which we take full responsibility.

A NOTE ON DATES, TRANSLITERATION, AND TRANSLATION

DATES ARE given according to the old style (o.s.; Julian) calendar used in Russia (and in many locations in the West), which, in the seventeenth century, was ten days behind the new style (n.s.; Gregorian) calendar. In some cases, for example when comparing contemporary accounts, we give both dates (for example, the False Dmitrii was killed on May 17/27, 1606). We use the Library of Congress transliteration system throughout, with a few exceptions for names and terms frequently encountered in English-language histories (for example, *boyar*). We have supplied all translations unless noted otherwise.

ABBREVIATIONS

ABBREVIATIONS: PRINTED AND REFERENCE SOURCES

Amburger-Datenbank	Erik-Amburger-Datenbank: Ausländer im vorrevolutionären Russland (https://www.amburger.ios-regensburg.de/)
ChOIDR	*Chteniia v Imperatorskom obshchestve istorii i drevnostei rossiiskikh*
DLB	*Dictionary of Literary Biography.* Vol. 150, *Early Modern Russian Writers, Late Seventeenth and Eighteenth Centuries.* Edited by Marcus C. Levitt. Detroit: Gale Research, 1995.
DNB	*Oxford Dictionary of National Biography* (www.oxforddnb.com)
DR	*Dvortsovye razriady po vysochaishemu poveleniiu izdannye II otdeleniem sobstvennoi ego Imperatorskogo velichestva kantseliarii.* 4 vols. St. Petersburg: Vtoroe otdelenie Sobstvennoi E. I. V. kantseliarii, 1850–1855.
DRV	*Drevniaia rossiiskaia vivliofika.* Edited by N. I. Novikov. 1st ed., 10 vols. St. Petersburg: Tipografiia Akademii nauk, 1773–1775; 2nd ed., 20 vols. Moscow: Tipografiia Kompanii tipograficheskoi, 1788–1791.

EEBO	Early English Books Online (eebo.chadwyck.com)
GMO	*Grove Music Online* (www.grovemusic.com)
JGO	*Jahrbücher für Geschichte Osteuropas*
OED	*Oxford English Dictionary* (www.oed.com)
OSP	*Oxford Slavonic Papers*
PDS	*Pamiatniki diplomaticheskikh snoshenii drevnei Rossii s derzhavami inostrannymi*. 10 vols. St. Petersburg: Vtoroe otdelenie Sobstvennoi E. I. V. kantseliarii, 1851–1871.
PKNO	*Pamiatniki kul'tury. Novye otkrytiia*
PSRL	*Polnoe sobranie russkikh letopisei*. Vol. 11. Moscow: Nauka, 1965; Vol. 18. St. Petersburg: M. A. Aleksandrov, 1913.
RBS	*Russkii biograficheskii slovar'*. 25 vols. St. Petersburg: Izdanie Imperatorskogo Russkogo istoricheskogo obshchestva, 1896–1918.
RIB	*Russkaia istoricheskaia biblioteka*. 39 vols. St. Petersburg and Leningrad: Arkheograficheskaia komissiia, 1872–1927.
RRD	*Ranniaia russkaia dramaturgiia (XVII–pervaia polovina XVIII v.)*. Edited by A. N. Robinson et al. 5 vols. Moscow: Nauka, 1972–1976.
SEER	*Slavonic and East European Review*
SRP XVIII v.	*Slovar' russkikh pisatelei XVIII veka* (http://lib.pushkinskijdom.ru/Default.aspx?tabid=460)
TODRL	*Trudy Otdela drevnerusskoi literatury Instituta russkoi literatury (Pushkinskogo doma) RAN*
VD16	Verzeichnis der im deutschen Sprachbereich erschienenen Drucke des 16. Jahrhunderts (https://www.bsb-muenchen.de/sammlungen/historische-drucke/recherche/vd-16/)
VD17	Verzeichnis der im deutschen Sprachraum erschienenen Drucke des 17. Jahrhunderts (https://www.vd17.de)
ZhMNP	*Zhurnal Ministerstva narodnogo prosveshcheniia*

ABBREVIATIONS: ARCHIVES AND
MANUSCRIPT COLLECTIONS

BAN	Biblioteka Rossiiskoi Akademii nauk (Library of the Russian Academy of Sciences), St. Petersburg

BN	Biblioteca nazionale, Florence
FB Gotha	Universitäts- und Forschungsbibliothek, Gotha
HAB	Herzog August Bibliothek, Wolfenbüttel
HHStA	Haus-, Hof- und Staatsarchiv, Vienna
IRLI	Institut russkoi literatury (Pushkinskii dom) Rossiiskoi Akademii nauk (Institute of Russian Literature, Pushkin House, Russian Academy of Sciences), St. Petersburg
LVVA	Latvijas Valsts vēstures arhīvs (Latvian State Historical Archives), Riga
MAP	Medici Archive Project (http://bia.medici.org/DocSources/Home.do)
RAC	Rigsarkivet (National Archives), Copenhagen
RAS	Riksarkivet (National Archives), Stockholm
RGADA	Rossiiskii gosudarstvennyi arkhiv drevnikh aktov (Russian State Archives of Ancient Documents), Moscow
RNB	Rossiiskaia natsional'naia biblioteka (Russian National Library), St. Petersburg
SBV	Stadsbiblioteket (City Library), Västerås
UUL	Uppsala University Library

RUSSIA'S THEATRICAL PAST

INTRODUCTION

The Comedians Come to Pskov

There was confusion on the outskirts of Pskov, a Russian town near the border with Livonia, in June 1644, when a group of visitors showed up unexpectedly. Fortunately, the bureaucrats knew exactly what to do: they kicked the problem upstairs. The local in charge of the border station, as per standard procedure, promptly dispatched the strangers into town, where the higher authorities could decide how to respond to their unplanned appearance. Those authorities, including the military governor and his staff, turned to the city's trade representative and to a Russian state translator, Matvei Veiger, in order to assemble the necessary information. Based on the documents the visitors provided to these officials, we can identify them as members of a German acrobatic troupe headed by Simon Dannenfels, a well-known itinerant tightrope walker and performer.[1]

By the time he found himself being interviewed in Pskov, the Strassburg-born Dannenfels was fifty years old and had been traveling internationally for at least half his life. Already in 1623–1624, when he was in his late twenties, he was performing in the newly founded Swedish town of Göteborg and corresponding with King Gustavus Adolphus; it appears that Dannenfels was the first foreign player to attempt, at his own initiative, to exploit the Swedish entertainment market. In his letter to the king, he described one of his routines: tightrope walking without a balancing pole while wielding bared swords. Following this Swedish excursion, he visited (probably) Cologne and then went back home to Strassburg, and at some point, he married and had children. He also traveled south, where he was recorded in Brixen (in

South Tyrol) in 1639 and Innsbruck, probably in the same year, as a tightrope flier (*Seilflieger*).[2]

The Pskov documents report that when he arrived there, Dannenfels was traveling with his wife, Rosina, and four children: two sons and two daughters. He had also acquired three other members for his troupe: Konrad, Matthias (a young trainee traveling with Konrad), and Samuel. The inquiries about the group's intended activities revealed that it was at the end of a very long tour. Dannenfels and his family had been performing in Holland beginning in May 1643. After that, they went to Denmark, and from there, in June, they crossed over to Stockholm. All of this was routine, not only for Dannenfels himself but also for other itinerant troupes—they were following familiar paths marked out by many other such traveling companies. The following year, in April 1644, they were in the Swedish Baltic territories, visiting first Reval (Tallinn) and then Dorpat (Tartu). In the latter city, they got a pass to continue on to Pskov.

The troupe members' intentions appear to have been modest: they simply wanted to perform their act in Pskov. They had no plans, they said, to go farther, asking only for permission to remain where they were and put on some shows. And to indicate what their act was, they handed over one of their posters—an extremely rare example of an advertisement by a strolling company, surviving when it was buried in the archives by the authorities in Moscow (see fig. I.1).[3] The all-purpose advertising copy underneath the illustration reads, roughly:

> We herewith announce to one and all that a foreign artist has arrived here, who will display many artistic and entertaining tricks, which will be of enjoyment to everyone. Namely, a young man and a girl may be seen; they most gracefully perform various beautiful dances on the rope; also a man, who will perform all kinds of dances on a higher rope, as shown in the illustration. There he will display marvelous and artistic acrobatic routines. There will also be shown various thrilling acrobatic leaps by two or three youths as well as by the aforementioned girl. In addition, they will run with bowls and glasses. And there will be tricks with two unsheathed swords, along with 50 or 60 threads threaded into one needle. Moreover, there will be masquerades and performances in the English comic style. Whoever wishes to see this performance should come to the place noted below [in the blank space at the bottom of the poster].

All of these marvels, and more, are illustrated in the drawing, which shows that the Dannenfels troupe delivered the entire package of contemporary

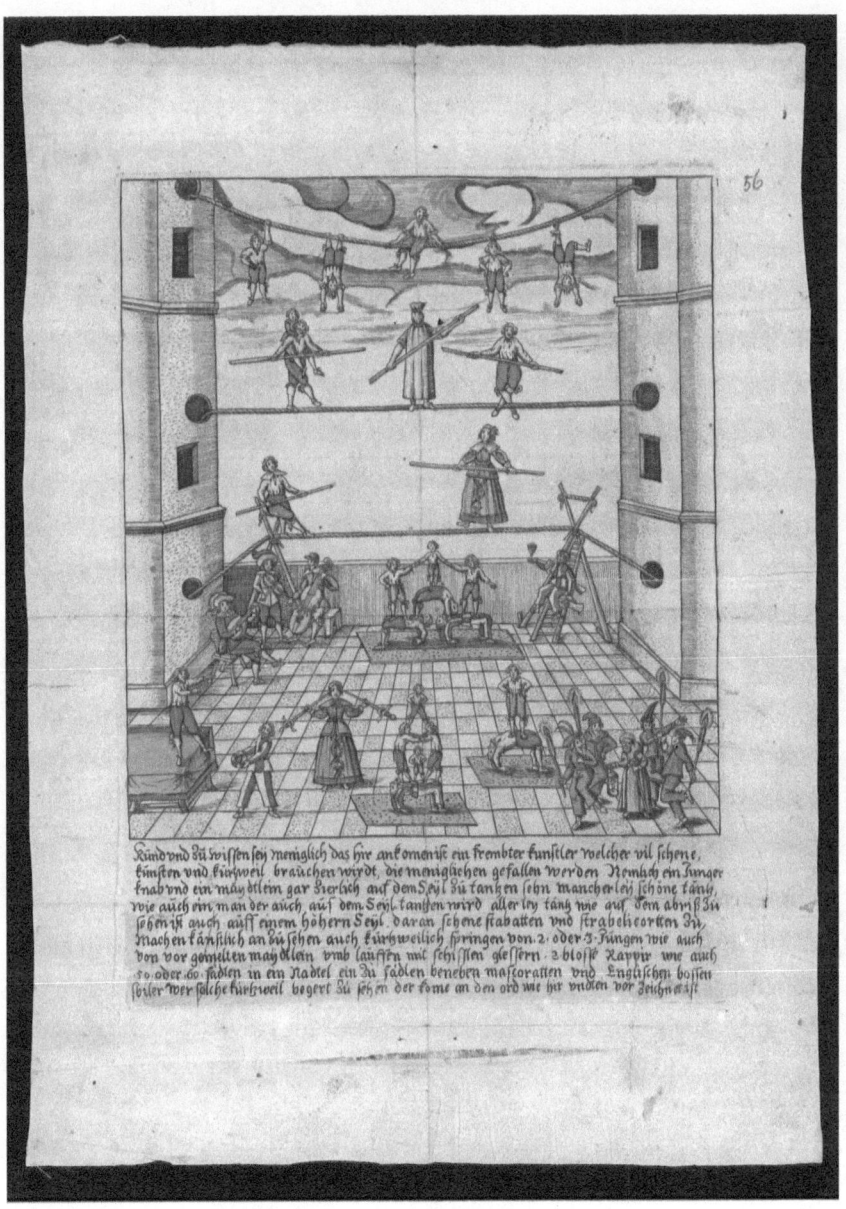

FIG. I.1

The Dannenfels poster
(RGADA, f. 53, op. 1, 1644, No. 6, fol. 56, used by permission)

popular entertainment. The images give us a sampling of various tricks one might see the troupe perform, each involving roughly the same numbers of performers as indicated in the text, about five or six total. Could this be Simon himself, with the striped clothing and the jutting beard, forming the bottom of the two human pyramids on the floor, holding out his hat (*front left*), and on the ladder (*right rear*), holding a goblet and pitcher? The masquerade (*lower right*) is advertised as being in the "English" style, reflecting the enduring popularity of the English performers who flooded the Continent beginning in the late sixteenth century and continuing through the seventeenth century. Advertising oneself as "English," whether or not there were any actual English performers, was a widespread and bankable tactic. The various tricks are accompanied by musicians tucked into the back left corner of the stage, playing lute, violin, and gamba. The rope setup is elaborate, providing for the thrilling performances at the highest level as depicted in the illustration, where we see creative methods of suspending what appears to be one of the young members of the troupe on a slack rope. The middle rope displays tightrope tricks (again, perhaps Simon himself, who may be carrying his youngest child on his back). The gimmick with the unsheathed blades is performed probably by one of the daughters, gripping the blades and threatening her eyesight; she is also depicted on the low tightrope. All in all, we get a real sense of the popular and up-to-date routines offered by an experienced group of players who had been plying their wares successfully for many years and in many places. Indeed, some of the same tricks displayed in the Dannenfels poster are mentioned in a later German novel, which includes advertisements for a rope-dancer's company that performed several skills requiring "naked swords," various "artistic jumps," a play, and—apparently still quite a draw—"a young lady who will thread one hundred and forty threads into a needle while turning them continuously."[4]

Clearly Dannenfels made an effort to provide the Pskov authorities with all the information necessary to describe their proposal, and following standard procedure, the locals in charge sent all of it to Moscow even though the answer to the troupe's request might have seemed obvious: go away. Indeed, when the documentation reached the Ambassadorial Chancery in Moscow, this is exactly the answer that was issued. The reply arrived back in Pskov on July 10, and three days later, the troupe was escorted to the border. So what, beyond normal bureaucratic punting, made the local officials hesitate in the first place? It is at this point that the request of this adventurous traveling troupe got caught up, purely coincidentally, with larger political goals of the Russian rulers.

A clue to the Pskov authorities' anxieties about this request lies in the location of the documents: in Moscow, they were filed in the Danish affairs section of the records (*Datskie dela*). Specifically, they were filed with other documentation that had been generated as a result of Tsar Mikhail Fedorovich's plan to marry his daughter, Irina Mikhailovna, to the Danish count Waldemar Christian, a son of the Danish king Christian IV. It was a messy and protracted affair that was probably hopeless from the start. The plans ostensibly foundered on Waldemar's refusal to convert to Orthodoxy, but the motivations for the initial proposal as well as the reasons for its failure were numerous and broad.[5]

Before the project failed completely (at one point, Waldemar attempted an armed breakout from Moscow), the Russians had worked to make a good impression on the intended bridegroom. In preparing for Waldemar's visit, the tsar sought out specialists who might add a bit of European luster to his court. Among the court's contacts abroad was one "Justus Filimonatus," a pseudonym for Laurentius Grelle, a news agent in Swedish service from at least the mid-1630s. By 1643 Grelle/Filimonatus—now stationed in Riga—had begun sending news compilations to Russia, using the pseudonym Filimonatus to keep his activities secret from the Swedish authorities. Some of his letters were read and translated in Pskov by the tsar's translator there, Matvei Veiger—the very same translator who was involved in interrogating the Dannenfels troupe about their plans. The well-informed Grelle was thus perfectly positioned to scout out possible hires for the court.[6]

Grelle reported specifically on his efforts to hire "a cook, players [performers], and entertainers" for the Waldemar effort.[7] *Entertainer* (*poteshnik*) was a kind of catchall word to indicate people who could do interesting and amusing things. For example, several times in Grelle's dispatches he describes "fire entertainers"—that is, people who could mount fireworks displays. Waldemar brought some fireworks experts in his entourage as well.[8] But the term also indicated the kind of staged entertainments the Dannenfels company might produce—indeed, in the Russian translation of the troupe's travel documents, Dannenfels is labeled as a "poteshnik" several times.[9] The Pskov authorities, and specifically those who had dealt with Grelle's communications in the past, would thus certainly have been alert to this word, as it fit into their concurrent hiring efforts in anticipation of the Danish bridegroom's arrival. It was only natural, then, that when the German "poteshniki" showed up in Pskov, the authorities there wisely decided to make no assumptions: as far as they knew, these entertainers might have been part of Moscow's plan.

There is no evidence that Grelle had anything to do with the Dannenfels troupe's excursion to Pskov or that the acrobats had been in Riga, where Grelle worked. However, he was certainly the right person to ask about such entertainers for the Danish bridegroom, for at the very time of this intensive exchange of information, in mid-1644, a traveling acting company did indeed appear in Riga. It was a large group, eighteen members, and they stayed for a fairly long time, from April 11 to May 24, 1644. This is almost certainly the same group of "English comedians" who submitted an application to the Danzig authorities in July of that year, having previously traveled to Riga and Königsberg.[10] Such a travel circuit made sense, as it prioritized areas that were relatively unscathed by what must have appeared, on the ground, as the endless ebb and flow of the conflicts collectively (and later) known as the Thirty Years' War.

Might Dannenfels have heard about Waldemar's wedding plans when his troupe passed through Reval or Dorpat in April 1644? If so, it would have been reasonable and enterprising to take advantage of the news, especially when he and the troupe were (relatively speaking) already in the area. Royal weddings had always offered good opportunities for traveling players, for example at the Danish-Saxon "Great Wedding" of 1634 in Copenhagen and, a little later (for the Dutch troupe headed by Jan Baptist van Fornenbergh), at the wedding at Gottorp Palace (1649).[11]

Putting all this together, one can understand why the Dannenfels troupe might have been willing to explore new territories by going to Pskov after its Baltic tour—other performing groups were active in roughly the same areas. As the documentation was moving between Pskov and Moscow and back again, the troupe remained in Pskov, where it stayed for about a month. We have no evidence indicating what the troupe members did there, and nothing to suggest that anyone in Pskov saw them perform. They would have had no other way to earn any money; a rather desperate plea from a different acting troupe, in Riga in January 1648, begs permission to perform publicly in order to fill its coffers so that it could move on to Stockholm, as it had planned.[12] Whether the Dannenfels group made a similar request in Pskov is unknown. It is likely that the troupe members went to Riga directly after they had been escorted to the Russian border, because the city council there decided, on July 30, 1644, that "a dancer ... who also has been dancing in Stockholm" and his group "cannot be allowed [to perform in Riga]"—the description fits the Dannenfels troupe's travel patterns.[13] After the summer of 1644, we have no other information about Dannenfels at all.

The arrival and departure of the Dannenfels party may seem like a small historical blip, perhaps a good story for the players to share when they returned to more familiar territory, but the contexts and ramifications of this likely nonperformance are telling. The preservation of the poster is, in itself, remarkable. Furthermore, as far as we know, this was the first time that a traveling foreign entertainment troupe had ever expressed interest in coming, on its own terms, to perform in Russian territory; as we shall see over the course of this study, it was not the last. All of the elements that made this story possible—the availability of itinerant players such as Dannenfels, the recruiting of entertainers for the tsar, the bureaucratic process and record keeping, the Russian interest in information gathering from the West—bring Russia firmly into the patterns of cultural commerce that have been so well studied in the context of Western theatrical and musical history.

The present study explores how performative cultures of the West, particularly theater and music, were imported, realized, transformed, and expanded at the Russian court in the seventeenth century. Our focus is on the establishment of a court theater for Tsar Aleksei Mikhailovich in 1672, for which multiple plays were written, performance venues established, acting troupes assembled, and elaborate visual and musical preparations supplied at great cost and effort—and to equally great delight on the part of the tsar and his family. In examining these transformations, we rely on approaches developed by historians of early modern theater in the West, especially on the concept of intertheater. As historian William West has written, "Intertheatricality is theatre from the bottom up. It is recognizing how performances are made up out of other performances, treating performance as its own archive."[14] Anston Bosman relies on intertheater in considering the movement of English players to the Continent, and particularly throughout Dutch- and German-speaking territories, at the beginning of the seventeenth century—in other words, describing precisely the activities that resulted in troupes like the Dannenfels players, with their "performances in the English comic style." As Bosman writes, the theater that emerged in the Netherlands and in Germany over the course of the century was neither

English nor German nor Dutch. Instead, he proposes, "we must recognize their theater as a hybrid, a developing phenomenon no longer English and not yet European, assimilable neither to a unidirectional model of cultural transference nor to a strictly reciprocal one of cultural exchange. To describe it will require a vocabulary that acknowledges both the continuum of transculturation across which this theater moves and the temporary stable configurations in which it can legitimately be arrested."[15] In Bosman's formulation, intertheater "draws attention equally to processes of interaction and interference between two established systems and to the production of a third intermediary norm." Such a measured evaluation was not always the case. In the words of an important early scholar of this repertoire, Albert Cohn, such Continental theatrical transfers "obliterated all traces of higher art in the dramatic treatment" of the English source plays, a view that made it difficult to plumb the cultural resonances of these renditions.[16]

In the context of our study, the multiple views and entry points provided by intertheater help us understand the Russian court theater as part of a broader continuum both geographical and repertorial and as just such an "intermediary norm"—a relevant and adaptable expression of its own place and time that can, simultaneously, be situated within theatrical presentations on the Continent. In a larger sense, the concept complements discussions among Russian historians, who have been exploring just such multivalent historical shifting points. These discussions have focused especially on the ramifications and boundaries of the periodization of Russian history, an issue particularly fraught given the impact of what one historian, Paul Bushkovitch, calls the "demiurge" Peter the Great. In addressing these debates, Nancy Shields Kollmann borrows an approach from the Polish historian Jerzy Topolski, which she characterizes, elegantly, as nesting: Topolski, she says, aims for a periodization of history that "retains multiplicity and multivocality," employing "nested stages of gradual change."[17] Bushkovitch has focused on both the speed and the role of cultural change, questioning, succinctly: "Why did the importation of culture and customs occur, and what difference did it make to Russia as an early modern society and state?"[18] We explore some of these interrelationships, particularly theatrical, but also in the context of broader cultural flexing points, throughout this volume.

One way in which the Russian elite was exposed directly to Western performance art was through diplomacy, and throughout this study, we consider how such exchange introduced Russian representatives to this cultural currency of Western politics. In his recent study of early modern diplomacy, Jan Hennings posits diplomatic practice itself as "a product of continuous cultural exchange," and this approach provides a useful model for our study as well.[19] The famous claim by the Courland native Jacob Rautenfels, in which he states clearly that the tsar was motivated to create his own theatrical entertainment after "hearing through reports" that such practice was popular in the West, strikes us as eminently true. Indeed, we see that it was largely in the context of diplomacy, in which the visiting dignitaries were, ideally, meant to be professionally open and curious about their hosts, that theatrical experiences were initially filtered back to the Russian court. But it was not only the great embassies that reveal details of Russian court culture—such concerns also feature in the more routine exchanges, particularly with one of Russia's closest neighbors, Sweden. The nearly constant representation of Swedish interests in Moscow, especially after midcentury, has provided us with some of the most vivid surviving descriptions of Russian court culture in the whole of the seventeenth century.

As Dannenfels's experience shows, bureaucratic protocol forms a crucial basis for our investigations. For diplomatic reports, such protocol determines not just what the Russian representatives observed but also why particular situations were worthy of inclusion in an official account at all. Although limited by the formal constraints of their reports, the visiting diplomats approached their assignments largely with gusto and curiosity—indeed, in their capacity as diplomats, such openness was part of their job description. Their awe at the spectacles they saw, especially in Italy, matches that of other eager travelers, and in some cases, we even see them abandoning their diplomatic dignity to ask in amazement how everything worked, to be shown the inner mechanisms producing the marvels they witnessed on stage.

More broadly, the government's bureaucratic organization, particularly for payment records, provides intimate glimpses of administrative preoccupations throughout the period. Although such records are especially important (and, fortunately, were published) for the few glorious years in the early 1670s when the official court theater functioned in Moscow, such records extend throughout the century, created by squadrons of scribes and secretaries laboring in the ever-flourishing Muscovite bureaucracy over this time. These bureaucrats, too, thus eventually played their own roles in the court theater and its other entertainments.

In addition to such internal record keeping, our study considers the wider context of the communications networks in the seventeenth century, a time during which, throughout Europe, there was a revolution in the means and efficiency by which news could be transmitted from place to place. Russia, although somewhat belatedly, joined this lively network, and this contact affected our specific areas of interest, particularly after the middle of the century. Letters could be posted with a fairly reasonable expectation of their being received, thanks to the postal system linking Russia with the developed networks, especially with the northern European states after the 1660s. Indeed, one of our participants could plausibly blame delays in communication on the post and could then turn around and use that same network to arrange future travel plans and propose alternative performance opportunities.

Another news route into Russia was via the *kuranty*, the translated foreign news excerpts selected for the tsar on an increasingly regular basis over the second half of the century. These summaries came from a variety of sources, primarily published and manuscript newspapers and also pamphlets. (The Russian name, from the Dutch *courant(e)*, indicates the general, primarily northern European, provenance of such news sources.)[20] The information and communications revolution, which influenced the tiny case of the Dannenfels party's travel adventures, created jobs for people like "Filimonatus" and hundreds of others, who made their living passing on news and information to governments and other willing recipients. Finally, because diplomatic exchange was often closely linked with the news agents who provided newspapers with items to print, we also see that information about the theatrical activities in Moscow occasionally spilled out into the Western press.

All of this brings us to another of our overall themes, one already touched on: the role of northern Europe in the culture of seventeenth-century Russia. The very nature of our source material—particularly kuranty summaries, reports from long-term diplomatic representatives stationed in Moscow, and newspapers—underscores this influence. It is especially prominent in the case of the court theater, for Moscow's Foreign Quarter, populated heavily by northern European commercial and military representatives, was the source not only of the planners, playwrights, and actors for the theater but also of the underlying experiences and assumptions of performance, based on this community's previous exposures to comedies performed by traveling players on the Continent, school plays, and other amateur productions.

This influence sets the stage for the interests so clearly demonstrated later by Peter the Great. Peter's interest in Holland and England, as we see in his own Great Embassy at the very end of the century, was naturally focused on scientific and technical (especially naval) expertise in these countries, but by this time, northern cultures had long permeated the Russian court. Peter was not the first Russian ruler to discover the delights of Moscow's Foreign Quarter; although his father, Tsar Aleksei Mikhailovich, did not (as far as we know) visit this neighborhood, he imbibed liberally of its talents, most obviously through the court theater. In this sense, it might be said that, instead of visiting the Foreign Quarter, Tsar Aleksei arranged for the Foreign Quarter to visit him. Artamon Matveev, the tsar's theatrical impresario and the closest and most influential adviser late in his reign, was well aware of the Foreign Quarter's resources, which functioned as his readily available talent pool from the very beginning of the theatrical project.

Our observations of the northern European (especially Dutch and German) roots for the Russian court theater thus emphasize a range of cultural networks that complement those traditionally considered for seventeenth-century Russia, which generally focus on Ukrainian and Belarusian church and intellectual traditions. The wide-ranging net cast by the language of intertheater is thus useful in a much broader sense—the concepts of "temporary stable configurations" and "third intermediary norms" are relevant in describing not just Tsar Aleksei's court theater but other aspects of Russian culture over this period as well.

One such evolving cultural process with wide ramifications in Russia during this time is what might be termed audience formation: that is, how the ruling elite, particularly the tsar and the royal family—frequent participants in sacred and secular ceremony—also became engaged in performing the role of an audience. Entertainments produced for the enjoyment of the ruling family were nothing new, as we see in several of our chapters, but over the course of the seventeenth century this process, like many others at the Russian court, became increasingly systematized. The combined interest in performative entertainment and its associated emphasis (actually, a requirement) on the assembly of an appreciative viewing audience can be illustrated by an important antecedent for the court theater: the regular productions of liturgical drama through the middle of the century, based on the story of the three boys cast into the fiery furnace, from the biblical book of Daniel.[21] This tradition seems to have died out largely in the 1640s, with some limited examples seeping into the 1660s, and so was not a direct inspiration for Tsar Aleksei's court plays. Nevertheless, such annual productions, performed on the Sunday of the Forefathers in mid-December and with dramatic theatrical effects (real fire in the furnace!), costumes, systematic instruction for the youthful performers, and continuing roles for certain players, were a highlight of the religious calendar, and the tradition must certainly figure, even if tangentially, into the court's assumptions of and organizational approach to dramatic performances.[22]

Such audience-building experiences were reinforced by the declamations created later by Simeon Polotskii, the erudite Belarusian-born, Kiev-educated cleric who brought his poetic skills, and his students, to the Russian court in the decade of the 1660s, where he produced a series of performed recitations in honor of court and church events.[23] Simeon's work dovetails with the theatrical interests and exposures of the Moscow court in many ways, in addition to providing "audience training" for the royal family. Simeon wrote a play on the theme of the biblical furnace story, the subject that had been the featured event over the first half of the century in the liturgical dramas; as we suggest briefly in our later discussion, Simeon's furnace play seems to have been written in response to, not in anticipation of or in coordination with, the successful productions at the tsar's court theater. With his reference to a familiar dramatically rendered story, reliance on his own declamatory performance style, and use of young students as performers, Simeon's furnace play represents his own "intermediary norm" by invoking existing, if not necessarily current, theatricalized subjects and contexts. Simeon's role in the performative life of the Russian court thus blurs a narrative that has traditionally focused primarily on his role as a representative of Belarusian and Ukrainian intellectual stimuli in Moscow. Although not denying in any way the importance of such intellectual traditions or Simeon's role in transmitting them, in the specific case of the plays, we see an artist like Simeon Polotskii not so much as a pathbreaker but as a respondent who is following, and reinterpreting, popular established court entertainments.

An example from the visual arts reinforces this wide-ranging cultural blend in late seventeenth-century Russia, for which academic debates among art historians interestingly parallel those by historians evaluating Continental theatrical productions of this same period. These debates focus on the artist Simon Ushakov, who was active at the Moscow court in the last third of the century. In analyzing Ushakov's artistic works, scholars have long considered the role of the models provided by the illustrated Bible (*Theatrum Biblicum*, 1643) by Jan Visscher (better known as Johannes Piscator), a "main source of the new elements evident in Russian painting of the last decades of the seventeenth century," as characterized by cultural historian James Cracraft. Did such influence impair or stimulate Ushakov's work, or as in Cracraft's summary of the long-standing art historical debates, was Ushakov a "tragic failure" who "slavishly" imitated Western models or was he a "hero of a golden age," creatively recombining received materials into a satisfying whole?[24] Intertheater offers a different vocabulary to describe such questions, in the same way it did for theater historians: a "third intermediary norm" (in place of a "slavish copy" or Cohn's "obliteration" of higher art in Continental dramatic renditions) seems tailor-made to characterize Ushakov's artistic creations.

One of the most popular elements in the court's theatrical productions was music, provided by singers and instrumentalists in a variety of dramatic and decorative contexts. Such music, like the performed dramas it enhanced, did not parachute into a void but emerged into a dense landscape of long-standing traditions of religious and secular music at court. Russia, of course, was awash in highly developed liturgical singing and the requisite professional ensembles that performed a wide range of monophonic and polyphonic styles.[25] The emergence, after midcentury, of the genre known as *kontsert*—large polychoral vocal works based generally on liturgical texts— featured musical effects that required trained singers who could slip readily between solo and ensemble textures, execute quick runs and imitative passages, and sustain the genre's large formal structures. The presence and development of kontserty reflect, in part, the effect in Russia of Ukrainian-influenced singing (which itself incorporated elements from points farther west), and parties of visiting Ukrainian clerics served as pools for musical recruitment by the Moscow court, as we will see in a variety of contexts. The intense cultivation of kontserty at the Russian court over the last third of the century also demonstrates the emphasis on hierarchical organization and regulation, with increasing, and increasingly specialized, ranks of singers necessary to perform such pieces, in addition to other kinds of music required for church services.

But the more relevant connection to the music of the court theater is, naturally, in the realm of nonliturgical singing and its associated performers.

As we see throughout our study, the court was frequently entertained by singing, often featuring styles and performers drawing on secular traditions. This kind of music making was not necessarily related to the itinerant countryside entertainers known as *skomorokhi* but reflects long-standing entertainment practices, often produced in house in relaxed, intimate settings, for the amusement of the royal family. (We pursue the distinction between secular and skomorokh music making at several points in our narrative: they were not synonymous.) Another relevant musical genre, in terms of the theater, is the *kant*, a Western-influenced style that was smaller in scale and less elaborate than the kontserty. Kanty were usually written for three vocal parts and were generally syllabic and strophic, much in the style of seasonal carols. Here, too, we can expand Simeon Polotskii's cultural footprint, in this case via his rhymed setting of the Psalter (which was, in turn, based on Polish poetic models and published in an edition featuring an illustration by Ushakov). Simeon's texts were set as a collection of kanty by the Russian composer Vasilii Titov, who also wrote many kontserty—the professional musical worlds of late seventeenth-century Moscow, like the professional musical worlds of all European courts, were small and overlapping.[26] As we suggest, such familiar, nonliturgical singing was a natural crossover point, one that could be easily understood and rendered by the young foreign performers in the court plays, following their own singing traditions (particularly Protestant hymns, which are also syllabic and strophic) yet equally appreciated by the royal audience. This malleable singing style made a big impression from the very beginning of the court's theatrical exposure, reflecting multiple traditions of entertainment for the royal family.

Our focus in this volume is narrow: court performances, especially the development of the court theater in the early 1670s. We use this tight focus, however, to highlight a much broader range of Russia's cultural interests and interactions, especially vis-à-vis the West. This book is organized roughly chronologically yet with this basic theme of performative culture at court and its sources in diplomacy and communication at its core. Chapter 1 introduces the importance of diplomatic contacts in exposing to the Russian court and its elite up-to-date Western performance styles, especially musical, and how they might have been realized in Moscow beginning in the mid-sixteenth century. We then explore the variety of court entertainments that emerged or were renewed after the establishment of the Romanov dynasty in the person of the teen-aged Mikhail Fedorovich, elected as tsar in 1613. Our work relies here on new archival documentation to amplify or correct previous scholarship, offering a fuller picture of how the Russian court viewed and produced entertainments for its members, and how they might have become acquainted with foreign performers and practices. We also keep in mind the notably bumpy path in such productions and acquisitions—the Russian court reacted, adopted, and adapted in fits and starts, influenced by both grand political occurrences and intimate domestic affairs.

In chapter 2, we focus intensively on the role of diplomacy in Russian exposure to Western entertainment, beginning in the mid-seventeenth century, when Russian diplomats had some especially thrilling encounters with Italian music theater in trips to the heart of the new genre of opera, the Venetian Republic, and other Italian states. Although, as our first chapter indicates, such encounters were not wholly new, the Russian diplomatic missions beginning in the 1650s seem to mark a kind of tipping point, when the reports from Russian emissaries abroad resulted, again in fits and starts, in cultural outreach projects of his own by Tsar Aleksei Mikhailovich (son and successor of the first Romanov ruler). Our study relies especially on richly informative Italian reports of the visiting Russian diplomats, accounts used only sparingly in other histories of performative culture.

In chapters 3 and 4, we see how such exposure and outreach was realized in Moscow. These chapters track the origins of the Russian court theater, beginning in early 1672 with a command performance for Tsar Aleksei by a group of foreign residents in Moscow, and expanding to the establishment of a continuing court-sponsored theater, one that produced multiple plays and lasted to the tsar's death, in 1676. Our study is more comprehensive than earlier surveys, offering unexpected and vivid views of the productions. Both the early 1672 performances and the later theater were widely reported by Western observers stationed in Moscow, and their descriptions enhance the extensive published Russian archival material, here fully integrated with the foreign accounts. Because this brief theater mania was so closely tied to the foreigners in Moscow who initiated these productions, we also discuss some of the relevant performance traditions from which these largely German players would have drawn. The concept of intertheater is relevant here, as it posits ways in which theatrical traditions might be realized on a continuum both chronological and geographical and how such interim iterations might be contextualized. How, for example, does a stock comic character like the anarchic Pickleherring make the transfer from northern European stages to the tsar's court in Moscow? Our answer: very readily. Our detailed source study shows the degree to which the Russian court was willing to dip into the capital's Foreign Quarter and its traditions to produce such entertainment. This is not just an important precedent for Peter's far-better-known sojourns into Moscow's Foreign Quarter but offers revealing glimpses into the dynamism and experimentalism demonstrated at Tsar Aleksei's court.

Chapter 5 reinforces the theatrical planners' reliance on Western sources by focusing on a single play produced in Moscow, on a theme with important and topical European-wide political ramifications: the story of Tamerlane, which was performed at two separate theatrical events for the Russian court in 1675. A theatrical production of a Tamerlane story inevitably brings to mind the most famous rendition of all, the thundering Tamburlaine of Christopher Marlowe's play (first published in 1590). Building on the theatrical and performative contexts we have developed in previous chapters, we discuss the possibility of what might loosely be called a Marlowe-Moscow axis within which we might situate this Russian play. We also suggest paths by which Western historians might consider echoes of Marlowe's great play on the Continent, for which there is otherwise no performance evidence.

Our final chapter brings us full circle, moving through the end of the seventeenth century and into the early years of Tsar Aleksei's eventual successor: his son, Peter the Great. Here we see how the diplomatic and performative links we have followed throughout the volume come together yet again, in the establishment, briefly, of a theater by an invited German troupe, on Red Square in Moscow. We thus return to some familiar territory: diplomatic exposure, repertorial links with Continental traveling troupes, the Russian court's desire to hire expertise from abroad, and the roles of northern European sources and performers. As Russian scholars of the late eighteenth century began to investigate these relatively recent Petrine-era theatrical activities, they also uncovered Tsar Aleksei's earlier productions, and here, too, diplomatic sources play an important role. We thus conclude with a brief historiography of Russian theater that tracks the publication of many of the source materials used throughout this study (for example, diplomatic reports and payment records). It was through these late eighteenth-century scholarly investigations and publications that knowledge of Tsar Aleksei's theater began to become known to Russian scholars and to work (or, more accurately, belatedly to rework) its way to the West.

Overall, our study is devoted to performed entertainment at the Russian court and the burgeoning world of communication that made the diplomatic and cultural exchanges we discuss so widely known and readily transmitted. When a Russian ambassador was in Florence in 1660, he sat alongside Grand Duke Ferdinand de' Medici with a map spread out on a table, examining together the travel routes to distant Muscovy and discussing the enticingly valuable animals of Siberia. They were, in a sense, putting Russia on the map. This study, too, is meant to put Russia unambiguously on the musico-theatrical map of Europe in the seventeenth century. In spite of all the differences—which are real and in certain areas deeply ingrained—Russia is very much a part of this European-wide cultural realm. This is the lesson of Dannenfels's encounter in Pskov in 1644, these are the implications of intertheater, and this is what we intend as the overarching theme of this book.

NOTES

1. This discussion is based on Maier and Shamin, "Pskovskoe teatral'noe leto," and their "Straßburger Mummenschanz," and on Maier and Schumacher, "Eine Straßburger Artistenfamilie."

2. Maier and Schumacher, "Eine Straßburger Artistenfamilie," 251–252 and n. 26; on other such "fliers," see Kröll, "Theatrum Mundi," 81–82; Katritzky, *Women, Medicine and Theatre*, 286–288.

3. Detailed discussion of the print itself is in Maier and Shamin, "Straßburger Mummenschanz," and see VD17 4620:750138Z.

4. From the novel *Güldner Hand*, by Wolfgang Caspar Printz (1675), quoted and translated in J. Alexander, "Ridentum dicere verum," 743–744.

5. Ellersieck, "Russia under Aleksei Mikhailovich," 132–141, gives an excellent survey of the events, and see the discussion in Martin, "Dynastic Marriages," esp. 143–152.

6. Filimonatus's identity was established independently by Daniel Waugh and Stepan Shamin in 2019. Many of Grelle's newsletters to his Swedish employers, together with manuscript newspapers and other attachments, are in UUL, Livonica 1; translations of his letters sent to Russia are in *Vesti-Kuranty* II. For the Swedish context see the forthcoming monograph by Maier and Waugh.

7. *Vesti-Kuranty* II:79, from December 11, 1643.

8. Fireworks are mentioned by Grelle/Filimonatus in *Vesti-Kuranty* II:66, 67, and, in Waldemar's party, on pp. 86, 250.

9. The word *igrets* ("player") in the Grelle/Filimonatus report is also interesting—as we see in later chapters, this word is used to describe people who were apparently participants in the Russian court theater.

10. The Riga listing is in Bolte, *Das Danziger Theater*, 70n1; the additional Danzig documents were uncovered by Limon, *Gentlemen*, 92–93, with a translation of the Danzig petition (declined by the city council), on 55–56. According to Limon, the Riga petition cited by Bolte is lost.

11. On the traveling troupes at the Great Wedding, see Wade, *Triumphus Nuptialis Danicus*, 261–270; on the Fornenbergh troupe in Gottorp, see Brandt and Hogendoorn, *German and Dutch Theatre*, 384.

12. Limon, *Gentlemen*, 92–93. The stranded troupe did eventually make it to Stockholm, where it performed for the queen in July 1648.

13. Maier and Shamin, "Straßburger Mummenschanz," 14.

14. West, "Intertheatricality," 155.

15. Bosman, "Renaissance Intertheater," 565.

16. Bosman, "Renaissance Intertheater," 565; Cohn, *Shakespeare in Germany*, cvi.

17. Kollmann, "Comment: Divides and Ends," 440, 442; she refers to Topolski, "Periodization," esp. 13, where he describes "a sequence of narrative wholes composed of other narrative wholes." Bushkovitch's "demiurge" is in "Change and Culture," 314.

18. Bushkovitch, "Change and Culture," 292.

19. Hennings, *Russia*, 8. A theatrical focus on diplomacy is in Henke, introduction to *Transnational Exchange*, 7–8.

20. See Waugh and Maier, "Muscovy"; Shamin, "Slovo." Pettegree, *Invention of News*, chapter 9, details the rapid development of printed newspapers in northern Europe in the early seventeenth century.

21. In addition to the obvious example of liturgical drama, there were other performative displays appearing throughout the century in venues ranging from church to court; Panchenko, "Deklamatsiia Sil'vestra Medvedeva," emphasizes a continuum of performance styles, for example performed readings at banquets on church or state occasions and recited declamations for the royal family.

22. The fundamental English-language study is Velimirović, "Liturgical Drama." See also the more recent survey in Stennikova, "Tserkovno-teatralizovannye deistva."

23. The declamations, especially later in the century, often included musical components; see, for example, Panchenko, "Deklamatsiia Sil'vestra Medvedeva" and Nikolaev, "Russkie intermedii."

24. Cracraft, *Petrine Revolution*, 94, 96, 98, with a general discussion on pp. 92–106. Even those who do not see influence from the Piscator Bible on Ushakov's work still discuss him in terms of models; Smirnova, "Simon Ushakov," 170, argues that Ushakov's work "does not provide evidence of any serious move toward a new artistic epoch in the second half of the seventeenth century," instead finding models from the medieval Orthodox culture of Byzantium.

25. On the singing ensembles, see Parfent'ev, *Professional'nye muzykanty*.

26. The musical setting of Simeon's Psalter translation was dedicated and presented to Tsarevna Sofiia Alekseevna during the period of her regency, in the mid-1680s; the large literature is summarized in Jensen, *Musical Cultures*, esp. 60–70 and 253n13.

1

COURT MUSIC AT HOME AND ABROAD

Osip Nepea, Russia's first ambassador to England, very nearly did not make it to London at all. This was not a case of a diplomatic mission metaphorically foundering on the shoals of political intransigence or blunder, although that happened often enough in future meetings—in this case, Nepea's ship, in 1556, literally foundered on the wild shoals of Scotland, killing many of the English sailing crew as well as members of the Russian party and destroying much of their precious cargo. The ambassador's life was spared, and this terrifying event served, in some ways, to solidify the fledgling relationship: the Crown (and the English merchants who were determined to develop the newly discovered trade opportunities) stepped in, providing for the "gentle comfortment and entertainment of the saide Ambassadour, his traine and companie" while in Scotland and escorting them safely to London, where they were lavishly provided for.[1] Although trade relations were the overriding concern of both the English and the Russian representatives, and would remain so for the next century, this shipwrecked mission also introduces the cultural contacts and interactions that are the primary concern of this study.

In this chapter, we highlight the entertainments offered to Russian diplomats abroad, how the visitors described them (if, in fact, they were able to describe them at all), and what the consequences of such exposure might have been. Two early examples, both commonly cited in studies of such encounters between Russian and Western cultural traditions, illustrate the different trajectories such contacts might produce. One of the Russian representatives to the Council of Ferrara-Florence (1438–1439), Bishop Avramii of Suzdal', famously reported on the elaborate productions of liturgical dramas he saw in Florence; such performed ingredients seem to have been incorporated later into the Russian *Play of the Furnace* (*Peshchnoe deistvo*), a liturgical drama that enjoyed its heyday from the mid-sixteenth to mid-seventeenth centuries. Although the results were not immediate, it seems plausible that Avramii's experiences of performed church drama were ultimately influential in Russia because of the shared traditions of liturgical drama in Eastern and Western rites. As the theater historian Petr Morozov pointed out, sustained interest in Avramii's theatrical descriptions in Russia is indicated by the fact that they were copied multiple times over the following years. Such shared traditions were likely bolstered by the influx of Italians (or Italo-Greeks) in the suite of Grand Prince Ivan III's bride, Zoe (Sofiia) Paleologue, the Italian-raised niece of the last Byzantine emperor (the marriage was in 1472).[2] However another trip to Italy shortly thereafter, also frequently cited in the music-historical literature, was less impactful. A Russian diplomatic mission to Rome, Venice, and Milan brought back to Moscow, in 1488, an Augustinian monk who was an organist; he remained in Moscow, converted to Orthodoxy, married, and was rewarded for his service to the tsar.[3] The appearance of this organist was certainly natural, given the Italian presence at the Russian court at this time. But in this case, the influence was restricted—organs were (and are) not used in Orthodox services, so if the organist was employed professionally, it must have been in a limited fashion, one that apparently did not continue, for example, by training students or hiring instrument builders. As we shall see, the performative keyboard tradition at the Russian court eventually emerged from different sources and different contacts and in wholly secular court entertainments.[4]

This opening chapter also highlights the possibilities and limitations of our source materials. In the case of Nepea, for instance, no Russian account survives, so we rely only on English descriptions of events that were, to the hosts, quite normal. For other ambassadorial trips, although we do have the Russian reports, we notice difficulties in describing musical performances that would have been simultaneously familiar and out of context—for example, singing in church but with instrumental accompaniment. As the music historian Dinko Fabris points out, most European travelers, whether diplomats or simply tourists, brought with them certain expectations. These savvy travelers were equipped with guidebooks and must-see destination points, and, just as important, they brought with them on their journeys their previous experiences from home: they could compare the theater of their own country to that of Italy or recollect musical performances as they exceeded or failed to live up to expectations.[5] For the most part, and particularly in the sixteenth century, this was not generally the case for the Russian ambassadorial personnel, and the novelty of their experiences is reflected only partially in their reports, which were fairly inflexible in their format. The ambassadorial party was not expected to produce an entertaining diary documenting its experiences but rather an account demonstrating how scrupulously it fulfilled the detailed operating instructions it was provided before leaving. Thus, in our context, certain activities were worthy of note—toasting at banquets, for example, or seating plans at entertainment events; these were matters of precedence and honor, and the reports describing them were filed away for future reference, as we see in later chapters.

Finally, in this context we approach, gingerly, the enormous divide between what was written down and what must have been communicated orally. We know that the exhilarating events experienced by Russian diplomats abroad were not confined to official written reports. One Russian ambassador, Grigorii Mikulin, who was sent to London in 1600–1601, talked frequently about his time abroad. As the Englishman Richard Barne wrote, from Arkhangel'sk in 1601, Mikulin "imparteth at large every particular of his entertainment: in which discourse he intermingleth commendations of our country and people." We necessarily rely on the surviving written accounts, with a rueful awareness of their shortcomings.[6]

We begin by providing some background to our main focus—the seventeenth century—in order to suggest the range of experiences such diplomatic interchange might generate. We survey primarily contacts with England and the Holy Roman Empire, adding a short overview of the musical consequences stemming from the Time of Troubles and the presence of the False Dmitrii's Polish cohort in Moscow. We then move to the world of entertainment established at the court of the first Romanov tsar, Mikhail Fedorovich, keeping in mind how the previous experiences may have rippled through the menu of amusements offered during his reign. Osip Nepea's visit to London thus serves as a useful embarkation point, one of a suite of diplomatic interactions that took place over decades.

THE BACKSTORY: *DIVERTISSEMENTS* FOR MOSCOW'S DIPLOMATIC CORPS

Nepea had been dispatched to London with the English navigator Richard Chancellor, who died in the disastrous shipwreck in Scotland. (Indeed, the origins of the English "discovery" of Russia was also the result of a seafaring mishap, when two of three English ships perished during their journey—Chancellor's was the only one to survive, finding the entrance to the White Sea and landing along its coast and then continuing overland to meet Tsar Ivan IV in Moscow.) After arriving in London, Nepea plunged into the ceremonies of diplomatic life. He hit the entertainment trifecta immediately, experiencing the delights of public, private, and sacred performances during the two months of his stay in the city. The climate-related travel times required by the northern sailing route, icebound most of the year, resulted in fairly long stays abroad for the Russian ambassadors, which gave them extra time to enjoy the delights of London life at roughly the same times in the year. This travel constraint also accounts for some of the overlap in the Russian ambassadors' experiences in England and, later, in the Italian states.[7]

The most generic of such diplomatic ceremony, processional fanfare, is the least documented of Nepea's experiences. Nepea's initial entry into the city, on February 27, 1557, is described in the diary kept by Henry Machyn (d. 1563).[8] Machyn had been a member of the Merchant Taylors' Company since 1530, so he had good reason to be interested in Nepea's visit, which was lavishly sponsored by the merchants of London. Machyn, perhaps naturally, described the pageantry with particular focus on the clothing that was displayed in the parade. Neither Machyn nor the contemporary English account of this mission specifically mentions music, although the large size of the greeting party and the high rank of the attending dignitary (Viscount Montague) suggests that there must have been some sort of accompanying fanfare. One assumes that Nepea's entrance would have been marked in a fashion similar to that of another Russian envoy to London, A. G. Savin, who, in 1569, was "saluted with [the] sound of Drums, noise of Flutes, Trumpetts &c" as his party approached the city.[9] A few weeks after Nepea's arrival, Queen Mary and King Philip made a procession into London, accompanied, as Machyn says, by "trumpets blowing with other instruments with great joy and pleasure and great shooting of guns at the Tower."[10] This rambunctious greeting was typical; as the Brandenburg traveler Paul Hentzner observed during his 1598 tour through England, the English "are vastly fond of great noises that fill the ear, such as the firing of cannon, drums, and the ringing of bells."[11] Nepea, waiting for his summons from the rulers, would surely have been aware of the joyous reception, which supports the idea of a similar (necessarily more subdued) fanfare for his own entry. Trumpets and percussion were standard military accoutrements in Russia also, mentioned in descriptions by English visitors a few years later.[12]

Nepea's audience was on March 25, 1557. About a month later, he was invited to accompany the royal couple to Westminster Abbey, where the remains of Edward the Confessor had recently been returned at Queen Mary's instigation. As Machyn noted: "The twentieth day of April went to Westminster to hear Mass and to the lord abbot's to dinner, the Duke of Muscovy, and after dinner came into the monastery and went up to see St. Edward's shrine new set up."[13] Machyn's reference to Mass suggests there was singing and perhaps an organ. A slightly later visitor to this shrine, Frederick, Duke of Württemberg, did hear organ music and singing there, in 1592, during Elizabeth's reign.[14] A few days later, on April 23, Nepea witnessed the festivities of St. George's Day and the ceremony of the Order of the Garter, and in this instance, Machyn reports that the ambassador heard Evensong at Westminster. The contemporary English account also mentions his presence at the services.[15]

But Nepea also had the opportunity to hear music in a less structured setting. Machyn writes about a March 31 dinner for the ambassador given by the Lord Mayor—apparently Machyn did not attend, for he describes only the grand procession there and back.[16] A month later, on April 29, Nepea attended a banquet at Draper's Hall given by the merchants of the city: "During his abode in London, [the merchants] did both invite him to the Maior, and divers worshipfull mens houses, feasting and banquetting him right friendly, shewing unto him the most notable and commendable sights of London.... And also the said 29. day of April, the said merchants assembling themselves together in the house of the Drapers hal of London, exhibited and gave unto ye said Ambassador, a notable supper garnished with musicke, Enterludes and bankets."[17] We have no record of Nepea's reaction to such amusement, but based on the account of the Englishmen who accompanied the ambassador on his return to Russia, we know the event would have been a novelty—at least, it was not the kind of entertainment provided in Moscow for a banquet attended by the English dignitaries. In Moscow, the visitors did hear some singing, and even though liturgical singing was developed to a very high degree in Russia at this time, the style was not to the Englishmen's taste; there is no hint of additional entertainment along the lines of the "musicke" or "Enterludes" provided by the London merchants. At the tsar's banquet in Moscow, "there came in six singers which stood in the midst of the chamber, and their faces towards the Emperour, who sang there before dinner was ended three severall times, whose songs or voyces delighted our eares little or nothing."[18]

For the mission to London headed by Fedor Pisemskii, in 1582–1583, we get a fuller picture of the Russian view of the events because we have the official ambassadorial account, or *stateinyi spisok*, the summary report of the mission; these were submitted to the Ambassadorial Chancery (Posol'skii prikaz) to document and confirm that all initial directives had been followed.[19] Pisemskii was accompanied by his second-in-command, Neudacha Khovralev—both are named throughout as attending the diplomatic ceremonies. They, too, saw the St. George's Day celebration, at which they were informed by the translator that the singing was from the psalms; this was followed by a banquet, with toasts to the rulers.[20] Two entries from Pisemskii's trip, however, introduce a new element: dancing. We do not know if Nepea witnessed any dancing, although it was very popular at Elizabeth's court, when Pisemskii was there several years later, and the sequential descriptions in his report seem to track the visitors' reactions. Dance was, of course, not unknown in Russia, but it was absolutely not part of official court ceremony and indeed had strong implications of un-Orthodox behavior. Nearly a century later, in the mid-1660s, the former Russian diplomat Grigorii Kotoshikhin stated that there was no dancing whatsoever at the Russian court, and this is consistent with other evidence, as we shall see: the Russian royal family did not dance.[21] Thus, as Pisemskii's account indicates, the sight of dancing by Elizabeth's courtiers required some explanation, although the report is accepting of the differences in custom, a flexible attitude we encounter many times in our survey.

Pisemskii's first (recorded) encounter with dance was at Richmond, one of Elizabeth's favorite royal retreats, preceding the party's first audience with the queen. This was on January 20, 1583, when a number of high-ranking courtiers, including one of the queen's favorites, Christopher Hatten (1540–1591), a member of the Privy Council, welcomed the guests to a banquet, after which they had their audience. The Russian account mentions several musical instruments, specifying *surny* (double-reed wind instruments, akin to the shawm or *Schalmei*) and horns (*truby*), which in this context probably indicate not fanfare-type trumpets but cornetts:[22]

> And at that time the players began to play on surny, and truby, and on many other instruments in that same banquet hall. And the queen's nobles began to dance with the noblewomen and girls. And the advisers said to Fedor and Neudacha: "In this do not censure our ruler, Queen Elizabeth, because they are dancing in your presence; for our ruler, our queen, this is customary; every day after the meal entertainments and dancing take place." And Fedor and Neudacha said: "As it pleases God and the queen: do not alter your customs for her on our account. It should be arranged as it suits her."[23]

The second reference to dancing is from several months later. In the report of their final visit with the queen, at Greenwich on May 26, 1583, the Russian account is matter-of-fact: dancing occurred but apparently merited no special observations or explanations this time. The account uses the same formulaic description of the accompanying instrumental music: "And when they entered the queen's chamber, there Fedor and Neudacha were met at the door by the queen's counselor Christopher Hatton. And when he had met Fedor and Neudacha, he asked them to go to the queen. And in the presence of the queen at that time players played on truby and surny and on many other instruments, and her noblemen danced with noblewomen and girls."[24]

At around this same time, other Russian diplomats were going through similar sorting processes, sifting out how Western courts incorporated entertainment that, to the Russians, might have seemed inappropriate. This was the case when the 1595 Russian embassy to Emperor Rudolph, headed by M. I. Vel'iaminov and A. I. Vlas'ev (who will reappear at other strategic diplomatic/musical intersections in our narrative), attended a banquet in Prague. There, the group heard entertainments by "imperial players" (*tsesarevye igretsy*). The Russians were disturbed because they were in mourning for the death of the tsar's daughter, Feodosiia, and they told their hosts that they were not permitted to engage in such apparent frivolities during this time. The answer was reassuring: the emperor was also grieving for his brother, Archduke Ernest, who had died earlier that year—the music they heard was appropriate, for the musicians were performing the psalms of David and other religious hymns.[25] A banquet held a few days later included the same kind of music as before—that is, appropriate religious singing.²⁶ Several weeks later, on their departure, they again heard musical performances at a banquet, which was contrasted with fanfare-style music that was played in the courtyard at the window. Although the performers are unknown, we do know that Rudolph had largely retained the substantial troupes of singers and instrumentalists that had been a feature of his father's reign, as well as the special squadrons of trumpeters.²⁷

Grigorii Mikulin's mission to London in 1600–1601 included some by now familiar ceremonies.²⁸ Mikulin enjoyed a star-studded reception at Richmond for his first audience with the queen, followed by a banquet on October 14, 1600. Following in the footsteps (and sailing times) of previous Russian ambassadors, he attended the St. George's Day festivities, which included the singing of psalms, described in language quite similar to that used by the Pisemskii mission earlier. Mikulin also noted the great fanfare for the queen's entrance into London on November 5, and he attended the impressive jousts held on Accession Day, an important part of Elizabeth's court pagentry.²⁹ But Mikulin also enjoyed some new experiences, one of the most important of which was the celebration of Twelfth Night on January 6, 1601. As argued creatively (and persuasively) by theater historian Leslie Hotson, this was the date Shakespeare's *Twelfth Night* premiered, and although Mikulin did not attend this performance, he did take part in the lead-up events at Whitehall.³⁰ Mikulin witnessed the preliminary religious services from the vantage point of the Queen's Closet, a private space from which he could observe the activities in the chapel.³¹ He apparently asked about the texts that were being sung but made no comment about the fact that there were accompanying musical instruments: "And when the queen had left her chambers, she went to the chapel, and the escorts took Grigorii and Ivashka to the chamber, and from this chamber the chapel was visible. And as the queen had entered the church, at that time they began to play in the church on organs, truby [again, probably cornetts], and on many other instruments, and to sing. And the escorts said that they were singing the psalms of David."³² The visiting Duke of Bracciano, Virginio Orsino, who also attended this series of events, was more lavish in his praise, portraying this chapel music as "wondrous."³³

At the banquet that followed, Mikulin enjoyed the privilege of dining with the queen, who rarely took her meals in public. There was musical entertainment, which was noted in the Russian account: "And when the banquet was going on, in front of her many players played many instruments."³⁴

Mikulin would have heard "the Musitions of the Citty" who were required "to be reddy to attend." These were probably the Lord Mayor's Waits, a large mixed-instrumental ensemble. Other music at the banquet was provided by the Children of the Chapel, who were "to come before the Queene at Dinner with a Carroll." Both were established and highly trained ensembles, and the Children of the Chapel had long performed musical and theatrical entertainments for the court, especially around Christmas.[35]

Church services, including instrumental music, figured in the accounts of other Russian ambassadors abroad. An early description, from a court widely acclaimed for its music (by no less than Orlando di Lasso), appears in the report of the Russian embassy of 1575–1576 that was sent by Ivan IV to Maximilian II. The account mentions a church service attended by the visiting diplomats along with many members of the royal family. It naturally included singers, labeled in the Russian account as *d'iaki* ("clerks"), reflecting the terminology used to describe Russian liturgical singers in this period.[36] Although many individual members of the imperial chapel choir are known—it was headed by the well-known composer Philippe de Monte— the Russian account gives no clues about names or numbers involved. The singers were accompanied during the service by truby—again, most likely cornetts, although the court was certainly well supplied with fanfare-type trumpets and percussion, which the guests heard on other occasions.[37] One of the terms used in the Russian account of this service gives us pause: a reference to the "tsymbalniki" who were accompanying the liturgical singing. In slightly later sources the word *tsymbaly* refers clearly to plucked (quilled) keyboard instruments; here, however, in the context of a religious service, it may indicate an organ. This is the earliest Russian usage of this term we have found in a secular account, and it is difficult to assign a precise meaning, although by this point, Russian diplomatic parties had presumably been exposed to both organs and plucked keyboards.[38]

Foreigners in Russia, for their part, made observations about the kinds of entertainment they experienced, or provided, during their stays. A series of visits, mostly occurring during the reign of Tsar Fedor Ivanovich (r. 1584–1598), suggest the range of such encounters. One of the longest-employed English representatives in Russia was Jerome Horsey (d. 1626), whose career spanned nearly twenty years. Horsey described his preparations in London, in 1586, for a return trip to Russia, emphasizing that he had assembled various keyboard instruments at the Russian court's request: "I... had made my provicion of... organes, virgenalls, musicions... and of other costly things of great value," Horsey wrote, "according to my commissions" from the Russian rulers.[39] Furthermore, Horsey reports that members of his party performed on these instruments for the Russian court, suggesting why he listed "musicions" in his account: the "Emporis" (this is Irina, Boris Godunov's sister) "admired especially at the organes and vergenalls, all gilt and enambled, never seinge nor heeringe the like before, woundered and delighted at the lowd and musicall sound therof. Thousands of people resorted and steyed aboutt the pallace to heer the same." Although we are taking Horsey's claim of "thousands" of auditors with a hefty grain of salt, at least it indicates that the instruments were played to good effect in the presence of the rulers. Such entertainment was regarded as private (even if the audience was large)—a quality that is essential in understanding the Russian court's approach to foreign entertainment. Horsey's conclusion affirms this: "My men that plaied upon them [were] much made of and admitted into such presence often wher myself could not com."[40]

The extent and success of these musical interchanges are clear from the terminology that emerged at this time and that would ultimately be used for over a century at the Russian court. Although the "tsymbaly" of the 1574 diplomatic account are a bit vague (a keyboard but likely an organ), the definition of *tsymbaly* (also *tsynbaly*) as a plucked, harpsichord-like keyboard instrument seems to have settled in fairly quickly.[41] The French trader Jean Sauvage made a short stay in the Russian North, in Kholmogory, in 1586; he apparently did not travel to Moscow but remained at this important, although remote, town, the nexus of the northern trade. Sauvage recorded a variety of terms for musical instruments (mostly folk instruments), as well as a separate listing of military terms, including percussion. But he also heard, or needed vocabulary for, other kinds of music, as indicated by his definition of a performer on the tsymbaly: "Ung Joueur d'espinette, Samballenicq" (i.e., tsymbal'nik). This may reflect ownership of such instruments by the many foreign traders in the Russian North, either for their own use or as valuable, and portable, items to pass on to Moscow; it might also reflect the interests of the many Moscow-based Russians who worked in the North. Sauvage's reference is clearly to a Western-style keyboard, for the épinette or spinet is a small plucked keyboard instrument, much like the English virginals.[42] An association of tsymbaly with virginals is made explicit in the glossary compiled by the Englishman Mark Ridley, who served as physician to the tsar in the 1590s and so had experience at court in Moscow. His definitions of keyboard instruments support Sauvage's information, for he defined *tsimbaldi* as "virginals" (and *organy* as "organs"), which seems to reflect court practice and/or ownership of such instruments by foreigners or Russians in the capital.[43] Ridley's stay in Russia began just after Jerome Horsey had brought his "organes and virgenalls" from London, so we know that such instruments were at the Russian court when Ridley was there.

The fate of Horsey's musically talented men is a blank, but there may be an echo of their activities in a slightly later account. Emissaries from the Holy Roman emperor to the Persian court were sent, via Russia, in 1602. During their stay in Moscow, they added three people to their party, including an organist who already possessed his own instrument.[44] This organist's identity and fate are unknown, but the ambassador, Stephan Kakasch (Kakas István), had been to England himself and had important connections with London traders, who knew him and were familiar with his mission. Given these direct ties, it may be that this imperial mission was aware of the presence of some foreign (perhaps even English) musicians or instruments in Moscow.[45]

Ridley's terminology may also help identify a privately owned instrument listed a few years later. An inventory of Mikhail Tatishchev's possessions compiled in 1608, after the death of this wealthy and high-ranking figure, includes a "broken tsymbaly," which was nevertheless purchased and, presumably, repaired.[46] This entry, short as it is, raises questions that take us into another period of concentrated exposure to Western entertainment in Moscow. Tatishchev's possessions were inventoried because he was put to death as a result of his complex activities during the tumultuous and deadly period between the end of the Russian Rurikid line (the last ruler of this line, Fedor Ivanovich, died in 1598) and the establishment of the Romanov dynasty (1613). During these years, known as the Time of Troubles, the Russian lands suffered through dynastic insecurity, famine, military invasion by Polish-Lithuanian forces, and brief occupation and rule by the so-called False Dmitrii (who claimed to be the miraculously living youngest son of Tsar Ivan IV and thus the true successor to the throne). We do not know how Tatishchev might have acquired his tsymbaly, although he had extensive contacts at the Russian court as well as diplomatic experience abroad, specifically, in Poland. Through whatever means the instrument came into his possession, though, it was clearly desirable, even in its poor condition, as it represented the objects valued at the court itself and was not tainted by association with the Polish cohort that had, literally as well as culturally, invaded the Kremlin—an association that did, ultimately, result in the execution of the tsymbaly's owner.

We focus on a concentrated period within the complex series of events that unfolded during the Time of Troubles: the half year between the proxy wedding of Dmitrii and his Polish bride, Marina Mniszek, which took place in Cracow (November 1605), and the deluge that overthrew and killed Dmitrii and most of his Polish cohort, in Moscow (May 1606). At each step of the way, Western musical traditions slammed directly into Russian customs and assumptions—the cultural collisions could not have been starker or more potent. Previous Russian ambassadorial parties had witnessed, queried, and accepted the performed entertainments they had seen on their missions, and similar entertainments (and entertainers) had appeared at the Russian court. All of this, however, was playing at the margins. This brief period in 1605–1606 brought these elements into contact with the central pillars of Russian life: the rulers, their church, and their essential rituals and responsibilities.[47] We can trace these confrontations through a familiar face, that of Afanasii Vlas'ev, whose activities reinforce the important confluence between diplomatic travels and cultural exposure.

We have already met Vlas'ev as the second-ranking member of the tsar's embassy to the Holy Roman Empire in 1595, when the Russians questioned the propriety of singing during a period of mourning. Vlas'ev returned, as the highest-ranking member of the party, to the imperial court in 1599–1600, when he also attended ceremonies and banquets highlighted by musical entertainment.[48] But all of this pales in comparison to his crucial role in the events surrounding the False Dmitrii, for he figured prominently in the very actions that precipitated the violence to come. Vlas'ev went to Cracow as Dmitrii's proxy in the betrothal ceremony to Marina Mniszek, and he then returned with the Polish party to Moscow, where the new bride/tsaritsa was to be installed. There were many disturbing aspects of the proxy wedding, but we highlight two familiar elements: instrumental music and dancing. It was one thing for a visiting Russian ambassador to witness Queen Elizabeth's courtiers dancing with each other to musical accompaniment. But Vlas'ev's activities and the proxy wedding itself were very different matters, carrying serious implications, because these activities not only involved the direct participation of the Russian ambassador himself but were also then taken to Moscow and displayed there in a much more public way than had ever occurred previously.

Vlas'ev arrived in Cracow after a stately two-month procession from Moscow, and the proxy wedding took place on November 22, 1605. The ceremony was held according to the Roman rite and concluded with celebrations that included partnered dancing, beginning with Marina and the Polish king. However, when Vlas'ev was invited to dance with Marina, he declined, saying he was not worthy of such an honor; when it was necessary to touch her arm to escort her, Vlas'ev did so only through a handkerchief.[49] Vlas'ev remained in Cracow after fulfilling his duty as proxy, playing a starring role at another wedding that occurred very soon afterward, when the Polish King Sigismund III Vasa married Constance of Austria—as the stand-in for Dmitrii in the betrothal that linked the two states, Vlas'ev was included in all of the festivities. The king's wedding was elaborately celebrated over several days with banquets accompanied by music (one description includes the seating plan, showing that the Russian representative was placed in what looks like splendid isolation on one side of the long table). Most impressive was the postwedding extravaganza on December 13, for which a complex suite of entertainments was offered, including instrumental music and singing, ballets with elaborate costumes, masquerades, comic theater, and even the creation of a model of Parnassus, featuring Apollo, his lyre resounding.[50]

When the Polish-Russian party escorting Marina made it back to Moscow, in May of the following year, 1606, it brought along many of these amusements. The lavish productions in Cracow were not direct models (least of all in terms of scale) but certainly represented what might be called aspirational goals of proper display at such an important wedding. Although no Mount Parnassus sprang up in Moscow, the Polish entourage brought instrumentalists and singers, whose performances accompanied partnered dancing that featured elaborate dress and masking.[51] It was these elements, particularly masking, that transgressed Orthodox wedding norms, because they most obviously duplicated (however unwittingly) activities associated with the resolutely secular itinerant entertainers, called skomorokhi, who were often associated with countryside wedding celebrations, much to the distress of church representatives and leaders. So, while Dmitrii and his Polish bride followed some of the rituals and formulas of the Orthodox royal wedding ceremony (which included noisy trumpet and percussion fanfares), the norms they violated were far more serious.[52]

On May 6/16, 1606, as a warm-up, forty instrumentalists performed for Dmitrii and a group of Russians. On the wedding day, May 8/18, after the church ceremony there was entertainment on a "richly ornamented stage" on which "an orchestra of musicians played all manner of instruments.... They were Polish, Italian, German, and Brabançon." (The international flavor of the musicians reflects that of the Polish court's establishment.)[53] Another observer described music in similar abundance: "The days of the wedding festivities were celebrated splendidly and joyfully with food, drink, singing, and acrobatics. There were not only all imaginable kinds of musical instruments playing but also an excellent choir with thirty-two voices, as fine as any potentate might desire, which Dmitry had summoned from Poland."[54] Furthermore, the Poles included, as a matter of course, the same kinds of partnered dancing witnessed (although declined) by Vlas'ev in Cracow at the proxy wedding and at King Sigismund's wedding shortly thereafter. This occurred in Moscow on several occasions and was described by different witnesses—only a few Russians were present at the elaborate sequences of dancing, which included banquet music, dancing in mixed-gendered pairs, and changes of clothing for Dmitrii. All of this would have been standard wedding fare, perfectly acceptable in any court in Europe except the court at which it was actually taking place.

But there was worse to come, again reflecting the recent experiences at the Polish royal wedding. Several sources refer to "mascarade" or "mascarata" in the context of the multiday celebrations marking the Polish king's wedding the previous year, and we see Marina industriously planning something similar, although necessarily on a much smaller scale. One account of Marina's and Dmitrii's last days in Moscow describes plans for a "mummerie," and the Dutch merchant Isaac Massa reports that on May 16/26: "The Polish lords were busy dancing with great ladies. The tsarina [Marina], with her maids of honour, was preparing disguises for a masquerade that she was planning to offer the tsar as an entertainment on the Sunday following."[55]

The reaction to all these outrages was violent, and although obviously prompted by far more than musical and choreographic transgressions, the Polish musicians were a special target of Muscovite wrath: apparently very few of them survived the assault when it came, on May 17/27. Why such focused anger, especially in light of previous ambassadorial exposure (including Vlas'ev's) and the delighted reception of Horsey's musicians at court?[56] Apart from the masking, deeply offensive because of its association with skomorokh transgressions, the most important violations appear to have been not necessarily in the music itself but in the realms of scope and privacy. Horsey's "thousands" notwithstanding, the large performing ensembles at Dmitrii's wedding flaunted their talents to a large audience—mostly Poles, granted, but there were also some Russian witnesses. Vlas'ev should have been able to take this in stride, although one reporter's comment—"the Russians were highly astonished at the orchestra's performance"—indicates the presence of less seasoned (or less hardened) Russians and their obvious disapproval.[57] The dancing was also far removed from anything one might have seen in Moscow, even if diplomatic reports had carried information of such doings to some Kremlin officials (as in Pisemskii's mission to Queen Elizabeth's court). Furthermore, this entertainment was provided not by small numbers of invited guests, as in the case of Horsey's men, but by large numbers of uninvited (or, at least, unregulated) guests. Finally, given the fact that Dmitrii and Marina *were* the Russian royal family, all of this was even more troubling.

Because these activities pushed so many cultural buttons, it is no wonder that the death toll for the Polish musicians in Moscow was so high. We emphasize the violence here because as soon as Mikhail Fedorovich Romanov became tsar, reestablishing a ruling dynasty, we see what looks like an instant resumption of the suite of entertainments from the "Horsey era"—not the dancing and certainly not the masking of Dmitrii's time, but the enthusiastic resumption, almost without missing a beat, of the other musical entertainments that had been so enjoyable before the Polish deluge. Although the events surrounding Marina's appearance in Moscow killed off many Polish musicians, they did not kill off the desire for Western-influenced court entertainment provided by foreigners. This is what Tatishchev's tsymbaly suggests as well—Tatishchev himself fell victim to the turmoils and violence of this period, but his property, even his apparently foreign-influenced property, was still desirable. And these desires are immediately visible at the court of the new tsar.

ENTERTAINMENT AT THE COURT OF TSAR MIKHAIL FEDOROVICH: STATUS QUO ANTE

Given the enormity of the convulsive decade-long trauma the country had lived through, it is remarkable how quickly the entertainments of the previous dynasty resurfaced. As historian Chester Dunning writes, the tasks facing the new and very young tsar and his officials comprehended such nonnegotiable items as the need "to assert the new regime's authority, to preside over the rebuilding of the Russian government, to mop up the last traces of the civil war, and to confront Polish and Swedish interventionists." The Kremlin itself had to be cleaned up. Between the time of Mikhail's election as tsar, in February 1613, and his coronation, in July, there are multiple orders for repairs to the Kremlin residence quarters in order to make them habitable for the incoming royal family.[58] Given all this political and physical upheaval, one would not think that tsymbaly would be on anyone's mind.

Yet the newly established Romanov court resounded with music and enjoyed its full measure of other amusements. All of these activities meshed readily with the court's desire deliberately to link the new dynasty to the previous, pre-Dmitrii, establishment, an effort assiduously cultivated in many political, social, and religious arenas.[59] It is thus natural that it returned to the familiar kinds of entertainments—Western or otherwise—that had been popular in the days before Dmitrii and his Polish cohort arrived. Judging from the archival evidence, this transition was swift and unquestioned, yet selective, jettisoning the undesirable elements and framing anew the returning amusements (or, echoing the great historian Sergei Platonov's remark about the aftermath of the Time of Troubles, the patient survived the illness but was not quite the same as before).[60]

A great deal of effort was devoted to providing entertainments for the new royal family, centered on an establishment that is first named in these early days of Mikhail Fedorovich's reign: the Entertainment Hall or Chambers (Poteshnaia palata, khoromy; the word *potekha*—"entertainment," "amusement"—is embedded in the Poteshnaia palata's name). Its associates were paid from government coffers, and it was up and running within months (at the latest) of the new tsar's installation. Although the designation Poteshnaia palata first appears in the early seventeenth century, it certainly reflects court entertainments familiar from the past. There is a hint, for example, of a similar special entertainment venue from the mid-1580s, around the time that Horsey's men were entertaining that earlier royal family. This reference is in the diary by Martin Gruneweg, a Danzig merchant who traveled to Russia in 1584–1585. In a diagram he sketched of Moscow, Gruneweg labeled one location a "Tantzhaus," a term that almost certainly carries a general meaning as a place of entertainment, not a venue intended solely for dancing.[61]

A similarly all-purpose use can be ascribed to another of the court's entertainment venues, the private family quarters, upstairs ("v Verkh")—this, too, has precedents in the late sixteenth century. In an often-quoted passage by the Englishman Giles Fletcher, who was in Russia in 1588–1589, he noted that, following evening worship, "for the most parte [Tsar Fedor] recreateth himself with the Empresse till supper time, with iesters, and dwarfes, men and women, that tumble before him, and sing many songs after the Russe manner."[62] The same kinds of entertainers—fools and dwarves, traditional singers and storytellers—are mentioned throughout the seventeenth century, most often in the context of family entertainment; many such performers lived at the court itself.[63]

Neither of these venues seems to be related to the itinerant, jongleur-like skomorokhi mentioned earlier. We do not minimize skomorokh activities in other aspects of Russian life in the seventeenth century—the voluminous complaints from religious figures certainly indicate their vivid presence. But the realms of court amusements—our specific focus—and skomorokh ribaldry do not appear to overlap. Thus, we do not automatically equate court entertainers and entertainment (whether at the Poteshnaia palata or in the private quarters) with skomorokhi—or, to put it slightly differently, references to musical instruments do not automatically invoke an assumption of skomorokh performance.[64]

The word *potekha* was widely used to describe all manner of divertissements, as the diplomatic reports from abroad indicate. At Tsar Mikhail's court, many different potekhi were provided by many different *poteshniki*, not just musicians but people, and even animals, with a variety of skills. Indeed, exotic animals were a valuable diplomatic commodity across Europe, the acquisition of which the Russian court participated in enthusiastically. The English rulers sent lions back to Russia as gifts after Nepea's visit to London, in the 1550s, and this gesture was reinforced later by Horsey's "commissions" from the Russian rulers, which also included lions (and bulls and dogs).[65] Trained elephants, gifts from the Persian shah, were sent to Moscow with a visiting embassy, and they entertained Tsar Mikhail twice, in 1625 and 1626, at his residence at Pokrovskoe (Rubtsovo), outside Moscow; as we shall see, such "off-campus" venues were crucial several decades later in establishing the court's theater. There is no evidence of the elephants' fate, although given the fact that they experienced frostbitten ears on their way to Moscow, it seems likely that they did not survive much longer; their handlers petitioned for, and received, fabric for winter clothing.[66] Animal-baiting, another "entertainment," was extremely popular all over Europe, and Mikhail Fedorovich's court engaged in this sport almost immediately, with reports of bearbaiting from January 1614.[67]

Human-powered potekhi continued along the lines suggested by Fletcher's "iesters and dwarfes"—organized groups were paid throughout the seventeenth century.[68] For example, there were payments from the Tsaritsa's Craftsmen Chancery (Prikaz Tsaritsinoi masterskoi palaty) to a series of female dwarves and fools and also to many blind *domra* players (the domra is a plucked stringed instrument with a rounded body and long neck). These were established groups paid over several years, including for the upkeep of their instruments, and sometimes linked in the payment records to the Poteshnaia palata. Other sources show Poteshnaia palata employees paying a group of male fools, providing them with elaborate costumes—again, the same names appear across different records.[69] All in all, much of this indicates the court returning to its entertainment comfort zone.

Instrumental music shows the same patterns: the size, composition, and public nature of Dmitrii's and Marina's musical entertainments were aberrations, but the fact of organized music at the tsar's court was not. When reestablished for the new ruler, such entertainments seem to have been more rigorously organized than previously, integrated into the bureaucratic structure. The link between the keyboard instruments that had been entertaining the Moscow court at least from the 1580s and those of Tsar Mikhail's establishment is especially clear through the continuation of the terminology established earlier. The seventeenth-century records appear overwhelmingly to refer to the same kinds of keyboard instruments used in previous decades, thus the tsymbaly/virginals/keyboard continuum, and not (or, at least, less commonly) the dulcimer/cimbalom meaning also sometimes carried by the term *tsymbaly*.[70] These keyboard instruments were also associated with the Poteshnaia palata. The authorities were thus able to reestablish musical instruments in properly private surroundings, under the purview of the Chancery of the Great Court (Prikaz Bol'shogo Dvortsa), headed by A. M. L'vov, who is mentioned throughout the documents we cite later in this chapter.[71]

References to keyboard instruments and to the Poteshnaia palata appear very early in the new reign, beginning in November 1613, when tsynbal'nik Tomila Mikhailov Besov delivered fabric there, an errand he repeated in March 1616. Because he delivered enough fabric to cover or decorate four doors and seven windows, the space seems to have been relatively large.[72] Organs were also associated with this venue, as indicated in a record from 1617, when fabric was sent to the Poteshnaia palata, "where the organs are located."[73] Organs, which were small and portable, also appeared elsewhere. For example in October 1625, a Poteshnaia palata employee, Patrekeika Luk'ianov, took silk fabric to the organs located in the private residence.[74] We do not know if any pre–Time of Troubles keyboards survived at court. The Kakasch mission, described previously, was able to resupply itself with an organist and an organ in Moscow before Tsar Mikhail's time, in 1602, and the Tatishchev tsymbaly survived, although in a damaged state. Given the speed with which keyboard music resurfaced at the new court, it seems possible that some instruments may have remained.

Instrumentalists wound up at the Moscow court in various ways, demonstrating an opportunistic approach to acquiring desirable talent that we will see throughout. Officials were adept at tracking interesting skills among visitors, as shown by their attention to Iurii Proskurovskii, who came to Moscow in the suite of the Orthodox bishop (later archbishop) Iosif Krutsevich, in August 1625. Later that month, we find Proskurovskii working at the Russian court as a trumpeter, and over the course of the next few years, he received in-kind pay regularly from the Armory (Oruzheinaia palata). Most of these payments list fabrics for splashy clothing: a striped sash, yellow boots.[75] Proskurovskii is generally identified in these records as a Pole. We encounter him in a different role, as an "organ master," a decade later, so his original contact with the court eventually expanded.

Royal weddings also prompted interest in instrumental music in the mid-1620s, although suitable performers had been assembled at the court before this time. There were two royal weddings within less than two years. Tsar Mikhail Fedorovich married Mariia Dolgorukova on September 19, 1624; immediately thereafter, the young bride fell ill, and she died less than four months later. Apart from the traditional fanfare provided by percussionists and trumpeters, little is known about other kinds of music that might have been provided for this celebration.[76] We do know that a tsymbal'nik was rewarded for his participation in the wedding, for an unnamed player is listed with others, including liturgical singers, who took part.[77] In addition, the "poteshnik" Proskurovskii was rewarded from the Tsaritsa's Craftsmen Chancery in September 1625; his duties are not specified, although earlier records in this sequence refer to the wedding.[78]

There is more information about the non-fanfare musical component of the tsar's second wedding, to Evdokiia Streshneva, on February 5, 1626. For this wedding, keyboards were positioned in the Faceted Palace (Granovitaia palata), attended by the same Poteshnaia palata employee, Patrekeika Luk'ianov, who had been paid the previous fall for attending to the organs in the private quarters.[79] A couple of weeks after the wedding, Melentii Tsynbalnik was paid for work that was almost certainly related to the celebrations. Soon after this, Proskurovskii was paid for a lengthy list of clothing items, suggesting that he, too, may have had wedding duties.[80]

Other musicians assembled for the 1626 wedding performed in the private "upstairs" quarters. One record lists a suite of instruments, some of which, particularly the domra, featured consistently in the private entertainment repertoire of the royal family; *gusli* players (the gusli is a multistringed plucked instrument) were also paid by the court.[81] This record describes the participants with the word *veselyi* (merry one, merrymaker) rather than the more common, and general, word *poteshnik*. We tentatively agree with the interpretation put forward by A. A. Pletneva, who suggests that *veselyi* is a broad and fairly neutral term (unlike *skomorokh*) to indicate some sort of entertainer.[82] Thus, in this private, wedding-related context, it seems likely that this mixed instrumental group, even though its composition at least partially reflects instruments that might also appear in skomorokh entertainments, was drawn from resources at the court itself or in the city: "February 10 [1626] ... the Tsar's payment to the veselye: Paramonka Fedorov, the gusli players Uezda and Bogdashka Vlas'ev, the domra players Andriushka Fedorov and Vaska Stepanov, and the fiddlers [*skrypotchiki*] Bogdashka Okat'ev, Ivashka Ivanov, Onashka, and the foreigner, the newly-christened Armanka ... because they were at the Tsar's wedding, in the private quarters, and entertained the Tsar."[83]

After the wedding, the court continued to bolster its keyboard menu by recruiting two Dutch brothers, who worked with organs and/or musical clocks from 1630 to 1638. The clockmakers Hans (or perhaps Johan) and Melchior (Melkhart) Loon (Luhn)—the spelling uncertainties reflect the fact that we have only Russian sources—arrived in Moscow by October 1630.[84] They came with other such specialists (silversmiths and a jeweler), and they also brought along two assistants. Hans died in Russia in 1637, and Melchior was given permission to return home the next year.

Melchior's 1638 departure records describe what the brothers had brought with them to Moscow initially. The intent seems straightforward: not only did they bring materials or constructed components to work with—the "strement na argannoe delo"—but also their skill in fabricating this "strement" was the motivation for hiring them in the first place. The language in the record is elusive, so we have provided some alternatives in the translation: "they brought with them from the Dutch lands a 'strement na argannoe delo' [an organ or components associated with organ making], and in Moscow they completed this instrument, and around this instrument they made a carved frame [or case], and painted it with paint and gold; and on this instrument they made a nightingale and a cuckoo with their voices [i.e., something that produced birdsong or other musical sounds], and when they play these 'argany' [the pipes/sounding element or the instrument as a whole] both birds sing all by themselves, without any human hand."[85]

The foreign glossaries cited in this chapter, as well as a few more from the 1630s–1640s, indicate that visitors to Russia were aware of organs and other keyboard instruments there. Adam Olearius, a member of a Holstein diplomatic delegation who traveled through Russia in the 1630s, uses *Positiv* to describe an instrument at the home of Nikita Ivanovich Romanov (the tsar's cousin). The Trondheim vocabulary, a Russian-German glossary from the mid-seventeenth century, has several organ-related terms: "*organy* – ein Orgel"; "*organshik* – ein Organist"; "*rygaly* – ein Real."[86] The word *strement* (or *strament*) also appears in later Russian sources to describe toys belonging to the young royal children, and keyboard historian Leonid Roizman believes these references indicate mechanical instruments.[87] It is possible that the Loons' "strement na argannoe delo" referred to mechanical components for a larger instrument, which they then completed in Russia.

It is unclear exactly how the Loons' instrument sounded (by means of a keyboard, with a turning handle, or both), and the terminology in the various Russian documents could be interpreted to mean either stand-alone, smallish organs or perhaps the elaborate mechanical clock organs that were so popular all over Europe. The Loons' "strement" could fit at any point along a continuum: clever musical clocks and automata were often and brilliantly joined together with clever keyboard instruments, and the skills for creating both required fine workmanship and tools as well as a knowledge of intricate mechanisms. Based on the description quoted earlier, the Loon instrument seems to tilt toward the mechanical clock-organ side of the continuum.[88]

Such mechanical curiosities had long fascinated the Russian court. The embassy from Emperor Rudolph to Tsar Fedor's court, in 1597, brought an elaborate chiming clock that featured mechanical actions and the sounding of musical instruments by figures "like living people."[89] In their turn, the Russians sent ambassador Vlas'ev to Poland with an impressive musical clock featuring an elephant surmounted by a tower as a gift to Marina Mniszek for the proxy wedding (1605). It sounded out "according to Muscovite custom," with various "loud and distinct sounds," including drums, twelve pipes or trumpets, and then, after a long display, flutes.[90] The 1654 inventory of the possessions of royal cousin Nikita Romanov—the owner of the Positiv—also associates complex Western workmanship with clock/instrument combinations. He owned a decorated box or chest with "tsynbaly" and a clock, as well as another foreign or German chest, inside of which was a "tsymbal" (in the singular) and on top a clock with military-style accoutrements.[91] On the more organ-like side of the continuum, however, an instrument created by the German composer Hans Leo Hassler recalls the Loon instrument. Hassler wrote that the mechanical organ for which he composed music "by itself, without the help of the hand plays several pieces." Even further along this continuum were the exquisitely decorated cabinets with many amusing components—the intricate and popular *Wunderkammern*—which often included small keyboards.[92] The elaborate outer decoration and cabinet that the Loon brothers created (or completed) in Moscow was also part of the appeal, recalling Horsey's virginals "all gilt and enameled" that had so delighted a previous Russian court.

Wherever it fell on the clock-organ continuum, the Loon instrument was popular at court. The tsar himself attended performances on two occasions and paid the enormous sum of 2,676 rubles to purchase it, in addition to payments to the brothers for their work. Melchior was given permission to leave with the option of returning to Moscow freely and was rewarded with a handsome monetary gift on his departure. He was requested to negotiate with two clockmakers, who were to come to Moscow and teach their skills there; they would replace the assistants the brothers had brought with them initially.[93] We do not know if there were any results from this request.

Throughout the Loons' residence, the Russian court continued to employ other keyboard specialists. The tsymbal'niki Andrei Andreev and

Melentii Stepanov were both provided with fabrics for what appear to be performance costumes (1631–1632). Stepanov had been involved in the 1626 wedding as well, so his tenure at court lasted for several years.[94] Another available tsymbal'nik was "young Gladko," who appears to have been a remnant of the party brought to Moscow by Bishop Iosif (the group also included Proskurovskii). A 1634 petition requested that Gladko (as well as another desirable young specialist, a clockmaker) be transferred from Suzdal' to one of the tsaritsa's relatives. As in the case of Nikita Romanov's Positiv and the other instruments he owned, the upper ranks were following the musical tastes of the court.[95]

At the time of Melchior Loon's departure, Proskurovskii reemerged, now referred to as an organ master ("argannyi master"). We do not know if he worked directly with the Loon brothers because there is a ten-year period in which Proskurovskii's name is absent from the records. He resurfaced only a few weeks after Melchior Loon departed and seems to have undertaken his duties immediately. Or, at least, he attempted to. Proskurovskii's December 1638 petition indicates that he was struggling to fill Melchior's shoes, so Fedor Zaval'skii was ordered to help him out. Apart from a reference in the 1638 Moscow census records, this is our last glimpse of Proskurovskii after a career of well over a decade.[96]

We know from later evidence that Fedor Zaval'skii, like Proskurovskii, came to Moscow in the obviously multitalented suite of Bishop Iosif, with whom he had been associated from his youth, as a servant. Although their paths crossed at several points, Zaval'skii's experiences in Russia were very different from those of his fellow traveler. In 1628, he was caught up in a series of petitions against his employer, Iosif, and wound up being hauled off in chains and sent into exile, where he remained for five years; Zaval'skii reappears in the records only in 1634, when he was brought back to Moscow.[97] After another archival gap, Zaval'skii pops up in 1638, when he was assigned to help Proskurovskii in his post-Loon assignment with the organ entertainment ("organnaia potekha"). As in the case of Proskurovskii, it is unclear where or when Zaval'skii acquired his keyboard skills, which at any rate seem to have been inadequate, for he failed to find permanent employment at the Poteshnaia palata. A petition from May 1639 mentions his work there over the previous six months but he was not a member of its ranks. Eventually he received some back pay for his work there with the organs (July 1640), although by that time, the keyboard position had been filled by another person, Iakushka Timofeev (June 1639), who had been listed as a "poteshnik" in the Moscow census records of 1638.[98]

In addition to this keyboard contingent, in the late 1620s and 1630s the court organized a separate group of entertainers with different skill sets. One long-standing participant was Ivan Semenov Lodygin. He emerges first in fully formed sartorial splendor in records from 1629 to 1631, although it is not clear what activities such splendor was meant to enhance. Nevertheless, he was supplied with a wardrobe in a rainbow of colors and fabrics, trimmed with fur and lots of silver buttons, so whatever he was doing, he was clearly doing it in style.[99] He is almost always mentioned by his full Russian (or russified) name, but this first group of records does not mention any specific skills, and he is not associated with the Poteshnaia palata. We get more details in late 1631, and given the importance of the audience, it is clear why Lodygin had to dress so nicely. For the December 6 holiday that year, he entertained the tsar and the almost two-year-old tsarevich, Aleksei Mikhailovich, with trained falcons.[100] The performance was successful although not without incident: somehow the other entertainers assembled for the festivities, the court fools, ended up tearing Lodygin's performing clothes. Eventually all was replaced in typically resplendent style.[101] In October 1632, he was issued a foreign costume ("nemetskii kostium"), but it was only two years later that he was listed explicitly as a foreigner. In December 1634 the "foreign entertainer" performed together with some unnamed cohorts as well as some students or trainees and, again, the court fools. For this performance there is a payment to a translator, implying not only that there was a spoken component to the entertainment but also that Lodygin could not handle it himself (or perhaps was too busy performing, or protecting his costume, to take on this linguistic task).[102]

This seems to have been so much fun that shortly thereafter, in January 1635, female "foreign" costumes were ordered for the tsaritsa's entertainment, and in the same month, there was another large production, which looks like a follow-up performance after Lodygin's December 1634 success.[103] This January event did not involve Lodygin but introduces two others who figure over the next several years: the foreigners Iurii Voin-Brant and Ermis. As in the December event, this January production required an interpreter, Fedor Ivanov, who had worked at Lodygin's show the previous year.[104] At around this point, then, in the mid-1630s, there was a real focus on providing a variety of performed amusements, and we see these three figures (Lodygin, Ermis, and Voin-Brant) appearing separately and together in various combinations.

References to Voin-Brant are concentrated in 1635, but Ermis appeared on the scene for a longer period. His name might be a *nom de théâtre*, from Hermes, perhaps a nod to his rope-walking talents; this was his occupation in the 1638 Moscow census and in later petitions, where he says, for example, that he taught rope-walking skills to youngsters.[105] Lodygin also taught rope walking and percussion (*barabany*, which are military drums); here he is explicitly associated with the Poteshnaia palata.[106] Ermis, too, ended up teaching other music-related skills, for later he, apparently quite reluctantly, taught trumpeters. After this point, in the early 1640s, Ermis departed for Siberia, where he apparently remained for the rest of his career.

The *barabanshchiki* (who played the barabany) were not the only percussionists at the Russian court, for a different ensemble was much more important in terms of its participation in court entertainments (as opposed to the barabanshchiki, who functioned primarily in military or processional ceremonies). All three of the entertainers we have been discussing were associated with performers on *nakry*, which are small, usually paired, bowl-shaped drums (the performers are called *nakrachei*). Nakry were of long-standing use at the Russian court, and they featured widely in both Eastern and Western traditions.[107] Like many other instrumentalists, nakry players, too, have fallen victim to the determination to equate all instrumentalists with skomorokhi—they are unrelated.[108] The ensembles of nakry players were characteristic in their organization into squadrons and the provision of costumes; they are also particularly delightful because of their association with the young tsarevich, Aleksei Mikhailovich, and later with his brother, Ivan Mikhailovich.

Tsarevich Aleksei's nakry players were organized in 1633, when a group of eighteen performers was assembled (and costumed) for the nearly four-year-old heir. The players themselves were young, following another group of (relatively) age-appropriate specialists assembled right after the tsarevich's birth: young liturgical singers.[109] Two years later, three nakry players were paid from a new government department established in the name of the tsarevich, and at this time, the young players were provided with foreign costumes; the transaction was handled by Lodygin.[110] There are many references to the nakrachei throughout the mid-1630s, indicating that Lodygin, Ermis, and Voin-Brant worked on a variety of tasks with them, in addition to their other entertainment duties. They must have been successful, for in 1635, another nakry ensemble was established for the heir's younger brother, Ivan. The tsarevichi themselves apparently also wanted to get in on the fun, for in late 1636 and early 1637, foreign costumes were made for them and for some of their attendants, with rich fabrics and furs and positively festooned with buttons. It is right after this that Lodygin was paid for teaching rope tricks and other entertainments at the Poteshnaia palata. The suite of amusements was also provided outside of Moscow, particularly in the royal retreat at Rubtsovo (where the tsar had seen the elephant performance earlier).[111]

During this energized period of court entertainments, two Russian diplomatic missions, both to Warsaw, witnessed the ways in which other rulers created elaborate productions in specially prepared venues. Earlier Russian diplomats had seen such performance spaces. In 1582, Iakov Molvianinov had dined and witnessed a "scena, musica et oration" at the as-yet-unfinished Teatro Olimpico in Vicenza; a later visitor noted that the Russians had been "very honourably entertained in this Theater with musicke and a banquet."[112] The two missions to Poland, in 1635 and 1638, brought Russian representatives face to face with the latest in Western entertainment: opera.

The Russian delegation sent to the signing of a peace treaty between Russia and Poland was led by A. M. L'vov (who headed the Chancery of the Great Court) and seconded by S. M. Proestev.[113] The main musical event was an opera, *Giuditta*, staged on April 24/May 4, 1635, the day after the treaty was signed. This was the first opera produced at the court of King Ladislaw (Władysław) Vasa (r. 1632–1648). The king was an early and fervent devotee of the new genre, and maintained an extensive musical establishment, with a full complement of singers, instrumentalists, and other necessary personnel (poets, set designers, and so forth).[114] *Giuditta* survives only in a published summary although the performance was reported widely; an Italian dispatch, for example, praised it as a "tragedy, recited to music in the Italian language, with changes of scenery and proper splendor."[115] The important Polish magnate Albrycht Stanisław Radziwiłł, grand chancellor of Lithuania, describes it as a "recitativa," and he offers some unflattering commentary about the Russian spectators: "In the evening there was an Italian comedy (called a *recitativa*), pleasantly sung by musicians in the presence of the Muscovite ambassadors and the one from Florence. The Muscovite ambassador, obese, was unmoved, and praised nothing but the comedies of their grand prince."[116] The cultural condescension (from both sides) indicated by this remark is particularly telling because the Russian ambassador in question, L'vov, probably knew more about the state of entertainment at the Russian court than any other official. As head of the chancery responsible for the court entertainments provided by the likes of Lodygin, Ermis, and others, L'vov certainly would have known that the "recitativa" was not only wholly uncharacteristic of the Romanov entertainments but also completely beyond the means of the Russian court's performers.

Whatever official disapproval the Russian party may have affected, its report documents this performance in (relative) detail. The Russian account refers to the production in general terms, beginning with the invitation to attend this "potekha" with the king, and then going to the palace to "see the history [i.e., story]." It concludes by noting that the performance took place in the king's "Poteshnaia palata," an accurate description reflecting not only Russian terminology but also the current state of the Polish court, for the production was at the palace but took place before the construction of the large, specialized theater.[117] The most detailed description relates to the all-important seating arrangements, protocols that warranted inclusion in the official report: the royal couple sitting in armchairs, L'vov at the king's right, the senators seated on benches behind them, and other dignitaries standing.[118] The Russian account summarizes the three-hour production as an "entertainment from rhetoric" taken from the Bible, in which Holofernes, the Assyrian king's general, comes to Jerusalem, and Judith saves Jerusalem.[119] The fluidity of the language in the Russian account matches that of the Italian and Polish descriptions (as a "comoedia Italica," a "recitativa," "una tragedia in lingua italiana recitata in musica"), but there is a difference. The Russian description relies on variants of the familiar term *potekha* but does not use *komediia*—this word appears in Russian reports shortly thereafter.

Almost exactly three years later, another Russian party saw an elaborate production in Warsaw, this time at the new Royal Theater.[120] There is some crossover in personnel, for Proestev, who had been the second-ranking member of the earlier mission, headed this 1638 visit. During the party's stay, its members attended *Narciso transformato*, a "favola pastorale recitata in musica," on April 23/May 3, 1638, which was given at the closing of parliament in a lavish production that concluded with a battle dance performed by the royal pages.[121] The Russian report does not describe the mythological subject matter, which, unlike the biblical story the visitors had seen earlier, would have been unfamiliar. The only hint of the variety the Russians saw displayed on the stage over the course of seven hours is in the comment: "And in the comedy the entertainment was [produced by] various clever contrivances."[122] But the Russian account does indicate a gradual settling of terminology, for the report, although invoking the familiar *potekha*, also consistently describes the production with the word *komediia*. Indeed, this 1638 report offers a brief definition—"komediia, in Russian, potekhi"—and after that proceeds to use *komediia* many times without further comment. Although such lexical choices do not necessarily reflect a straightforward selection process, we do see overall the gradual incorporation of terminology necessary to describe what the ambassadors were seeing in person and what the kuranty translations were reporting.[123]

In the midst of such interesting reports from abroad and entertainment efforts at home, however, the situation at the Russian court changed. There is no reason to think that the performers or their repertoires were suddenly deemed objectionable in and of themselves; it was, instead, the sad turn of events experienced by the royal family that blunted their interest in such frivolities. The most devastating were the deaths of two of the tsar's sons, the five-year-old Ivan and the newborn Vasilii, both in early 1639, following a sorcery incident uncovered the previous fall.[124] The family was plunged into mourning, and this probably accounts for the disappearance or reassignment of Lodygin and Ermis at around this time. It was only several years later that the court seems to have regained its entertainment equilibrium, and this is the period with which our study opened, in the early 1640s, with the appearance of the Dannenfels troupe attempting to peddle its wares in Pskov at the same time that the court was trying to hire entertainers to impress the Danish count (and hoped-for bridegroom) Waldemar. Given the court's previous engagements with musical entertainments, acrobats, and rope walkers, the Dannenfels troupe, and any other hires from the West, would have fit right in.[125]

The expectations and exposures that developed in Russia over nearly a hundred years, from the mid-sixteenth to the mid-seventeenth century, set the stage for future encounters. When the political and military environment, in the 1650s, resulted in more extensive diplomatic interactions with Western powers, the visiting Russian ambassadors and the staff at the Ambassadorial Chancery would thus have had some acquaintance with the entertainment landscapes they were to encounter—almost. For these midcentury trips took them to the very heart of Western performance, particularly operatic, traditions: Italy. These experiences are the subject of our next chapter.

NOTES

1. The English account of this mission is in Hakluyt, *Hakluyt's Collection of the Early Voyages*, 318–324; here, 319 (henceforth cited as Hakluyt, *Voyages*).

2. Morozov, *Ocherki*, 29–33, discusses Avramii's account; it is published in *DRV* 17:178–185 (all references are to the second edition unless otherwise noted). Another Russian delegate to the conference described a puppet show in Lübeck (*Biblioteka literatury* 6:468–469). See Velimirović, "Liturgical Drama," on the Byzantine-Russian connections.

3. The mission was headed by D. I. Ralevyi and M. I. Ralevyi (see Skrzhinskaia, *Rus', Italiia i Vizantiia*, 154–156; *PSRL* 18:272–273, 276). We thank T. A. Matasovaia for advice on these events. This is the organist known in Russian sources as "Ivan Spasitel'," usually assumed to be a rendition of "Giovanni Salvatore."

4. We emphasize here a practical performance tradition. Late sixteenth-century Russian sources featured organs prominently in imagery depicting, especially, King David's composition of the Psalter (see Roizman, *Organ*, esp. 33–38). An early unsuccessful attempt at hiring an organist from the West is noted in this chapter.

5. Fabris, "Italian Soundscapes," with references to relevant travel literature.

6. Barne is quoted in Evans, "Meeting," 528. Waugh, "What Was News," discusses oral transmission and how it might be traced.

7. Sowerby, "Material Culture," 54, also emphasizes the length of the diplomats' stays. On Nepea, see Baron, "Osep Nepea."

8. All entries from Machyn's diary (*London Provisioner's Chronicle*) are quoted from the modern translation edited by Richard Bailey, Marilyn Miller, and Colette Moore, available online; entries are identified by date, here, February 27, 1557. The names and places in Machyn fully correspond to the contemporary English account in Hakluyt, *Voyages*, 320. Nepea's entry is discussed in Sowerby, "Material Culture," 49. On Machyn, see Mortimer, *DNB*, s.v. "Machyn, Henry"; Marsh, *Music and Society*, 505–525, surveys musical elements in his diary.

9. Vinogradoff, "Russian Missions to London," 41. On Savin's mission, see Willan, *Early History*, 112–117.

10. Machyn, *London Provisioner's Chronicle*, March 23, 1557; Hakluyt, *Voyages*, 321, mentions the royal arrival but includes no description.

11. Rye, *England as Seen by Foreigners*, 201n34.

12. Military instruments and salvoes, for example, are in Berry and Crummey, *Rude and Barbarous Kingdom*, 185, 335.

13. Nepea's procession to the royal audience is in Machyn, *London Provisioner's Chronicle*, March 25, 1557, and Hakluyt, *Voyages*, 321. The diplomatic implications of Nepea's route and reception are in Sowerby, "Material Culture." The Westminster Abbey visit is in Machyn, April 20, 1557; as the editors remark, Machyn seems to have been inclined toward Catholicism, so appears to note this excursion with approval.

14. Rye, *England as Seen by Foreigners*, 10; on the use of organs, see Marsh, *Music and Society*, 394–404, 422 (with reference to Machyn, who mentions organs and "regals" several times, for example, *London Provisioner's Chronicle*, September 28, 1553; June 8, 1556; May 11, 1562).

15. Machyn, *London Provisioner's Chronicle*, April 23, 1557; Hakluyt, *Voyages*, 321. Sowerby, "Material Culture," 51, discusses the spatial architecture of this event. Evensong takes the *Magnificat* from Vespers and the *Nunc dimittis* from Compline (see Harper and Le Huray, *GMO*, s.v. "Service").

16. Machyn, *London Provisioner's Chronicle*, March 31, 1557. A description of a later dinner given by the Lord Mayor (1611) shows that it might be accompanied by instrumental music and singing (Rye, *England as Seen by Foreigners*, 145).

17. Hakluyt, *Voyages*, 322. Machyn's diary has no entry under this date.

18. Hakluyt, *Voyages*, 353. The description emphasizes Tsar Ivan's religiosity, so it seems most likely that these were liturgical singers. From the English point of view, the court at this time (in the late 1550s) seemed devoid of entertainment: "Hee [Tsar Ivan IV] delighteth not greatly in hawking, hunting, or any other pastime, nor in hearing instruments or musicke, but setteth all his whole delight upon two things: First, to serve God, as undoubtedly he is very devoute in his religion, and the second, howe to subdue and conquere his enemies" (Hakluyt, *Voyages*, 357). The report of a foreign organist, Danilo, at Ivan's court is in error (see Shamin and Dzhensen, "Inozemnye poteshniki," 34–35).

19. Russian diplomatic practices are summarized in Hennings, *Russia*, chap. 2. On the stateinye spiski, see Rogozhin, *Posol'skii prikaz*, esp. 101–109; Likhachev, *Puteshestviia*, 326–329. Rankings of diplomatic staff are discussed later in this chapter and in chapter 2.

20. Likhachev, *Puteshestviia*, 136–138.

21. Kotoshikhin (d. 1667) wrote about the Russian state from exile in Sweden; his remarks on dancing are in Kotoshikhin, *O Rossii*, 27 (fol. 19), in the context of a royal wedding.

22. Surny (plural; players are called *surnachei*) are identified as reed instruments in several sources. A late sixteenth-century glossary by the French trader Jean Sauvage lists "ung joueur de hault boys, Sounachay" (i.e., surnachei; Larin, *Tri inostrannykh istochnika*, 102), and a slightly later source defines "surenka" as "ein Schallmey" (Sverdrup Lunden, *Trondheim*, facsimile fol. 90v). On the cornett, see Baines and Dickey, *GMO*, s.v. "Cornett," which suggests the indoor use described earlier (especially, as the authors note, in the chapel, where cornetts appear "along with trombones and organ as support for choral music"). In these Russian accounts, *truby* thus seems to function as an all-purpose word for something that looked generally horn- or trumpet-like but was not necessarily a military trumpet, especially when applied to indoor use.

23. Likhachev, *Puteshestviia*, 128.

24. Likhachev, *Puteshestviia*, 140.

25. *PDS* 2:336 (August 19/29, 1595); highlighted in Gruber, "Muscovite Embassy," 20–21.

26. *PDS* 2:339. This banquet was on August 24 / September 3 and is described in Western reports (Klarwill, *Fugger-Zeitungen*, 187, which mentions "Musici").

27. *PDS* 2:360 (September 17). On Rudolph's court music and his retention of his father's establishment, see Lindell, "Music and Patronage," and Lindell and Mann, *GMO*, s.v. "Monte, Philippe de."

28. Recent studies of Mikulin's mission are in Sowerby, "Material Culture," and Musvik, "And the King of Barbary's Envoy." See also Evans, "Meeting," and Mikulin, "Kommentarii"; the stateinyi spisok is published in Likhachev, *Puteshestviia*, 156–205.

29. Contemporary descriptions of the Richmond gathering are in Evans, "Meeting," 517; the Russian account is in Likhachev, *Puteshestviia*, 164–169. On the St. George's Day celebrations (which Nepea, Pisemskii, and Mikulin all attended), see Musvik, "And the King of Barbary's Envoy," 235–236; the Mikulin account is in Likhachev, *Puteshestviia*, 183–184, with the queen's London entrance and Accession Day Tilts on pp. 171–173.

30. This discussion is based on Hotson, *First Night*, chap. 8; the English document describing the events is in R. Alexander, "Record" (Hotson interleaves the Russian report with rearranged portions from the English account). Hotson is the source for Crewdson, *Apollo's Swan*, 57–61. Another near miss by a visiting Russian diplomat was a performance by women entertainers planned for the Russian ambassador, Istoma Shevrigin, when he passed through Ferrara en route from Rome, in 1581—could this have been the famous *concerto delle donne*? See Dubrovskii, "Novye dokumenty," 65.

31. Hotson, *First Night*, 188–191; R. Alexander, "Record," 15 ("to heare service"). Sowerby, "Material Culture," 54 and figs. 1 and 3, discusses the layout of the space.

32. Likhachev, *Puteshestviia*, 176.

33. Hotson, *First Night*, 199.

34. Likhachev, *Puteshestviia*, 177.

35. Hotson, *First Night*, 181; R. Alexander, "Record," 17; Crewdson, *Apollo's Swan*, 59–61. There is a description of a performance by the Children of the Chapel the following year, 1602, when they played at Blackfriars; see "Diary of the Journey," 26–29, and Chambers, *Elizabethan Stage* 2:46–47. The description mentions their use of lighting effects and their excellent musical abilities.

36. *PDS* 1:680–681. On the Russian liturgical singing ensembles (*pevchie d'iaki*), see Parfent'ev, *Professional'nye muzykanty*; other references are summarized in Jensen, *Musical Cultures*, chap. 2. Lasso's widely quoted description is in Lindell, "New Findings," 231.

37. For example, *PDS* 1:677. On Maximilian's fanfare and chapel musicians, see Pass, *Musik und Musiker*; on other chamber ensembles, see Lindell, "New Findings," and Seifert, "Institution," esp. 42–43.

38. Nepea, for example, had heard organs in religious services and, because he was so closely attended by the wealthy London merchants, would likely have heard virginals or other keyboards in these surroundings or at court. Roizman, *Organ*, 38–39, discusses *tsymbal* or *tsimbany* in association with images of organs in late sixteenth-century Russian miniatures.

39. Bond, "Russia at the Close of the Sixteenth Century," 217; modern edition in Berry and Crummey, *Rude and Barbarous Kingdom*, 321. The commissions were presumably general in nature, corresponding to Horsey's "costly things of great value."

40. Bond, "Russia at the Close of the Sixteenth Century," 222; Berry and Crummey, *Rude and Barbarous Kingdom*, 325. In Croskey, "Composition," the chart on p. 375 indicates that these recollections of the gifts are from the initial period of the work's composition, in 1589–1590, so Horsey's enumeration seems reliable, although he may have inflated his role in the requests. This situation—servants could go where Horsey could not—suggests that the English, too, were trying to sort out appropriate behaviors for visiting dignitaries.

41. As we shall see, *tsynbaly* could sometimes indicate a dulcimer-like folk instrument. See Roizman, *Organ*, 53–55, although he concludes that in seventeenth-century court practice—as depicted in the sources discussed here—it generally indicated a keyboard instrument; he notes (pp. 54–55) that records describing repairs point to such keyboards and also (p. 45) that *vargany* (used in the plural) in the seventeenth century generally referred to an organ.

42. Sauvage spent about a month in 1586 in Kholmogory, where his glossary was initially compiled; the musical instruments are in Larin, *Tri inostrannykh istochnika*, 102 (see Jensen, *Musical Cultures*, chap. 4, for more detailed discussion). The keyboard terms are in Ripin and Whitehead, *GMO*, s.v. "Spinet," which explicitly links the terms *épinette* and *virginal*.

43. Ridley's musical terms are in G. Stone, *Dictionarie*, 437 (*tsimbaldi*), 264 (*organy*). One wonders if the use of the plural, *tsymbaly*, reflects the frequent use of plural for *virginals* (the word is plural in the uncertain 1574 usage also).

44. Schwarcz, "'Iter persicum' Tectanders," 201: "und noch andere drey Diener angenommen/ unter welchen einer ein Organist/ so sein eigen Regal gehabt."

45. The ambassador's strong English ties and the contemporary English translation of the mission's account are discussed in Ács, "Iter Persicum." There was an earlier attempt to bring organs to Russia. Hans Schlitte was sent by Ivan IV to the empire to bring some craftsmen back to Russia; he apparently sought out a "Cantor" and an "Orgelbauer," although there is no evidence that any of these specialists made it to Moscow. See Batalov, "Evropeiskie arkhitektory," 16, cited (and slightly corrected) in Shamin and Dzhensen, "Inozemnye poteshniki," 34.

46. Hellie, *Economy*, 617 (although he calls it "cymbals"), citing "Opis'," 32 ("Tsymbaly poporcheny"). Given the ambiguity of the term, it is possible that Tatishchev's instrument was a dulcimer type, but his strong court associations and the item's valuation in the inventory at one and a half rubles suggests a keyboard. On the owner, see *RBS* 20, s.v. "Tatishchev, Mikhail Ignat'evich."

47. This discussion is based on Jensen, *Musical Cultures*, chap. 1, and Shamin and Dzhensen, "Inozemnye poteshniki."

48. Gruber, "Muscovite Embassy," chaps. 2–4; *PDS* 2:esp. 742, 744 (where there is an unfortunate break in the source just as the conversation turns to entertainments at the Russian court; the focus appears to be on animal baiting). On this mission, see also Lavrent'ev, *Tsarevich*, 96–97 and 113n72. Vlas'ev was also involved in sending some young Russian students abroad for language training (see Maier, "Habent sua fata litterae").

49. Liseitsev, *Posol'skii prikaz*, 70–71. Vlas'ev's unworthiness is in a Polish dispatch describing the proxy wedding, published in *Dnevnik Mariny Mnishek*, 175 (from *RIB* 1:65).

50. A contemporary published description, including the seating plan, is in *Polnische königkliche Hochzeit* (1606), although some of the dates in this pamphlet are incorrect (referring to November rather than to December). See also Szweykowska, "Widowiska baletowe," and Leitsch, *Das Leben* 2:923–938, 3:1420–1437 (esp. 1427–1430). These reports enhance the minimal information in *Dnevnik Mariny Mnishek*, 32 (Marina did not attend, as she had not yet been officially designated as tsaritsa [Lavrent'ev, *Tsarevich*, 84–85]).

51. Lavrent'ev, *Tsarevich*, chap. 4, emphasizes the importance of the Polish context in the later events in Moscow. On the foreign musicians in Moscow, see Shamin and Dzhensen, "Inozemnye poteshniki," esp. 41–42 (no matter how they might have been counted by various observers, they were numerous). The sources for these events are detailed in Jensen, *Musical Cultures*, chap. 1.

52. Martin, "Dynastic Marriage," chaps. 2–4, compares the Dmitrii/Marina wedding structure to other Russian royal weddings. Jensen, *Musical Cultures*, esp. 20–22, discusses the overt connections made by contemporaries between Dmitrii and skomorokhi.

53. Massa, *Short History*, 133. The forty musicians are reported in *Dnevnik Mariny Mnishek*, 42. On the Polish court's musical environment, see Przybyszewska-Jarmińska, "Habsburg Queens of Poland."

54. Bussow, *Disturbed State*, 61.

55. Massa, *Short History*, 136; the "mummerie" is in "Reporte," 42, and see also *Moskovskaia tragediia*, 50.

56. Vlas'ev (and some of his diplomatic regalia) survived Dmitrii's fall (see Lavrent'ev, *Tsarevich*, 201–208). Vlas'ev died shortly thereafter in Ufa, where he was the military governor.

57. *Dnevnik Mariny Mnishek*, 42.

58. Dunning, *Russia's First Civil War*, 443; DR 1:1141–1142, 1153–1154, noted in Topyčkanov, "Die Musik," 44.

59. Dunning, *Russia's First Civil War*, chaps. 24–25. For example, liturgical drama was immediately evident at the new court; Viktorov, *Opisanie* 1:102, 104 (November and December 1613).

60. Platonov, *Lektsii*, 299.

61. Khoroshkevich, *Martin Gruneveg*, 208, and see 303–304n505 on the general meaning of *Tantzhaus* in this context. A similar meaning appears in a 1606 complaint from the Pomeranian town of Loitz, where traveling comedians had taken over a church; in so doing, a petition states, they turned this sacred space into a theater or a dancing place ("ein Spielhaus, ein Tantzplatz")—the same generalized meaning, not necessarily specifying only dancing (Limon, *Gentlemen*, 83, 168n4). Gruneweg had two musical encounters shortly after leaving Lemberg (L'viv), in the region of Bryn'; see Khoroshkevich, *Martin Gruneveg*, 186, 195.

62. Berry, *English Works of Giles Fletcher*, 297.

63. See Zabelin, *Domashnii byt* 1:pt. 2 (1915), 281–283.

64. The instrument/skomorokh assumption, for example, appears in one of the few English-language studies of the skomorokhi, Zguta, *Russian Minstrels*, 42; Roizman, *Organ*, 56, also seems to make the association between the Poteshnaia palata and skomorokh-like entertainments.

65. Nepea's lions are in Hakluyt, *Voyages*, 323; Horsey's commissions are in Berry and Crummey, *Rude and Barbarous Kingdom*, 321.

66. Shamin, "Tsirk," 138; we thank Vera Chentsova, Dmitrii Liseitsev, and Maksim Moiseev for archival documentation about the elephants and their trainers (the elephantine ear damage was due, apparently, to drunkenness on the part of one of the handlers en route).

67. Shamin, "Tsirk," 137; Viktorov, *Opisanie* 1:105. Rye, *England as Seen by Foreigners*, has references to animal baiting throughout, and, as noted earlier, this seems to be the direction of the broken-off discussion of Russian court entertainments by the 1599–1600 embassy to the imperial court. See also Kleimola, "Hunting for Dogs," esp. 478–479.

68. Fletcher's "iesters" were probably what are called *duraki* ("fools, idiots") in the seventeenth-century Russian sources; they received assistance in collecting their payments, unlike the dwarves, who collected payment on their own (Shamin, "Tsirk," 137–138).

69. For example, Zabelin, *Domashnii byt* 2 (1901): 695–705; Shamin, "Tsirk," 137–138.

70. Roizman, *Organ*, 53–55. A likely example of the dulcimer-like meaning of *tsymbaly* relates to a talented family of runaway serfs who passed through Moscow before 1625. According to the petition by their aggrieved owner, one member was not only literate but played the tsimbaly quite well. The petition says only that the family fled to Moscow and then to Siberia—it is not known if they had any contact with the court musical establishment, although it seems unlikely. Given the nature of these performers, *tsymbaly* here might suggest a dulcimer, not keyboards. See Preobrazhenskii, *Ural i Zapadnaia Sibir'*, 128.

71. L'vov also signed payments for other groups, for example, the court fools. P. Brown, "Muscovite Government Bureaus," 307, notes the expansion of the Chancery of the Great Court during Tsar Mikhail's reign, a convenient way to provide sinecures for the ruling family's supporters.

72. Viktorov, *Opisanie* 1:102 (November 1613 and the fabric for the Poteshnye khoromy). Tomila Mikhailov is also mentioned in May 1614 in Viktorov, *Opisanie* 1:107; March 1616 in Zabelin, *Domashnii byt* 2 (1901): 629.

73. On the same day, other entertainers (storytellers, a domra player) were paid in fabric; Zabelin, "Dopolneniia," 1 (1882): pt. 2, 103.

74. Zabelin, *Domashnii byt* 2 (1901): 645; on organs at this location, see also Zabelin, *Domashnii byt* 1:pt. 2 (1915), 283–284. The famous illustration of the organ in Karion Istomin's 1694 primer indicates the instruments' small size late in the century ([Istomin], *Bukvar'*, under the letter O), as does the frequent transport of the organ to different venues for the court theater in the early 1670s.

75. Information on Proskurovskii from Oparina and Shamin, "Biografii inozemnykh poteshnikov," which clarifies and corrects Zabelin and Roizman. On Bishop Iosif, see Gorbatov, "Novye materialy."

76. On the fanfare component of Russian weddings, see Jensen, *Musical Cultures*, 18, 77–79, based on the excellent studies by Russell Martin, "Choreographing" and "Dynastic Marriage." In the latter work (pp. 75–76), Martin provides context for the (relatively) delayed marriage plans for Tsar Mikhail.

77. RGADA, f. 135, otd. IV, rubr. II, No. 15 (September–December 1626); the numerous fanfare musicians are in Martin, "Choreographing," 806.

78. Zabelin, *Domashnii byt* 2 (1901): 691 (wedding payments), 692 (Proskurovskii). Proskurovskii's payment came after the tsaritsa's death but the funding source suggests he performed for her.

79. Zabelin, "Dopolneniia," 3 (1882): pt. 1, 445–446. Martin, "Choreographing," 806, notes that the tsar and his bride banqueted at the Faceted Palace. Perhaps this is the location hinted at in a passage from the much later account by Jacob Rautenfels that seems to suggest organs placed in Orthodox churches. In his description of the succeeding ruler, Aleksei Mikhailovich, Rautenfels says that the tsar, influenced by his confessor and his wife, removed the organ located in the main church of the Kremlin. This would be a highly unlikely place for an organ—perhaps Rautenfels actually meant the Faceted Palace, a far more likely location ([Rautenfels], "Skazaniia," 289). Roizman, *Organ*, 47, does not address the instrument's placement but suggests that Rautenfels refers to the Loon brothers' organ (see later in this chapter), which was located not in a Kremlin church but at court in the 1630s; Roizman, *Organ*, 76, 94, discusses organs at the Faceted Palace later, in the 1660s and 1680s.

80. Zabelin, *Domashnii byt* 1:pt. 2 (1915), 663–664 (Melentii's payment, February 24, 1626, and Proskurovskii's, February 28, where he is labeled a Pole but with no other identifying associations).

81. Shamin, "Tsirk," 138, and see the discussion later in this chapter.

82. Pletneva, "*Skomorokh*," esp. 100–101; *veselyi* appears in the 1638 Moscow census records (*Perepisnaia kniga*, 86, 131); see also Jensen, *Musical Cultures*, 263–264n42.

83. Zabelin, "Dopolneniia," 3 (1882): pt. 1, 440. The group, probably significantly, does not include any wind instruments, which were consistently associated with skomorokh practice. The keyboard player Zaval'skii, discussed in this chapter, also had to be rechristened after a spate of troubles (Gorbatov, Oparina, and Shamin, "Biografii inozemnykh poteshnikov," 108).

84. RGADA, f. 396, op. 2, ch. 1, No. 286, 7139 g. (1630/31), fol. 60v (October 14, 1630). Although their name is generally rendered as "Luhn," we are opting for "Loon" here, primarily because of an admittedly tenuous coincidence with a Dutch clockmaker by that name in the early eighteenth century; see *Catalogue of the Museum*, 51 (the Nelthropp collection), item 19, which has an entry for a clock movement attributed to "Wm. Loon," of Dordrecht.

85. *RIB* 8:284; RGADA, f. 150, op. 1, 1638, No. 3: "а превезли они с собою из Галанские земли стремент на арганное дело, и тот они стремент на Москве доделали и около того стремента станок зделали с резью и разцветили краскою и золотом, и на том стременте зделали соловья и кокушку с их голосы, а играют те арганы и обе

птицы поют собою без человеческих рук." *Slovar' russkogo iazyka* 28, s.v. "strement" [стрементъ], cites this source to define *strement* as a musical instrument, a definition that seems a bit too specific.

86. Olearius, *Vermehrte Newe Beschreibung*, 302, and *Travels*, 263 (where *Positiv* is translated as "harmonium"); *Positiv[e]* can refer to a small organ (Williams and Thistlethwaite, *GMO*, s.v. "Positive") and also to a mechanical barrel organ. The Trondheim vocabulary is in Sverdrup Lunden, *Trondheim*, facsimile fols. 90v–91. The problem, as always, comes with *tsymbaly*, defined in the Trondheim source as *ein Rausimbel*, which has associations both with organs (*Zimbel* is an organ stop) and with dulcimer/cimbalom types (Williams and Owen, *GMO*, s.v. "Organ stop," and Kettlewell, *GMO*, s.v. "Dulcimer").

87. Roizman, "Iz istorii," 596–597; he does not make a connection between these later *stramenty* and the "strement na argannoe delo" in the Loon documents. On the later keyboard instruments (including the *stramenty*), see Zabelin, *Domashnii byt* 1:pt. 2 (1915), esp. 119–121, and chapter 6 of this volume.

88. Roizman, *Organ*, 61–62, places their "strement" firmly on the pipe-organ side. The association with clocks continues in descriptions of the organs Simon Gutovskii constructed later for the court, which were dispatched as gifts in the 1660s; see Roizman, *Organ*, 72–76, with an English translation of the description of one of the instruments in Velimirović, "First Organ Builder," 222.

89. Gruber, "Muscovite Embassy," 21–23, discusses the ambassadorial party; the clock is described in Zabelin, *Domashnii byt* 1 (1895): 224. Emperor Rudolph had a special interest in such elaborate mechanical objects; see Morsman, "Quicquid rarum."

90. *RIB* 1:74. The same clock is apparently listed in *Dnevnik Mariny Mnishek*, 32, although with no reference to the elephant. Tsar Mikhail received an elephant clock from a visiting Polish embassy in 1645 that included "argany" and twelve performing figures (Zagorodniaia, "Chasy," 76). Spectacular contemporary elephant clocks are in Maurice and Mayr, *Clockwork Universe*, 262–265.

91. "Rospis'," 42, 60. A similar item was listed at court in 1640, when supplies were provided to repair "tsynbaly" that were decorated with dancing foreign figures: "к государевым цынбалом х починке, что скачут у цынбал немцы" (RGADA, f. 396, op. 2, kn. 635, 7148 g. (1639/40), fol. 55). A later reference, from 1675, reports that a clockmaker repaired the "clocks with organy" belonging to the tsarevich (*Sbornik vypisok* 1:14).

92. Hassler is quoted in Leichtentritt, "Mechanical Music," 19; see also Blankenburg and Panetta, *GMO*, s.v. "Hans [Johann] Leo Hassler." Such precision workmanship is associated with the Biderman [or Bidermann] family of Augsburg. Although there is no evidence of any link between the Loon brothers and the Biderman family, there is, in St. Petersburg, a mechanical ottavino spinet in a writing cabinet that, according to keyboard historian Robert Karpiak, is "reminiscent of the type made by the German builder Samuel Biderman," and there is a signed Biderman spinet there as well (Karpiak, "Researching Early Keyboards," 5–6; Lefeber-Morsman, "Augsburger Instrumentenbauer").

93. *RIB* 8:284–286.

94. Zabelin, *Domashnii byt* 1:pt. 2 (1915), 665–666 (Andreev on March 23, 1631; Stepanov on March 19, 1632).

95. Petition from V. I. Streshnev, March 24, 1634, in Gorbatov, "Novye materialy," 24. Streshnev maintained a large residence in Moscow (Crummey, *Aristocrats*, 144). If Gladko was a youngster in 1634, he must have been just a child when he arrived nearly ten years earlier. Perhaps this abundance of musical instruments among these high-ranking families indicates that Olearius's well-known remark about Nikita Romanov was a bit of an exaggeration:

"The Germans, however, are permitted to have music in their homes, as is the great magnate Nikita, the friend of the Germans.... There is little the Patriarch can say to him" (Olearius, *Travels*, 263).

96. Roizman, *Organ*, 63–64, where Zaval'skii is instructed not to perpetrate any tricks ("khitrosti") during his employment.

97. Gorbatov, Oparina, and Shamin, "Biografii inozemnykh poteshnikov." Gorbatov, "Novye materialy," is a detailed study of the complex accusations, which were resolved (or wiped out) with the death of Patriarch Filaret (Tsar Mikhail's father), in 1633; Zaval'skii petitioned for release directly thereafter. The reference to "Feska Tsymbal'nikov" as a servant (*keleinik*) comes from a statement by the drummer Gubarevskii, from 1634, before Zaval'skii had demonstrated any keyboard skills—either he had already displayed such talents or the nickname derived from his father.

98. Roizman, *Organ*, 63, lists Iakushka Timofeev as a student of the Loon brothers, apparently based on the chronological proximity of his appointment; we have not been able to document this association. Timofeev is listed in the census as a "poteshnik," along with his brother, Luk'ianka (*Perepisnaia kniga*, 244); they lived next to another of the tsar's entertainers, the gusli player Liubimka Ivanov, who, in 1629, was also paid for his skills (Shamin, "Tsirk," 138).

99. On Lodygin, see Shamin, "Tsirk"; on clothing and fabric, see Hellie, *Economy*, chaps. 16–18.

100. There is a much earlier reference to an "Ivan Lodygin" as a falconer in 1617 (RGADA, f. 396, op. 2, kn. 279, 7125 g. (1616/17), fol. 420); the next reference to Lodygin is more than a decade later, so it is hard to be absolutely certain that this is the same person, although the association with falcons continues in this 1631 reference.

101. RGADA, f. 396, op. 1, 7140 g. (1631/32), No. 1954 ("А дураки, государь, теша тебя, государь, издрали на мне однорядочку да шапочку"); the episode is mentioned in Shamin, "Tsirk," 139.

102. Shamin, "Tsirk," 139, focuses on the terms describing Lodygin's foreign costumes, which are different from the other, traditional, garments provided for him. The records are in RGADA, f. 396, op. 1, No. 2853, 7146 g. (1637/38), fols. 1–2 (Lodygin and students) and RGADA, f. 396, op. 2, kn. 290, 7143 g. (1634/35), with the name of the translator.

103. Zabelin, *Domashnii byt* 1:pt. 2 (1915), 289.

104. RGADA, f. 396, op. 2, kn. 290, 7143 g. (1634/35), fols. 288–288v; Shamin, "Tsirk," 141–142.

105. On Ermis see Oparina and Shamin, "Biografii inozemnykh poteshnikov," and Shamin, "Tsirk," 140–141. Ermis converted to Orthodoxy and married a Russian woman; in the 1638 census he is listed as "the foreigner Ermil, who walks on the rope" (*Perepisnaia kniga*, 74). Ermis and the other entertainers may have been tightrope walkers but they may also have displayed other rope tricks; see the description of rope dancers, for example, in Vander Motten, "Jacob Hall," 45.

106. Shamin, "Tsirk," 143, citing petitions from June and July 1637 (the Poteshnaia palata association), both of which mention teaching students to walk on the rope and dance ("учеников по конатам ходить и тонцовать" in the June petition).

107. Blades and Bowles, *GMO*, s.v., "Nakers," where the Arabic term is given as *naqqāra*, and Bowles, "Impact"; they are widely illustrated in Western processions.

108. See Shamin, "Nakry," 322; the present discussion is based on this study.

109. Shamin, "Nakry," 334–336; on the young singers, see Zvereva, "Gosudarevy pevchie d'iaki," 362.

110. The same three players are named in July 1637, with Ermis in charge; Shamin, "Nakry," 335–336.

111. Other entertainments at Rubtsovo in 1631 included a blind performer (probably on the domra) and bearbaiting (Shamin, "Tsirk," 137–138).

112. Dubrovskii, "Novye dokumenty," 56 and n. 116; the later report of the event, from [Coryate], *Coryat's Crudities* 2:86 (1611), is based on travel experiences in 1608—so the Russians' attendance was still worth reporting more than two decades after the fact.

113. *RBS* 10, s.v. "L'vov, kn. Aleksei Mikhailovich" (L'vov had been to the West previously, on a mission to the Danish court in 1621) and *RBS* 15, s.v. "Proestev, Stepan Matveevich"; Crummey, *Aristocrats*, 183–184, summarizes their careers.

114. Przybyszewska-Jarmińska, "*Dramma per musica*" (on p. 29, she suggests that the librettist was probably Virgilio Puccitelli; the composer is unknown); Żórawska-Witkowska, "*Dramma per musica*." The Russian diplomatic mission is surveyed in Solov'ev, *Istoriia Rossii* 5, book 9: 171–175.

115. Translation from Przybyszewska-Jarmińska, "*Dramma per musica*," 212, a dispatch from G. B. Tartaglini to Tuscany (with the original in n. 34); also published in Buturlin, *Documenti*, pt. 2:67 (Italian)/273 (Russian translation). On Buturlin, see chapter 2 of this volume. Żórawska-Witkowska, "*Dramma per musica*," 43, indicates a three-week rehearsal period for *Giuditta*.

116. Radziwiłł, *Memoriale* 2:98 (Polish translation in *Pamiętnik* 1:452). The passage is puzzling; we take it up from the final phrase quoted earlier: "The Muscovite ambassador, obese, was unmoved, and praised nothing but the comedies of their grand prince, which should rather be called tragedies performed on their cruelly scourged backs; hence, in pitiful crying, they were shouting [in a fashion that], according to the opinion of the Italian musicians, should be placed above the eunuchs' [i.e., castrati] trilling" (Moschis immotis crassitie assueta nihilque laudantibus praeter magni illorum ducis comoedias, quae potius tragoediae vocitandae dorsis illorum flagellis crudelibus expositis, hinc voces eiulantium erumpunt, quae musicorum sono Italicorum eunuchis ipsorum iudicio antelatae). We thank Bartosz Awianowicz for advice on this difficult passage.

117. Żórawska-Witkowska, "*Dramma per musica*," 45, suggests that such performances generally took place in the dining hall.

118. The seating arrangement is quite similar to one for a production at the Royal Theater in 1638 (Żórawska-Witkowska, "*Dramma per musica*," 47; Limon, *Gentlemen*, 138).

119. RGADA, f. 79, op. 1, kn. 49, 1635, fols. 767v, 769, 769v–770 ("А потеха была из ритории, что написана из Библеи, как приходил к Ерусалиму Асиреиского царя воивода Алаферна, и как Юдиф Ювеенина спасла Иерусалим"). Excerpts quoted in Solov'ev, *Istoriia Rossii* 5, book 9:174. The Russian description, which omits the name of the town of Bethulia, does not necessarily reflect ignorance of the storyline (as suggested in Przybyszewska-Jarmińska, "*Dramma per musica*," 212)—Bethulia seems to be located on the way to Jerusalem, so Judith's deed does end up saving the city.

120. King Ladislaw had built this venue for his wedding, in September 1637. The Russians had been invited, tardily, but were able to get to Poland only later, in the spring of 1638 (Solov'ev, *Istoriia Rossii* 5, book 9:179–180). On the Royal Theater, see Limon, *Gentlemen*, 137–140, in addition to the studies cited earlier.

121. On *Narciso*, see Żórawska-Witkowska, "*Dramma per musica*," esp. 30, 39, 42 (we know of one participating singer, the castrato Kaspar Förster, because he wielded a prop shepherd's flute as a weapon, bloodying composer Marco Scacchi, with whom he had been arguing for days); see also Przybyszewska-Jarmińska, "*Dramma per musica*," 215. The Radziwiłł diary

errs in calling this performance a setting of Daphnis, a natural mistake given the similarities in subject matter (Radziwiłł, *Memoriale* 2:269).

122. RGADA, f. 79, op. 1, kn. 60, 1638: "А на комидеи потеха была великими розными играми."

123. *Komediia* is used without comment in a 1646 kuranty translation to describe a production in Innsbruck for a royal wedding (*Vesti-Kuranty* III:125) but with a bit more explanation later, in a 1650 report of a Nuremberg banquet (*Vesti-Kuranty* IV:185). A new term, *balet*, appears in a 1649 report (*Vesti-Kuranty* IV:159; the work is identified in Dzhensen and Maier, *Pridvornyi teatr*, 155–156n190). Various translators were responsible for these kuranty translations, so usage would reflect general consensus but not necessarily a rigid standard. Berkov, "Iz istorii," 280–282, shows that contemporary Ukrainian usage was quite familiar with the term *komediia*.

124. Shamin, "Tsirk," 145, and sources cited there.

125. There was a very hostile description of the musical entertainments produced by Waldemar and his party in Moscow that, given the activities recounted here, should not have seemed out of place at the Russian court at this time. However, the language emphasizes the non-Orthodox transgressions of the foreigners, including a reference to the pipes (*piski*) and wild antics commonly associated with skomorokhi, thus reinforcing the inappropriateness of the behavior (and making explicit the pipes-skomorokh connection); the report also reflects the antiforeigner bias engendered by the marriage project: "Over the course of these days, living in the quarters prepared for him [Waldemar], he began to celebrate wildly, according to their unorthodox [transgressive] custom and belief, playing on trumpets, *organy*, and on various kinds of pipes" (Golubtsov, "Pamiatniki Prenii o vere," 6 [*organy* in this context might have a general sense of "instruments"]). The antiforeigner bias is described in Ellersieck, "Russia under Aleksei Mikhailovich," esp. 134–137.

THE THEATER OF DIPLOMACY

With the presence of the English "organes and virgenalls," the rope walkers, and the instrumentalists—not to mention the elephants!—the Muscovite court was clearly a lively place. But how did all of this add up? Although the Russian diplomatic missions we have surveyed certainly contributed to the court's familiarization with Western entertainments, we propose that during the period we have covered so far, they constituted a somewhat piecemeal foundation. In this chapter, we identify what might be called the tipping point, that is, the beginnings of sustained cultural influences at the Russian court as a result of diplomatic encounters during the later 1650s and through the 1660s. Because of the changing political and military landscapes in these decades, diplomatic exchanges were carried out more frequently and more grandly. The intensity and richness of the visitors' encounters with performed entertainment in the West made their mark in Moscow, and it is precisely such diplomatic contacts that were named specifically as stimulating the tsar to create similar private entertainments for himself, beginning in the early 1670s.[1]

What happened during these decades to promote such a sea change, particularly in light of the many encounters dating back a century or more? Some of the answers lie in the personality and growth of the tsar, Aleksei Mikhailovich (r. 1645–1676), whose carefully cultivated entertainments as a youngster we traced in our previous chapter. By the late 1650s, Tsar Aleksei had been ruling for almost fifteen years and was approaching his thirtieth birthday. He had formed a broad diplomatic and military vision regarding his two powerful neighbors, Poland-Lithuania and Sweden, and he had assembled experienced officials to help guide these efforts, particularly Afanasii Ordin-Nashchokin, who was to be his primary policy adviser for the next decade and more. The interactions among these three powers and their crucial (and shifting) Cossack alliances, through successes and failures in the military conflicts between 1654 and 1667, are tangled but the overall impact of this period on Russian culture was profound. In the broadest sense, the Muscovite military successes, especially the rapid victories in 1654–1655, when the cities of Smolensk, Polotsk, Wilno (Vilnius), and others fell to the tsar's large armies, commanded the attention of Western powers through newspaper reports and diplomatic communiques. This attention was strengthened by means of the generally low-level but numerous exchanges of representatives. All were motivated in some fashion by the military conflicts and, from the tsar's side, all had as their aim the consolidation of support (or at least the maintenance of neutrality) regarding the Russian position.[2] In some cases, the results of such diplomatic exchanges were interesting but not particularly consequential, at least from our focused view. F. F. Poroshin, for example, went to the Berlin court of Elector Friedrich Wilhelm, where he spent about two weeks in July 1654. Poroshin was treated rather more elaborately than his fairly lowly position, as messenger (*gonets*), warranted, and he was received with some honors, including a banquet. The musical entertainment that was supposed to end the evening, however, was canceled, due to the arrival of news about the untimely death of Ferdinand IV (son of Emperor Ferdinand III). Poroshin did, however, manage in his brief visit to sit for a portrait.[3]

In other cases, such outreach might actually have been detrimental, at least in terms of the general impression made by Russian diplomacy and diplomats. The Russian party that arrived in Paris later in the same year, 1654, was poorly informed (it was the first Russian mission to this country) and, according to the account (and assumptions) of the French master of ceremonies, poorly behaved. Although the Russians' elaborate attire—compared, inevitably, to Turks—was impressive, their unwillingness to leave their lodgings prevented any influential contact with Parisian culture. A Russian mission to Vienna, dispatched at the same time, was reported widely in the French press; both missions seem to have been carried out with the requisite pomp although neither appears to have enjoyed any special entertainments.[4]

The same initially mixed impact holds for foreign parties sent to Moscow, as illustrated by the experiences of Alberto Vimina, a representative from the Venetian Republic, who spent the last half of 1655 in Russia.[5] The Venetians were looking for Russian assistance in their protracted campaign with the Ottoman Empire over Crete, although trade issues were also of interest; the time seemed right in light of the favorable reports about the tsar's victorious Smolensk campaign. Vimina's difficulties were compounded not only by war but also by the envoy's illness, which delayed him in Smolensk; he never made it to Moscow. This setback, however, was only tangentially responsible for the mission's lack of success, since the tsar was, in any event, not in Moscow but in the field with his troops near Wilno.[6]

Indeed, the tsar's own travels in the early phase of the wars proved to be influential. In 1654, Tsar Aleksei became the first Russian ruler in the seventeenth century to leave the borders of Russia when he led his troops against the Polish forces in Smolensk, then in Wilno in 1655, and Polotsk (twice) in 1656 (in Polotsk, the tsar was waiting for the Truce of Wilno to be signed; Polotsk had come under Russian control in mid-1654). Although Russian forces took a number of cities during this phase of the conflicts, these three seem particularly influential. The English physician Samuel Collins, who was at the Russian court in the 1660s, pointed to the tsar's wartime travels as introducing him to the look and feel of a Western city: "Since his Majesty has been in Poland, and seen the manner of the Princes houses there, and ghess'd at the mode of their Kings, his thoughts are advanced, and he begins to model his Court and Edifices more stately, to furnish his Rooms with Tapestry, and contrive houses of pleasure abroad."[7] Music historians have long focused on the career of the Smolensk-born organ builder Simon Gutovskii, who, like many other skilled craftsmen from the newly taken territories, ended up in Moscow, where he remained for over thirty years, playing an important role in the music supplied for the court theater and, more generally, for the royal family. Gutovskii, for example, was responsible for the repair of many keyboard instruments belonging to the next generation of royal children. Another future theater musician, the trumpeter Johann Waldonn, also had connections with the Russian forces in Smolensk, and in general, after 1654, the tsar's representatives actively sought out trained workers from these areas and brought them back to Moscow, where they plied their skills in the Armory.[8]

The tsar's travels to the smaller city of Polotsk also proved to be of lasting significance. In July 1656, he passed a short time in Polotsk, where another Simeon (known in the literature as Simeon Polotskii), a monk at the Theophany Monastery, and twelve of his young students recited a declamation for the royal guest. A few months later, in October, as the tsar was returning back through Polotsk, Simeon's students again performed for him. Aleksei's favorable impressions were picked up quickly. The next year (November 1657), the Russian patriarch, Nikon, sent instructions for an elaborate reception to mark the tsar's visit to the Iverskii Monastery. It was to include not only the most modern singing style ("po partesu," in multiple vocal parts) but also an oration ("oratsiia") to be performed by twelve youngsters.[9]

Yet despite the flattery of imitation, the patriarch's influence was on the wane, and this, too, can be traced through our focus on performative culture. Simeon and some of the same youngsters from Polotsk went to Moscow, where they performed declamations on many occasions at court during their nine-month stay in 1660.[10] The reason motivating this trip highlights another point of change in the young tsar's reign. Not only was he exercising his military authority by going into the field himself, but he was also handling an extraordinary religious crisis that eventually resulted in the dismissal of Patriarch Nikon, one of the most powerful figures of his early reign. Nikon, who had enjoyed the support of the tsar since his elevation to the patriarchate in 1652 for his reform efforts, eventually overstepped this relationship by insisting on the priority of his spiritual position over the status of the tsar. The patriarch removed himself from Moscow, not officially resigning but presumably expecting to be recalled. The tsar, in effect, called his bluff, convening a council of church authorities to consult on appropriate measures. It was this council that Simeon and his young students attended in Moscow in 1660. (Nikon was finally removed from office by the council that convened in 1666–1667, although the reforms he had promoted were upheld.[11]) Shortly after Simeon's return to Polotsk, the city fell back into Polish hands (1661), an event that may have helped to motivate the poet's eventual permanent relocation to Moscow in around 1663–1664, where his writings and teachings were enormously influential in the court's literary and performative culture.[12]

THE TIPPING POINT: LIVORNO, FLORENCE, AND VENICE

It is against this complex background of the 1650s that we are able to track impacts on Russian court culture from diplomatic exchanges through what might be called the intertheater of diplomacy, borrowing from a definition of intertheater proposed by William West as "unfolding a net of possible connections and necessary spaces rather than a particular meaning that might be transmitted directly and unidirectionally."[13] Our rich source materials allow us to trace this "net of possible connections" through the range of entertainments presented, assessed, and adjusted by the hosts, the immediate reactions of the visitors, and the ways in which such responses were filtered through the constraints of the official reporting documents.

Some of the most spectacular experiences witnessed by the Russian diplomatic corps in the period resulted directly from Vimina's star-crossed mission in 1655: the encounters of the ambassadorial party headed by Ivan Ivanovich Chemodanov to the Republic of Venice the following year, 1656–1657. Chemodanov had spent his career in military service and as a member of the tsar's service nobility, holding the rank of table attendant (*stol'nik*). He had served at court as a ceremonial bodyguard (*rynda*) in the late 1620s, attending banquets for visiting dignitaries in the years following; he had also taken part in the military campaigns of the 1650s. So, although Chemodanov did not have any diplomatic experience abroad before this assignment, he was certainly familiar with diplomatic ceremony and protocol as it was practiced at the Muscovite court.[14] At the time of the Venice assignment Chemodanov was about sixty years old, and his secretary, Aleksei Posnikov (Postnikov), was about forty; in the estimation of one of their Italian hosts, Antonio Serristori (governor of Livorno), both were imposing and well-formed men ("grandi e formati"; see fig. 2.1).[15]

The dignified presence of their representatives (as well as their sartorial splendor, widely admired) showed Russian familiarity with the crucial concerns of precedence and form in the diplomatic arena. As cultural historian Helmer Helmers puts it, the Russians, like their European counterparts, were fully aware of public appearances as a "communicative event" that helped to define the diplomatic process itself.[16] In this sense, then, Chemodanov and his party were traveling on familiar territory.

Yet in other arenas, the Chemodanov mission would have found itself on terra incognita that went beyond the unfamiliar cities and landscapes

FIG. 2.1

Justus Sustermans, portrait of Chemodanov (Wikimedia Commons)

it encountered. Although the missions to the Polish court in the late 1630s had introduced Russian diplomats to the latest in Western staged entertainments, their impact was muted by the sad events at the Moscow court that occurred shortly afterward—there seems to have been no immediate interest in following up on these experiences. The Chemodanov mission, dispatched to the heart of the operatic world nearly two decades later, was thus largely unprepared for the intensity of the cultural extravaganzas that awaited it. This was certainly to change, and later Russian envoys learned to expect such encounters as part of their diplomatic perquisites. But for the Chemodanov party, the dazzling encounters in Italy were particularly impactful because they were so unanticipated, and the reports of the Russians' reactions add a humanizing dimension to the rigid and wordy protocols through which contemporary diplomacy was practiced—the spirit of adventure from both sides is palpable.

The voyage undertaken by Chemodanov and Posnikov was nothing less than epic. They left Moscow in early July 1656, heading for Arkhangel'sk, where, in early September, the party boarded two Dutch ships; passage had been arranged by the English trader John Hebdon (1612–1670), who worked extensively for the Russian court. From Arkhangel'sk, the ambassadors essentially circumnavigated western Europe, arriving in late November of that year in Livorno.[17] The three-month sea voyage—necessitated by the land wars that motivated the mission in the first place—was, quite simply, terrible, with huge storms and danger from privateers in the Mediterranean, in addition to the usual ailments and delays. The official account records all of these miseries, and when asked by the curious hosts, in some awe, about their long journey, the visitors never hesitated to launch into a recap of its horrors.

The ambassadors planned to disembark in Livorno and go through Florence to Venice. But their stay in Livorno set the tone for the rest of the trip and, indeed, for other Russian embassies that followed. The Italians had been well informed regarding the whereabouts of the visitors along the way; by early November the Livorno-based Venetian representative Giuseppe Armano had reported their departure from Arkhangel'sk to the Venetian resident in Florence, Taddeo Vico.[18]

When Livorno city officials, including Governor Antonio Serristori, boarded the Russians' ship, on November 27/December 7, 1656, they not only discussed politics but had their first experience of the grand Russian tradition of toasts. The papal correspondent detailed the ambassador's splendid, jewel-encrusted garments and the elaborate toasts featuring beautiful goblets and a variety of drinks. The next day, the ambassadors were taken into the city for a tour by their hosts, including Charles Longland, a prominent English merchant who lived and worked in Livorno. The Russian account identified him as a friend of John Hebdon, who had arranged their passage from Arkhangel'sk, and they lodged at his house.[19] The political talk and the toasting were all part of the official account; the tour of the city appears in a separate appendix or addendum to the report.[20] The description of the city formed a brief guidebook, outlining important sights (for example, the *Monumento dei Quattro mori*) and characterizing its architecture. These responses might be compared to the tsar's view of Wilno several years previously; one wonders if this earlier strong impression on the tsar prompted the amplified descriptions in the addendum.

Throughout their three-week stay in Livorno, the Russian party attended many banquets, "official" entertainments that were filled with the requisite toasts to the health of the tsar and to the Livorno hosts and, therefore, dutifully noted in the visitors' account. These banquets were a clear matter of honor and precedence and, thus, obviously belonged in the official report. But there was another series of entertainments, off-book as it were, that took place generally at Longland's house, although not necessarily limited to this venue. These were not recorded in the Russian accounts, and we know about them only from descriptions by the Livorno hosts, who, from almost the moment of the Russian party's arrival, had planned what they probably regarded as normal entertainment for important visitors but as something new and exciting for their Russian guests. (In this, they may have been relying on information relayed from Hebdon to Longland, Armano, or others among his extensive contacts.) On almost the very day of their arrival, the Venetian representative in Livorno, Giuseppe Armano, wrote of his upcoming plans, with special emphasis on the display of beautiful women: "here at home I will organize a party with beautiful ladies. For them [the Russians] it will be something new that they have not seen because in their country the women are covered in the Turkish way."[21]

Entertainments were lavishly provided. Governor Serristori observed (December 11, 1656): "It seems that they liked instrumental music, dancing, and singing, because every night these entertainments are made at Mr. Longland's house and they enjoy these activities very much."[22] This reference to parties given "every night" is reflected only faintly in the official Russian report, which mentions the banquets and toasts and omits the rest. Based on these enthusiastic responses, however, the hosts readily supplied more. On December 15, Serristori wrote to Florence, saying that he had decided to provide something similar for the visitors himself.[23] He followed up on this plan the next week, finding that the grand duke was in favor of the scheme: "I propose to invite on Thursday evening [December 21] local ladies for dancing, and on this occasion, to organize a musical performance, because I noticed that this, more than anything else, is to the taste of the ambassadors."[24]

A long report written a week later, on December 26, summarizes the activities over the past week, including this and several other parties, all of which involved the lovely ladies of Livorno and featured dancing and beautiful music.[25] The ambassadors declined to dance but feasted their eyes on the women, as Serristori remarked in his long summary report: "In the ballroom, they remained in their prepared places and did not take part in the dancing but they accepted drinks several times, and over the whole evening they stared at the women; on their return home they didn't talk about anything else at dinner except the grace of these women dancing at the ball, and they continued to talk about them [next] morning and evening at mealtimes."[26] Their fascination with the women continued in a less savory way. In the same long report, Serristori described the older ambassador as "a very lascivious man" who constantly spoke about women and was "very lustful toward them."[27]

Serristori was relieved when the Russians finally left for Florence. His long report of December 26 was filled with complaints about their behavior. Table manners and their violent treatment of servants—echoing some of the complaints about the 1654 Russian party to Paris—were especially singled out; in both cases, expectations and behavioral norms of host and guest were clearly divergent. It must also be admitted that Serristori was a fairly supercilious host, opining, for example, that in the group's frequent religious singing, headed by the Russian mission's second-in-command, "their melodies are worse than cats' music." The fact that the guests were stingy with their purses was also a sore point.[28]

The Florentines clearly relied on such advance information from Livorno. The Russian party's formal entry into Florence took place on December 25/January 4, as described in the court's Diario di Etichetta, when it was received by Prince Leopold and Grand Duke Ferdinand II and later by Cardinal (and Prince) Giovan Carlo as it made its way to the Pitti Palace. An anonymous letter describes the ceremony, adding that the entertainment began immediately. When the group got to the palace, a buffoon, Gabriello the dwarf, appeared, to much merriment; this was Gabriello Martinez, a well-known entertainer at the Medici court (see fig. 2.2).[29] This was certainly a promising start to the visit, and this first bit of comic amusement would have been familiar from the Russian court.

The Florentines offered their guests a grand city tour, which was reported in the official Russian account and, at greater length, in the appendix.

FIG. 2.2

Gabriello Martinez, entertainer at the Florentine court
(Florence, Gallerie degli Uffizi, used by permission)

They went through palaces and gardens, saw the armory and other workshops, and described the rich interiors and the tourist curiosities.[30] The Florentines were well prepared to satisfy the newly discovered musical enthusiasms of their visitors. The musical entertainments in Florence, as in Livorno, do not figure in the Russian account but are detailed in the Italian sources. They began in earnest the day after their arrival, December 26, 1656/ January 5, 1657. At the palace, properly costumed for their grand reception, the Russian party met members of the ruling family, including Cosimo, son of the grand duke, who inquired with interest about the visitors' long journey. Although Cosimo, when he succeeded his father, in 1670, was not particularly interested in music, he did seem to have been curious about Russia; perhaps this initial encounter, as well as with the Russian party that came to Florence a few years later, was the stimulus for such interest. One of the important texts about seventeenth-century Russia, Jacob Rautenfels's

De Rebus Moschoviticis, was written at Cosimo's court (and later published, with a dedication to Cosimo, in 1680).

This first greeting ceremony in Florence included a concert in the throne room (the Jupiter Room, Sala di Giove), where, seated with Grand Duke Ferdinand and Prince Leopold, the guests heard singing by castrati and women. The anonymous letter, dated on the same day (January 5), shows that the Florentine hosts were responding promptly to the tastes of their guests: "When the grand duke understood that they liked music very much, he invited almost every musician to his palace and had them come in and sing in the audience room."[31]

The amusements continued on the following day. In the anonymous letter describing the visitors' activities, a postscript mentions that there were two musical events on that day. The first was a song of thanksgiving offered spontaneously by the Russian party when they heard that the tsar had signed a peace treaty with Poland (the Truce of Wilno, which had been signed in November 1657 and which the grand duke had just learned of). The second was another musical entertainment provided for the visitors: "When the grand duke received the announcement that their emperor had made peace with the Poles, they all gathered together and sang for a long time in thanks.... Later, they went back to their rooms to get ready to go to the grand duke's rooms in order to listen to the singing and other different *zimphonie*."[32] The next day they went to the Piazza di Santa Croce for a *calcio diviso* match, a typical pre-Lenten athletic contest played by two opposing teams; they received as a gift some embroidered garters.[33] In the evening, there was a "festino di ballo" at the Salone Regio dei Principi Forestieri, a large hall in the palace used for receptions. The Russians were fascinated with the elaborate dancing.[34]

But these were just warm-ups. The most extravagant entertainments were the evenings at two of the important theaters in Florence, on January 8 and 9 (n.s.), 1657: the Cocomero and the Pergola. The Russians had not seen such elaborate performances in Livorno; the party given there by Governor Serristori was a musical evening, not a theatrical one.[35] Monday, January 8, opened with an archery session, during which Chemodanov apparently acquitted himself well. In the evening, the entertainment switched gears, when the grand duke, his wife, and all of the princes went to the Cocomero theater accompanied by the two Russian dignitaries; the court diarist recorded: "In the evening, they watched a comedy in the Via del Cocomero in the Academy de' Sorgenti's room. The comedians acted and presented *Il convitato di pietra*. It was enriched with nice music, interludes, machines, and *balletti*. The grand duke, the grand duchess, and all the princes were there, and also some women were invited. The ambassadors went [to the theater] and returned with the grand duke."[36]

The account in the anonymous letter, written on January 11, the day the Russians left, summarizes the events of the previous week. It paints an elaborate and well-attended performance, reinforcing the official court diarist's description, although the writer points out some flaws in the production (which, however, did not seem to hinder the Russians' enjoyment): "They went to the Via del Cocomero for the comedy where there were many women and a lot of gentlemen. At the same time, the grand duchess and the grand prince arrived in this order: 1, the grand duke; 2, the grand duchess; 3, the little prince [Cosimo]; 4, the older ambassador [Chemodanov]; 5, the young one [Posnikov]; 6, Leopoldo. They stayed in the box seat in the center [of the theater], and even though the machines did not work very well, they enjoyed it."[37]

Everything about this choice of venue, genre, and even the performers and audience made perfect sense from the hosts' point of view (and was certainly not planned specifically for their lucky visitors). The Cocomero theater was one of the institutions sponsored by Cardinal Giovan Carlo, a brother of the grand duke and a munificent patron of music and other arts. At the time of this visit, Giovan Carlo and the Accademia dei Sorgenti, one of several Florentine academies devoted to performance and theater, had taken over the operation of the theater in the via del Cocomero. The theater had been constructed beginning in 1650 by yet another academy sponsored by the cardinal, the Accademia degli Immobili. Part of this latter group decided to build a larger theater, in the via della Pergola (a theater our Russian party attended on the following evening), and the smaller Cocomero theater came under the patronage of the Sorgenti in 1655. The Cocomero, with seating for around five hundred, plus about fifteen boxes, was not the largest theater in Florence, but for the Russian guests, who had never previously attended any theater at all, the impression must have been stunning.[38]

The court diarist reports that the Russians saw *Il convitato di pietra*, a story with a long history on European stages. Although there is no surviving text from this Florentine production, it was one of many works, especially Florentine, based on Spanish originals—in this case, Tirso de Molina's early seventeenth-century play *El burlador de Sevilla*, the original and fertile source for the many subsequent retellings of the Don Juan story. Spanish drama was widely known throughout Europe, providing source material for many artistic treatments, as we see in later chapters. This single performance thus succinctly encapsulated the theatrical, musical, and literary interests of the Florentine hosts.[39] Although the names of the performers at this event are not given, there is strong evidence to suggest that the Russians saw two well-known commedia players, Giovan Battista Fiorillo and Marco Napolioni. Both actors were in Florence at this very time, and both received a generous payment from the grand duke (probably reflecting the fact that there was a second performance of *Il convitato di pietra* on January 19, after the Russians had departed).[40]

These performances had wide ramifications, with unexpected connections to later Russian diplomatic experiences. Shortly after the 1657 Florentine productions of *Il convitato di pietra*, a group of Italian commedia players visited Paris, where they stayed for about a year. In their repertoire was *Il convitato di pietra*, the first rendition of a Don Juan play in that city, performed in 1658. It is not known if Giovan Battista Fiorillo made this trip, but his brother, the famous Scaramouche Tiberio Fiorillo, did, possibly playing Don Juan's servant in the Paris performances.[41] After this visit, the Italian company returned to Paris later, and during this second stay, the Fiorillo comedians shared the Théâtre du Palais-Royal with the Molière company—it was this theater and these two companies that another Russian ambassador saw in 1668. At the time of this 1668 visit, the Italians were still performing *Il convitato*, as a surviving scenario attests. There must have been many differences among these Paris and Florence productions, as the performers were probably different for each, even if the general traditions of the Fiorillo family survived. Nevertheless, there may have been distant echoes from Chemodanov's first theatrical encounter, at the Cocomero in Florence, in the Paris productions the Russian diplomats saw a decade later.

On the day following its trip to the Cocomero, the Chemodanov party remained busy. As reported in the Diario di Etichetta: "The ambassadors went to the stables to see the horses and then went to the new hall for comedies in the Via della Pergola, and in the evening, the grand duke went to visit them."[42] This was shortly before the first opera was produced at the Pergola (February 5, 1657), so it is hard to say what the visitors might have seen there. Whatever the specifics, the surroundings alone would have been impressive, as the theater was spacious and luxurious, with a deep stage designed for the many special effects created by the machines.[43]

The Russian party was given a big send-off at its departure, which included the composition of some festive sonnets, probably written by Girolamo Bartolommei.[44] The report by Pignatelli, papal nuncio in Florence, confirms the impression of the weeklong stay, describing the nonstop entertainments, with *festi*, comedies, and music, noting that the guests particularly liked the music.[45] With this, the ambassadors embarked on the last leg of their journey to Venice. They traveled through papal cities (Bologna, Ferrara), and in Bologna, especially, they raised a great deal of interest. Cardinal Lomellini, the papal legate there, gave a sense of the city's fascination with them, echoing the interest expressed by the Livorno ladies: "The people of the city were very interested in them, especially some of the ladies, who wanted to go to visit them; the women were received very graciously but the invitation that day to attend a *festino* at the home of one of the gentlemen that evening was declined, on the basis that their duties and the lack of time prevented this entertainment."[46] The Russian account mentioned the invitation, omitted the ladies, and confirmed the necessity of declining.

They were greeted by Vimina, Venice's resident Russia expert, when they arrived at the border, on January 7/17, 1657. They spent several days on the outskirts of the city, leaving from Chioggia on January 11/21, in a parade of boats, accompanied by two trumpet players, to the shouts of "viva" by the populace and the roar of a military battery. The Russian reports convey the marvels of Venice, including the many "gunduly" and bridges that graced the city, and they visited palaces and the armory, with their displays of precious jewels and religious relics. These excursions provided welcome distraction from their work, for they met diligently with numerous representatives, both from Venice itself and from other cities.

Theater, however, was not forgotten in all this official business, and Carnival afforded plenty of opportunities for such show—familiar opportunities, because the Russian *maslenitsa*, or Butter Week, which was celebrated the week before Lent, was also a traditional period for entertainments and role-playing. This Carnival timing was fortuitous, determined by the climate-related departure schedule from Arkhangel'sk, but it meant that the Russian guests arrived when the theaters were in full swing. Several reports by Italian observers mention the Russian party's enthusiastic attendance at the Teatro SS. Giovanni e Paolo and the Teatro Sant'Apollinare (Sant'Aponal), two of the very important and active theaters in this most theatrically active city. A summary report to the Vatican, written on February 10, mentions visits to both theaters. On February 7, at a performance at the Teatro SS. Giovanni e Paolo, the Russian ambassador was "amazed by the quality of the scenery, costumes, and machines."[47] The Carnival opera playing at this theater was Cavalli's *Artemisia*, which was very popular and would have been performed throughout the season, although not necessarily every day—nevertheless, it is a good guess that this is what the Russians saw there. The convoluted plot, set in Venice and with some historical characters, although focusing primarily on multiple amorous intrigues, required eight different stage sets (nine including the prologue, which is missing), and it featured ballets at the ends of the first two acts. The opera house itself was large, described in a popular city guidebook in 1663 as including "marvelous mutations of sets, majestic and most rich costumes, and miraculous flights."[48] The Russians, in other words, would have seen a great show there.

The same report described the ambassador's experience a few days later, on February 10, at the Teatro Sant'Aponal: "[the ambassador] was amazed at the flight made by the *Prologo* from the ground to his box in order to present the [program of the] opera into his hands. Then he wanted to see the sets and how they were changed."[49] The action, hand-delivering the program to the ambassador in the box seats, was typical of the spectacular theatrical flights (*voli*).[50] The regularity of the Venetian Carnival productions suggests that the Russians saw *Le fortune di Rodope e Damira*, composed by Pietro Andrea Ziani to a libretto by Aurelio Aureli (and famous for its mad scene, performed by the well-known singer Anna Renzi). This would have been near the conclusion of the run, for Carnival ended on February 13. Another account, also from February 10, confirms the visitors' interest in the stage machinery. According to Urbano Gransbarra, the Florentine resident in Venice: "In these theaters, His Excellency was left astonished by the changing of scenery and he wanted to understand how it worked by looking inside."[51]

The Mantuan resident in Venice, Leonardo Villeré, also tracked the visitors' musical tour of the city, observing that "every evening they take them to see an opera, to their great delight and wonder, and often when they see the flights, they exclaim 'grande, grande Venetia.'"[52] He goes on to describe a special event at the Teatro SS. Giovanni e Paolo on February 10, 1657—that is, on the very same evening they also went to the Aponal: "This evening they are going to the Teatro Giovanni e Paolo, where they will listen to a *canzonetta* in the Russian language."[53] This must be the first time Russian was heard on a Western stage. The diplomats had probably already seen *Artemisia* during their previous visit to this theater, and this little Russian song would have been devised specially for them, perhaps on one of the off nights late in the production run—an amuse-bouche offered up before they were taken to the other theater later that evening. (The description as a canzonetta implies a light, fairly simple secular song.) With the many exchanges among various representatives of the Republic and the tsar, someone might easily have contacted a member of the Russian party and worked up a number to perform for the appreciative guests.[54]

These descriptions focus on the Russians' responses to the visual wizardry enveloping them, and this is also the case for their reactions later to Florentine theater. Indeed, even for experienced audience members, it was the spectacular stage effects that made the greatest impression. For example, the Englishman Robert Bargrave, a talented amateur musician who gave knowledgeable accounts of musical performances on his travels, was overwhelmed by the production values of the Venetian theaters. Bargrave was in Venice at the same time as the Chemodanov party, and his account echoes the Russians' awe-struck reactions upon encountering the same effects at the same theaters. As Bargrave writes, the Venetian theaters intermix the "most incomparable apparitions and motions in the aire and on the Seae, governed so by Machines, that they are scarse discernable from the reall things they represent." He says that he saw one opera there "about 16 severall times" and that "so farr was I from being weary of it, I would ride hundreds of miles to see the same over again."[55] If an experienced and musically educated traveler could be so overpowered by the extravagances of Venetian opera, it is no wonder that Chemodanov and his party were mystified, even requesting to see how the machinery worked "by looking inside."

Such overwhelming production values may account for the ways in which the Russians reacted, responding to the most unfamiliar effects. The singing styles they would have heard during this trip, as well as the interaction between the singers and the instrumental ensembles, would have been equally alien, although they did encounter singing that would have been more familiar, in church services they attended.[56] They also enjoyed singing in a setting far more comprehensible than the elegant private and public performances they witnessed. During the Venetian portion of the trip, the party encountered a peasant singer on the road; as the party's guide noted: "They enjoy instrumental music and songs, and during the trip when they heard a peasant woman singing, they stopped to listen; when she stopped singing they begged her to keep singing and gave her a pearl necklace worth 70 ducats as a present."[57]

This account is by Angelo Correr, one of the Venetian dignitaries assigned to the Russian party (and related to one of the Teatro Sant'Aponal's owners).[58] Correr had other opportunities to observe his guests' reactions to Venetian culture, specifically, to the tradition of masks they encountered during their Carnival-period trip. The Italians were aware that this custom could be troubling to their guests, and as we have seen, they were correct: masking had specific and wholly negative associations in the Russian Orthodox world. The Florentine resident in Venice, Angelo Popoleschi, had expressed concern before the Russians arrived in the city, writing that "the ambassadors will arrive at the height of Carnival, Venice's most sinful time," which "during the day is full of masks and during the night full of games, *balli*, musical presentations, and comedies."[59] The issue arose several times during their stay in the city. Urbano Gransbarra, another Florentine representative in Venice, reported after their arrival that the Russian ambassador, although he had enjoyed the hospitality he had received in Florence, had objected to the masks he saw men and women wearing there. When he got to Venice, Gransbarra said, the ambassador wanted to retire immediately to his room because he saw many masked people in the hall. Correr, however, was able to reassure him, explaining that the people wearing masks were gentlemen and ladies from Venice who had come to see him. Chemodanov acquiesced, and even though he remarked that people should show themselves and not wear masks, he nevertheless "walked around the hall greeting everybody."[60] This flexibility is reported directly by Correr in his own account:

> He was surprised to see people wearing masks. He asked why people were covering their faces when they were free to do what they wanted without a mask. He said that in his country this [custom] would not be popular and, on the contrary, it would be considered a shame and an infamy. Since God created man in his own image and likeness, and this is the greatest privilege that man enjoys, covering one's face would mean for a person to be unworthy to bear God's image on his own face.... I [Correr] answered that people were wearing masks because it was Carnival time and this happened not only in different regions of Italy but also in other countries; [wearing a mask] was

not considered bad and it was for amusement and fun. He said that he did not condemn this custom because in every country the local custom needs to be accepted without scruple. He said that their custom is different and what is good here is not good in our country [Russia].[61]

Chemodanov was evidently able to reconcile himself to the portions of the Italian Carnival celebrations he enjoyed and to dismiss the rest. A report sent to Rome on February 7/17 noted that "even though he [Chemodanov] went to see musical presentations, he has nonetheless mocked the other Carnival vanities."[62]

Masking continued to be noticed by Russian travelers. Petr Tolstoi was sent by Peter the Great to study maritime skills in Venice between 1697 and 1699. In his detailed diary, Tolstoi described the masking he observed in Venice in late 1697 and early 1698 with a passage that might have been lifted from Chemodanov's (or Bargrave's) experiences, saying that the theaters in Venice are "impossible to describe adequately, and nowhere in the whole world are there such marvelous operas and comedies." Tolstoi continues: "Many people come to these operas in *mashkarakh* ... in Slavic, in masks, so that no one will recognize them if they are at the opera.... Also all through the carnival all the men and women and girls walk in masks, and they stroll about freely, wherever they please, and no one knows anybody."[63]

Another, slightly later, example of the continuing Russian uneasiness with masks comes from a different diary, one kept by a young Italian castrato singer, Filippo Balatri, who lived with the aristocratic Golitsyn family in Moscow and, later, in Vienna. During their stay in Vienna, from 1701 to 1704, the Russian visitors had no problem with the idea of going to theaters but they did have some trouble finding appropriate entertainment. As Balatri recounts in his diary, they were able to persuade the Orthodox priest in their establishment "to attend a drama of Judith and Holofernes by telling him it was an edifying biblical story with no masks." Balatri explained the negative Russian view of masks by noting that they were forbidden by the Orthodox church.[64]

The Chemodanov party left Venice and returned home, via Amsterdam, arriving back in Arkhangel'sk in midsummer of 1657. Nowhere in their detailed report or in the addendum were there any descriptions of the parties, musical performances, and theater visits that were highlighted in the Italian accounts. Indeed, as we have seen throughout in the reporting on this mission, officials on both sides held divergent opinions about what constituted salient information. Nevertheless, the travelers must have said something that sparked the tsar's interest. This is evident by the commission to John Hebdon, the well-connected English merchant who had arranged the ships in Arkhangel'sk to take Chemodanov and his associates to Italy. Hebdon had been dispatched on similar errands for the tsar in 1652, when he went to the Venetian Republic in search of luxury goods, and again in 1656, when he made a brief trip to Venice, returning to Arkhangel'sk by August in time to help arrange transport for Chemodanov. There would have been some overlap between the Chemodanov party's return (presumably by September 1657) and Hebdon's next trip, to the Dutch Republic.[65]

We have not uncovered any detailed dispatches for Hebdon's two earlier trips, so we cannot track any possible shifts in his commissions for the Russian court. However, a retrospective listing, compiled between September 1657 and August 1658 (that is, after Chemodanov returned from Venice), indicates items Hebdon had been ordered to find, with annotations noting whether or not he was successful. The list shows that Hebdon was requested to find people who knew how to put on comedies (variants of *komediia* are used throughout): "masters who know how to make various birds sing and walk about and bow down and talk, as is done in a comedy. And this master should also know how to create a full comedy." Hebdon was not entirely successful; for the request about the master who can "create a full comedy" the anonymous annotation says "no." There were other unfulfilled requests, including one for a self-playing instrument ("argany") that is placed or built in a table and can play twelve pieces—apparently referring to the mechanical creations, perhaps built into a cabinet, that had long been prized by the Russian court.[66] There is no annotation next to a request for royal trumpeters and percussionists, but some birds, of which the tsar was very fond, were purchased.

Overall, although the tsar's wish list for Hebdon represents a miscellany of long-standing desires, the request for a master who could produce a "full comedy" may relate specifically to the recent experiences of Chemodanov's embassy. The word *komediia*, although previously known in Russia, must have been bandied about very frequently, given the party's multiple visits to theaters where various *commedie* were performed. However they were expressed, Chemodanov's encounters with Italian theatrical spectacle seem to have made an impression back home, for the next mission to be sent there, leaving Moscow in July 1659, resulted in the fullest account of music and theater to appear in any Russian report of the period. At least this next party, headed by Vasilii Likhachev, might have had an inkling of what was in store for them.

THE FOLLOW-UP IN FLORENCE

Likhachev, like Chemodanov a member of the service nobility, was accompanied by the state secretary (*d'iak*) Ivan Fomin and a large party.[67] Their mission is described in two published documents. The longer (and drier) account clearly represents the official mission report written for the Ambassadorial Chancery and preserved in its archives. The other account, shorter and quite vivid, was written by an unknown eyewitness participant.[68] It includes travel distances as reckoned for Chemodanov's previous embassy, indicating that these reports functioned as general reference works, in addition to being records of individual missions.[69] In spite of the uncertainties surrounding this shorter account, the relationships between the two reports bring to mind intertheatrical approaches, in which "shared memories of actions... can be called up to thicken present performances"—in comparing these two reports, the "thickening" of "shared memories" is evident.[70]

The mission headed by Likhachev and Fomin took the same long route as did Chemodanov's party, via Arkhangel'sk, where transportation was also arranged by John Hebdon. The Russians boarded their ship in September 1659, arriving in Livorno on January 5/15, 1660. They went first to the governor's residence, where they were received with honors, and then, like the Chemodanov mission before them, they met Charles Longland, at whose home they, too, stayed.[71] During their few days in Livorno, they worked through Alessandro Cerchi, the grand duke's representative assigned to arrange their transport to Florence.[72] Their short stay in Livorno included at least one of the private entertainments that had been provided so abundantly for the previous Russian mission. Cerchi, in a long series of communiques dated January 20, 1660, wrote that he dropped in on an evening party taking place at their residence, at Longland's house. Not only was there dancing and singing, but both Likhachev and Fomin also offered their hands for one of the female guests to kiss.[73] This mission was indeed better prepared to interact with women.

Although their stay in Livorno was shorter than for the previous Russian mission, the ambassadors spent more time in Florence, where they remained for about a month. Their first few days in the city were devoted to establishing the requisite protocol—the visitors were particularly intent on having an audience with the grand duke. These days were filled with standard tourist fare during which they were shown decorative boxes ("shkatuly") that had been given to the ruling family, one of which especially impressed them: when opened, people appeared, moving around as if they were alive. They also enjoyed music, and the January 14/24 report by the Florentine court diarist indicated that the guests were actively requesting such entertainment: "On Saturday the 24th, they asked to listen to violin playing, therefore in their rooms a *sinfonia* of instruments was organized."[74]

The impressive banquet that was held on January 19/29 was most definitely a matter of performance, an atmosphere certainly heightened by the paintings and other artistic works that surrounded them. The escort conducting the Russian visitors to the banquet inquired about the images portrayed on the tsar's seal, asking about the two-headed eagle and the lance-wielding figure on horseback. And then, lo and behold, when they entered the hall, they saw three eagle representations, at the head, center, and foot of the table, each in the image of the tsar's seal and decorated with precious stones. Grand Duke Ferdinand asked if these eagles were correct; yes, they replied, but—ever the sticklers for protocol—they noted that the tsar's titles, which were supposed to be encircling the images, were lacking. Ferdinand graciously apologized, claiming lack of time to add the proper titles.[75] The Italian account mentions a performance by one of Prince Mattias's men on a chitarrone (theorbo) at the banquet. The Russian description includes additional banquet music, with keyboard instruments ("kimvaly" and "organy") as well as two trumpeters (possibly cornett players) and additional wind instruments ("gudtsy," or pipers), which was followed by a large dance later in the evening.[76] Several additional *balli* took place, and the visitors also attended calcio games on more than one occasion.[77] But there was, very shortly, a more awe-inspiring spectacle to come.

On January 24/February 3, 1660, the first day of Carnival, the Russian party attended a comedy at the Pergola theater, the first theatrical visit during the group's time in Florence. The Italian diarist records that: "On the 3rd, the Cardinal's sung comedy took place in the via della Pergola. The grand duke, la Serenissima [his wife], and all the princes were present. The Muscovites were sitting in a box to the side of the one where the grand duke was sitting. They admired the machines and the flights, and often crossed themselves in wonder."[78] Because the Russians attended this performance on the first day of Carnival, we can be fairly certain that the commedia they saw at the Pergola was *La serva nobile*.[79] They arrived at a good year for the Florentine Carnival performances because ballets had been reinstated between the acts and, in general, the production was more elaborate than in the previous year. *La serva nobile* was the work of librettist G. A. Moniglia and composer Domenico Anglesi, who was associated with Cardinal Giovan Carlo, patron of the Accademia degli Immobili; it was this academy that produced the opera at the Pergola. The plot is comic, with largely domestic action and many disguises, yet the machine effects were obviously impressive.[80] The Russians made an unaccompanied repeat visit to the theater, apparently to see the same opera, on January 27/February 6.

The guests also attended some private performances. For example, on January 28/February 7, the court celebrated the birthday of the grand duchess with a commedia and other entertainments: "On the 7th, on the Serenissima's birthday, in the morning, they went to the Nunziata to talk, and in the evening to the Sala dei Forestieri [the large reception hall in the palace] to see the pages' comedy with equestrian jumping, combat presentations, and two ballets. It was very much appreciated.... The Muscovites watched everything from the door of their room."[81] They witnessed another staged battle from the same vantage point a few days later, on January 30/February 9: "In the evening, at the Palace, a comedy by young gentlemen was exhibited together with an *abbattimento* and a dance. The Muscovites watched from their doorway."[82]

The Florentine hosts were not only carefully tracking the visitors' activities but also clearly aiming to make the guests easier to handle through this overwhelming cultural deluge. It was at around this point, on February 12, that Cardinal Giovan Carlo's secretary described the progress of the visit: "These Muscovite lords are becoming more tractable every day: they attended some *feste*, calcio games, and some comedies performed during the current Carnival."[83] They witnessed the Turkish procession ("la processione turchina") on February 4/14, an annual celebration in honor of Ferdinand I and his role as a victor over the Ottomans (memorialized in the Livorno statue *Monumento dei Quattro mori*, which had been featured on Chemodanov's city tour); they saw other Turk-related art and artifacts in Florence on their guided excursions.[84] They most likely attended the large concert on February 9/19, featuring a work by Anglesi and Moniglia, the creators of *La serva nobile*, the opera the Russians had seen twice; these two artists were the court's season favorites.[85]

THE THEATER OF DIPLOMACY 79

Their final trip to the Pergola, on February 10/20, 1660, produced the most sustained description of a performance in any seventeenth-century Russian account—indeed, it rivals many of the frequently cited descriptions of Italian operas by other, Western, observers. It appears in the shorter Russian account:[86]

> The prince ordered [the entertainment] to start and chambers [*palaty*] appeared, and there was one chamber, which sank out of sight, and in this way there were six changes [of scenery; *shest' peremen*]; and in these chambers the ocean appeared, disturbed by waves, and there were fish in the sea and people rode on the fish, and at the top of the chamber was the sky and people sat on the clouds. And the clouds with the people on them were lowered down, and they grabbed a person on the earth under his arms, and they went back up again. And the people sitting on the fish also rose up to the sky after them. And then a man sitting in a carriage was lowered from the sky onto a cloud, and across from him in another carriage there was a beautiful maiden, and the valuable horses beneath the carriages moved their legs as if they were alive. And the prince said that one represented the sun and the other the moon. And in another change [of scene], in the chamber there appeared a field full of human bones, and ravens flew in and started pecking at the bones. And then the sea appeared in the chamber, and on the sea were small ships and people inside were sailing [them]. And in another change [of scene], there appeared about fifty men in armor, and they started fighting with sabers and swords and they shot from firearms [harquebuses], and it was as if three men were killed. And many marvelous young men and maidens came out from behind the golden curtain and danced and did many wonderful things. A young boy came out and started begging to eat, and they gave him many loaves of plain white bread but could not fill him up.[87] And that entertainment was given eight weeks before the ambassadors [arrived], and it cost 8000 *efimki* [thalers]. This same comedy was presented as a gift to the Spanish king when he had a son. And there were three different comedies when we were in Florence.

We begin our examination of this action-packed description with the final sentence: "And there were three different comedies when we were in Florence." This, as we have seen earlier, is true or, at least, just about true. The Russian party attended the Pergola theater three times, seeing a total of two different comedies (*La serva nobile* they saw twice).[88]

The clue to identifying the work they described is near the end of the passage: "And that entertainment was given eight weeks before the ambassadors [arrived], and it cost 8000 *efimki*. This same comedy [or, this same kind of comedy] was presented as a gift to the Spanish king when he had a son."

The wording here is a bit ambiguous but the information seems clear enough.[89] The work produced as a gift to the Spanish king for the birth of an heir was Francesco Cavalli's *Ipermestra*, which was performed at the same theater, the Pergola, in 1658. Although this does not mean that the ambassadors saw a hitherto unrecorded encore of Cavalli's *festa teatrale*, the link to *Ipermestra* is made explicit in the Italian court diarist's account of the visitors' activities on that date: "On the 20th, they went again to a sung comedy in the via della Pergola, where all the machines of *Ipermestra* were used. It was managed well and they were greatly astonished. The grand duke, the grand duchess, and all of the princes were there."[90] With this direct association, the other information in the account falls into place. The Russian description specifies that this entertainment had been given eight weeks before the ambassadors arrived. They reached Florence in late January 1660, so the performance in question would have been in late November 1659. Felipe Prospero, the Spanish prince in whose honor *Ipermestra* was written, was born on November 28, 1657, and was still alive in early 1660, when the Russian party saw this production; he died in 1661, just short of his fourth birthday.[91]

There was a tradition of marking the young prince's birthday with theatrical performances, even after *Ipermestra*. An avviso sent to Florence from Spain notes that on November 27, 1659, a "bellissima commedia" was given to celebrate the prince's second birthday.[92] The tradition continued, for a December 1660 issue of the Paris-based *Gazette* reports that a comedy was performed in honor of the little prince's birthday.[93] The Florentine hosts obviously told the visiting diplomats about this Spanish connection; otherwise, how would the visitors have known about the original context for this work? Clearly the Florentines were flattering their guests with the high cost of the entertainment and its previous association with royalty. Equally clearly, the Russians carefully reported what they had heard.

The Russian description includes many actions for which the sets and machinery originally constructed for *Ipermestra* might have been used. We cannot identify each scene or set precisely, but some rough comparisons are possible. For example, the author begins by saying that there were a total of six changes of scenery, which would correspond roughly to the three acts in an opera, concluding with some comic action.[94] This might follow generally some of the action (or, at least, the situations) in *Ipermestra*, as summarized by art historian Phyllis Massar: "The Prologue had sky and sea scenes, with gods and goddesses floating about. Phoebus Apollo arrived from the heavens

FIG. 2.3

Ipermestra, set for the prologue, 1689 print
(University of Washington Libraries, used by permission)

aboard his chariot, Venus soared in on a cloud, and Thetis floated on a shell, surrounded by nereids, tritons, dolphins, and marine monsters—these sea-creatures being a Florentine specialty often worked into their productions."[95] The Russian party saw something similar at the beginning, with the ocean waves, the fish in the sea, and the carriage lowered from the sky. It is for this section that the prince described what was happening on stage—the visitors' amazement must have been palpable. Although such stage action might appear in many productions at the Pergola, the carriages do match pleasingly with the often-reproduced imagery from the printed libretto of *Ipermestra* (fig. 2.3).

Massar's summary of *Ipermestra* continues, describing the combat at the end of act 2: "Orazio Rucellai, the author of the *Descrizione*, which details the action of *Hipermestra*, describes the fighting as so realistic that some among the audience, particularly the women, overtly showed fear for their loved ones among the combatants [i.e., members of the Immobili]." The Russians, too, were impressed by the battle scene, which ended after swordplay and firearms, "and it was as if three men were killed."

The realism of the production was felt by other, more experienced travelers. An Englishman who attended the premiere of *Ipermestra* described his impressions in stunned shock: "I may pretend to some Skill in Perspectives; but cou'd never till now believe, 'twas possible so much to deceive my sight, as it has been twice this week by the Machines of this Famous Opera. A little Rhetorick wou'd perswade me, that I have been a spectator to the reall sports of the Poeticall Gods in the Clouds; & to the Noble Actions of the old Greeks in their famous City of Argos."[96]

Massar continues her summary by describing the third act, in which "the despairing Hipermestra is saved by a swooping eagle in the course of her suicide leap from a tower." A similar action impressed the Russians: "And the clouds with the people on them sank down, and they grabbed a person on the earth under his arms, and they went back up again."

The lingering associations of *Ipermestra* were not surprising, then, given the memorable impressions of the original production. Because the little prince's birthday was marked in subsequent years by theatrical performances, the explanations given to the Russian visitors fit nicely. The tsar's representatives were being honored by a performance that was, quite literally, fit for a king.

The shorter Russian account also reports on other delights of Florence. The pleasure gardens were astonishing in their abundance and the fountains were like magic, although the writer diligently attempts to describe their mechanisms. The gardens also featured musical entertainment: "And then there were many performances, and *organy, kimvaly*, and [instrumental] music. And other people played the organs but no one touched them. And I cannot describe this in another way, because no one who did not see this can understand it."[97] But the novelties ran in both directions, for the Florentine hosts were curious about their visitors' lands as well. The ambassadors sat with the grand duke and examined maps of Siberia, discussing the wild animals that lived there.[98] All in all, then, Likhachev's theatrical experiences in Florence seem to have built on Chemodanov's recent operatic encounters there and in Venice, probably solidifying their impact by being written down in such vivid detail.

These impressions appear to have been reinforced by subsequent missions abroad. Likhachev's party got back to Moscow in the summer of 1660, and that fall, John Hebdon was on the move again, sent to Amsterdam and London.[99] As in the case of Hebdon's mission after Chemodanov returned from Venice, we cannot document a direct cause and effect; nevertheless, Hebdon's post-Likhachev assignment similarly included a search for entertainers. We have two documents relating to Hebdon's Amsterdam/London trip. The earliest is a long listing of items Hebdon was to look for; this seems like an interim draft, with annotations apparently in the tsar's own hand, dating from late 1660.[100] This list indicates that Hebdon was still seeking masters who could create a comedy, one of the unfulfilled requests from the previous trip. It also asks for "masters who can make birds sing in trees, and also people who can play the trumpet"—the first item may indicate actual birds or it might imply some sort of mechanical item (the "organs that play by themselves" was among the unsuccessful requests from his earlier trip). They did, however, need a resupply of real birds, as the specimens sent back previously had all died, not surprisingly, over the winter.[101]

A dispatch from London later the following year, November 1661, shows that Hebdon had persisted in his efforts, making inquiries and getting cost estimates. He reports that it would be very expensive to find people who could put on comedies, saying that such troupes would ask for between three and four hundred rubles per day to come to the Russian court. Other entertainments would be less expensive; for example, what appears to be a puppet theater could be hired much more cheaply.[102] We have not uncovered any response to this alternative, and at any rate, based on the previous requests, a puppet theater is not quite what the tsar had in mind. Nevertheless, the court had obviously reiterated its desire for performed entertainment, and Hebdon was actively scouting possibilities. Hebdon's long stay in London takes us into our next section: the impacts of Russia's resumed relationship with England.

RESTORING TIES AFTER THE RESTORATION: ENGLAND AND RUSSIA

Tsar Aleksei Mikhailovich had been a steadfast supporter of the future King Charles II, and the two rulers had exchanged friendly letters immediately after Charles's accession to the throne. The Russian embassy sent to London in 1662, headed by Petr Prozorovskii, was thus a high-profile affair. John Hebdon, already in London, remained there to assist with this mission.[103]

On their arrival in London in November 1662, the Russian party was greeted with the unusual honor of being heralded by the king's trumpets. They made an impressive appearance, with many observers remarking on the exotic birds and other animals they brought with them.[104] Newspapers enumerated the tsar's lavish gifts, and an enterprising publisher advertised what appears to be a tie-in to the embassy: an English translation of Adam Olearius's well-known book about Russia.[105] At the formal audience with the king in late December 1662, the Russian party was accompanied at Banqueting House, according to John Evelyn, with "Wind musick playing all the while in the Galleries above." After this, they were escorted by the Master of Ceremonies to York House for a big (and expensive) banquet.[106] In spite of all this goodwill, however, there is no evidence that the Russians participated in the lively theatrical and musical events of London, which were thriving after the Restoration. This may have been, in part, due to the ambassador's long illness, which delayed their formal reception at court by a month.[107] The embassy's departure was much less elaborate, reflecting not only their failure to agree on trade issues but also the early departure of part of the group before this. Ivan Zheliabuzhskii, the second in rank after Prozorovskii, left in February with a small detachment for a brief mission to Florence and Venice. These visits, too, were unproductive, and there is no suggestion that the visitors were taken to any theaters or offered other special entertainments.[108]

It was the English mission sent to Russia as an immediate response to Prozorovskii's embassy that offered a new window onto the cultural influences we have been tracking. The mission entrusted to Charles Howard, First Earl of Carlisle, was part of the continuing attempt at revitalizing the England-Russia trade relationship, and although it was not a diplomatic success, it was nevertheless full of pungent interactions that brought Western performances in music and dance directly to at least some Russian spectators. The Earl of Carlisle—although he proved to be a rather intolerant diplomat—was a logical choice for this mission. Carlisle and his secretary, the poet Andrew Marvell, were knowledgeable supporters of trade and shipping interests in the north of England, a group naturally invested in promoting ties with Russia.[109] The embassy's diarist, Guy Miege, lists somewhat different qualifications for the ambassador, writing that the Earl of Carlisle was "in all respects proper for the employment. For, besides that he was of a comely and advantageous stature ... he had a peculiar grace and vivacity in his discourse" (Miege, 4).[110] This "peculiar grace" (and the desire to display it) proved influential in the actions of this mission.

The embassy was large and included a musical contingent: two trumpeters, six musicians, and a music master. The fanfare musicians were deployed in the usual ways, to announce the group's entry into towns and to show approval or, sometimes, disapproval (for example, by silencing the trumpets as it approached the capital to indicate displeasure at the confused state of its reception [Miege, 116]). The party's observations began immediately after disembarking at Arkhangel'sk (August 1663): the dancing of Samoeds was "the most ridiculous in the World" (Miege, 84–85), and Russian dancing was no better, for "it is so absurd and ridiculous, that the Bears they teach to dance there acquit themselves better than themselves" (Miege, 56).[111] In Vologda, where the group waited for several weeks before continuing on to Moscow, Carlisle had a chance to demonstrate true elegance in the art of dance, with displays before a Russian audience to the accompaniment of the musicians in his suite: "Our dancing also, which the Ambassador used sometimes upon occasion of this Musique, was no less admired by them [the Russians], who in their Dances knew nothing but brutish and uncomely Postures" (Miege, 100).

The English party displayed its musical talents as well. Another remark from Vologda, where the party had time to engage in such pastimes, also indicates a Russian audience for such performances: "Our Musique was most commonly at Dinner, at which time there was nothing to be heard but Trumpets and Viols, whose delightful and agreeable Harmony, did sometimes so charm the Russes, that it drew great Company of them to hear it. And indeed the Musique was very good, being managed by one of the best experienced Musicians of England, who from time to time composed new aires" (Miege, 99–100). The visitors also engaged with the English merchant population in Vologda, in one instance introducing a theatrical element, a "farce of Mascarads," on November 5, to celebrate Guy Fawkes Night (Miege, 100).[112]

The party's formal entrance into Moscow (February 1664), although marred by some miscommunication, was a grand affair. The English contingent was headed by its own trumpeters, but the greatest musical contribution was made by the Russian military musicians, deployed en masse, which the English party regarded with some degree of respect. Opportunities for musical exposure continued in the capital. At one point, for example, the English party members were escorted back to their lodgings to enjoy a meal the tsar had sent to them. This banquet was attended by some high-ranking Russians, who had to be appeased by musical entertainment when they were not furnished with the beautiful silver plate from which Carlisle alone dined: "the Boyars not liking that Ceremonie seemed to look upon it with a jealous eye; yet his Excellency kept them as cheerful as he could, both by his graceful presence of spirit and the sweetness of his Musick."[113]

There was other homemade entertainment by the English visitors during their stay, not witnessed by Russian spectators but certainly known to their hosts, who kept very close track of all visiting parties. Their efforts follow along the lines of the "Mascarads" produced in Vologda, generated by the same causes: boredom and the need to find something to do. At their residence in Moscow, twelve members of the party formed teams "to play at Foot-ball" (see fig. 2.4 for an earlier example of field games played by a visiting embassy). They also turned to theatrical entertainment. "Our Musiquemaster," reports Miege, "composed a handsome Comedie in Prose, which was acted in our House" (Miege, 142).[114] Previous diplomatic encounters in the West had emphasized the suitability of all kinds of entertainment for women as well as for men—surely this was one of the lessons provided by the bold ladies of Livorno—and, because Carlisle's wife accompanied the embassy, the improvised theatricals would only have reinforced this point.

As soon as Carlisle and his party crossed the Russian border on their way home, they reencountered entertainments that would have seemed standard for visiting dignitaries: a splendid reception in Riga and balls and other elegant music in Stockholm and Copenhagen, recalling the amusements provided in Livorno and Florence. Nevertheless, in spite of the party's palpable relief at returning to familiar entertainment environments, Miege's account indicates that there were some, limited, opportunities for cultural interactions between the English visitors and their Russian hosts.

ANNOUNCING THE PEACE: POLAND AND PARIS

Another of Moscow's diplomatic endeavors during the 1660s resulted from the signing of the Treaty of Andrusovo, in early 1667, an armistice ending the military conflicts with the Polish Commonwealth that had stretched back to the 1650s and produced the important diplomatic missions of that earlier decade. The signing of the armistice stimulated ceremonial receptions that were inflated to heights of grandeur. The Polish party that came to Moscow

FIG. 2.4

The Mayerberg party in Moscow playing field games at the ambassadorial residence, 1661 (from Adelung, *Al'bom Meierberga*; University of Washington Libraries, used by permission)

to formalize the treaty was received magnificently, with endless processions of dignitaries, military escorts, and, of course, musical accompaniment. The Scottish general Patrick Gordon, a mercenary in the longtime employ of the tsar, wrote a series of letters about this conference, emphasizing the Russians' efforts to produce a truly "gallant show."[115] The show was indeed gallant, as described not only by Gordon (who mentioned the "drummers being all in dutch habite" and who "made the brawest show of all") but by a Polish observer as well. This Polish report also focused on the enormous parades, accompanied throughout by Russian trumpets and percussion at the entry and at the visitors' procession to their audience with the tsar, echoing the impressions of the Carlisle mission.[116] (The observer also described, in a kind of culinary stupor, the immense banquets and toasts that took place, with the glittering plate for which the tsar's court was famous.) Although the Russians were adept at such spectacle, for this particular occasion, they might have remembered an account of a similar event produced earlier by the Poles, in 1661, for a very different parade, one celebrating a Polish victory in this protracted military contest. This description, originally published in a Polish newspaper, was very quickly translated into a Russian version that preserved the emphasis on the multitudes of soldiers and the constant musical accompaniment.[117] The Russians certainly did not require a guide for their Andrusovo celebrations but it might have been useful to know what they needed to surpass.

As Gordon wrote after the accord was signed, the Russians were "busy in dispatching messengers to most of the Christian Princes"; one of these missions was headed by the same Ivan Zheliabuzhskii who had gone from London to Florence and Venice a few years earlier.[118] This time he was sent to Vienna, and even though he arrived too early for the stupendous production there of the opera *Il pomo d'oro* (July 1668, for the marriage of Leopold I), the Russian government was nevertheless kept abreast of the celebrations: a kuranty report datelined Vienna, December 1, 1667, mentions the festivities in the works, including the construction of triumphal gates, entertainments, and comedies.[119]

Another Russian mission, however, continued to enjoy the entertainments witnessed by the earlier ambassadorial trips to the Italian states. This was the embassy headed by Petr Potemkin, who was embarking on a long and distinguished career that would ultimately take him to many states (and many theaters) throughout Europe. The account of his first sojourn, to

Spain and France, shows why: he appears to have been diligent and curious, a much better representative than the members of the 1654 Russian mission to Paris had been, willing to explore the city and clearly eager to partake of its amusements.

Petr Ivanovich Potemkin (d. 1700) had taken an active role in the conflicts of the mid-1650s before being dispatched, along with Semen Rumiantsev, on the post-Andrusovo mission to the West.[120] The party left Moscow for Arkhangel'sk in July 1667, following the northern sea route established by earlier missions, and arrived in Cádiz in December of that year. This was Tsar Aleksei's first embassy to the Spanish court. They were received graciously throughout their journey via Seville to Madrid, where they finally arrived in late February 1668 and had their first audience with the young King Charles II and his mother in March. Although there are many references, in the Russian account, to entertainments (*potekhi*) at the royal court in Madrid and elsewhere, these seem to indicate excursions, particularly in garden settings ornamented by fountains, statues, and the like.[121]

Potemkin's visit took place in the nearly five-year interval following the death of King Philip IV, in September 1665, during which court theatrical presentations were shut down.[122] There were, however, large public displays during this period. The year before the Russian party arrived, the birth of a daughter to Maria Theresa of Spain, wife of Louis XIV, was marked in Madrid with banquets, music, fireworks, tableaux, and even a "supurbe Machine d'Artifice"—so, even though the court closed down its theatrical productions, opportunities for impressive display remained.[123] The public theaters were also closed down in mourning but more briefly, and by the time of the Russian party's arrival, they were open again.[124] During this time, Spanish actors did perform for private gatherings. The diaries of the English ambassador, Edward Mountagu, First Earl of Sandwich, describe entertainments that recall the homemade productions created by the Carlisle mission to Moscow a few years earlier, although on a grander scale. For a celebration of the English king's birthday, Mountagu notes that not only did he and his staff perform English comedies but that the guests were entertained with "a Spanish Comedy and Entremeses" (short comic intermezzi), adding that "I had presented mee *entremeses* by the Comedians of Madrid . . . the best actors, men and women out of their companies joyned together."[125] We have, however, found no evidence suggesting that Potemkin and his party witnessed such lavish public or private performances.

The Russian party left Madrid in mid-June, and by early August, it had arrived in Bordeaux and met up with its French escort, the Sieur de Catheux; as in the case of previous Russian embassies, it is the host's account that offers a more vivid picture of the visitors' occupations.[126] Both French and Russian reports mention the standard elements of an ambassadorial tour, with ceremonies of greeting along the way, accompanied by respectful military-type fanfares. In this early stage of the trip, Catheux observed that (quite unlike a previous Russian ambassador, the "uomo lussuriosissimo") Potemkin could not admire the beauty of some women they had encountered because, being married, he could not examine the women in question closely enough to comment.[127]

The Russian party's entry into Paris was noted in the *Gazette* (September 7, 1668), and its members were lodged at the Hôtel des Ambassadeurs extraordinaires. Over the first weeks of their stay, they arranged the most important event, their formal reception by the king, which was performed with proper fanfare (Catheux mentions "un grand nombre de trompettes en haut qui sônaient incessament").[128] In subsequent days, they were taken to see the sights: Versailles, the Louvre, the Gobelin factory, gardens, and so on—all of which is reported faithfully in the accounts of both parties.

Their theater visits took place on September 6/16 and 8/18; they are not mentioned in the Russian account, although Catheux and other Parisian sources report them. Catheux noted in his journal that on September 16, "the Ambassador, his son, the Chancellor [Rumiantsev], and all their entourage attended the performance of the comedy *Les Coups de la fortune*, performed by the Marais troupe with set-changes and ballet entrées, which they greatly enjoyed."[129] This was a revival of Boisrobert's tragicomedy, which originally had not called for incidental music but for this performance was given with interludes of music and dance.[130] We do not know if this enhancement was created specifically for the visitors, although such elaborations were increasingly common during this decade for special occasions. Two nights later, the party attended another such enhanced performance at a different theater: "On the eighteenth [of September] the troupe of Sieur de Molière performed *Amphitryon* with machines and ballet entrées, which greatly pleased the Ambassador and his son."[131]

We know more about this performance because the gazetteer Charles Robinet described it in his letter of September 29, saying that "the Italians" appeared as well—this is the Fiorillo commedia dell'arte troupe, which shared the Théâtre du Palais-Royal with Molière's company.[132] It is this performance that may echo Chemodanov's earlier encounter in Florence, where he (almost certainly) saw Giovan Battista Fiorillo in *Il convitato di pietra* at the Cocomero theater (January 1657). The story was still in the company's repertoire a decade later, in Paris, where Potemkin saw the Fiorillo troupe, and although there would have been many changes, the traditions of the company and of the genre itself might have provided some unifying threads.[133] It is unclear why Potemkin's report did not mention these experiences, as the vivid description of the operatic performances in Florence (although not part of the official account) certainly indicated interest in such events; a few years later, Potemkin himself would offer a brief description of an opera he attended in Vienna.

The party's departure from the capital, on September 16/26, 1668, did not conclude its association with Parisian theaters.[134] Its final audience with the king was at Saint Germain on September 13/23. This important event naturally superseded all other plans, and everything else was postponed or canceled. One of the canceled engagements was a third visit to a Parisian theater, the Hôtel de Bourgogne. The Russian diplomats, in their roles as audience members, had been drawing great crowds to the theaters they attended, to such an extent that the cancelation of their visit was noticed and lamented by the acting company, which had hoped to profit from their presence. As the actor and playwright Raymond Poisson explained, the change in plans "obliged me, on the encouragement of several of my comrades, not being able to have the real Muscovites, to cook up some fake ones. And since five or six days sufficed for this, everyone easily sees that these Muscovites were made in haste."[135]

Poisson's resulting one-act farce, *Les Faux Moscovites*, is a riot of stereotypes, some drawn from recent experiences and some seeming to reflect long-held views of the rough and alien Russians.[136] It touches on French hilarity regarding the Russian language and the prolix speeches unfurled by its representatives, something Catheux also observed in his journal.[137] Feasting is highlighted in the play, a trait mentioned by contemporaries, for example gazetteer Charles Robinet, who refers to another of their fascinating attributes, their "bizarres ornemens."[138] The play also features a rowdy chase scene that is characterized as ordinary postprandial exercise—although the members of Potemkin's party do not appear to have engaged in any physical violence toward their servants, this behavior is mentioned, very negatively, by the French hosts of Russia's first embassy to Paris, in 1654, as well as by the Italian hosts of previous Russian missions. The Russian party was scarcely out of Paris before *Les Faux Moscovites* was performed, in October, and it was apparently popular, at least temporarily, because Robinet recalled it with pleasure about a month later.[139]

One of the last large Russian missions to be sent abroad in the decade of the 1660s was headed by the chief of the Ambassadorial Chancery himself, Afanasii Ordin-Nashchokin (1605–1680), and it introduces us to the pivotal transitional period that laid the groundwork for the court theater. Ordin-Nashchokin had been deeply involved in facilitating the many news and communications networks we have been relying on. He planned a three-party meeting, to be held at the ducal court in Mitau (now Jelgava), in Courland, gathering representatives from Russia, Poland, and Sweden, with the aim of clearing the way for a permanent peace after the Andrusovo armistice. The diplomatic issues to be covered spanned the range of treaties that had ended the multifront conflicts of 1654–1667. None of these issues, however, was addressed in Courland because, as the result of a series of political missteps, neither the Poles nor the Swedes showed up to the conference, and Ordin-Nashchokin, after leaving Moscow with great ceremony in May 1668, was left hanging in Courland.[140]

The ramifications of this failure, both for the larger contexts of Russian international affairs and for our focused narrative, are considerable. This meeting marked the beginning of the end for Ordin-Nashchokin in terms of his position at court and his influence with Tsar Aleksei. The shift is palpable even at the outset of this unsuccessful mission. A description of the grand departure from Moscow in 1668 not only mentions Ordin-Nashchokin as the leader of the delegation but also notes, in the same entry, that Colonel Artamon Sergeevich Matveev, who was serving as the head of the guard (*strel'tsy*) on that occasion, remained at court after their departure.[141] It was Matveev who was to take over as head of the Ambassadorial Chancery and who, as we see in our next chapter, spearheaded the series of entertainments that resulted in the formation of the court theater. Matveev's rise can be traced during the period of Ordin-Nashchokin's absence in Courland, where he stayed for about a year. One of the indicators of Matveev's increasing influence is the prominence of Colonel Nicolaus von Staden, a well-known "creature of Matveev" who made several trips of his own to Courland during this time, possibly to light a fire under Ordin-Nashchokin, who, to the tsar's immense frustration, was lingering in Courland and its environs.[142] Von Staden, as one of Matveev's associates, was also active in the plans for the court theater.

This pivotal period at the end of the 1660s also included the loss not only of Tsaritsa Mariia Il'inichna, who died in childbirth in February 1669, but also the death of the heir to the throne, the fifteen-year-old tsarevich, Aleksei Alekseevich, a year later. The tsar was truly grieved by the death of his wife but the death of his oldest son so soon afterward made the necessity of a second marriage, and the production of another son, even more urgent, especially given the physical frailties of the new, surviving, heir (Fedor). In this matter, too, Matveev played a crucial role, introducing the ruler to Natal'ia Naryshkina, who would become the tsar's second wife.

Finally, the Courland mission involved one other person of interest to our narrative, the young student Vasilii Repskii, who was assigned to the Russian diplomatic party. His story links many of the threads that come together to create the court theater, including influences from Ukrainian religious culture (especially music) and contacts with northern European traditions. The young Repskii was a singer (*vspevak*) who traveled from Kiev to Moscow in the entourage of Bishop Mefodii in 1660–1661. His abilities impressed the Moscow authorities, and after he started on his return trip home, he was called back to Moscow and assigned to the court, where he was engaged as a singer for four years. We know this through a petition Repskii wrote in 1676, after Tsar Aleksei's death, in which he detailed the varied career in Moscow that developed from this initial contact. After being assigned to study Latin with Simeon Polotskii for more than three years, Repskii and his fellow students accompanied Ordin-Nashchokin on the Courland mission, in 1668.[143] It is not known for how long Repskii stayed there. The Russian group did not spend the entire period at the ducal capital, but Repskii and the others would likely have been exposed to the court's ceremonial culture, including its music; just a few years later, Courland provided the Russian court with theatrical musicians. After his return to Moscow, Repskii went to the nearby royal retreat at Izmailovo to study painting and "perspektivy" (the term refers to theatrical scenery and, more generally, to Western-style painting); at Izmailovo he studied with the foreign artist Peter Engels, who also worked on the court theater's productions. According to his petition, Repskii's art studies lasted for three years, which would coincide roughly with the first year or two of the court theater.[144] It was this training that caught Matveev's interest.

This notice resulted in a dramatic turn in Repskii's fate. At some point, Repskii signed (willingly or not) papers redefining his status as a legal bondsman, an onerous duty that included playing musical instruments at Matveev's orders for theatrical performances. Repskii specifies that this activity took place at the Posol'skii dvor, a residence in Moscow which was one of the venues for theatrical rehearsals: "And seeing, Lord, my artistic knowledge and study, boyar Artamon Sergeevich Matveev took me unwillingly by force to the residence and held me, Your servant, confined to the Posol'skii dvor in chains for a long time and starved me nearly to death. And, Lord, when I was with him, at his command I played the organ and violins at comedies many times against my will."[145] How or when Repskii picked up his instrumental skills is unknown, but the complaint reflects the kinds of music that were indeed associated with the court theater.

The ill-fated mission to Courland, which shifted power at the Russian court dramatically through Ordin-Nashchokin's fall and Matveev's rise, thus also introduces the network of connections and people who came together to create the Russian court theater. Beginning in early 1672, and in combination with the powerful and repeated impressions of other court entertainments witnessed by Russian ambassadorial parties abroad, we see how all of this begins to play out in Moscow itself.

NOTES

1. Earlier historians discussed these diplomatic experiences in the context of the court theater: for example, Morozov, *Ocherki*, 132–133; Veselovskii, *Zapadnoe vliianie*, 29–30; *RRD* 1:47–48, 68–70; Kholodov, *Teatr i zriteli*, esp. 25–27.

2. Overviews are in Frost, *Northern Wars*; Ellersieck, "Russia under Aleksei Mikhailovich," chap. 4; Longworth, *Alexis*, chap. 5. A detailed study is in Floria, *Russkoe gosudarstvo*, and bibliography is assembled in P. Brown, "How Muscovy Governed," 470–471n25. On the newspaper and kuranty compilations, see Waugh and Maier, "Muscovy," and Shamin, *Kuranty*, esp. 147–161.

3. The portrait is reproduced in Köhne, "Poroschin in Berlin," 7; on the mission, see Prudovskii, *Rossiia i Prussiia*, 454–459. Earlier Russian parties commissioned portraits, for example, the Mikulin mission to London in 1600 (Likhachev, *Puteshestviia*, foll. p. 160). On portraiture in diplomatic ceremony, see Helmers, "Public Diplomacy," 404–405, 409.

4. On the Paris mission, see Rambaud, *Recueil des instructions*, 43–44. The Vienna mission, headed by I. I. Baklanovskii, is summarized in Bantysh-Kamenskii, *Obzor* 1:20. Their entry and audience are in *PDS* 3:196, 200–205, 239–240; the Paris *Gazette* (no. 151, November 21, 1654), in an article datelined Vienna October 25, mentions the richly dressed Russian suite. The papal nuncio in Vienna also described the procession (October 7/17) (Theiner, *Monuments historiques*, 4–5).

5. Longworth, "Russian-Venetian Relations," 384–386; Russian accounts in *PDS* 10:809–930.

6. After falling ill, Vimina was quarantined in Smolensk due to fears stemming from the plague outbreak the previous year (Longworth, "Russian-Venetian Relations," 385). As Frost, *Northern Wars*, 165–166, emphasizes, Smolensk, after surrendering to Russian forces in September 1654, was in very bad shape, never having recovered from the damage caused by the Polish siege in 1632.

7. Collins, *Present State of Russia*, 64–65; quoted, for example, in Longworth, *Alexis*, 108–109.

8. On Gutovskii, see Roizman, "Iz istorii," and his *Organ*, 69–79; payments in *Sbornik vypisok* 1:esp. 9–13 (from 1674–1675). Other specialists who came to Moscow are surveyed in Hughes, "Moscow Armoury"; Cracraft, *Petrine Revolution*, esp. chap. 3.

9. *Akty istoricheskie* 4:251–254. The label "po partesu" derives from the Latin *partes*.

10. Hippisley, *Poetic Style*, chap. 1; the students are named on p. 24.

11. Longworth, *Alexis*, chap. 6; Bushkovitch, *Religion*, chap. 3.

12. Vroon, *DLB* 150, s.v. "Simeon Polotsky," 294, notes that the Polotsk Theophany Monastery was Orthodox, so the change to Polish rule may have had a special impact on Simeon, who had been so publicly noticed by the Russian tsar. See also Hippisley, *Poetic Style*.

13. West, "Intertheatricality," 160; see also Hennings, *Russia*, esp. 109.

14. Beliakov, "Posol'stvo Chemodanova." The article in *RBS* 22, s.v. "Chemodanov, Ivan Ivanovich," relies, in places, on the erroneous dates in Buturlin, *Documenti* (see later in this chapter). Stol'nik was one of several court ranks occupied by the service elite (Crummey, *Aristocrats*, 21–22). Before embarking on the mission, Chemodanov was given the title *namestnik*, which is a viceroy in a provincial office (Shmurlo, "Posol'stvo Chemodanova," 2). Following this mission, Chemodanov resumed his duties in Moscow (*Dneval'nye zapiski*, 79).

15. Serristori is quoted from Crinò, "Rapporti," 252; see also Buturlin, *Documenti*, IV, 7/158 (citations are from the document number, in roman numerals, and the pages, in Italian/Russian translation; unless marked, all citations are from part 1). Buturlin's edition is marred by transcription errors and by his misunderstanding of the dating system used in the Italian states, which results in incorrect ordering. All texts and dates cited here are from later, far more reliable archival studies; we include references to Buturlin because his work has been widely cited. On *d'iak* (state secretary) Aleksei Pos(t)nikov, see Veselovskii, *D'iaki*, 426; this was Posnikov's first assignment abroad. (*RBS* 14, s.v. "Postnikov, Aleksei," mistakenly names him as participating in a diplomatic mission abroad in 1616, a mission that was actually carried out by Fedor Postnikov; see Veselovskii, *D'iaki*, 428; Bantysh-Kamenskii, *Obzor* 1:19, 2:255, 260; Demidova, *Sluzhilaia biurokratiia: Spravochnik*, 448–449, 451). The *d'iaki* (state secretaries) and *pod'iachie* (sub-clerks or secretaries) were members of the professional administrative classes; see P. Brown, "How Muscovy Governed"; Hennings, *Russia*, 75–76.

16. Helmers, "Public Diplomacy," 404.

17. The mission report is in *PDS* 10:931–1150, 1151–1176 (the addendum; see later in this chapter), and in *DRV* 4:142–339 (no addendum; all references are to the second edition unless otherwise noted). Longworth, "Russian-Venetian Relations," 389, quotes an admiring report from Venice describing the "remarkable" voyage of circumnavigation.

18. Di Salvo, "La missione," 100–101; on Armano, see also Villani, "Ambasciatori russi," 39.

19. Shmurlo, "Posol'stvo Chemodanova," 4, describing the toasts related in *PDS* 10:948–955. On Longland (d. 1688), see Venning, *DNB*, s.v. "Longland, Charles"; Villani, "Ambasciatori russi," and his "'Republican' Englishman."

20. The tour is in *PDS* 10:1154–1158, and see Kazakova, "Stateinye spiski," 272; the sources are described in Rogozhin, *Posol'skii prikaz*, 174–175; Brikner, "Russkie diplomaty-turisty,"

18–19. There are different interpretations of this addendum (*rospis'*, "depiction," "description"; literally, "painting," "portrait") and how it fits within the generally narrow parameters of the stateinyi spisok: Kazakova, "Stateinye spiski," 270, indicates that it was kept separately from, but in parallel with, the longer official account; Longworth, "Russian-Venetian Relations," 392, describes it as a supplementary report requested by the tsar.

21. Di Salvo, "La missione," 107.

22. Crinò, "Rapporti," 252 (the entire report is on pp. 252–254); Buturlin, *Documenti*, IV, 7–8/159. Such private performances were not widely described in contemporary Western accounts, either, so these glimpses are valuable in a broader context; see Murata, "Musical Encounters," esp. 42–43.

23. Crinò, "Rapporti," 256; Buturlin, *Documenti*, VI, 10/164.

24. Crinò, "Rapporti," 256 (December 19); Buturlin, *Documenti*, VIII, 14/169.

25. One of the parties was again at Armano's house; this would be at least his second such gathering (the first one was shortly after they arrived); see Crinò, "Rapporti," 260, on Sunday, December 24; Buturlin, *Documenti*, XIII, 23/183. This long report (in Crinò, "Rapporti," 257–263) is particularly ill-served in Buturlin's edition, covering items IX, XI, XIII, VII, and X (in that order).

26. Crinò, "Rapporti," 261; Buturlin, *Documenti*, VII, 11/165–166.

27. Crinò, "Rapporti," 257: "Il piú vecchio degli ambasciatori è uomo lussuriosissimo, non ragionando mai d'altro che di donne, delle quali si vede ch'haverebbe gran desiderio . . ." (Buturlin, *Documenti*, IX, 15/172).

28. Crinò, "Rapporti," 258 (musical references throughout this report); Buturlin, *Documenti*, IX, 17/174 and XI, 19/176.

29. Crinò, "Rapporti," entry on pp. 238–239; the anonymous letter, dated January 4, on pp. 243–244. Gabriello's portrait (fig. 2.2), by an anonymous painter ca. 1640, was featured in the exhibit "Buffoni, villani e giocatori alla corte dei Medici" (2016) at the Uffizi.

30. Described in the addendum, esp. *PDS* 10:1158–1162; also Kazakova, "Stateinye spiski," 273–274; Longworth, "Russian-Venetian Relations," 392.

31. Crinò, "Rapporti," 239, 246.

32. Crinò, "Rapporti," 247.

33. Weaver, "Florentine Comic Operas," 40, describes the game as "a more sanguinary version of rugby"; the garters are in Crinò, "Rapporti," 240.

34. Crinò, "Rapporti," 240, where the motions are described as "capriole intrecciate." Alm, "Dances," 248, describes capriole as "jumps with beats of the legs or feet," a style typical of Italian stage dance. On the venue, see Satkowski, "Palazzo Pitti," 341. The anonymous letter from January 11, which summarizes the events over several days, also notes this *festino di ballo*, specifying that although the ambassadors did not want to dance, they did enjoy the dancing, especially "la copata" (Crinò, "Rapporti," 248); we have not identified this particular dance or style.

35. There was a performance of Cavalli's *Giasone* in Livorno just after the Russians left, for Carnival 1656–1657, by the traveling Fedeli company; a new theater began offering performances shortly thereafter, in 1658 (Chiti and Gianturco, *GMO*, s.v. "Livorno").

36. Crinò, "Rapporti," 241. This passage is highlighted in Testaverde, "Le 'riusate carte,'" 430, noting also the Russian ambassadors' attendance. Archery was a valued pastime at the Russian court (Shamin, "Tsirk," 137).

37. Crinò, "Rapporti," 248. This account puts the Cocomero visit on Tuesday, although it describes the same large party and the same performance at that theater on the previous day.

38. A few performances had been given in this theater in previous years; see Michelassi, "Il Teatro del Cocomero," esp. 156–159, 185–186; Leve, "Humor and Intrigue," 22. Surveys

of these two theaters are in Leve, "Humor and Intrigue," 31–37; Weaver and Weaver, *Chronology*, esp. 22–28; Holmes, *Opera Observed*, esp. 13–14.

39. Michelassi and Vuelta Garcia, "Il teatro spagnolo," studies this repertoire in depth; on this performance, see item 15 (pp. 99–100) in their chronology. See also Testaverde, "Le 'riusate carte,'" and Leve, "Humor and Intrigue," chap. 5, with extensive bibliography. A broader discussion is in Sullivan, *Calderón*.

40. Michelassi, "Il Teatro del Cocomero," 172–174 (in the context of the Russians' visit), 186; Michelassi and Vuelta Garcia, "Il teatro spagnolo," item 11 (p. 96, from 1651) and item 15 (pp. 99–100). On Fiorillo's career, including the payment, see Megale, *Dizionario Biografico degli Italiani*, s.v. "Fiorillo, Giovan Battista."

41. Tiberio had performed in Paris earlier, and it is possible that the other Florentine actor, Napolioni, had been there also; Scott, *Commedia*, 49 (Napolioni), 77 (Tiberio), 70–77 (the scenario).

42. Crinò, "Rapporti," 241, 248 (the anonymous letter).

43. On the Pergola theater, see Massar, "Costume Drawings," 244–248.

44. Crinò, "Rapporti," 249. The anonymous letter, dated January 11, says that the party left on Monday; it includes the two sonnets (Crinò, "Rapporti," 250–251; Buturlin, *Documenti*, XIX–XX, 32–33/197, but not translated into Russian, as Buturlin judged them to be "quite bad"). Villani, "Ambasciatori russi," 71n69, also suggests Bartolommei as the author.

45. The report is dated January 13 (Shmurlo, "Posol'stvo Chemodanova," 5 and 19n21); in the same report, the papal nuncio noted that one of the ambassadors knew Latin quite well. See also Sharkova, "Posol'stvo I. I. Chemodanova," 213–214 and n. 28. On knowledge of Latin among the Russian elite, see Bushkovitch, "Cultural Change."

46. Shmurlo, "Posol'stvo Chemodanova," 21n39; Russian translation on p. 8. The account in the stateinyi spisok is in *PDS* 10:esp. 1000–1001.

47. Di Salvo, "La missione," 106 (this report follows one about a later visit, on February 10; see the discussion later in this chapter).

48. The theater is described in Francesco Sansovino's *Venetia città nobilissima*, quoted in Glixon and Glixon, *Inventing the Business*, 228. On the opera, see Cavalli, *Artemisia*, ix, x–xvii (plot summary and analysis), xxx–xxxi; the editor, Hendrik Schulze, notes that the work's popularity was evidenced by productions in other cities shortly thereafter.

49. Di Salvo, "La missione," 106: "La medesima sera poi si portò all'opera, che si rappresenta in musica a S. Aponale, nella quale restò ammirato del volo che fece da terra al suo palco il Prologo che gli presentò l'opra in mano, che volle anche vedere le scene e mutazioni loro"; on the opera house, see Glixon and Glixon, "Oil and Opera."

50. See Glixon and Glixon, *Inventing the Business*, esp. 246–248, on the flying effects; they note that the prologue was one of the places in which such spectacular effects were concentrated. See Larson, "Giacomo Torelli," on stage machinery at the Teatro SS. Giovanni e Paolo in 1664, shortly after Chemodanov's visit.

51. Di Salvo, "La missione," 106n35. Gransbarra replaced the former Florentine resident, Angelo Popoleschi (Di Salvo, "La missione," 100n10, 103n26). On the opera, see Rosand, *Opera*, 124 (Anna Renzi's performance), 176.

52. Di Salvo, "La missione," 106.

53. Di Salvo, "La missione," 106.

54. We thank Beth and Jon Glixon and Hendrik Schulze for information on opera performances during Carnival and their thoughts on this little song. Glixon and Glixon, *Inventing the Business*, 302–304, note that operas were popular among visiting diplomats, and boxes at the theater were hard-to-obtain currency.

55. Tilmouth, "Music on the Travels," 156; Tilmouth suggests that this was *Artemisia*, at the Teatro SS. Giovanni e Paolo.

56. *PDS* 10:964–965 (Livorno), and 1054–1055 (Venice); in both cities, the Russians were invited to attend Greek churches.

57. Di Salvo, "La missione," 111.

58. Glixon and Glixon, *Inventing the Business*, 187–188.

59. Di Salvo, "La missione," 103–104n26, citing Popoleschi's report from January 6.

60. Di Salvo, "La missione," 103–104n26. Di Salvo identifies Gransbarra as Popoleschi's replacement as the Florentine resident in Venice (p. 100n10); Villani, "Una finestra," 170, indicates that Gransbarra was the legation's secretary.

61. Di Salvo, "La missione," 103–104. Longworth, "Russian-Venetian Relations," 392, attributes this account to "Angelo Cornaro"—probably a misreading of "Correr."

62. Di Salvo, "La missione," 106n35 ("vanità carnevalesche").

63. [Tolstoi], *Travel Diary of Peter Tolstoi*, 153–154.

64. Schlafly, "Filippo Balatri," 195. The description of the Judith drama is Schlafly's summary, not a direct quote from Balatri's diary; the singer stayed with the family in Vienna only until 1703. We return to Balatri in chapter 6.

65. *PDS* 10:1150, follows the Chemodanov party back as far as Iaroslavl' (late August 1657) but does not give the exact date of their return to Moscow. Bantysh-Kamenskii, *Obzor* 1:185, says that Hebdon was dispatched in March 1658. Hebdon's duties included collecting news for the Russian court (Waugh and Maier, "Muscovy," 85).

66. RGADA, f. 27, op. 1, No. 118, ch. 5, fol. 48: "мастеров таких, чтоб умели то зделать так, чтоб всякие птицы пели и ходили и кланелись и говорили, как в комедии делаетца. И чтоб умел тот мастер полную камедию делать," and fol. 49: "Арганы в столе чтоб сами играли двенатцать штук." (The latter phrase is open to some interpretation; it might also be inferred that the order is for twelve such self-playing items.) The date in this source is given only as [7]166, i.e., between September 1657 and August 1658. The addendum to Chemodanov's report mentions the skilled gold- and silver-workers in Augsburg and their wide influence in these trades (*PDS* 10:1169).

67. On Likhachev, see *RBS* 10, s.v. "Likhachev, Vasilii Bogdanovich," and *Slovar' knizhnikov* 2:299–300; like Chemodanov, Likhachev was given the title of namestnik before embarking on his mission. On Fomin, whose earlier experiences included some exposure to Polish/Lithuanian culture through his diplomatic assignments, see Veselovskii, *D'iaki*, 549; Demidova, *Sluzhilaia biurokratiia: Spravochnik*, 599 (the article in *RBS* 25, s.v. "Fomin, Ivan," appears to conflate two different people).

68. The longer account is in *PDS* 10:509–670; sources in Rogozhin, *Posol'skii prikaz*, 217. The shorter account is in *DRV* 4:339–359; the source for this publication is unclear (although see Starikova, "U istokov"). Scholars differ on how to characterize this shorter report; see Kazakova, "Stateinye spiski," 278–279. Klautova, "Zapadnoevropeiskoe iskusstvo," 434–435, sees the shorter account as following the model of the Chemodanov party's report—that is, split into two sections, with different types of observations. Chertkov, "Opisanie posol'stva," 324n, suggests that it may have been produced as a private record (as was, for example, Tolstoi's diary, mentioned earlier; see [Tolstoi], *Travel Diary of Peter Tolstoi*, xix). Whoever wrote this account, he evidently attended all of the vividly described official entertainments discussed here.

69. Kazakova, "Stateinye spiski," 279–280; Nikolaenko, "K voprosu." Even much later, in 1677, during the reign of Tsar Fedor Alekseevich, the stateinye spiski for the voyages we are considering here were consulted by government officials (*RIB* 21:337–341). These reports

were also collected in a different office, the Privy Chancery (Prikaz Tainykh Del), which was specifically associated with the tsar himself; see *RIB* 21:5.

70. West, "Intertheatricality," 155. The important study by Starikova, "U istokov," explores the context for the recopying of this source in the 1730s, which is also related to West's concept of shared memories—we return to Starikova's work, and this source, in chap. 6.

71. *PDS* 10:esp. 513–516, 536–544; *DRV* 4:esp. 343–344. Longland's notification of their arrival in Florence is in MAP document 14677.

72. Villani, "Ambasciatori russi," 46; correspondence with Cerchi is in Crinò, "Rapporti," 269–270 (cf., partially, Buturlin, *Documenti*, XXVIII, 44–45/212–215); additional correspondence is in Buturlin, Nos. XXXIV, XXXV, and XXXVI (these sections are particularly error-filled).

73. Buturlin, *Documenti*, XXXVI, 67–68/250; also cited in Villani, "Ambasciatori russi," 47.

74. Magli, "Nuovi materiali," 215. The decorative boxes are in *DRV* 4:347–348.

75. *DRV* 4:349–350; cf. *PDS* 10:590–595 and Magli, "Nuovi materiali," esp. 217. The shorter Russian account puts this description under the date January 20/30, which appears, based on the listing of the guests, to have conflated two different banquets. The *PDS* and Italian accounts agree on the previous day (January 19/29).

76. Magli, "Nuovi materiali," 217; *DRV* 4:350.

77. Calcio games in *DRV* 4:351 (date not specified); Magli, "Nuovi materiali," 220 (entries for February 1 and 2, 1660). For the corresponding days, *PDS* 10:599–601 does not mention any such entertainment, although it describes a city tour on one of these dates; a break of several days follows this entry.

78. Magli, "Nuovi materiali," 220.

79. Weaver, "Florentine Comic Operas," 61, notes that the dedication was dated January 31, so it is possible that the performances began on that date.

80. Plot summary in Weaver, "Florentine Comic Operas," 63–65, and 61 on the ballet; on the latter, see also Leve, "Humor and Intrigue," 123. There is no information about a prologue, although the previous Carnival opera (*Il vecchio*) included one; this is a likely position for elaborate stage effects. See also Magli, "Nuovi materiali," 220 (which mentions injuries sustained in the "abbattimento" that day, apparently associated with the production of this opera—it opened with a duel but this may refer to a separate combat action); the repeat visit is on p. 221.

81. Magli, "Nuovi materiali," 221. There was another performance a few days earlier, although it is unclear if the Russians attended. On January 25/February 4, there was a "commedia all'improvviso dagl'Accademici del s[ignor]e P[rincipe] Leopoldo" (Magli, "Nuovi materiali," 220); in n. 77, Magli identifies this as the Accademia del Cimento—it seems more likely that this was the Affinati (see, for example, Goudriaan, "Cultural Importance," 223 and references therein).

82. Magli, "Nuovi materiali," 222. Massar, "Costume Drawings," also emphasizes such battle scenes in the context of the various academies.

83. Thanks to Nicola Usula and Christine Jeanneret for this reference (and translation) and for their insights into the Florentine context. The letter is in Mamone, *Serenissimi fratelli*, 511, dated February 12, 1659 ab incarnatione (=February 12, 1660).

84. Magli, "Nuovi materiali," 222. As Magli explains, this celebration generally took place the previous week, but it was adjusted due to the grand duchess's birthday. *DRV* 4:348 also mentions arms captured from the Turks on display.

85. On Anglesi, see Kirkendale, *Court Musicians in Florence*, 390–393, noting that many of Anglesi's large works are lost. Magli, "Nuovi materiali," 222–223, describes the concert with instruments and forty voices, naming Moniglia and Anglesi as the authors.

86. *DRV* 4:350–351, under the heading "On Comedies." This passage is also highlighted by Klautova, "Zapadnoevropeiskoe iskusstvo," 434–435, Longworth, *Alexis*, 210 (with a partial translation), and elsewhere.

87. *DRV* 4:351: "да вышед малый и почал прошать есть, и много ему хлебов пшеничных опресночных давали, а накормить его не могли." This apparently describes a commedia dell'arte-like turn at the end of the performance.

88. They also saw at least two additional private performances at the palace, on January 25/February 4 and January 30/February 9.

89. *DRV* 4:351: "Такова же комидия послана в дар к Испанскому Королю, как сын у него родился."

90. Magli, "Nuovi materiali," 223: "A dì 20 andarono di nuovo alla commedia cantata in via della Pergola, arricchita con tutte le machine dell'Ipermestra. Riuscirono bene e con grande stupore loro. Vi fu il G[ran] Duca e la G[ran] Duchessa con tutti i P[rincipi]."

91. His birth date is given as November 28 in Stein, *Songs of Mortals*, 261, and as November 27 in Shergold, *History of the Spanish Stage*, 319.

92. MAP document 13389, written on November 29, 1659: "giorno natalizio del Serenissimo Principe di Spagna, complendo felicemente l'A.S. due anni, la Corte si messe in gala et la sera si fece in Palazzo una bellissima commedia."

93. The newspaper is available online; the article is datelined Madrid, December 9, 1661 (sic: 1660). This is apparently the comedy referred to in Shergold, *History of the Spanish Stage*, 324n3, which mentions a performance that was probably intended to celebrate the prince's birthday in November 1660 (here given as November 28) but was postponed to December of that year. Shergold identifies this as Calderon's *La púrpura de la rosa*; Stein, "Opera," gives the context in Franco-Spanish political events, which are also emphasized in the *Gazette* account.

94. Glixon and Glixon, *Inventing the Business*, 229, say that generally there were at least two set changes per act (in a three-act Venetian opera) plus a prologue, so this description of six changes suggests a fairly extended program.

95. *Ipermestra* plot summary here and in the following passages from Massar, "Costume Drawings," 253.

96. Brennan, *Origins of the Grand Tour*, 170. This letter, by the English traveler William Hammond, is dated June 1656, when Hammond was first in Florence. According to editor Michael Brennan, the letter indeed fits with Hammond's return trip to Florence, at the time of the *Ipermestra* production there (email communication June 30, 2014). Murata, "Musical Encounters," 49n65, independently came to the same conclusion (also assisted by the patient Michael Brennan).

97. *DRV* 4:353.

98. *DRV* 4:351–353, a general summary of impressions without specific dates. *PDS* 10:601–602 includes a visit to Anna, presumably Anna de' Medici, the grand duke's married sister.

99. *PDS* 10:665 documents the Likhachev party's return to Vologda in July. Hebdon, after arranging transport for them in Arkhangel'sk, returned to Moscow by December 1659 (Gurliand, *Ivan Gebdon*, 10) and saw the tsar in February 1660 (*Dneval'nye zapiski*, 58). He left Moscow in late June 1660, arrived in Arkhangel'sk in October, and then went on to Amsterdam, where he stayed, with a trip to The Hague, from November through late December 1660, at which point he went on to London (Gurliand, *Ivan Gebdon*, 19–20, 25).

100. Gurliand, *Ivan Gebdon*, 16, 46–49 (the date in late 1660 is based on comparisons to a later listing, on pp. 62–72, dated February 25, 1661).

101. Gurliand, *Ivan Gebdon*, 49, 57.

102. RGADA, f. 27, op. 1, No. 118, ch. 8, fol. 95 (November 20, 1661): "А мастеров, которые делают комидою, то тебе, великому государю, твоей государевой казны станет в большие деньги. И здесь, государь, оне добывают на всякой день рублев по триста и по четыреста. И не поедут хотя им давать две тысячи рублев на год. Только государь будетъ изволишъ такова мастера с игрушками – добуду: дело, государь, потешно, а не з большие деньги станет." Many thanks to Kirill Khudin for information about this report.

103. Gurliand, *Ivan Gebdon*, 26–27. Hebdon had been involved in financial transactions between the tsar and the future King Charles II, beginning in 1651 (*DNB*, s.v. "Hebdon, Sir John").

104. Venetian representatives in London tracked the mission (*Calendar of State Papers*, 216–231), and they noted the special honor of the king's horse guards and trumpets (p. 219), which irritated other diplomats (for example, Hennings, *Russia*, 127–139; Konovalov, "England and Russia," 61–62). On the live gifts, see Konovalov, "England and Russia," 60; *Calendar of State Papers*, 219, 226 (January 19, 1663, including not only "teeth of sea horses" but "pelicans and other live animals"). John Evelyn visited the pelicans at St. James's Park a few years later, as he noted in his diary (Dmitrieva and Abramova, *Britannia and Muscovy*, 207); their descendants are still at the park (Murdoch, *Exhibiting the Renaissance*, 8).

105. *Kingdomes Intelligencer*, December 29, 1662–January 5, 1663, Issue 1, under "Advertisements." This is the London, 1662, edition of Olearius's work printed for Thomas Dring and John Starkey. Another work seems to have been timed to coincide with the embassy's appearance in London: *The Rarities of Russia* (see Dunning, "Lost Chapters").

106. Evelyn is quoted in Konovalov, "England and Russia," 61; see also Murdoch, *Exhibiting the Renaissance*, 6–7. Lodyzhenskii, "Russkoe posol'stvo," 449, mentions the toasts at the banquet.

107. London's artistic life is recorded in Orrell, "New Witness," based on extracts from the diary of the Florentine resident there; this supplements the many references in *London Stage*. The party did sit for a portrait, which is widely reproduced (for example, in Konovalov, "England and Russia," foll. p. 60).

108. The Italian trip is reported in *Calendar of State Papers*, 226, 229–230; Crinò, "Rapporti," 276–278; *PDS* 10:671–802. See also Longworth, "Russian-Venetian Relations"; Lodyzhenskii, "Russkoe posol'stvo." Zheliabuzhskii (d. after 1709) went on to a long diplomatic career; *RBS* 7, s.v. "Zheliabuzhskii, Ivan Afanas'evich."

109. Dunning, "Lost Chapters," 136–137. Prozorovskii and Carlisle had met in London, where they contracted "great amity," but they did not meet again until well into the English party's stay in Moscow (Miege, *Relation*, 299–300; henceforth cited in the text as Miege). On Marvell, see Kelliher, *DNB*, s.v. "Marvell, Andrew."

110. Hennings, *Russia*, 140–141, also cites this description, and see also pp. 139–159. Russian documents are in *DR* 3:553–584.

111. The party ultimately took several Russian bears back home with them, one of which "was so gentle, that one might beat him or play with him as with a Spaniel" (Miege, *Relation*, 378).

112. It was in Vologda that the English party saw the performance of a liturgical drama (Miege, *Relation*, 104, from December 18, 1663), a very late reference to such productions. The visitors also continued to interact with the English residents they encountered, for example in Iaroslav (Miege, *Relation*, 111).

113. Miege, *Relation*, 183. The spectacular silver presented to the tsar is reproduced in Dmitrieva and Abramova, *Britannia and Muscovy*, which also summarizes this mission (pp. 116–117, including a portrait of the ambassador, by Sir Godfrey Kneller).

114. The author of this "handsome Comedie" is unknown. Although the mission included the poet and writer Andrew Marvell, we have no evidence for his participation in this production.

115. Konovalov, "Patrick Gordon's Dispatches," 10 (August 1667); these letters were addressed to Joseph Williamson, editor of the *London Gazette* and undersecretary to the secretary of state (Marshall, *DNB*, s.v. "Williamson, Sir Joseph"). On Gordon, see Waugh, "Best-Connected Man."

116. Konovalov, "Patrick Gordon's Dispatches," 14; see also Buturlin, *Documenti*, pt. 2, CXXI (musicians on 156/396 and 158/399). This was one of the first public appearances of the tsarevich, who had just been formally named heir to the throne (Gordon's description of the investiture is in Konovalov, "Patrick Gordon's Dispatches," 11–12).

117. The account was published in the *Merkuriusz Polski Extraordynaryiny*, no. 36, June 17, 1661, 385–390 (available online); the account was probably translated into Russian a second time. See Krol', Malov, and Shamin, "Pol'skii triumf."

118. Konovalov, "Patrick Gordon's Dispatches," 9 (letter from July 1667).

119. Zheliabuzhskii was in Vienna in the fall of 1667; *PDS* 4:561–674. The Paris *Gazette* published several bulletins on his stay there; the separate kuranty account is in *Vesti-Kuranty* VI:335.

120. Biographical surveys in Likhachev, *Puteshestviia*, 426–428; *Posol'stvo P. I. Potemkina*, 69–80. Potemkin held the rank of stol'nik and, as was the custom, was awarded the title of namestnik before embarking on his journey; Rumiantsev was a d'iak. The Spanish portion of their embassy is in *DRV* 4:360–457, with a new edition in *Posol'stvo P. I. Potemkina*.

121. For example, *DRV* 4:427–429; *Posol'stvo P. I. Potemkina*, 114–115.

122. Weiner, "Death of Philip IV," 184 and n. 25. The Russian visitors passed by the Salón de las Comedias during their procession through the Palacio Real but did not enter; see also *Posol'stvo P. I. Potemkina*, 345.

123. The events are described in the Paris *Gazette*, no. 32, under the dateline Madrid, February 11, 1667, and the special issue, No. 33, dated March 18, is devoted to the festivities. Spanish descriptions of the Russian party's processions include much pomp and ceremony but do not specify fanfares or other musical entertainment (for example, *Posol'stvo P. I. Potemkina*, 345–347).

124. Shergold, *History of the Spanish Stage*, 331, says that the public playhouses reopened at the end of 1666 (and the theater at the Buen Retiro, although shuttered, was apparently accessible, based on a letter from the French traveler Muret). Weiner, "Death of Philip IV," 183 and n. 24, describes productions beginning, with difficulty, in two theaters in Madrid in 1667 (one in May, before Potemkin departed).

125. Harris, *Life* 2:88–89.

126. The French portion of Potemkin's trip is in *DRV* 4:457–564; Likhachev, *Puteshestviia*, 227–315; "Journal du Sieur de Catheux," 1–30.

127. Greeting ceremonies are in Likhachev, *Puteshestviia*, 242, and "Journal du Sieur de Catheux," 6, with Potemkin's views of women, expressed at a gathering in Orléans, on pp. 10–11.

128. "Journal du Sieur de Catheux," 15–19; Likhachev, *Puteshestviia*, 254–260. On their entry into Paris, see Hennings, *Russia*, 99–100. Russian records indicate payments to substantial numbers of royal fanfare players and to the king's "music," implying other types of musical entertainments (*Posol'stvo P. I. Potemkina*, 149).

129. "Journal du Sieur de Catheux," 22; Jensen and Powell, "Mess of Russians," 133, 140n17. All translations from French in this article are by John Powell.

130. This performance was almost certainly not of the Quinault play of the same title (Jensen and Powell, "Mess of Russians," 133, 140nn18–19).

131. "Journal du Sieur de Catheux," 22; Jensen and Powell, "Mess of Russians," 133, 140n17. Curtis, *Crispien Ier*, 324n13, says that the date September 18 is surely an error and (p. 192) gives the date as September 17—his reasoning is unclear.

132. Parfaict and Parfaict, *Histoire* 10:336.

133. Scott, *Commedia*, 71, notes that *Il convitato* was in the Italian company's repertory in Paris in February 1668 and November 1669.

134. The Russian party reached Calais a few days after leaving the capital, at which point Catheux's diary comes to a close; their trip home was via Amsterdam and Riga to Pskov and thence back to Moscow.

135. Parfaict and Parfaict, *Histoire* 10:337–338; Jensen and Powell, "Mess of Russians," 134, 141n23.

136. Plot summary and printed sources for the play in Jensen and Powell, "Mess of Russians," 141nn21–22; Curtis, *Crispien Ier*, 195–196; Parfaict and Parfaict, *Histoire* 10:340–343. A brief discussion of the Parisian context is in Powell, *Music and Theatre in France*, 40–41, and in Curtis, "Theatre," esp. 238, where he describes the play's context in a true contemporary account of "faux" ambassadors exploiting their supposed status at an inn. On Western stage portrayals of Russians, see Jensen and Powell, "Mess of Russians," 137–138, and Jensen, *Musical Cultures*, esp. 215–223; see also Greenhill, "From Russia with Love"; Irvine, "'Oriental' Ambassador," chap. 2.

137. "Journal du Sieur de Catheux," 18.

138. Curtis, *Crispien Ier*, 191, cites Robinet's letter from September 29.

139. Robinet mentioned the success of Claude Deschamps, sieur de Villiers, a member of the Marais troupe, playing two roles in this farce (October 1668; Parfaict and Parfaict, *Histoire* 10:338–339n), and he mentioned the play again at the time of its publication, in 1669 (Curtis, *Crispien Ier*, 194–195).

140. Floria, *Vneshnepoliticheskaia programma*, 418–429; Ellersieck, "Russia under Aleksei Mikhailovich," esp. 189–191; Chistiakova, *"Oko vsei velikoi Rossii,"* esp. 140–142. Ordin-Nashchokin's place in Tsar Aleksei's government is stressed in Bushkovitch, *Peter the Great*, esp. 51–55 (where he emphasizes Ordin-Nashchokin's "personal fortress of chancelleries," an accumulation of power taken up more aggressively by his successor, Artamon Matveev).

141. *Dneval'nye zapiski*, 279.

142. Ellersieck, "Russia under Aleksei Mikhailovich," 194.

143. Repskii's petition and the related testimonies are in Starikova, "K istorii," 56–60; additional bibliography in Jensen, *Musical Cultures*, 247–248n67.

144. Starikova, "K istorii," 58. The word *perespektivy* is used slightly later to describe theatrical decorations in [Tolstoi], "Puteshestvie," 106, and it appears in the German-language reports we examine in chap. 3; on the term, see Hughes, "Moscow Armoury," 208 (the 1681 petition in question is published in *Slovar' russkikh ikonopistsev*, s.v. "Poznanskii, Vasilii," 486, in the context of his wide-ranging artistic skills). Likhachev, *Poeziia sadov*, 120, gives greater perspective on Engels's "perspektivy," noting that his later work at Izmailovo was connected with the gardens there, providing decorative backgrounds to the other garden ornaments (citing Zabelin, *Opyty* 2:296).

145. Starikova, "K istorii," 57; see chapter 4 on the Posol'skii dvor venue.

3

Introducing Pickleherring

The Origins of the Russian Court Theater

The series of plays produced for Tsar Aleksei Mikhailovich from 1672 to his death in early 1676 have long formed an important story in the history of Russian culture, and it is easy to see why. The plays themselves are (relatively) lively, with music and comic characters scattered throughout and featuring dramatic figures from biblical and even secular history. With Sergei Bogoiavlenskii's publication, in 1914, of an extensive collection of payment records, scholars have had a glimpse into the lavish productions, with elaborate costumes, heavy rehearsal schedules, and tantalizing views of props and other matériel assembled for the performances. These records, along with the publication of the play texts themselves, in increasingly full and multiple versions, offer a window into what has been called Aleksei Mikhailovich's "renaissance" years, at the end of his reign following his second marriage, to the young Natal'ia Naryshkina, when the tsar's curiosity and spirit of inquiry were set free to a degree not seen in his earlier years.

Previous studies of the plays have laid out their rich contexts in Western theatrical history as well as in the court culture of Tsar Aleksei's reign, and they have drawn on archival collections in Russia and Western Europe, where copies of play texts have been found and examined.[1] In the following two chapters, we amplify the Pan-European context of the tsar's theater and clarify many remaining puzzles by turning to a type of source that has not been emphasized previously: namely, accounts by foreign observers—all from northern European states—in Russia. This new documentary evidence expands on and, in some cases, alters significantly previous scholarship.

These chapters are further enriched through the frame of intertheater. Tsar Aleksei's theater was essentially a private one. This does not mean that he and his immediate family were the only audience members, for there were other, although limited, spectators. However, unlike the theaters of Florence and Venice, which functioned not only as public venues but also in the service of the rulers (as desirable locations to take visiting diplomats, for example), the tsar's theater was restricted. Although foreigners participated in, witnessed, and reported back to their governments about his theatrical endeavors, they were not generally high-level visiting ambassadors but rather the embedded longtime representatives of important nearby states (Sweden, especially) or merchants. This gives the tsar's theater a special flavor, one of domesticity and even intimacy, opening windows not only into the Moscow court's interests and desires but also into the cumulative knowledge and experiences of the people who created it—people who happened to be working in Moscow at that particular time and who were certainly not recruited for their theatrical know-how or experience. In this way, the Russian productions tell us a great deal about the theater of the West, not from the perspective of professional playwrights and acting troupes, but from the ground level, from the students and audience members who attended performances and absorbed its traditions and who were, suddenly and entirely unexpectedly, made responsible for realizing these traditions on a foreign stage, for a foreign ruler.

BEGINNING WITH "BALLETS": FEBRUARY AND MAY 1672

Although the Russian court had heard a great deal about the wonders of Western theater from the diplomatic reports we have surveyed in previous chapters and had enjoyed the performed recitations offered by Simeon Polotskii and his students beginning in the early 1660s, the date of the true premiere of Western-style theater in Russia is easy to pinpoint: February 16, 1672. This is the date on which a dozen or so residents of Moscow's Foreign Quarter put on a show for the tsar and the royal family, and this wildly popular entertainment, repeated in May of the same year, set the stage for the subsequent productions that lasted until Tsar Aleksei's death. Indeed, these first performances established the theater's essential foundation, its set of fundamental assumptions, as it developed over the next several years.

An account by the Courland native Jacob Rautenfels (d. 1681), who was in Moscow from 1670 to 1672, includes a passage about the origins of the tsar's theater. In his book *De Rebus Moschoviticis* (Padua, 1680), Rautenfels gives some brief context (here and throughout, italics indicate terms used in the original sources):

> Moreover, in recent years he [Tsar Aleksei] allowed some foreigners who live in Moscow to present for himself a dancing scene [*scenam saltatoriam*], and also the story of Ahasverus and Esther, described in a comical way [*comicè descriptam*]. Since he had been hearing through reports from time to time that different plays, dances, and other amusements are often given for European princes, in order to pass the time and disperse boredom, he suddenly ordered that an example of such a production in the form of some sort of French ballet [*in tripudio aliquo Gallico*] should take place. Thus, in view of the shortage of time, in one week with all possible haste everything necessary for the staging was prepared.[2]

Thus, according to Rautenfels, there were two separate performances, the "dancing scene" and the biblical story of Ahasuerus and Esther, which was performed as a play (indicated by the phrase "in a comical way"). We begin with the "dancing scene," which Rautenfels describes as resulting from the enticing reports of entertainments abroad. In contrast to the rendition of the biblical story, which was a full-length play, the "dancing scene" was something less formal, "some sort of French ballet," and put together quickly. What was this performance, and how did Rautenfels come to know about it?

The answers are in a series of letters from Moscow that were sent to Narva, to the governor general of Swedish Ingria, Simon Grundel-Helmfelt (1617–1677), and from there, copies were sent on to Stockholm and other places. These letters were part of the regular reporting system established to keep the Swedish government informed about its crucial neighbor. The individual Moscow reports were unsigned; they were collected together under a short cover letter signed by Grundel-Helmfelt and dispatched weekly. However, although these gathered reports were not signed individually, we know that Grundel-Helmfelt's Moscow correspondent was Christoff Koch (1637–1711). Koch was born into a wealthy German-speaking merchant family living in Reval (Tallinn); he came to Moscow as a young man, in 1655, and remained there, apart from a few short intervals, until 1690. He had begun sending newsletters to Grundel-Helmfelt (in Narva) in 1666, and Grundel-Helmfelt appointed Koch as his designated correspondent in Moscow in

1671.³ Koch's political observations were regarded as being astute and accurate; equally important, Koch was also quite familiar with the organizer of the theatrical events, Artamon Sergeevich Matveev (1625–1682).

Matveev's star, at this time, was rising—and rising fast, as we noted in our previous chapter. His long association with Tsar Aleksei Mikhailovich, stretching back to childhood, extended throughout his active military and diplomatic career, but it was capped by the tsar's choice for his second marriage, in 1671. The new tsaritsa, Natal'ia Naryshkina, was what might be called a shirttail relative of Matveev's in-laws—English-language accounts have called her a "ward" of Matveev. After this marriage, Matveev became, as historian Robert Crummey has written, the "nearest thing to a royal in-law" at court.⁴ Matveev was well connected with the foreigners in Moscow, including Koch, to the irritation of other, less favored, correspondents. Koch's counterpart, the Danish correspondent Frederik Gabel (1645–1708), was aware of this access: "It was partly of Koch that Gabel was complaining when he wrote in November 1676 that the Swedes had been 'wandering in and out of the chancellery like natives.'"⁵ Gabel was not exaggerating. In an (unsigned) report that Koch sent to Grundel-Helmfelt on October 29, 1672, shortly after he had watched an encore performance of the first court play, Koch says that he had dined with Matveev the day before both attended the comedy, and he included details from their political conversation at dinner. This was not an isolated occurrence.⁶

These largely Swedish documents clarify and greatly expand on the "dancing scene" mentioned by Rautenfels. They report initially on activities that were being planned for the near future. This information appears in an enclosure dated February 13, 1672, sent with a letter by Grundel-Helmfelt addressed to the Swedish king, providing the immediate background to the festivities Rautenfels described: "In this Butter Week [the last week before Lent], His Tsarish Majesty is entertaining himself with fireworks given by foreigners and with bears, wolves, and other wild animals for baiting. At the order of Ertemon Sergiofvits [i.e., Artamon Sergeevich Matveev] and at the expense of His Tsarish Majesty a *ballet* is being produced this week by some foreigners, which His Tsarish Majesty himself is going to watch." A Russian document from the previous day almost certainly reflects the preparations underway for this upcoming performance: on February 12, a large quantity of rich fabric was ordered, and although the *ballet* is not specified in this requisition, the scarlet velvet and satin match later descriptions of the rich costumes used in the production.⁷ Fireworks and animal baiting did form part of the pre-Lenten holiday festivities (*maslenitsa*) along with the performance; indeed, this was a natural time of the year for comic role-playing and entertainment.

Another enclosure, dated Moscow, February 20, 1672, and forwarded from Narva a week later by Grundel-Helmfelt, described the *ballet* more fully. This report was apparently sent to Bengt Horn (1623–1678), governor general of Estonia, and it contains a description of the event that had been in the planning stages in the previous report. It begins by providing a clear date, February 17, the death of Patriarch Ioasaf, and then continues:

> Last Friday [i.e., February 16] His Tsarish Majesty, his spouse, and the whole family watched a *ballet*, arranged by 12 persons, mostly foreign merchants. Its author was Dr. Rosenburg's son, who came to this country recently, and His Tsarish Majesty liked it very much. He was sitting very close and was visible, whereas the women were hidden behind a red curtain, however in such a way that their faces were perfectly visible. When the *ballet* was finished, His Tsarish Majesty's thanks were expressed and it was said at the same time that they [the performers] should come back on the next day toward the evening. However, since the patriarch passed away the following day, this did not come true.

The novelty of this production is reflected in the writer's (probably Koch's) further comments, in which he mentions by name the character Pickleherring, the comic figure widely known on European (especially German) stages:

> One is astonished that His Tsarish Majesty, together with his whole family, watched something like this, since previously it had never been permitted to watch anything similar. His Tsarish Majesty and the women laughed several times so that one could hear it, especially at Pickleherring's antics and faces. During the whole presentation—which lasted for more than three hours—nothing was said, except that Dr. Rosenburg's son at the beginning and at the end directed a speech in German to His Tsarish Majesty. The costumes cost about 200 rubles. The stage [or performance space; *Theatrum*] was covered with carpets and green fabric.⁸

At about this same time, the interest in such goings-on in Moscow spilled over into the public press. Readers of Western newspapers, as we have seen in previous chapters, were certainly familiar with seeing Russian names and events. However, the article datelined "Moscow 23 February" that appeared in Georg Greflinger's Hamburg newspaper *Nordischer Mercurius* in

March 1672 was something entirely new, offering a glimpse into uncharted domestic territory, worlds away from the pomp of diplomatic ceremony. This article clearly describes the same event mentioned in the report given earlier:

> His Tsarish Majesty has been amusing himself before Lent with bearbaiting, fireworks, and similar things. On the 16th of this month, 12 Germans presented a *ballet* for His Tsarish Majesty in the palace of the tsar's father-in-law, Ilia Danielowiz. It consisted of 4 Romans, 4 wild men, 2 drunk peasants, and 2 cutpurses, to whom was added an amusing Pickleherring. The stage [*Theatrum*] was very beautiful, and His Tsarish Majesty was sitting quite close to it with 4 of his princes and most important ministers. The tsaritsa or empress was sitting with her state ladies behind a scarlet curtain, which afforded a glimpse of their beauty and allowed them to see the *ballet* clearly. They were shining like brilliant stars through small clouds, and since this *ballet* was the first that has ever been seen in Moscow, it provoked a great deal of interest. The tsar together with his 4 princes and most important ministers as well as the tsaritsa with her ladies were so pleased with it that they often almost shook with laughter, and after the end they asked for another presentation on the following day. However, the next morning the patriarch died, and therefore it was asked to postpone it until Easter. The participants were presented with wine and mead, which is considered to be a great honor here. There was also hope of getting some presents from the tsar, especially sable furs, and there is still no reason to question this [future] grace. The music consisted of 2 violins, 1 viola da gamba, and 2 singing voices, which [altogether], as could be noted, amused the ladies very much, as being an unusual [kind of] music. This is being written to show that something that is very common for our German people is seen as something new in these parts.[9]

Greflinger's source would have been some sort of written newsletter, and the publisher, to his credit as a writer and poet himself, obviously enjoyed the intimate details of the royal family's reactions. It is impossible to know if Greflinger enhanced this report with any editorial flourishes of his own. Two additional brief reports appeared in Western newspapers a few weeks later. The first was in the Dutch newspaper *Oprechte Haerlemse Courant*, which published a short notice dated Moscow, March 1, in the April 9 (n.s.) issue. The second was in *La Gazette d'Amsterdam* for April 12, 1672, datelined "De Hambourg le 8 Avril." Neither of these very short accounts adds any new information, and the specific route by which the story circulated to these two newspapers is uncertain (although the event was probably known from the Hamburg article).[10]

After the *Nordischer Mercurius* article, with its dateline of February 23, our final report is, almost unbelievably, an eyewitness account from the very stage itself (see fig. 3.1). Although this report is not signed, it is reasonable to propose Koch as the author. The document, written in a professional chancery hand, is not dated, and the identification "attachments to letter of 29 December 1671," added in pencil by a late nineteenth- or early twentieth-century archivist, is undoubtedly wrong: this report clearly follows up on the February 20, 1672, enclosure previously discussed, and other internal evidence makes a date at the very beginning of March 1672 a reasonable proposition.[11] The opening description clearly meshes with our previous sources, especially the report in the *Nordischer Mercurius*:

> His Tsarish Majesty let himself be entertained during this period of fasting with all kinds of amusing things, namely bearbaiting, fireworks, and finally a big *ballet*, which the 12 of us presented at the castle, in the tsar's mother-in-law's, Ilian Danilowitz's,[12] residence, in such a way that, without boasting, His Tsarish Majesty, his wife, and also the princesses and the honorable State Counselors were very pleased with it. His Tsarish Majesty was sitting right in front of the stage [*Theatrum*]. The same is true for the aforementioned royal women, who, however, were screened off with red drapery. However, soon they cut up big holes through which they could look. The tsar was in a very merry humor.

After a brief description of the performance space, to which we will return shortly, the author lists the names of the players and their roles:

> In this *ballet* were the following participants, namely Doctor Rosenborg's two sons, and also his house teacher [*Studiosus*], Mons. Trautenberg; Mr. Butinant's house teacher; both Misters Siwerts—the elder brother was *inventor* and author, along with Mons. Rosenburg, who personally was acting in the role of four different characters, namely as *Mercurius, Orpheus*, a Moor, and, in the fourth place, as a wild man. Mons. Christo[ffr] Roden was a hunter in green morocco [leather] clothes, along with three other persons: Rautenberg and Hasenkrach—who was also a skillful Pickleherring [*ein artiger Pickelherung*], in another role—[and] Paridon Voos. Mons. Hindrich M[ü]nter, Mons. Fabbert, and also the embassy's honorable former stable master were drumming on stage while I along with Mons. Münter were playing the roles of two wild men, and afterwards of two foolish peasants.[13] You should have seen the curious jumps in the air, as can be attested some time in the future by Mr. Butenandt, to whom we gave a pass [*Axal*[14]], *pro forma*, so that he, too, was able to see it—otherwise, it was guarded, so that nobody could come in, except the great boyars, such as Arctemon Czergowitz Trokunow[15] and similar persons, who were very eager to see

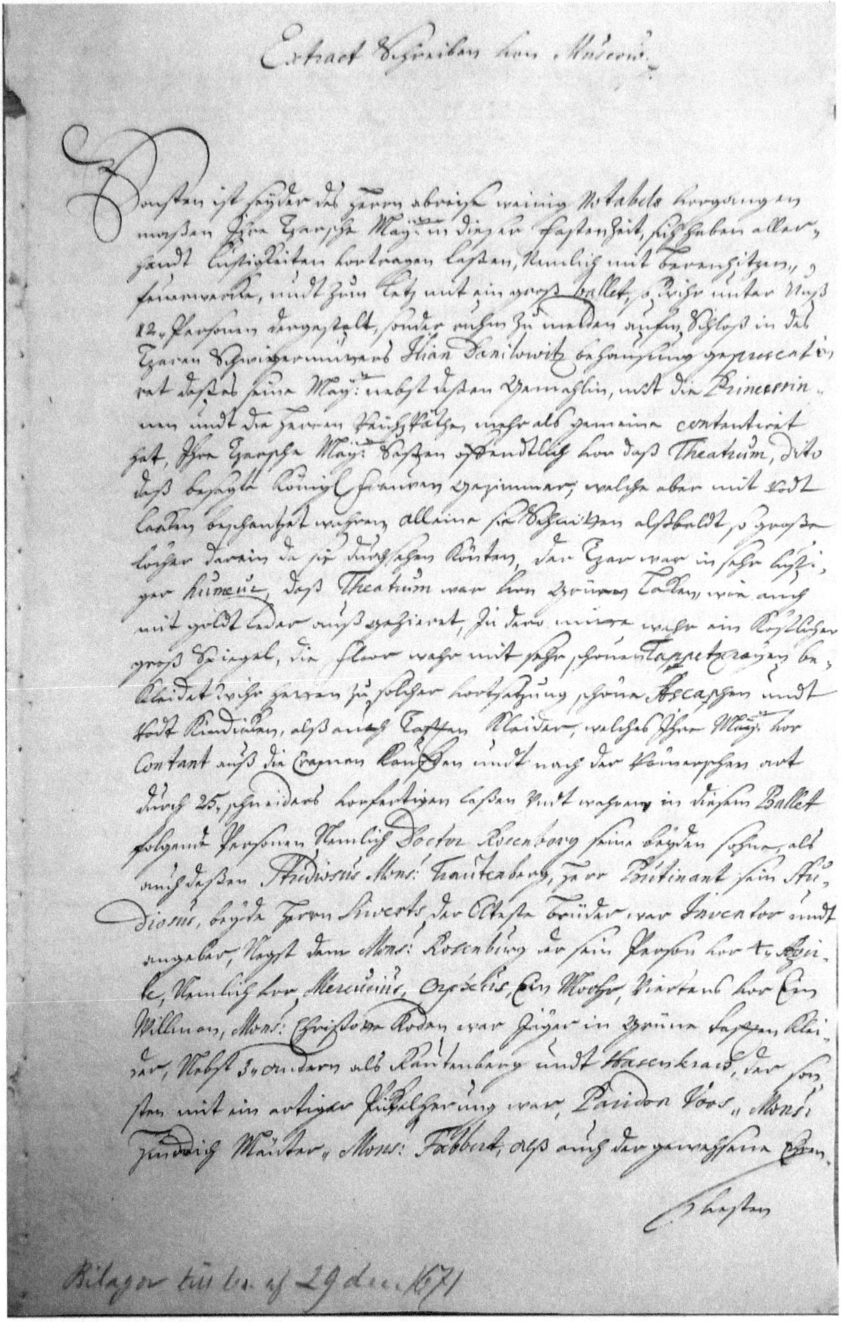

FIG. 3.1

"Extract Schreiben von Muscow" (RAS, Livonica II, vol. 180, used by permission)

our presentation [*Theatrum*]. His Majesty and the above-mentioned women liked it so much that they shook with laughter several times, especially the tsar. And they had such great patience that they sat for more than three hours with the greatest pleasure. They also permitted us music, specifically, two violins, one viola da gamba, and flutes, as well as transverse flutes. When it had come to an end, His Tsarish Majesty thanked us all through Mr. Artemon Sergowitz. He also asked us to repeat the presentation the next day, which we accepted, obediently. Yet to our disadvantage—since His Tsarish Majesty had planned to give us an excellent reward—the patriarch died the next day. At Easter, undoubtedly, we will have to give the continuation—probably then we will get our reward. Hereby is attached [*ergehet*[16]] the song that was sung in a very enjoyable way by Mons: Hinrich Münter in this presentation, accompanied by a viola da gamba. This is indeed something special and extremely new in this place, since nothing similar has been heard before. This happened on the 16th past [of February].

This, then, is the context for Rautenfels's account, which was written several years after the performance and published only in 1680. Rautenfels's commentary at the beginning of his description, regarding the novelty of the production for the Russian audience, mirrors the report in the *Nordischer Mercurius* article. He then describes what is clearly the same performance that our other contemporary reports outlined, providing an appropriate and accurate context for this important account. The Rautenfels description of the event continues:

Whereas this performance would not have been able to be seen without anticipated apologies in any other place but Moscow, to the Russians it appeared unique and artistic since the new kinds of costumes, the unfamiliar appearance of a theater stage [*theatri insolita facies*], even the marvelous idea that it was something foreign, and also the strains of the music, never heard before, easily awoke their admiration. At first, it is true, the tsar did not want musical instruments to be used, as being something new and rather pagan, but when the dancers argued that they could not present a decent dance without music, just as it is impossible to dance without legs, he—a little unwillingly—left everything to their discretion. The tsar watched the entire presentation sitting in an armchair in front of the stage; the tsaritsa, however, and the royal children watched through a lattice, or rather through slits, from a wooden platform built opposite [the stage], separate from the audience. The aristocrats (everybody else had been ordered to stay away) were standing on the stage. The celebratory verses to the tsar, declaimed by Orpheus, before he began to dance between two moving pyramids, were rude and inelegant; however, I find it necessary to quote them here, out of respect to the most honored Aleksei.[17]

> On that same day—namely, the penultimate day of Shrovetide[18]—the tsar also organized a hunt on the Moscow River, which was frozen over. There large English dogs and other kinds of dogs fought with some white Samoyed bears, a spectacle that was all the more entertaining, the more they stumbled on the slippery ice. In the evening, however, the tsar went to see fireworks on the same ice.

All of our accounts, whether written at the time or a few years later, thus agree on the success of this exciting new entertainment. Such a triumph demanded an encore—the death of the patriarch precluded any immediate repeat performance, however, and no sequel would have been possible after that date due to the Lenten fast and then the Easter celebrations. But no one forgot about it, for in May, after Easter, the much-delayed encore finally took place (as the author of our long report from the stage had predicted).

We know about the May 1672 encore from two sources: one a signed letter and the other a brief description in a report, probably by Koch, from Moscow that was sent to Stockholm via Narva. The letter was written in Novgorod by the Lübeck merchant Philip Vinhagen on May 29, 1672; he describes an interesting performance he had heard about (although he had not seen it), which had taken place on May 18. In his letter, Vinhagen uses the term *ballet*, which he seems to assume refers to dance alone (unlike the more general meaning in the rest of our sources): "On the 18th of this month some German merchants danced a *ballet* for His Tsarish Majesty, which was said to have pleased his Tsarish Majesty very much. The tsaritsa watched it, too. According to report, she was sitting in plain sight [*unverdeckt*], which is something strange to hear, because up to now nothing like this had ever happened. One assumes that the dancers will be well rewarded for this."[19]

In addition to Vinhagen's brief observations, a longer dispatch, headed "Moscow May 28, 1672," does not provide a specific date, merely noting that the performance took place "last week," which would be consistent with the date given in Vinhagen's letter. This report shows that Matveev had not wasted his enforced Easter break: the encore performance was twice the length of the original and, presumably, involved more participants. The favorite, Pickleherring, returned, bolstered by other comic characters identified as Swabians. Orpheus and Mercury also reappeared, along with new characters and scenarios (farmers, shepherds and shepherdesses, bears, and others), and with what appear to be scenes or vignettes displayed for the royal family. Such tableaux vivants were extremely popular in Dutch theater, especially, and were common in Western theatrical performances during the seventeenth century, so this would have been a natural addition for performers tasked with repeating, even exceeding, their previous success:

> Last week some Germans again performed a *ballet* for His Tsarish Majesty, which consisted of Peace and War, the 4 Seasons, 4 State Persons [*Staats Personen*],[20] a beggar, Pickleherring and Swabians, 2 shepherds and 2 shepherdesses, Orpheus and 4 bears, 3 hunters, 4 farmers, 8 Romans, and Mercury. Altogether it lasted over 6 hours. The tsar and his closest boyars, who were sitting nearby, completely visible, saw it all with great pleasure, as it seems. The tsaritsa was screened off with other women so that no one could see them. Afterwards His Majesty had Artamon Sergeevich thank them for him, and they were promised an invitation to the tsar's table; everybody was also supposed to get some sable furs.[21]

This May performance is also documented in Bogoiavlenskii, as the first of the records he published, dated May 10, 1672; this second "ballet" performance took place just over a week later. The May 10 funding request is for supplies to be used at the Miloslavskii house, "where the comedy is to take place," and is for rich fabrics in green and scarlet, apparently to be used as decorations or hangings.[22]

This second, May, performance seems to have cemented the court's desire to create a more substantial theater, for plans began in earnest over the summer of 1672. In fact, the "ballet" dispatch previously quoted, from May 28, concludes by observing the activities of Colonel Nicolaus von Staden, who was employed by the Russian court for all kinds of miscellaneous duties; the report says that von Staden was planning to leave very soon on a recruiting trip to hire various craftsmen to work in Moscow. It is von Staden who was described by historian Heinz Ellersieck as a "creature of Matveev," and his rise in prominence mirrors the rise of Matveev, at the end of the 1660s, as we saw in our previous chapter; von Staden was thus a natural choice for such international errands.[23]

Taken together, then, this series of letters, reports, and newspaper articles from February to May 1672 provides a range of information about these initial "ballet" productions. They give us that most fleeting of all moments, an intimate glimpse of the royal family at leisure, laughing and happy, marveling at the stage business they saw and the music they heard—a humanizing view of the stiff formalities captured, and at that only partially, by other records from the Russian court. Most of our accounts mention the presence of other audience members, in addition to the royal family, for both the February and May performances. Even though the Russian court theater has been characterized as "a theater for one," it is clear that the entertainments were, from the beginning, shared—not necessarily widely but shared nevertheless. We get an equally intimate view of the performers, who brought with them their own, informal knowledge of what a theatrical performance was "supposed to be." None of the foreigners involved in these proceedings would have anticipated such a command performance during their posting in Moscow, so what they produced gives us an understanding of their shared theatrical assumptions, what they took for granted in the comedy routines, vignettes, dances, and music so popular throughout Western Europe, particularly in German lands. This is, in a sense, domestic theater at its purest, from the point of view of both the performers and their exalted audience.

SETTING THE SCENE: PLAYERS AND ROLES, PROPS AND SPACE

Given the intensely mercantile concerns of the Swedish reporters, it is unsurprising that they focus on the fact that the players were not only foreigners but also, more specifically, "mostly merchants." This is indeed the case. Of the performers named in the long account (written by a participant) that we have been able to identify, most are merchants. Dirck Hasenkroeg (Dietrich Hasenkrug) was one of the most prominent figures in the two productions, in the role of Pickleherring, and he was one of the oldest active participants, for he was probably around forty years old at the time of the spectacle.[24] Hasenkroeg was likely born in the early 1630s, since already in 1656 he was employed as an assistant merchant in Moscow. From the 1660s, he was working independently on behalf of different Hamburg- and Amsterdam-based trading houses; he died in Moscow in 1683.[25] Hasenkroeg was involved in the tsar's theater to the very end, even beyond the very end.

Another of the players mentioned in the eyewitness report, Heinrich Münter, is often noted as a Swedish merchant in the scholarly literature; his roots were probably in Livonia. Münter began his career in Moscow in the late 1660s. He must have been quite young in 1672, since he was still alive almost fifty years later, and his career in Russia was active throughout that time. In the February "ballet," Münter had roles as a wild man and as a farmer (both roles together with the anonymous author), and he also sang a song, accompanied by a viola da gamba. The two Mr. Siwerts, mentioned as participants but without any specific roles, are probably the brothers Peter and Johann Sievers, merchants from Hamburg. Peter was mentioned as an "author" of the February production, along with one of the Rosenburg sons (probably Bernhard), and he was involved in supplying the later theatrical productions at court, apparently because of his trading connections.[26] Fabbert, described as drumming on the stage along with the Swedish embassy's "honorable former stable master" in the February performance, may be identified with Ägidius (or Egidius) Tabbert or his brother. Both later became quite prominent in Russia. Paridon Voos must be Paridom Voss, described in Russian sources as a Hamburg merchant. He was active in Moscow from the 1650s to the 1670s, and his trade in luxury goods brought him into contact with the Russian elite and the court. Our Moscow correspondent, Koch, was also a merchant, serving as the Swedish trade representative in the Russian capital.

Jacob Rautenfels may also have had direct connections with the players: the "house teacher, Mons. Trautenberg" we believe to be Rautenfels himself. Rautenfels spent about two years in Moscow, from 1670 to the spring of 1672. It is not known exactly when he arrived there, but since Rautenfels says in his book that he had seen the tsar's second wife twice when she was still unmarried, he must have arrived before January 22, 1671, the date of the royal wedding.[27] These encounters were likely at Matveev's residence. During his time in Moscow, Rautenfels lived in the house of the tsar's personal physician, Dr. Johann(es) Coster von Rosenburg, where he probably worked as a private tutor for the doctor's children; unlike the other resident foreigners, Rautenfels was not in the service of the tsar.[28] On March 8, 1672, Rautenfels and one of the doctor's sons received permission to leave Moscow. Rautenfels was to accompany the son, who was going to study at the Jesuit university in Wilno, and they must have left Moscow at some point between mid-March and the end of May 1672. Because Rautenfels describes the February performance but not the encore production in mid-May, it seems likely that he had left Russia by that point.[29]

After this, Rautenfels made his way to Italy, where he arrived by 1673, and it was there that he wrote his book about Russia, which includes the description of the February "Orpheus" performance in some detail, and the brief reference to the play based on the Esther story, mentioned only in passing. Rautenfels must have had some communication about events in Russia after his departure, for he notes the death of Tsar Aleksei (in early 1676) and describes the funeral. He finished his manuscript in Florence, at the court of Grand Duke Cosimo III (r. 1670–1723), and then departed from Italy in November 1677, leaving his book manuscript, or a copy, in Cosimo's library. Given Cosimo's earlier exposure to Russian diplomats, this connection certainly makes sense. At some point after this, an unknown German scholar found the text in the library, and with the permission of library director Antonio Magliabechi (a friend of Rautenfels), he was allowed to make a copy. This is the text published in Padua in 1680 as *De Rebus Moschoviticis*.[30]

We know from the descriptions of the February production in Moscow that Dr. Rosenburg's son played a very important role, declaiming a speech in German at the beginning and at the end, which were the only spoken portions of the performance. Given Rautenfels's close association with the Rosenburg family, it seems reasonable to suggest that one of these declamations included the German-language poem that appeared later in Rautenfels's book (although how accurately it might have been reproduced years later we cannot say). Indeed, Rautenfels himself may have written these lines, a job that may well have fallen into his hands during his time as a private teacher in the Rosenburg family.

Overall, then, our sources describing these two early 1672 "ballets" seem to be reliable and accurate, reflecting the activities of many people who were in a position to participate in or report on the exciting performances. We do not know the precise route of the request (or command) for the original production, although presumably it was initiated by the tsar, who would have expressed interest to his right-hand man, Matveev, in some sort of unspecified entertainment like those he had been hearing about. Matveev, in turn, would have directed his attention to the people he knew, or knew of, in the Foreign Quarter. These "volunteers" produced exactly what one might have expected, reenacting the skits and characters that were familiar from their experiences and upbringing in the German- and perhaps Dutch-speaking world. Primary among these experiences would have been the comic anarchy of Pickleherring, who turned out to be as popular in Moscow as he had been on the Continent, especially in Germany. Although scholars have written with subtlety and impressive archival persistence about the origins of this character in English practice and via the English actors who went to the Continent in the 1590s and beyond, by the time of the Moscow vaudeville, the character was firmly entrenched in German stage practice, and it is surely from this tradition that Pickleherring ended up performing for the tsar on that memorable day in February.[31]

In his work on intertheater, Anston Bosman presents Pickleherring as a key figure for reasons relating to both the accessibility and the function of this and other comic characters: "the clown," he writes, "emerges as the archetype of the traveling theater. An artist of the space between, he worked to bridge the acts, the costumes, and the languages of the performance." This was Pickleherring's role in German territories in the early seventeenth century, as documented in the famous 1620 print *Engelische Comedien und Tragedien*, which includes a separate series of short Pickleherring actions in addition to full-length plays.[32] This is precisely the role Pickleherring played in Moscow. Like the early performances of the "English comedians" on the Continent, there was a language barrier, initially, between performer and audience, a barrier that was broken, or transcended, by comic routines and also by musical numbers; it is no coincidence that Pickleherring is often associated with music, along with frenetic activity, leaps, and dancing.[33] Many descriptions of the early performances by the English players on the Continent emphasize this language barrier. Some actions, for example, were entirely mimed, such as the 1608 performance by the Englishman William Peadle in Leiden, where he was permitted to engage in "various beautiful and chaste performances with his body, without using any words" at a church in the city.[34] In other early performances, the comic character provided linkage, although not necessarily translation. In 1602, English actors in Münster performed a series of plays in English, but as a contemporary account explains, "they were accompanied by a clown, who, when a new act had to commence and when they had to change their costume, performed many antics and pranks in German during the performance, which amused the audience."[35] Although there has been a great deal of speculation about the language of the earliest plays performed for the Russian court, particularly for the first full-length play, there is no question about the language of this February offering: our eyewitness reports that it had no spoken component at all, except for the German-language recitations at the beginning and at the end. Based on Pickleherring's delighted reception at the tsar's court, it appears that the comic character, as always, needed no translation.

Pickleherring is precisely the kind of character these amateur players would have known about and been able to reproduce—anarchic leaping and some sort of dancing would presumably have been within the abilities of the forty-something Hasenkroeg, and certainly such antics would have been readily reinforced by the other, generally young, male actors who appeared with him. Indeed, the "curious jumps in the air" mentioned in our long account from the stage echoes another description from Leiden, documenting a performance by the English company headed by Robert Browne, which included "diverse comedies and histories" as well as "diverse leaps."[36]

Other scenarios and character types in the February program are also what we would expect from this group of actors. The characters drawn from mythology, Orpheus and Mercury, would certainly have been known to the foreigners, who would have been literate and educated (both prerequisites for their work as traders or teachers). Mercury was especially relevant to the merchant-actors, for in his placement within the Roman pantheon, he was closely associated with commerce and finance. Mercury was also associated with speed, for example in the title of the newspaper *Nordischer Mercurius* (and many other contemporary newspaper titles).[37] Mythological characters were also known at the Muscovite court. Orpheus was invoked by Simeon Polotskii in his *Orel rossiiskii* (The Russian eagle, 1667), written in honor of Tsarevich Aleksei Alekseevich's elevation as designated heir, certainly a work familiar to the royal audience. Orpheus was generally familiar as a foreign musician through the many *azbukovniki*, alphabetic word lists that circulated in Muscovy throughout the seventeenth century, and the Orpheus legend was also known in Matveev's circles at about this time. The translator and writer Nikolai Spafarii (Nicolae Milescu) mentions Orpheus as a musician in his book about the seven liberal arts (1672), a copy of which was produced for Tsar Aleksei's book collection.[38]

The character translations need not have been exact—that is, the allusions would have been comprehensible from both sides of the stage even if they did not evoke precisely the same images. This, indeed, is the nature of intertheater, which, as in Bosman's formulation, focuses on the "processes of interaction" and "the production of a third intermediary norm." The Swabians of the May program might not have been readily identifiable as such to the Russian royal family, but their traditional comic bumbling would have been amusing nevertheless. Finally, there is a calendrical connection relevant to both sides of the stage, for the Pickleherring character was associated with Shrovetide in the West, which meshes with the same period, maslenitsa, in the Russian tradition (and reinforces the earlier Carnival reports submitted by the visiting Russian ambassadors in Italian states).[39]

The Swedish diplomatic communications, in combination with Rautenfels's long-known account, provide details that help us visualize the later court theater productions more fully.[40] In fact, the descriptions of the February performance, particularly in the long account from the stage, are more detailed than we have for any of the other plays. They are not technical but rather emerge from the same milieu as the performances themselves, that of interested nonprofessional circles, and they describe the effects used in the production as well as the reactions by the royal audience. We thus return to the long account in order to present some of the specific descriptions of the staging and the many rich costumes created for the performance: "The stage [*Theatrum*] was covered with green cloth, and also with gilded leather; in its center was a marvelous big mirror. The floor was covered with very beautiful carpets. To this purpose we had beautiful clothes made of nice Asian [*Aseaschen*] and red cotton [*Kindiaken*] and also taffeta [or satin; *Taften*] fabric, which His Majesty had ordered to be purchased in cash from kiosks and had sewn up by 25 tailors in the Roman manner."[41] In a slightly later passage, this account offers additional details of the production:

> This *ballet* started with a perspective performance [i.e., referring to theatrical scenery[42]]: The doctor's son, dressed very beautifully, was sitting on a chair; he saw Mercurius—with wings at his head and feet—standing in front of a mountain, nicely made of branches, and behind the mountain a lighted double red-painted eagle appeared. At that time two pyramid mountains became visible in a very pleasing way. Münter and I stood in front of the door opposite each other with clubs on our shoulders, ready to attack. To sum up, it was really nice and everything went well. His Tsarish Majesty would have liked to have kept sitting and watching more but we did not have anything left to perform. His Tsarish Majesty laughed a lot at Pickleherring and this Heinrich Ballon (the Pickleherring was played by Hasenbruch, and the other one was barber)[43] and, at the end, at the silhouette play [*Schatten werck*], which was quite successful. Thanks to God that his Majesty and the other spectators liked it so much.

We add here a reminder of the description of the May performance, which lasted six hours and included: "Peace and War, the 4 Seasons, 4 State Persons, a beggar, Pickleherring and Swabians, 2 shepherds and 2 shepherdesses, Orpheus and 4 bears, 3 hunters, 4 farmers, 8 Romans, and Mercury."

The planners of the February performance obviously put a lot of effort into the costumes, and the rich fabrics they describe reflect the importance of such luxury goods in court circles as a whole. Although the planning period was short, they were able to find the appropriate fabrics from local sellers and then put a large force of twenty-five tailors to work in order to meet their performance deadline. The considerable sum of two hundred rubles was invested in these costumes. Several of the players themselves were engaged in such high-end trade, so this is another natural tie-in to the production—one wonders if this is why Matveev focused on foreign merchants in the first place, perhaps anticipating that their trading stock might prove as important as their acting talents.

Furthermore, the creation of beautiful costumes was something for which local expertise already existed—there was no need to find foreign specialists as the court was well supplied with tailors and others who could create impressive clothes.[44] Costuming was thus an aspect of the performance that reflected the aesthetic values as well as the skills available at court, even if the twenty-five tailors may have needed some input into the design of appropriate clothing for some of the characters. The long account from the stage, which was written by someone wearing one of these newly produced costumes, does not provide much detail about the dress or props, although the author says that Roden and the three other hunters wore green morocco clothes and that Mercury had "wings at his head and feet." The Romans mentioned for the May performance would probably have worn some sort of appropriately classical garb; they may also have appeared in the February program, as the account mentions that the costumes were sewn up "in the Roman manner." The four bears would have appeared in some sort of furry costume—furs of all sorts were staple items at the tsar's court. As we shall see, for one of the final plays created for the court theater, in January 1676, four bear costumes were created and four actors trained to perform in proper ursine fashion.

The most intriguing costuming possibilities relate to Pickleherring. This figure was so uniformly, and thus apparently so readily, identified by the foreign observers that one assumes he was wearing some of the character's traditional accoutrements. This might have been generally "foolish costume" or maybe something a bit more specific: a big ruff, stripes, even possibly certain colors, all of which were associated with the character.[45] Another of Pickleherring's traditional attributes, silence, was also observed in these two early performances (and, as we see in chap. 5, also in the Tamerlane play produced later for the court).

Both the long account from the stage and the February 20 report (sent to Bengt Horn) try to set the scene in general, giving their overall impressions of the physical arrangements. The production took place in the home of the tsar's late father-in-law—that is, in a place not intended for such entertainments but obviously spacious enough to accommodate what appear to be separate performance areas as well as the small (male) audience sitting near the performers and the screened-off female family members, who were seated together. Both accounts mention the carpeted floor and the green cloth covering the performance space; the long account also mentions gilded leather. There is also agreement on the use of red fabric to screen the royal women (although Rautenfels, writing several years later, mentioned some sort of wooden slats). The "marvelous big mirror" may have served as decoration but it might also have functioned to amplify the lighting.

There were some lighting effects, for example the "lighted double red-painted eagle." The "two pyramid mountains [that] became visible in a very pleasing way" may have been revealed by lighting or through the removal of drapery or perhaps moved by hand into view. The tableaux vivants of the May performance would have required some sort of screening or drapery in order to produce an effective reveal. There must have been some explanation of these scenes for the audience—especially for the tableau with the *Staats Personen!*—but they would have required no actual dialogue and so would fit the bill quite readily. The reference to the silhouette play also implies some sort of lighting effects, although we are at a loss to define them: perhaps through puppetry or by means of the exaggerated images created by a magic lantern effect, in which light directed on small figures produces large shadows on surfaces behind them (although, admittedly, we have no evidence that such equipment or technical know-how was available either to the foreigners or at the Russian court). Fireworks displays might also have provided some inspiration—at least later, in the 1690s, celebratory Russian fireworks included transparencies that were lighted from behind. Here, too, Russian expertise would have been available.[46] At any rate, however the effects were produced, the tsar laughed as much at the Schatten werck as he did at Pickleherring's antics.

Our accounts do not mention many props, but like the lighting effects or the use of curtains or drapery, all of the descriptions seem well within the range of the amateur actors and organizers, especially as they may have been familiar with such production basics from their own experiences either as students or as audience members before coming to Russia. The accounts include reference to "a mountain, nicely made of branches," to clubs held by the two participants guarding a door, and a chair, and one also presumes that some characters would have held appropriate props: perhaps a lyre for Orpheus, tools for the farmers, and other implements associated with the hunters, shepherds, and so forth.

Each of these theatrical building blocks set precedents for later productions at the court theater, creating expectations for characters, for the theatrical setup, for the use of music, and most fundamentally for the presentation of these actions by foreigners. The selection of the Foreign Quarter's Lutheran pastor, Johann Gregorii, as the playwright and organizer for the court theater naturally brought in students as performers, following a tradition that would have been familiar to the foreigners from their own schooling and equally familiar to the court from the declamations performed by Simeon Polotskii's well-drilled pupils. It also made available a group of actors who would not have to take time away from their professional employment, unlike the merchants who, presumably, lost at least a week's worth of work during the intense preparations for the February spectacle (although, apart from the fact that they could hardly have refused, they may have made up this investment in time through the provision of fabrics and other matériel; this was certainly the case for Peter Sievers). Many elements of the subsequent series of plays thus mirror and expand on these beginnings.

The sense of a two-way street—the experiences of the foreign amateur players and the reception of those experiences by the Russian royal family—fits comfortably into the overall patterns of the expansion and integration of English theatrical traditions throughout northern Europe over the course of the seventeenth century, as the intertheater concept suggests. There is another kind of context to consider as well, the spectacle and pageantry that already existed at the Russian court: the impressive religious rituals performed not just in and for church services but on a large-scale outdoor theater (the Palm Sunday rituals or the Blessing of the Waters—this latter so interesting to Westerners that they made special requests to see it[47]); the grand ceremonial entrances of diplomatic missions and departures of military forces; and especially the existing entertainments routinely provided for the tsar and his family. The royal family was already accustomed to hearing declamations and large groups of church singers, private performances on Western-style musical instruments, and amusements by traditional entertainers (storytellers, singers, and so forth). In other words, and particularly in the context of the declaimed readings, the Russian royal family had become acclimated to playing the role of an audience long before they took their seats on February 16, 1672, to see the delights Matveev had concocted for them.[48]

Without pushing the point too far, one might consider parallels to the fantastic displays arranged in the West to celebrate weddings and dynastic reaffirmations, peace treaties, and other such grand events. Indeed, such spectacle had regularly been brought to the attention of the Russian court through diplomatic and news reports. Just as the elaborate performances in the West were aimed widely but meant different things to different audience members, depending on their experience and education, so in Moscow was there sufficient overlap for things to make sense, for everyone involved to meet in the middle somehow.[49] It was not necessary for the players and audience to share fully in the expectations or interpretations of the "ballets"—they were enjoyable from a range of perspectives. That both performers and audience in Moscow were successful and satisfied in this confluence is evident by the immediate plans to create a more permanent structure to reproduce these pleasures, permanent in terms of physical constructions and, even more important, in the formation of a designated core of organizers and actors who could create all of this at will—at the tsar's will, that is. It is this process of solidification and regularization that we trace in the next section.

RECRUITING FOR THE TSAR'S THEATER

The dispatch from Moscow, May 28, 1672, which has the longer description of the May encore, also reports that Colonel Nicolaus von Staden, Matveev's "creature," was ordered to go abroad; this initiates a period extending for well over a year in which von Staden carried out complex and often confusing negotiations to hire players and musicians for what would become Tsar Aleksei's court theater. The author of the May 1672 dispatch writes that von Staden "has already received his traveling order and plans to leave next Monday and go from here toward Novgorod and Riga. As far as I can hear, he is to travel to Courland and Brandenburg to hire some craftsmen who are needed here." The "next Monday" would be on June 3. The writer was well informed, because according to the document published by Bogoiavlenskii, the order had been issued on May 15, and von Staden was indeed ordered to go to Novgorod and Pskov and then to the court of Jacob, Duke of Courland, where he was to look for, among other specialists, two trumpeters, the best and most learned, and also two people who knew how to mount various comedies.[50] As we will see, the search for trumpeters was expanded to include other instrumentalists as well. Von Staden's orders stipulated that if he could not hire these specialists in Courland, he was to go to Sweden and Prussia to find them and either bring them back to Moscow or send them on ahead through Pskov. Von Staden was also ordered to keep in touch, via the post, with Moscow.

The colonel eventually fulfilled most of his theatrical orders, although not without significant confusion and not in time for the October opening of the court theater. His zeal nevertheless deserves a brief review because his contacts included one of the best-known acting troupes in Western Europe, who seemed genuinely interested in exploring this Moscow commercial opportunity. Von Staden reached Pskov on June 29 and headed for the border a few days later. He wrote to Matveev from Riga on July 18, in a dispatch that was translated in Moscow on July 31. There must have been at least one additional intervening communication because this July 18 report begins by mentioning information he had sent in a previous mailing. Now he asks for a response to his question about possible hires. He says that he had found eight willing actors (*komedianty*), and these actors say that if this is not enough, it will be possible to augment their ranks in Moscow. Von Staden goes on to discuss financial arrangements, saying that the actors would be conveyed to Moscow at the tsar's expense and that for "every performance or comedy" they present for the tsar, they are to be paid fifty rubles; furthermore, they are to be allowed to offer paid performances for any interested people who want to see them. Otherwise, the actors would receive no additional salary from the court. Von Staden then reports on the trumpeters he was looking for, saying that he has not been able to find experienced players who want to come, although he was offering a great deal of money; he has, however, found two players who have recently learned and who can play various pieces and might learn more. They would be suitable as actors as well. They are to be paid six rubles per month, and they, like the actors, will have permission to perform elsewhere for money (pp. 2–3).

So, over roughly two weeks in Riga, von Staden made contact with a group of actors and searched for trumpeters, and he was able to report these hiring possibilities back to Moscow. Apparently, however, he had said something slightly different in the earlier (lost) communication, because just a day before this letter was translated for Matveev (on July 31), the tsar sent directions from Moscow to his agents in Pskov (p. 2). This order refers to a larger group of actors, numbering fourteen, and instructions were issued so that the Pskov agents would be prepared for this and have permission to pay for their travel to Moscow. Perhaps, then, this larger number explains why von Staden was at pains to assure Matveev that, although the number he proposed in his July 18 account—eight players—might have been considered small, it could easily be augmented. These arrangements, both numbers and salaries, are confirmed by Matveev on August 2—that is, just days after the translation of the report—and were followed by an order to the Pskov authorities in a dispatch sent from Moscow on August 10 (pp. 3–4).

The next surviving report shows, unsurprisingly, that things did not work out quite as planned. In a report written in Riga on October 10 (translated in Moscow on October 25), von Staden says that he had just returned from Stockholm. Among other topics, he says that he has found a trumpet player (who wanted to bring his brother along) as well as three other young people who play on instruments that have never been heard in Moscow. He also says that he had broken his leg in Sweden and that he planned to return to Moscow after it had healed a little more. The documents support his claims, for the trumpeter Johann Waldonn signed a contract with von Staden in Stockholm on September 10 (pp. 5–6, 18).[51] A few weeks earlier, von Staden had signed a contract with four (not three) other musicians in Mitau, the capital of the Duchy of Courland (the site of the unsuccessful meeting discussed in our previous chapter). This contract, signed on August 25, specified that the musicians' monthly salaries were to start on September 1, with payment for travel to Moscow provided. They, too, were guaranteed the option of leaving the tsar's service if they so chose and given permission to play for others when not needed by the court (pp. 6, 18–19). This assurance of their freedom to leave was probably not coincidental: according to von Staden's report, local specialists were unwilling to enter into Russian service due to the experiences of some earlier hires, who had not been allowed to leave and were even threatened with exile to Siberia (p. 3).

Von Staden showed up in Pskov on November 4 with the numbers laid out in these contracts, but the Pskov authorities, working from the earlier numbers, wrote back to Moscow to try to clear things up, probably a hopeless task.[52] When von Staden finally got back to Moscow, his report, dated

December 3, gives the final accounting, which meshes with the contracts he signed with the trumpeter and the four other instrumentalists (and with the numbers he had ultimately brought to the confused authorities in Pskov). These musicians came with him to Moscow, and Matveev's response, a few days later, confirms the arrangements for payment (pp. 6–7).

There were two separate contracts, one with the trumpeter Waldonn and another with the four other musicians (*muzykanty*). Waldonn, it turns out, had previously been in the tsar's service, for he had participated in the siege of Smolensk, in 1654, along with other foreign mercenaries.[53] Although it seems unlikely that von Staden sought Waldonn out specifically because of this earlier service, it does suggest how von Staden's inquiries, in Stockholm, about a trumpeter to work in Russia might have come to Waldonn's attention. Waldonn signed himself as a "Felt Tromp[e]ter," and his duties, spelled out in the contract, were to serve as "Hoff und Feltrompetter." Waldonn would thus have served at court (in the context of the theater) and in a military capacity (presumably reflecting his earlier experience in Smolensk). Although von Staden's initial report refers to Waldonn as an imperial trumpeter (p. 6), later Russian documents consistently refer to him as a Swedish resident; when he was released from service, in June 1674, he was headed for Sweden (p. 40).

The joint contract for the four musicians von Staden hired in Courland lists them individually: Gottfried Berge (from Danzig), Christopher Ackermann (from Saxony), Friedrich Plattenschläger (from Prussia), and Jacob Philips (from Courland). Ackermann was apparently fairly young, for in one of his later petitions, he called himself a student.[54] Their joint contract lists the various instruments they brought with them and could play: "Orgeln, Trompeten, Trompeten-Marinen, Cinchen, Dulcian und Posaunen, Violen und Viol de Gambe, auch die vocalische Music dabey, und noch andere Instrumente mehr." In combination with the specialist trumpeter, this list shows that von Staden had made provision for a varied ensemble, with performers on organ; brass and wind instruments, including trumpet, trombone (Posaune), cornett (Cinchen, probably Zincken or Zink), and Dulcian (or Dulzian, an early bassoon); and strings, including the tromba marina, which was quite popular in the second half of the seventeenth century. All this is in addition to singing and the miscellaneous "other instruments" they could play.[55] In his December 3 report, von Staden said that the five musicians brought with them seven instruments (p. 6); apparently, they were not expected to bring an organ, and by the time they arrived, in December, the problem of acquiring an organ for the tsar's new theater had been solved (by appropriating one owned by Hasenkroeg; see chap. 4). This mixed ensemble thus reflects and expands on the kinds of music that our eyewitness described as being a highlight of the February 1672 "ballet," which featured strings and flutes, with particular praise for Heinrich Münter, who sang a song accompanied by a viola da gamba. The musical enumeration in the *Nordischer Mercurius* article is very similar, omitting only the flutes. Von Staden's musical hires clearly aimed at enhancing one of the most popular features of the previous performances.

The contracts also hint at the seeds of contention regarding payment, a running argument, provoked by several causes, that was to thread its way throughout these musicians' employment in Moscow. The first difference of opinion was about their start date. Although the contract specified that their wages were to begin on September 1, the musicians were paid only for December, when they finally arrived (p. 7). The reason for the delay is not given in their petition for these promised funds, but one suspects that it was not their fault; it seems likely that they hesitated to come on their own to Moscow, preferring to wait for von Staden to recover sufficiently from his injury so that he could accompany them. At any rate, in spite of appeals, they were not to receive this stipulated payment—Matveev was interested only in the fact of their arrival in December, not in the corollary that they apparently had to cool their heels in Riga for a couple of months before they could start collecting that salary.

In addition to enumerating the musical ensemble, von Staden's December 3 report adds some very important names connected with another of his assignments, the hiring of an acting troupe to come to Moscow. In this report, von Staden said that he had arranged for the comedians of *"magister* Felton and Charlus," twelve people, to entertain the tsar. They were to come to Moscow at the tsar's expense but would live there without a regular salary; when the tsar requested a performance, they would be paid fifty rubles. They were waiting in Riga for orders to come. In his response to this report (December 10), Matveev gave permission to von Staden to tell the waiting troupe in Riga that they might proceed, and he also arranged for the Pskov authorities to be notified of their impending arrival (pp. 6–7). Thus, as far as von Staden knew at this point, everything was approved and the troupe was waiting for their orders to come to Moscow. The arrangements for the komedianty to be paid fifty rubles when they played for the tsar and to have permission to give paid performances elsewhere in the city was the same proposal von Staden had described in his July 18 dispatch, and it seems reasonable to assume that these arrangements applied to the same group of players in both reports.

Although at this point, in December 1672, the tsar's court theater had already performed (and encored) its first play, this effort to contract with an existing Western acting troupe deserves careful attention. All of von Staden's theatrical recruiting efforts took place in the summer and fall of 1672. His report on the "Felton and Charlus" actors was dated December 3, after he got back to Moscow, and permission to write to them in Riga was given by Matveev a week later (December 10; p. 7), which, presumably, von Staden did fairly expeditiously. The following spring, von Staden received a letter from one Anna Elisabeth, written in Copenhagen on April 4, 1673 (pp. 20–22; see fig. 3.2). It is this letter, and the name of the writer, that solidifies the identification of the komedianty as the Paulsen-Velten troupe, headed by Carl Andreas Paulsen, Anna's husband and clearly the "Charlus" of the Russian sources.[56] In 1664, Paulsen had brought Johannes Velten into his troupe, luring him away from another well-known acting group headed by M. D. Treu. Velten (1640–1692)—obviously the "Felton" of the Russian sources—is one of the most important figures in seventeenth-century German theater history.[57]

Anna's letter is consistent with von Staden's recruiting trip to Riga the previous year. We know from its petitions to the Riga city council that the Paulsen-Velten troupe was performing there in May and June 1672. Riga was a frequent destination for traveling acting companies, often as a stopping point on the way to Sweden, so this was a natural place for von Staden, Riga-born himself, to begin his search for actors.[58] He arrived there in July, a few weeks after the troupe's departure. He had relatives in Riga: Anna's letter mentions his cousin, and there is a Russian translation of a letter to Nicolaus von Staden from an uncle there, so it would have been easy for him to learn about the troupe's recent performances as he made his inquiries into available actors and musicians.

Anna opens her April 1673 letter by saying that she had received letters the previous day from von Staden, from his cousin, and from her own son-in-law. These letters had been delayed, Anna writes, but through no fault of her own, for the postmaster in Königsberg had not forwarded the mail from

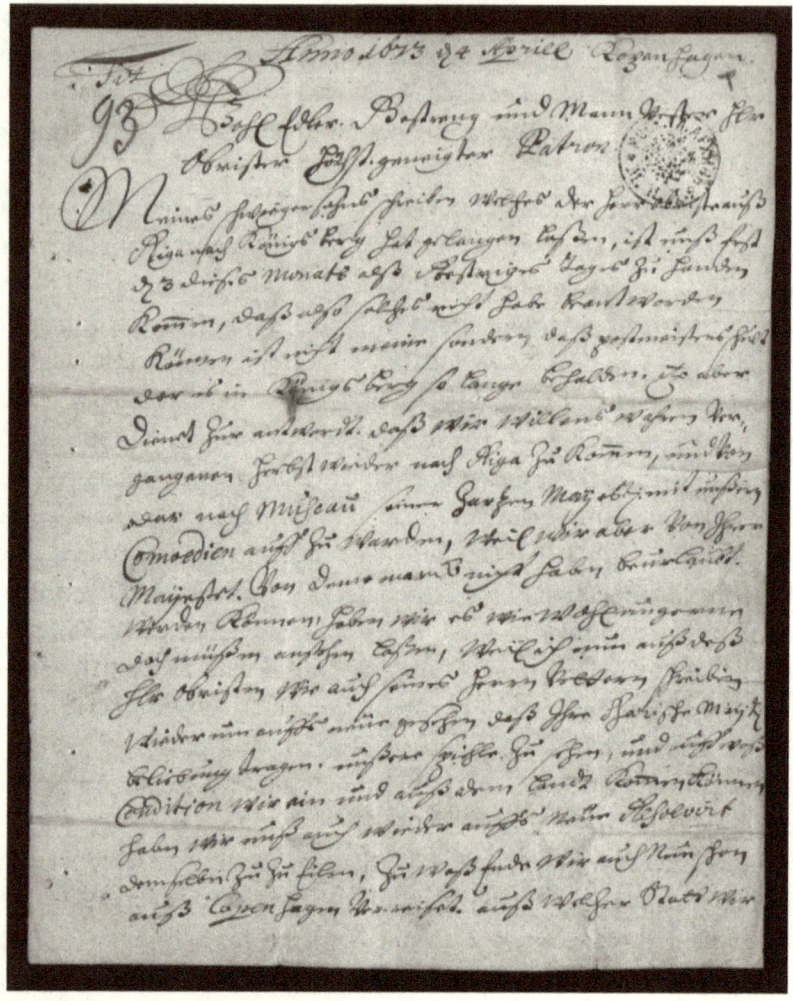

FIG. 3.2

Anna Paulsen's letter to von Staden, first page
(RGADA, f. 150, op. 1, 1672, No. 1, fol. 93, used by permission)

Riga in a timely fashion.[59] In her letter, Anna explains that, although the group (an unspecified "we") had intended to come to Moscow from Riga the previous fall (1672), it had been impossible to break its contract with the Danish king. The troupe was indeed engaged in a long contract with the Danish court, and its trip to Riga in the spring had been a quick excursion squeezed into this existing commitment. Now, however, as Anna reports in her April 1673 letter, the players were free and still interested in coming to

Moscow; furthermore, judging from the (delayed) letters they had received from von Staden and his cousin (who was apparently involved in the transactions), they understood that the tsar was still interested in seeing their performances.[60] Anna says that the company planned to be in Riga again in the fall (that is, in the fall of 1673) and that it would be ready to come to Moscow at any moment, whenever the tsar summoned.[61] She also mentions making arrangements for the troupe's stage machinery. Meanwhile, it was looking for a good (male) singer and a lutenist, as von Staden had requested earlier. This last bit of information shows that discussions between a representative of the acting troupe and the tsar's emissary had indeed taken place, just as von Staden had said in his December 1672 report to Matveev. The lutenist would further enhance the instrumental ensemble von Staden had been assembling, and the specialist singer would replicate Münter's popular appearance in the earlier production(s).

Finally, Anna signals her diligence and eagerness to close the deal by mentioning that she had dined three times with the Russian representative (she calls him "Herr Obriste") in Copenhagen and that he had written a good letter of recommendation for the company. The representative (unnamed in Anna's letter) was Emel'ian Ignat'evich Ukraintsev (1641–1708), who was in Copenhagen from the end of January through April 1673. This lengthy stay would have given Anna ample opportunity to visit him on three different occasions.[62] Ukraintsev would have known of the tsar's interest in theater, for he had left Moscow just after the premiere of the first full-length play (described in chap. 4). To our great regret, Ukraintsev's recommendation letter seems not to have survived—one wonders if it was based solely on his meetings with Anna or if he had actually seen the troupe perform.

The letter to Nicolaus von Staden written by his uncle, Johann (Riga, March 7, 1673), introduces another thread we will follow throughout the period of the court theater: the context in the Russian and, indeed, Pan-European fears of the Turks during this time. In his letter, Johann tells his nephew that the unnamed actors had written of their concerns about traveling to perform in Moscow due to their fears that the tsar was going to march against the Turks.[63] It seems that perhaps Johann, in Riga, was able to calm the actors' fears, and then, when Anna Paulsen had the chance to talk to Ukraintsev in Copenhagen later, she decided it was safe to proceed, and thus wrote her letter to Nicolaus von Staden, in April. The fears were real, for the Turks had crossed the Danube in the summer of 1672; this is what motivated the tsar to send Ukraintsev (and other emissaries) to Western Europe that fall. So, as we will see, the "Turkish threat" hovers over the theater almost from its inception and is finally manifested most clearly in the play written on the subject of Tamerlane and Bayezid (which we discuss in chap. 5).

In February 1673, Matveev ordered payment for von Staden's expenses from the previous year, including those he had incurred for his efforts to hire the instrumentalists, all of whom came in December, as well as for his efforts to hire the twelve komedianty (p. 24). This was before von Staden received Anna's letter, in which she delayed the troupe's proposed trip to Moscow until the fall of 1673, so the plans were, at this point, clearly still under consideration. As a follow-up, in September 1673 the tsar wrote to inform his representatives in Pskov about the imminent arrival of comedians from abroad, who were coming on the authority of a letter by von Staden. The Pskov officials were told to facilitate the troupe's travel to Matveev, to the Ambassadorial Chancery in Moscow (p. 23). This fall arrival would thus confirm Anna's proposal in her own earlier letter, saying that they would be in Riga in the fall of 1673 and would come to Moscow at any time the tsar wished.

Thus, over a period of about a year and a half, and nearly a year after the premiere performance at the new court theater, the idea of bringing an established acting troupe from abroad was still being actively pursued. Although there is no evidence that the Paulsen-Velten troupe ever made it to Moscow, these extended negotiations surely tell us as much about its business interests as about the tsar's (or Matveev's) desire to see it perform.[64] These extended efforts to hire "authentic" German actors also testifies to the continuing importance and resonance of the February and May "ballets." Matveev's goal seems to have been to replicate this initial success as faithfully as possible, and the best way to accomplish this would be to do exactly what von Staden attempted: hire ready-made professionals, in line with the other technical specialists they had so often sought (and did indeed seek on this same trip by hiring the instrumentalists). It thus follows along the lines of the court's earlier attempts to hire knowledgeable theatrical personnel from abroad, for example, by John Hebdon a decade earlier. In the context of the early 1672 performances, it may not be a coincidence that the Paulsen-Velten troupe was known for its Pickleherring, played by Christian Janetzky, who had been associated with the acting company since the mid-1660s (see fig. 3.3).[65] A good Pickleherring would certainly be a bonus.

FIG. 3.3

Christian Janetzky, the Pickleherring of the Velten troupe (HAB, Lo 3396.1, used by permission)

Our next chapter follows up on the experiences of February and May 1672, tracing the efforts to build a permanent theatrical infrastructure for the Russian court.

NOTES

1. Nineteenth-century studies include Tikhonravov, *Russkie dramaticheskie proizvedeniia* 1:esp. xiii–xxiv; Morozov, *Ocherki*, chap. 5; Veselovskii, *Zapadnoe vliianie*, chap. 1; and, later, the important surveys in *RRD* 1 and 2 (with extensive bibliography and source information). Recent studies, including the dissertation by Ekaterininskaia, "Pridvornyi teatr" and several articles by Kaplun, are based on these earlier fundamental works.

2. This section is based on sources originally published in Jensen and Maier, "Orpheus" and "Pickleherring Returns"; all quotations are from these published translations (with some slight modifications), and all original texts appear in full in these articles; this passage is in "Orpheus," 151–152, with the Latin original as Source One, p. 180. In the printed book from 1680, the author's name is given as "Reutenfels" (fol. a3v), a spelling that does not appear in any of the known historical documents (for example, Stensen, *Nicolai Stenonis epistolae* 1:301, 307, 326, uses "Rautenfelz" or "Rautenfels"). We use the spelling "Rautenfels" (except in some bibliographical references). A detail that strengthens the Rautenfels spelling comes from the career of our Filimonatus, Laurentius Grelle, who was ennobled as L. von Rautenschildt in 1650. *Raute* is a geometrical form (rhombus, diamond, lozenge), an important element in heraldry.

3. The reports we discuss here are in RAS, Livonica II, vol. 180. Biographical information from Droste and Maier, "Christoff Koch"; Elgenstierna, *Den introducerade svenska adelns ättartavlor* 4:229. In addition to his work as correspondent in Moscow, Koch was the official Swedish commercial representative (factor) there. This was not unusual; the other regular correspondents from Russia, Hans Deyne in Novgorod and Hermann Herbers in Pskov, were also commercial representatives.

4. An overview of Matveev's career is in Bushkovitch, *Peter the Great*, 55–79; Longworth, *Alexis*, 11–12, 53, 90, 105–106, and chap. 9 (p. 199 as "ward"); Crummey, *Aristocrats*, 101 (as "ward" and Matveev as royal in-law). Bushkovitch, *Peter the Great*, 58–60, 63, explains more precisely that Matveev's "wife's niece was the wife of Natal'ia's uncle" and doubts that Natal'ia spent much time in the Matveev household.

5. Ellersieck, "Russia under Aleksei Mikhailovich," 52n40; this was during the reign of Tsar Aleksei's successor, Fedor Alekseevich.

6. RAS, Livonica II, vol. 180. Other such invitations appear throughout the reports in RAS, Diplomatica Muscovitica, vol. 604.

7. The February 12, 1672, source is RGADA, f. 396, op. 1, ch. 10, No. 13674, fol. 1, published in Dzhensen and Maier, *Pridvornyi teatr*, 68n71.

8. RAS, E 4304 (Bengt Horns Samling). Complete translation in Jensen and Maier, "Orpheus," 159–160, with the German original as Source Three, p. 182.

9. The *Nordischer Mercurius*, founded in 1664, was issued twice weekly during this time, and this article appeared in the last of the ordinary issues for March 1672. The individual issues had no separate title or printing date; instead, the newspaper was paginated continuously. See Jensen and Maier, "Orpheus," 155–156, where the article appears in full on pp. 156–158 (original text as Source Two, pp. 181–182).

10. See Jensen and Maier, "Orpheus," 170–171, and "Pickleherring Returns," 8, on these small articles.

11. This source is presented in full in Jensen and Maier, "Orpheus," 183–184, as Source Four. We note here that the documents in the RAS collections we are using for our study are rarely foliated. Internal dating of the source under discussion here is provided, in part, by details about a visiting Polish embassy ("Orpheus," 169–170). This source—and additional letters, arguably also from Koch, written during that same period—contains unusual lexical items and grammatical forms, as compared to literary Early Modern German style (e.g., *dwer fleutz, des Tzaren Schwiegermutters*). The character of such "mistakes" suggests that the secretary responsible for writing out these communications was not a native speaker of German but rather a Dutch speaker.

12. The original has "des Tzaren Schwiegermutters Ilian Danilowitz," which makes no sense either grammatically or semantically (Il'ia Danilovich Miloslavskii was the tsar's deceased father-in-law). The letter *n*—*Ilian*—might reflect a possessive adjective, Ильина, "Il'ia's (wife)," which might have sounded like a female name to a foreigner. We have been unable to discover the date of the widow's death, nor do we know if she would still have owned the house in which the performance took place.

13. The *Nordischer Mercurius* article has "drunk" peasants, but this author (or copyist) clearly writes *drumbene*, not *drunckene*. The exact meaning of this word is unclear, although the Low German *Drümpel* indicates a "rube, muddler, or fool." The most likely explanation is a copying error, *druncken* becomes *drumben*.

14. This word seems to indicate something like an extraordinary authorization to enter. Any such pass would have been authorized or provided by Matveev, so the statement that "we gave an *Axal* [to Butenant], *pro forma*" suggests that the participants may have circumvented the authorities and allowed him access on their own. *Axal* could also refer to an object, something Butenant was given so that he would appear to be a supernumerary or an assistant and thus allowed access. Heinrich Butenant (d. 1701) was a well-known merchant and, later, diplomat in Moscow.

15. The reference here, we believe, is to Artamon Sergeevich Matveev. However, it is unclear if there was an additional person—"Trokunow"—who was also among the spectators. See Dzhensen and Maier, *Pridvornyi teatr*, 59–60n59 (including a possible identification with the Troekurov family).

16. This understanding of *ergehen* appears to be the most likely one here, although the verb had many meanings in Early Modern German and we were unable to document exactly this meaning elsewhere. If our interpretation is correct, the "attached" song was not filed with this document. Either it was not forwarded to the Swedish government or it was filed elsewhere in the archive. As we will see, the author was correct in linking the next performance opportunity to Easter.

17. We omit the poem here; see Jensen and Maier, "Orpheus," 154, with the original text as Source One, pp. 180–181.

18. In the Russian translation a concrete day of the week (Saturday) was given instead: "V etot zhe den', subbotu na maslenitse" ([Rautenfels], "Skazaniia," 302).

19. Jensen and Maier, "Pickleherring Returns," 12–13, with the original text as Source Eight, p. 54. The letter was originally published in Harder-Gersdorff, "Lübeck," 134. One other source uses *ballet* in this limited sense, a dispatch from Grundel-Helmfelt (Narva, February 29, 1672), with enclosures from Moscow, February 6 and 13 (that is, written before the first performance had taken place). Perhaps, in this instance, the use of *ballet* reflects Grundel-Helmfelt's own associations. This dispatch is written in Swedish, whereas Grundel-Helmfelt's letters are generally in German (RAS, Livonica II, vol. 180).

20. This expression (and its context) is unclear; the German phrase can have other meanings, with the general sense of an important person or dignitary. It may also refer to the

concept of the Four Estates—in Sweden, for example, these were the nobles, the priests, the burghers, and the farmers, and they sometimes appeared on stage in ballets and pageants, as in the Carousel for the Accession of Charles XI in December 1672; see Rangström, "Certamen Equestre," 304 (English translation on p. 305). There was a depiction of the Four Seasons at the tsar's Kolomenskoe residence (Bushkovitch, *Peter the Great*, 47n72), and see later in this chapter on the Orpheus figure in Russian sources.

21. Jensen and Maier, "Pickleherring Returns," 9–10, with the original text as Source Seven, pp. 53–54. On Dutch tableaux (*Vertoningen*), see Brandt and Hogendoorn, *German and Dutch Theatre*, 365 and 420–422, and J. Alexander, "Ridentum dicere verum," 740. We have so far found no evidence that the promised banquet took place.

22. Bogoiavlenskii, "Moskovskii teatr," 1 ("gde byt' komedii"). This is apparently the first Russian-language reference to these productions; in later Russian sources, they are called "balety" (see chap. 4).

23. Ellersieck, "Russia under Aleksei Mikhailovich," 194–195.

24. This discussion is based on the more detailed information and bibliography in Jensen and Maier, "Pickleherring Returns," 16–20. According to Martens, *Hamburger Kaufleute*, 12, almost all of the Hamburg merchant families in Moscow had originally immigrated from the Netherlands; this might explain the characteristic Dutch spelling *Hasenkroeg(h)*, and also the German and Dutch forms of his Christian name (Dietrich/Dirck).

25. Hasenkroeg owned a house in Moscow by 1674; earlier, in 1672, his house (whether he owned it or not) was known to Matveev, as discussed in chapter 4. Hasenkroeg thus seems to have been well established in Moscow at this point.

26. The family was German (not from a family originally from Holland, like Hasenkroeg).

27. Reutenfels, *De Rebus Moschoviticis*, 97; on pp. 97–98 he gives a lively description of the new tsaritsa's beauty and character (see also [Rautenfels], "Skazaniia," 297). Other details of Rautenfels's career are in Jensen and Maier, "Orpheus," 148–150.

28. According to a June 20, 1674, letter by Count Valerio Zani, sent from Bologna to the Florentine librarian Antonio Magliabechi, Rautenfels spent more than two years in Dr. Rosenburg's house in Moscow (Stensen, *Nicolai Stenonis epistolae* 1:42; the letter is in Florence, BN, Magl. VIII 1079, fols. 12r and 15v). For details about Rosenburg and his family, see Dumschat, *Ausländische Mediziner*, 477–479, 588–590, and the same author's entry in *Biographisches Lexikon*, s.v. "Coster (Köster) von Rosenburg, Johann(es)." Although Rautenfels has been identified variously as a physician (Bushkovitch, "Cultural Change," 95, 100) and a "Polish agent" (Martin, "Muscovite Esther," 25), we have found no evidence for these specific occupations.

29. Rautenfels is listed as a *plemiannik* ("nephew") in one source, but we have not been able to verify any familial relationship with Dr. Rosenburg; the word was not necessarily as specific in earlier usage as it is in modern Russian (Jensen and Maier, "Orpheus," 148n9). Kholodov, *Teatr i zriteli*, 65, says that Rautenfels must have left Moscow after May 30, 1672, the date the tsarevich was born. His conclusion is based on the Russian translation of Rautenfels, which says that Tsarevich Petr (the future Peter the Great) was born "nezadolgo do nashego ot"ezda" ([Rautenfels], "Skazaniia," 297). However, the Latin version has: "In secundo matrimonio, *sub nostrum ex urbe Moscua discessum*, Regina Natalia filium principem, Petrum nomine, felici in lucem dedit partu" (Reutenfels, *De Rebus Moschoviticis*, 98). The time frame expressed in the italicized phrase is best translated as "around the time of our departure," meaning that he could have left a couple of days or weeks before the tsarevich's birth on May 30.

30. Neither of the two manuscripts—Rautenfels's original or the German scholar's copy—seems to have survived. A German version of the work was published in Nürnberg

in 1687 by Johann Christoph Lochner (1653–1730). The complex relationship between the Latin and the German versions is beyond our present scope; however, the German text does not seem to be an exact translation of the Latin (indeed, the preface mentions using "other authors," although they are not specified; [Reutenfels], *Das Grosse und mächtige Reich Moscovien*, ij verso). Rautenfels almost certainly wrote his original (lost) version in Latin. See also Jensen and Maier, "Orpheus," 150n14.

31. There is extensive literature on the English comedians on the Continent and on the Pickleherring character; a brief summary is in Jensen and Maier, "Pickleherring Returns," esp. 32–35 (and see later in this chapter). Nineteenth-century Russian scholars noted this connection in the context of the Russian court theater that emerged shortly thereafter, for example, Tikhonravov, *Russkie dramaticheskie proizvedeniia* 1:esp. xx–xxiv; Morozov, *Ocherki*, esp. 147–155.

32. Bosman, "Renaissance Intertheater," 564. The 1620 print is available in *Spieltexte*; see also (among many other sources) Cohn, *Shakespeare in Germany*, esp. cvii–cxiii; Haekel, *Die Englischen Komödianten*, esp. 116–131, 205–212. Lande, *Persistence of Folly*, esp. chaps. 1–3, focuses on the actions of the comedians on the Continent.

33. Pickleherring's traits are sketched out, for example, in J. Alexander, "Ridentum dicere verum," and the same author's "Will Kemp" and "Pickleherring: An Early Modern Clown" (although some of the musical transcriptions in this latter article are puzzling). See also Katri(t)zky, especially "Pickelhering and Hamlet," and "A Plague o' These Pickle Herring," and Hilton, "Pickelhering."

34. Quoted in Riewald, "New Light," 76; a slightly different translation is in Bosman, "Renaissance Intertheater," 569.

35. Quoted in Bosman, "Renaissance Intertheater," 564.

36. Quoted in Bosman, "Renaissance Intertheater," 569; a more complete transcription is in Brand and Rudin, "Der englische Komödiant," 120.

37. The association with speedy news delivery began early on, with the Wolfenbüttel *Aviso*, which, beginning in 1609, depicted a winged Mercury "soaring over a landscape populated by busy news-bearers" (Pettegree, *Invention of News*, 184).

38. Spafarii's book is *Kniga izbranaia vkrattse o deviatikh musakh i o sedmikh svobodnykh khudozhestvakh* (A brief book on the nine muses and on the seven liberal arts). The Matveev-Spafarii connection is emphasized in Bushkovitch, "Cultural Change," esp. 96–97; on Aleksei Mikhailovich's library, see Waugh, "Library," with references to O. A. Belobrova's extensive studies of Spafarii. Other references to Orpheus are in Ioannikii Korenev's *O penii bozhestvennom* (On sacred singing), which dates from this time (the earliest version is from 1671). Korenev also mentions Amphion as another musical figure from the ancient world, and both names appear in Nikolai Diletskii's 1679 *Grammatika*, a music-theoretical treatise; see Jensen, *Musical Cultures*, 177–178, with updated references to Korenev's treatise in Vorob'ev, "Kliuch razumeniia." The play later written for the court theater on the biblical story of Judith also includes references to classical gods; the comic character Susakim refers to "Zeves, Aris, [and] Afrodita," and other characters in this play refer to Jupiter, Mars, Mercury, and Venus (*RRD* 1:376, 448; Kaplun, "Personazhishuty," 64).

39. On the Shrovetide associations for Pickleherring, see, for example, J. Alexander, "Will Kemp," 464–466, and Katritzky, "A Plague o' These Pickle Herring"; for the Russian context, see Likhachev, Panchenko, and Ponyrko, *Smekh v drevnei Rusi*.

40. In addition to Morozov and other nineteenth-century scholars listed earlier, comparisons with Western staging practices are in Bulgakov, "Komediia"; Flemming, "Deutsches Barockdrama"; J. Stone, "Pastor," and others.

41. *Aseaschen* may be related to the Russian word *aziiatka*, a type of traditional women's dress; see Dal', *Tolkovyi slovar'*, s.v. "aziiatka"; Hellie, *Economy*, 346, lists *aziam* as a caftan. On *Kindiaken*, see Hellie, *Economy*, 285; *Slovar' russkogo iazyka*, s.v. "kindiak" [киндякъ].

42. "[Z]ur anfenglichen praesent in selbigen Ballet war einer verthönung perspectiv-weis" (Jensen and Maier, "Orpheus," as Source Four, pp. 183–184); the word *perspektivy* was used in Repskii's account (cited in chap. 2 of this volume), and see also chapter 4.

43. The meanings of "Heinrich Ballon" and "barber" are unclear; in both cases, the author may be indicating either a character in the performance or a personal name (thus "Heinrich Ballon" might have played the role of a barber or perhaps someone named "Barber" played another comic role). A play called *Pickelhäring ein Barbier* is listed among a series of Pickleherring plays in the late seventeenth century, performed in 1668 (Heine, *Johannes Velten*, 23, citing Fürstenau, *Zur Geschichte* 1:228). *Balloon* as a noun is used in seventeenth-century English accounts as a recreation or game, so it is possible that this word refers to some sort of physical exhibit on the stage (*OED*, s.v. "Balloon"); in dance terminology, *ballon* refers to lightness in jumping.

44. See chapter 4, however, on a foreign fabric cutter who helped with costumes for the first court play.

45. Descriptions of Pickleherring's costumes are in J. Alexander, "Ridentum dicere verum," 740 (the "foolish costume," quoting Samuel Sturm's novel *Der Geist von Monsieur Pickel-Hering*, from 1666) and 747–748; see also Katri(t)zky, "Pickelhering and Hamlet," and Asper, *Hanswurst*, images 3, 5, 14–16; Hansen, *Formen der Commedia dell'Arte*, 39–56.

46. Bredekamp, "*Kunstkammer*, Play-Palace," includes images and descriptions of *laterna magica* effects. Kitching, *Europe's Itinerant Players*, 66, 121, 196, notes a 1680 petition from the performer Michel Bichel to authorities in Reval for a program involving what Bichel called an "Optica," a projecting device that created shadows, so there were such effects familiar from traveling theater. On fireworks displays, see Maggs, "Firework Art," esp. 27. Russian interest in such displays is familiar from accounts of the 1640s, described in our introduction; the Dutch diplomatic mission headed by Koenraad van Klenk, en route to Moscow in November 1675, saw such a display ([Coyett], *Posol'stvo*, 63 [Dutch text]/344 [Russian translation]).

47. For example, members of the van Klenk mission, in January 1676, were disappointed that their entrance into Moscow would take place after the Blessing of the Waters ceremony, so they made arrangements to sneak in quietly to observe it; their account includes a detailed description ([Coyett], *Posol'stvo*, 88, 90–96/373–374, 376–382). On the ceremony, see Bushkovitch, "Epiphany Ceremony."

48. Hippisley, *Poetic Style*, 34, emphasizes that Simeon Polotskii was well aware that he was writing for a "real and living audience, almost always in the form of the Tsar and his family and court"; Vroon, *DLB* 150, s.v. "Simeon Polotsky," 302, also points to the differences between works written for performed declamation and those written for silent reading.

49. See Aercke, *Gods of Play*, on the idea of discourse in Western private festive performances.

50. Bogoiavlenskii, "Moskovskii teatr," 1–2 (throughout the remainder of this chapter, references to Bogoiavlenskii will be placed in the text identified with page numbers only). Previous scholars have surveyed these valuable theatrical records, for example, Kudriavtsev, "Artakserksovo deistvo"; Beliakov, *Sluzhashchie*, 199–204, and throughout the *RRD* volumes.

51. Here and in the following discussion, we are using standardized German spellings for the names of these foreign musicians, in order to avoid the wondrous orthographic variety appearing throughout the Russian documents. For the trumpet player Johann Waldonn,

for example, the Russian spellings include: Ian Valdon, Ivashko Valdov, Ivan Vandon, Ivan Vaidon, and Ivan Polmon (Bogoiavlenskii, "Moskovskii teatr," 6, 17, 26, 27).

52. The documents in Bogoiavlenskii, "Moskovskii teatr," 5–6, trace the fluctuating confusion. In November, authorities in Pskov wrote to Moscow, referring to previous orders, from August 6 and 20, that said that von Staden had hired twenty-two comedians, two trumpeters, and two other specialists. But then, on November 4, von Staden had showed up with only six foreigners; he claimed that they were part of this group of komedianty and that the remaining hirees would arrive later. On November 11, the Pskov authorities sent von Staden and his group on to Moscow, asking what to do if the remaining komedianty showed up. If von Staden did indeed hire twenty-two players, this would be a rather large ensemble, as the discussion of the Dannenfels troupe in our introduction indicates.

53. This previous Russian contact is mentioned in a later petition (1672) in which a merchant attempted to collect on an old debt from Waldonn (RGADA, f. 150, op. 1, 1672, No. 1, fol. 127).

54. Bogoiavlenskii, "Moskovskii teatr," 6, 18–19; as in our discussion of the other foreign hires, spellings here are regularized. On Ackermann, see also RGADA, f. 150, op. 1, 1672, No. 1, fol. 166.

55. On the tromba marina, see Adkins, *GMO*, s.v. "Trumpet marine."

56. The letter is written in a single hand throughout. There is an annotation in a seventeenth-century chancery hand noting that it was delivered by N. von Staden on May 16, 1673 (possibly to Matveev himself [RGADA, f. 150, op. 1, 1672, No. 1, fols. 93–95]). We refer to Anna Elisabeth Paulsen simply as Anna; there is room for confusion because not only does the scholarly literature refer to her as Anna Paulsen (or Elisabeth Paulsen), but there was another Anna Elisabeth Paulsen, born in 1673 (Heine, *Johannes Velten*, Appendix I), apparently Carl and Anna Paulsen's grandchild. On Carl Andreas Paulsen, see Scherl and Rudin, *Theater in Böhmen*, s.v. "Carl Andreas Paulsen" (ca. 1620–1687) and "Catarina Elisabeth Velten" (d. 1712). The letter is in Bogoiavlenskii, "Moskovskii teatr," 20–22, and see the transcription in Jensen and Maier, "Pickleherring," 54–55, as Source Nine.

57. On Velten, see Heine, *Johannes Velten*, an important early study yet with some serious omissions (see Jensen and Maier, "Pickleherring," 28n43); see also Wesselofsky, *Deutsche Einflüsse* (on the "Russian episode" in Velten's life, which became generally known later through Nehring, "Eine unbekannte Episode"); Günther, "Das Moskauer Judithdrama," 194–196.

58. There are petitions to the Riga city authorities in May and June 1672 from a group described in the sources as "die Hochdeutschen Comoedianten"—this is clearly the Paulsen-Velten company; see Bolte, *Das Danziger Theater*, 97; Scherl and Rudin, *Theater in Böhmen*, s.v. "Carl Andreas Paulsen." The documents are in LVVA, fonds 673-1-246, pp. 92–95 (Ratsprotokolle). In May, the company asked about a reduction in the city fees it was required to pay and also permission to raise ticket prices; in June, it requested an extension of the period for its performances (which were in a stable!). We thank Kaarel Vanamölder for examining these documents for us in Riga and Heiko Droste for his help in transcribing them. On visiting troupes in Riga from a slightly earlier period, see Limon, *Gentlemen*, 91–93.

59. Waugh and Maier, "Muscovy," 93–94, highlight the importance of the connections from Königsberg to Riga. It is possible that the packet Anna mentions included the letter von Staden had received permission to write from Moscow on December 10, presumably giving the group official approval to come.

60. In her letter, Anna noted that "we have left Copenhagen," although she herself was still in the city; was she no longer active as an actor, or did she simply stay behind to conclude their business affairs?

61. We have no evidence indicating that the troupe was actually in Riga in the fall of 1673. Bolte, *Das Danziger Theater*, 98, says that it was in Copenhagen again from December 19, 1673, to January 12, 1674, but does not mention any trips to Riga. Perhaps this Riga trip was canceled due to the change in plans regarding Moscow—that is, if the troupe decided not to go to Moscow at some point after Anna wrote this letter, then perhaps it did not need, or want, to make this extra trip to Riga.

62. *PDS* 4:903–904. Ukraintsev was listed as a gonets for this mission; we appreciate the clarification in Gus'kov, "Dumnyi d'iak," 88. On his career, see also Veselovskii, *D'iaki*, 531–532.

63. "Да комедианты ж писали, что они проведали, что его царское величество хочет иттить самъ противъ турского салтана войною и они в такую дальнюю дорогу иттить не хотят, для того что опасаютца, что имъ то помешаетъ" (RGADA, f. 155, op. 1, 1672, No. 7, fol. 225). On the margin, by the name "Яганъ фон Стаденъ" there is an annotation: "дядя Миколаю" (Nicolaus's uncle). The letter, dated March 7, 1673, was translated in Moscow on March 20. This is additional evidence that Nicolaus was using family connections in Riga to fulfill the request for actors. We assume that the komedianty mentioned here are indeed the same actors under discussion, those of the Paulsen-Velten troupe.

64. Overskou, *Den danske Skueplads* 1:112–113 apparently thought that Anna Paulsen actually went to Russia; see also Katritzky, *Women, Medicine and Theatre*, 281, who says Anna performed in St. Petersburg in 1672 (the city was founded more than thirty years later, by Peter the Great).

65. Møller, "Københavns første Teater," 633–634, refers to a "Christian Scountskee," who arrived in Copenhagen in September 1666, and this date is also given in Nystrøm, *Den danske Komedies Oprindelse*, 26. Dahlberg, *Komediantteatern*, 247, reproduces an image of Christian Janetzky ("Janetschky"); see also Hansen, *Formen der Commedia dell'Arte*, 50–51; Asper, *Hanswurst*, images 14–15. J. Alexander, "Ridentum dicere verum," 742, emphasizes the Saxon connections for a group of traveling companies (including the Paulsen-Velten troupe) strongly associated with Pickleherring plays. The source for our illustration in figure 3.3, the book *Janetzkius Redivivus*, appears to date from around 1700, that is, after Janetzky's death (the date "ca. 1670" in the HAB catalog seems to be erroneous).

The Plays and "Ballets" for the Tsar

OPENING NIGHT AND ENCORES (FALL 1672 TO MID-1673)

All of the detailed back-and-forth presented in our previous chapter was, in a sense, just icing on the cake, as Artamon Matveev had hedged his bets from the outset, contracting with Johann Gregorii, a Lutheran pastor in Moscow's Foreign Quarter, to write a play at almost the same time as Nicolaus von Staden was dispatched on his hiring trip. One wonders if von Staden knew about Gregorii's assignment, which might have removed some urgency from his mission. Russian officials were certainly familiar with Pastor Gregorii, as he had been involved in a long dispute in the Foreign Quarter over church funding and patronage, which had ultimately been resolved by the Russian authorities.[1]

Planning began soon after the May encore, and Matveev, in dipping into the available resources at the Foreign Quarter, returned to the community that had produced the February and May successes. Although the organizers did hire other personnel from abroad, and the negotiations with the Paulsen company were continuing, the readily available pool of talent from the local foreign population proved to be the most stable source for creating the theater. The initial order to Pastor Gregorii, issued on June 4, 1672, includes the basic elements necessary for establishing the performances, elements we see addressed consistently throughout: choice of play topic, preparation of an appropriate venue, and funding: "[7]180 [1672] June 4, the Great Lord ordered the foreign teacher Iagan Godfrid [Johann Gottfried

Gregorii] to create a comedy, and the comedy is to be performed from [based on] the Bible, from the book of Esther, and for this action a building is to be newly constructed, and for the construction of this building and for the necessary items for it [funding] from the Vladimirskaia Department."[2]

From this time on, plans were carried out on a large scale. The contract established the initial location of the theater at Preobrazhenskoe selo, a nearby village retreat, and large quantities of building materials were ordered, totaling over 1,000 rubles. Indeed, the detailed order indicates that plans had been under discussion for some time (pp. 8–10). Over the next few months, between June and October, considerable allocations were made for payments to Gregorii and the youngsters who were to perform the play, and for costumes, props, and artists (both foreign and Russian) to create the sets and scenery (perspektivy). One of the artists was the foreigner Peter Engels, who, by this point, had had a long career in Russia; one of his duties was to teach "perspektivy" to Vasilii Repskii, the young musician mentioned in chapter 2 as an unwilling instrumentalist at theatrical performances.[3] The venue at Preobrazhenskoe was also decorated appropriately to accommodate the royal audience (pp. 10–11).

It may be that the plans could go forward so expeditiously—regardless of von Staden's recruiting results—because the February and May performances not only had given the planners a good idea of the materials and space they needed but had also acquainted them with useful suppliers. The trader Dirck Hasenkroeg, the popular Pickleherring, was listed in September and October as providing costumes for the new theater—he not only had access to these goods as a merchant but also had firsthand experience with the court's theatrical expectations.[4] Hasenkroeg also provided the organ used for the production. In July 1676 (after the theater had been closed down), he petitioned for reimbursement for the organ, valued at 1,200 rubles, that Matveev had, significantly, seen at his house and acquired for the theater in October 1672 (p. 76). The time frame makes sense, for it would have been in October that final preparations were underway, and it must have been apparent that local resources for the music were necessary, as von Staden's musical hires had not yet arrived.[5] At any rate, Matveev would have had ample opportunity to inform (and avail) himself of the necessary supplies and suppliers in the period between the February show and the October premiere of *Artakserksovo deistvo*, The Play of Artaxerxes (Ahasuerus in the biblical book of Esther).

It is not known who decided on Esther as the subject of the new venture, but it was certainly meant to be more substantial than the mélange of acts offered earlier. The play was intended from the beginning to have a clear storyline and plot, as indicated by the consistent use of the term *komediia*, which is also used in the May 15 dispatch ordering von Staden to go abroad.[6] Gregorii's play is closely based on the biblical story, in which the Persian king Ahasuerus chooses a new wife, a Jewish orphan named Esther, who had been raised by her uncle, the wise counselor Mordecai. Although the court's evil Haman plots to hang Mordecai, Esther is able to save him, and all the Jews, by her loyal appeal to the king. The gallows are ultimately used not for Mordecai but for Haman himself. The story had a natural crossover appeal, familiar to both Russians and foreigners, and Gregorii would also have been able to draw on the long tradition of Esther plays from Lutheran and school drama traditions, as well as from the many retellings produced on Western stages.[7] As in so many cases regarding the court plays, the story answered equally well to the expectations of the Russian audience and the experiences of the foreign playwright and players, with the added benefit (not coincidental) of aligning well with the current situation at the Russian court. As in the biblical story, the Russian court in 1672 had an all-seeing ruler, a young second wife, and a wise and trusted adviser (Matveev, of course). Indeed, as the scholar A. N. Robinson has pointed out, Simeon Polotskii had invoked the image of Esther to describe the new tsaritsa, so the comparison was front and center (quite literally) in the context of this royal audience.[8]

The surviving sources preserve a remarkable snapshot of how the performance was put together: intertheater in action, as it were. The Esther play is preserved almost completely (an epilogue appears to be lost), in both German- and Russian-language versions, reflecting the working process of the German playwright and his assistants.[9] There have been many speculations about the language of the premiere performance, but in both versions (German and Russian), the Hebrew texts recited in the play are written in transliteration, suggesting that this sort of rote syllabic performance was feasible for the young actors, at least in limited sections.[10] If the performance was in German, the Russian-language text might have functioned as a supplement, read aloud in alternation with the actors or read silently to aid in following the familiar action. The transliterated Hebrew sections would fit into either scenario, and their inclusion results in (nearly) full textual records in both languages.

The structure of *Artakserksovo deistvo* is more complex than for any of the other surviving Russian play texts, at least as indicated in the copy preserved in Lyon, published in 1954 by André Mazon and Frédéric Cocron. This source, in addition to the (almost) complete play text in German and Russian, includes a summary outline highlighting the main plot content for each act, with references to the many songs that appear throughout, a cast list, and a series of what are labeled "interscenia," which appear to be brief comic interludes positioned between some of the acts. This outline is likely the work of Laurentius Rinhuber, one of the Foreign Quarter residents heavily involved in the preparations for this first full-length play. With the exception of a character named Mops, the interscenia feature a set of characters separate from those appearing in the Esther narrative, although some of the interscenia roles were performed by the same boys who appeared in the main play, as the cast list indicates.[11] This layout, with the major storyline presented in the seven acts of the play and the comic interludes distributed throughout (following acts 1, 3, 5, and 7), thus combines two features that had already been popular at court: the comic turns that were such a hit in the February and May sketches and the singing, probably accompanied by instruments.[12]

There are no surviving texts for the interscenia (indeed, they may not have been written out at all), although the brief Latin descriptions in the summary seem to point to a series of increasingly violent interactions between the lovers (or married couple) Elena and Mops.[13] The annotation for the first interscenium says "Mops et Elena amorosi" (Mops and Elena are lovers); the second and third indicate escalating trouble: "Sibi imminent" (they threaten each other) and "Semet percutiunt" (they hit each other). The final interscenium is labeled "Mops strangulat Muischelowum" (Mops strangles Muischelow), a deed that parallels the main action of the play, underscored particularly because the character Mops steps out of the interscenia to appear in the play as Haman's hangman. The Russian text makes this clear in the list of characters, where Mops is described as "the hangman as well as the fool."[14] Such a dual role was familiar in German settings of the Esther story, for example in the 1620 publication *Engelische Comedien und Tragedien*, which opens with a "Comedia" on this popular narrative. In this German text, the clown figure, Hans Knapkäse, appears throughout in conflict with his wife, and he, too, is the hangman who accompanies Haman to the gallows.[15] The complex structure of *Artakserksovo deistvo* appears to have been unique among the Russian plays. Later surviving play texts show that although the comic elements were retained, they were integrated into the action of the main storyline, not sequestered into separate actions.

Artakserksovo deistvo premiered on October 17, 1672, according to Laurentius Rinhuber, the probable annotator of the Lyon copy, who wrote about it several months later during an extended trip to the West. Rinhuber had originally come to Russia in 1668 as a medical assistant to Laurentius Blumentrost, the tsar's physician (and Pastor Gregorii's stepfather). After arriving in Moscow, Rinhuber tutored the Blumentrost children and then taught at Gregorii's Lutheran school in the Foreign Quarter—he was thus well ensconced in the milieu from which the theater emerged and well positioned to participate. Rinhuber's often-cited description of the court theater, given below, was written after he left Moscow to accompany Major Paul Menzies, a Scottish officer in the tsar's service, on a diplomatic mission to Venice and Rome.[16] They departed on October 20, 1672, just three days after the premiere. This was one of three missions sent out at this time, each tasked with engaging Western states to join in the fight against the Ottoman Turks who, in July, had crossed the Danube in force.[17] (This is also the context for the letter by von Staden's uncle, discussed in chap. 3.)

The Menzies mission, with Rinhuber as secretary, traveled overland through Berlin, Halle, and Leipzig, reaching Dresden on March 9, 1673. They stayed there for about two weeks, as Menzies was engaged in negotiations with the elector, Johann Georg II. It was during this stay that Rinhuber contacted Ernst I (der Fromme), duke of Saxe-Gotha, who had a long-standing interest in Moscow's Lutheran community. Duke Ernst had donated money to Pastor Gregorii during the latter's 1667–1668 fundraising tour through German territories, so Rinhuber's reference to the theater and to Gregorii's role in it would certainly have raised interest.[18] On March 10, Rinhuber wrote:

> The Great Tsar of Muscovy heard of dramatic works and desired to see a comedy. The question was who could take charge of this matter. Nobody daring it, Mr. M[agister] Gregorii the Pastor was secretly recommended. It was reported that he was able to write a play. He [Gregorii] was initially indecisive but then he was compelled either through the tsar's benevolence or—on the contrary—danger [that is, the risk of refusing]. Thus he wrote, involving me as his assistant, the tragi-comedy of Ahasuerus and Esther, which I taught, over the course of three months, in German and in Russian [to] youngsters who [later] performed it. The performance itself took place

on October 17, 1672. The Great Tsar was entranced by the performance and watched it for ten hours, without moving from his place. This event no doubt will be the beginning of a better fortune. After the presentation of the play, the Great Tsar showed his gratitude and favor to Mr. Gregorii and to Mr. Blumentrost's son, who had played the main roles and had been performing better than the rest of the youngsters. On that same day, the above-mentioned most noble Mr. Paulus Menesius, His Most Serene Tsarish Majesty's major [Major] and envoy, wished to have me with him as a travel partner, planning to make use of my labor [opera]. Therefore I obtained my dismissal from the Great Man Mr. Artemon Sergeiovits [Artamon Sergeevich Matveev]; meanwhile, somebody else had to take over my position.[19]

Rinhuber thus took pains to emphasize his personal contributions to this project. His reference to work over the course of three months coincides with the Russian payment records, which begin in the summer of 1672. Rinhuber's ten-hour performance is generally cited with amazement—however, the Russians were certainly no strangers to very long church services (even visiting clerics, for example Paul of Aleppo, complained of these marathon sessions). If the premiere had indeed been offered, in some fashion, in both German and Russian, the leisurely performance time might not be much of an exaggeration. Rinhuber does not say that the premiere took place at Preobrazhenskoe, although this was certainly the case.

Rinhuber's description of the theater project (part of a longer discussion of Moscow's Lutheran contingent) stimulated a series of questions by the duke's secretary, Job Ludolf (1624–1704). Rinhuber responded, and in his answer, written in Vienna in 1673 (as he was continuing on the trip with Menzies), he confirmed some of the theatrical information: "From May to October 1672, at his Tsarish Majesty's order, I had to teach in the school the boys who were to play in the future, in rehearsals. Whether there is anybody else who is teaching [them] now, and who, I do not know."[20] This second report verifies the importance of the May 1672 "ballet" encore: Rinhuber specifically mentions that he worked from May to October on the comedy (rectifying and amplifying his previous statement). He mentioned his Russian theatrical experiences still later, in a memoir written around 1679, so some seven years later, Rinhuber was still dining out on the story of his involvement in the tsar's theater.[21]

There were other theater-related tasks assigned to the three diplomatic parties dispatched in October 1672, for they were also instructed to find trumpet players, with the requests implying that these musicians might also take part in the new court entertainment. The Menzies group, for example, was ordered "to engage in the Great Lord's service two of the very best trumpet players, who have demonstrated their training [and] can play dances on the high trumpet."[22] The final reports by the Menzies mission and another of the parties sent out at the same time, Andrei Vinius's mission to London, Spain, and France, explained that they had tried to recruit such trumpeters but failed, due to the small salaries they were offering.[23] The third of the parties sent out at that time was headed by Emel'ian Ukraintsev and sent to Amsterdam and Copenhagen; it was in the Danish city that he met three times with Anna Paulsen, of the Paulsen-Velten acting troupe, and wrote her a letter of recommendation. Vinius, in London, was taken to theaters.[24]

If the weeklong preparations in February had created such a sensation, the months of planning and rehearsing between May/June and mid-October clearly resulted in an even greater success. After the premiere on October 17, 1672, we can trace encore performances through a combination of familiar sources: payment records and reports from foreign observers in Moscow. The earliest evidence is in an unsigned letter, presumably written by the regular Moscow correspondent, Christoff Koch, and sent to Governor General Simon Grundel-Helmfelt in Narva. The letter is dated October 29 (a Tuesday, Koch's regular day to send reports as this was when the post was dispatched). Koch begins by mentioning "the day before yesterday," which would have been Sunday, October 27, and then continues: "Last Saturday, I was at Herr Artemon's place for dinner. On this occasion he asked me whether I had any news about the Swedish envoys. . . . On the following day he saw me at the comedy." Koch would thus have seen an encore performance on Sunday, October 27, ten days after the premiere. So far, this is the earliest indication of an encore. Although there are no entries for October 27 and 28 in the records of the tsar's daily activities, the entries for the surrounding days indicate that he went to Preobrazhenskoe on October 26 and left on October 29.[25]

Other encores seem to have been given in quick succession. On November 2, the records of the tsar's activities note that, in the evening at Preobrazhenskoe, he attended a comedy and saw a performance given by foreigners.[26] Theatrical historian E. G. Kholodov examined a listing of the Russian elites who were known to be at Preobrazhenskoe on this date; although they were not mentioned as having attended the performance, he concluded, reasonably, that this was a likely audience.[27] As we see later, this is indeed the sort of audience that attended comedies at this venue.

About two weeks later, on November 19, the Danish resident in Moscow, Mogens Gjøe, reported to the Danish foreign secretary, Conrad Biermann, about theatrical activities, again in the context of the Turkish threat that was so palpably on people's minds: "Since they have recovered from the fear the Turks inspired in them, the first minister's [i.e., Matveev's] most important occupation is to ensure the performance of comedies, appearing in the theater himself in order to maintain discipline among the children who are performing."[28] This report does not refer to a specific performance, although it suggests that Gjøe might have been indicating a possible third encore production (that is, after October 27 and November 2), one that took place at some point before his report on November 19. The records of the tsar's rounds are incomplete, but the entries following the November 2 encore are all from Preobrazhenskoe.[29]

After Gjøe's reference to the mid-November performances, there are payment records for expenses related to *Artakserksovo deistvo* through roughly the first six months of the next year, 1673. There is no evidence for preparations or performances of any other play during this period. There was, however, a flurry of activity over the last two weeks of January 1673 that might reflect continuing interest in *Artakserksovo deistvo*. On January 21, 1673, Pastor Gregorii was paid over 100 rubles in sables for his work on the comedy about Artaxerxes, and on the same day, Matveev ordered repairs to be made at the school in the Foreign Quarter, where Gregorii was teaching the children for the comedy (pp. 23, 28).[30] The next day, Matveev ordered Gregorii to be provided with necessary materials for the comedy: replacing some of the missing costumes, repairing props that had been damaged, and providing supplies such as candles and paper. For these funds, the teacher Georg Hüfner signed for Pastor Gregorii, noting that the money was intended "zu reparirung einiger Sachen zur Comoedie"; this marks the beginning of Hüfner's long association with the court theater (p. 29).[31] On the same day, there was a separate order for firewood for the school in the Foreign Quarter, where Gregorii was teaching the young actors (p. 28).[32] It thus appears that rehearsals were gearing up again, perhaps after a break following the performances during the previous fall.

But the plans went beyond this, with the introduction of a new performance venue. On the same day Gregorii's school was supplied with firewood, January 22, 1673, an order was issued to create a space for the performance of a comedy on the upper floor of the building housing the court Apothecary (*Apteka*). This long entry names the carpenters who did the work, with the explanation that it took place over five days, from January 25 to 29 (p. 29).[33] Creating a performance space easily accessible to the court would make sense; Preobrazhenskoe, although close to the city, nevertheless required the tsar to leave his residence and journey forth. A closer and more convenient venue would seem appropriate.

However, because the surviving documents indicate that work on this new venue was ordered only on January 22, if other performances of the Esther play were to be offered, they would have to take place at Preobrazhenskoe. Thus, also on January 22, Matveev ordered the theatrical materials to be assembled in the Preobrazhenskoe venue. The orders are confusing, for Matveev first said that all of the carpets, fabrics, and costumes at the former home of I. D. Miloslavskii, items that had been taken from Preobrazhenskoe, should be removed from the Miloslavskii residence and transported back to Preobrazhenskoe. The Miloslavskii house was the site of the February and May 1672 "ballet" performances that had started the whole theatrical craze in the first place; some of the equipment used at Preobrazhenskoe may have been taken there, perhaps for storage. Matveev's order goes on to say that all of this should take place so that everything would be ready for a performance on January 23 (p. 31).[34]

Meanwhile, on January 23, orders continued to be issued regarding the new space over the Apothecary, with requisitions including hardware and other construction materials (p. 30).[35] However, this seems to indicate a change of plans, for now, the carpets and cloth are ordered to be removed from Preobrazhenskoe and delivered to this new venue in Moscow. Sixty children—the young actors—are to be transported from the Foreign Quarter, where they lived, to court (that is, to the Apothecary, or Apteka, performance space). This is roughly the number of actors required for *Artakserksovo deistvo*, so this seems to be the play in question. The orders also specify transport from the Foreign Quarter (where von Staden, the musicians, and Hasenkroeg were apparently involved in preparations) to the new Apteka theater; they were ordered to be in the (new) comedy venue for an entertainment ("dlia potekhi"). Finally, blue fabric is purchased to decorate four *balety* at the new comedy venue (p. 30).

So, what is happening here? We have no records independently verifying a performance at this time, either at Preobrazhenskoe or at the new space over the Apteka, or both.[36] Perhaps there was indeed a performance at

Preobrazhenskoe on January 23, and the orders continue afterward, bringing everything back to Moscow, to the new venue that was being prepared. (The distances are not long, so this would be possible.) Whatever the case, on January 23 the sets ("ramy perespektivogo pisma") from Preobrazhenskoe were ordered to be taken to Moscow, to be placed in the theater over the Apothecary, even making provisions to add hardware (hinges, for example) so that the larger pieces would fit through the doors. A final payment from this series, for some rich fabrics, is dated January 25 (pp. 30–31). The reference to the four balety suggests that the smaller and less formal "ballets" were still on the entertainment menu. As we shall see, this is clearly the case for later performances described by foreign observers.

The time frame outlined here makes sense, as does the haste, for as in the previous year, such a performance would have occurred right before the beginning of Lent, when such entertainments would have been impossible. Indeed, just after Easter (March 30), the tsar invited Pastor Gregorii and the "komedianty" of *Artakserksovo deistvo*, a total of sixty-four people, to his presence. They spent the night at a residence near the Kremlin and the reception took place on the next day, April 6.[37] This is just about as soon after Easter as possible for such a visit.

On May 22 of this year, 1673, Matveev ordered that the organ and the scenery, which were at the Apothecary, should be moved to Preobrazhenskoe and that the theatrical rooms there should be prepared "as before" (pp. 31–32); the artist Engels was involved in this work. Just a few days later, however, Matveev was injured, as reported from Moscow by the Danish observer, Gjøe (May 26): "His Tsarish Majesty showed such great concern over this serious accident that he shed tears and postponed the comedy and the ballet which were to be performed that same evening." Gjøe was correct, for the tsar was indeed worried about Matveev and even went to visit him.[38] The performance, which must have been the Esther play, seems to have been canceled permanently, for we have found no indication that it was rescheduled.

Over this same spring, conflicts between the foreign instrumentalists von Staden had hired and the Russian bureaucrats intensified. In early April 1673, just after the tsar's post-Easter reception of the young actors, the instrumentalists petitioned for wages that were in arrears, claiming that they had not been paid for March and (in advance) for April. They had indeed participated in theatrical productions, for there are payments covering their transport to the Preobrazhenskoe venue earlier that year (p. 30). Their petition also claimed that they had not yet received the contractual payment for September through November of the previous year. Matveev ordered payment for their work in March and April but not for the previous fall (pp. 25–26). At this point, another bone of contention appears. The payment in advance for April was not the custom; the clerks issued payment on the next day yet with a notation indicating that now, the instrumentalists had to request payment by means of a special petition each time, and not the originally specified monthly food wages ("pomesiachnyi korm"; p. 26). The musicians' petition for July shows that they were paid only part of their salary and were required to receive the rest in kind, as sables from the Siberian Chancery (p. 27). This slow walk on the part of the clerks was not necessarily malicious. The foreigners were likely unaware of the custom of tipping the clerks, and the clerks, for their part, were facing continually declining salaries throughout the century and depended on such gifts.[39]

EXPANDING FORCES, 1673–1675

It is only in June 1673 that we see the first records indicating plans for an additional play, and over the course of the next two years, the organizers created three new plays—on the biblical stories of Tobit and Judith and on the history of Tamerlane—and solidified the two performance venues they had set up. Increasing the numbers of plays meant enhancing the ranks of performers. Beginning in June 1673 and proceeding regularly into October—the regularity and even the willingness to pay in advance clearly signaling the intensity of purpose—a group of twenty-six young actors consistently described as "meshchanskie deti" were assembled and paid (pp. 26–28). This designation indicates that the youngsters were from the families of the newly designated city suburb or quarter made up of merchants and artisans from the Polish-Lithuanian Commonwealth (the Meshchanskaia Quarter; a *meshchanin* is a small-level trader). This is the origin of the second performing troupe recruited for the tsar's theater, and we can trace, broadly, these two groups (from the Foreign and Meshchanskaia Quarters) for the rest of the theater's existence. A later account by a foreign observer calls these "meshchanskie" players "Polish," which may reflect their geographical origins (including Ukraine) but not necessarily their ethnic heritage. The surviving names of this initial group of players (Luka

Stepanov, Timoshka Moksimov, Rodka Ivanov) do not appear to be Polish, although they do suggest actors who could handle performances in Russian more easily than the German youngsters from the Foreign Quarter. Their teacher, Ivan Feodorov Volosheninov, was from Nezhin (a city that came under Muscovite control after the Russo-Polish conflicts of 1654–1667).[40] This expansion of the acting forces also drew in participants from other government departments. Vasilii Meshalkin, a clerk at the Vladimirskaia Department (one of the funding agencies originally connected with the court theater), began what would be a long association with this group of actors (p. 26); we can trace him to the closure of the theater.

Clearly this new group was busy rehearsing something specific over the summer, but the first reference to a named play comes only in October 1673, in a payment to Pastor Gregorii for his work repairing the dress or costume for angels, for "young Tobit," and for his companions (p. 29).[41] The biblical narrative of Tobit (or Tobias) had long formed an important part of the German Lutheran play tradition, as this story (along with that of Judith, the subject of the next Russian court play) had been singled out by Martin Luther himself as "useful and good," whether the events were true or fictional. Pastor Gregorii may have been familiar with some of the previous settings, many intended for school productions. The payment records confirm that the character Tobit the Younger, the focus of the biblical story, appeared in the Russian play.[42]

Tsar Aleksei was at Preobrazhenskoe in early November, and on November 11, the Swedish envoy, Adolph Eberschildt, reported to his king that the tsar was entertained there with hunting, comedies, and ballets.[43] This would have been the first performance opportunity for the new play, presumably offered along with *Artakserksovo deistvo*, for these are the only two plays listed by name (or by subject) to this point in the Russian documents.[44] Eberschildt's observation also distinguishes between "comedies" and "ballets" (both in the plural), which suggests that some of the less formal performances, consistently called "ballets" by the foreigners, were still part of the entertainment picture (this separation of genres also appeared in Gjøe's report about Matveev's injury).[45] The Tobit play was apparently unsuccessful, for there are no subsequent references to performances.[46] No text survives, but if it was based on the biblical narrative, it would have offered a complex history that unfolds across a wide geographical range, unlike the character- and plot-driven dramas of the first three surviving play texts.

Given the focus on and integration of the comic elements in the following two court plays, as we discuss later in this chapter, perhaps *Tobit* did not provide suitable opportunity to incorporate such interludes.

The first reference to the next play, based on the biblical story of Judith, appears early the following year, on February 15, 1674, when Gregorii was paid for the creation of the comedy about Holofernes, and costumes were created for the people of Bethulia (p. 38). These references reflect the familiar story, which, like that of Esther, focuses on opposing groups and strong dramatic confrontations.[47] The play opens at the Assyrian court of Nebuchadnezzar as he dispatches the armies of Holofernes, and it continues with the anxious anticipation of the Jews—all of this takes place over the first three acts, with many shifts in scene. After a section labeled "Mezhdosenie" (literally, a "between scene"), in which the four kings captured by Holofernes lament their fate, the action moves to the threatened town of Bethulia and the actions of Judith, who appears for the first time in act 4. The fifth and sixth acts show Judith learning about the fate of her city and forming her plans; act 7 presents the banquet, Judith's (and her servant's) appearance there, and the final reckoning with Holofernes. The play also includes comic elements revolving especially around the character Susakim, a soldier. The role was complex, for Susakim not only performs in the comic scenes but takes part in the dramatic action as well.

Unlike the separate interscenia in *Artakserksovo deistvo*, the mezhdosenie in *Judith* is clearly related to the main action of the play, with one of the characters (Odid, an Assyrian) appearing in both and with references in its dialogue to the main storyline. It opens with the spoken laments of the four kings taken captive by the Assyrians and concludes with a song ("pesn'"), which each of the four kings is directed to sing sorrowfully or mournfully ("zhalobno"), one after another, written in a series of six-line strophes. Although the kings themselves do not appear outside this scene, the dramatic situation of the mezhdosenie underscores the events of the play, and it appears roughly at its center. There is not as much (labeled) singing in *Judith* as in the Esther play, although there is still strophic singing associated with comic characters (for example, the drunken soldiers, act 5, scene 2) as well as ensemble singing at the conclusion.[48]

After the first reference to the Judith play, in mid-February, there was another flurry of theatrical activity late in the month, the week before Lent started. As in the previous year, there was a great deal of transportation from the theater above the Apothecary out to Preobrazhenskoe and back again; this occurred between February 24 and 27. At the same time, repairs and improvements were being carried out at the Apothecary theater (p. 39).[49] We do know that comedies and ballets, both performed by "Germans," were presented in the days following February 25, although it is not clear at which venue(s) this took place. A newspaper article datelined Moscow, March 13, describes a fire that had broken out in Moscow on February 25, saying that the tsar was very distressed and that "to improve his mood about this, he has ordered, some evenings later, on the one hand, ballets and dances, partly by Germans, and comedies to be played by [people from] that same nation, and also, during the daytime, leopard, bear, and wolf hunts."[50] Given all this activity, it seems likely that the Judith play was performed at some point in February 1674.[51] It was quite popular, performed at least through the end of 1675.

There is an undated annotated cast list preserved for *Judith*, which presents the characters in the play, roughly in the order of their appearance. Next to each character is the name of the actor who performed the role, indicating whether or not he had learned his part. For example, the role of the comic soldier Susakim was performed by one Vaska Andreev, judged initially as not having mastered his role, although later he seems to have shaped up properly; such multiple evaluations give us good reason to sympathize with those in charge. The annotations indicate the difficulties the young actors experienced in learning their roles, suggesting that the list dates from the initial preparations for the play, in early 1674. Presumably, things would have been smoothed out for subsequent performances. The cast seems to reflect generally the new group from the Meshchanskaia Quarter, although the names themselves are a little too generic to be absolutely certain of individuals.[52]

During this same period, over several months of 1674, we observe another protracted series of petitions regarding payments owed to the foreign instrumentalists, this time directed to a different office, the Apothecary Chancery (also part of Matveev's purview). The January petition, requesting payment dating back to the previous September, lists the five musicians (the trumpet player and the four other instrumentalists); their payment included a higher proportion in kind (sables, from the Siberian Chancery; p. 35). In a petition written several months later, September 1674, we find that, in fact, they had not been paid from the Apothecary Chancery, despite Matveev's orders.

Furthermore, this September petition lists the names of only three of the four instrumentalists; there is no information on Friedrich Plattenschläger, whose fate is unknown (he may have died, as there is no evidence that he was officially released from his duties). The trumpeter, Johann Waldonn, had left in June 1674 for Sweden but died en route, in Novgorod (p. 40).[53]

The Kievan play *Aleksei chelovek bozhii* (Aleksei, Man of God, 1673–1674) suggests the ripple effect of the tsar's theatrical interests at around the time of the plans for *Judith*, although it was not written for the Moscow court theater and reflects the very different performance traditions of the Kievan Academy. The play was written for a planned, but unrealized, visit by the tsar to Kiev; the project was spearheaded by Prince Iurii Petrovich Trubetskoi, a prominent boyar who, based on his rank alone, would most likely have witnessed the successful fall 1672 performances of *Artakserksovo deistvo*—the 1672 "ballets" provide an even longer period during which prominent people would have assessed the popularity of this new entertainment at court. Furthermore, the political context of the Kievan play echoes that of the court dramas, for it refers to the Turks, who were of consistent concern over the entire theatrical period.[54]

The two popular court plays, on the Esther and Judith stories, were performed multiple times in the fall of 1674, again along with what appear to be the less formal "ballets."[55] For this period there is, oddly, an embarrassment of documentary riches, for we have three different foreign reports, all of which mesh perfectly with an important series of Russian court records. These accounts confirm several important things: first, two plays, on Esther and Judith, were being performed during this time; second, the "meshchanskie deti," originally assembled to perform the Tobit play, were now assigned to the Judith play (certainly with some reorganization); and finally, in addition to these full-length plays, the court continued to enjoy what the foreigners unanimously call "ballets," as distinguished from "comedies."

The first report is from November 10, when the Danish resident, Gjøe, wrote that the court was at Preobrazhenskoe: "His Tsarish Majesty with the court is continuing his stay away from here [Moscow] at a residence called *Pria Brazenza* [Preobrazhenskoe], where he passes his time watching ballets and comedies, which the foreigners try to produce as best they can in order to entertain them."[56]

Gjøe was correct in observing the continuing stay, for the tsar and the royal family had arrived on October 28.[57] A week after Gjøe's account, the ever-reliable Koch reported on these activities in a letter from November 17 that indicates the widening scope of the productions: "Moscow, November 17, 1674. His Tsarish Majesty and the whole court are still at *Prijobrazenska*, where, during the days before the fasting period[58] started, they had comedies performed and ballets danced. They had so much pleasure in all this that they say an order will be given to bring a good dance master and actor [*Comoediant*] here, whose task will be to improve and teach the boys further. In the ballets mentioned above, a Livonian, or more precisely, an Estonian peasant [farmer's or rustic] dance was presented."[59]

Finally, the December 9 report by Hermann Dietrich Hesse of Brandenburg, describing events that had taken place over the past three weeks, is explicit about the acting troupes and their repertoire. Hesse writes that "we" had taken part in a "ballet" performance, indicating that he was one of the participants. As always, the court (probably Matveev) was willing and able to incorporate the talents of foreigners as the opportunity arose; this may have been the case for the rustic Estonian dance mentioned in Koch's earlier report. Hesse writes: "[December 9, 1674] Three weeks ago, we presented for His Tsarish Majesty a *Ballet*, after which every participant was invited to his table. At the same time, two comedies were presented, one played by Polish boys on the subject of Judith and Holofernes, and the other on the subject of Ahasvero, played by German boys."[60]

The Russian documents show that planning for these performances was underway in mid-October, when Matveev approved the payment, in advance, to the "meshchanskie" actors (p. 37). Starting on November 9, 1674, and continuing into December—exactly when the foreigners wrote their reports—the Russian records show a series of payments and arrangements for the two groups of actors, forty-eight "meshchanskie" youth and thirty-six from the Foreign Quarter. Transportation, as before, was arranged to take them to the Preobrazhenskoe venue, and, also as before, Hasenkroeg was involved in assembling the necessary supplies. Payment records from November 26 refer by name to the foreign children who performed the characters Artaxerxes (Fredrik Gosens), Esther (Ivan Berlov), and Haman (Germas Klifmas, probably Hermann Kliffmann)—the same players for these characters are in the cast list in the Lyon source: "Fridr." Gosens, M. (probably "Mons.") Berner, and Klifman.[61] At this point, these three young actors would have been performing the same roles for over two years.

It was certainly in the context of this batch of performances that a copy of the Esther play was bound, in early December (p. 38).

All this provides context for an important series of entries in the published Russian court records describing performances of plays as well as what appear to be the "ballets" mentioned by the foreign observers.[62] The first entry names the new, Judith, play and indicates a large audience: "In that same year [1674] there was, for the Great Lord at Preobrazhenskoe selo, a comedy, and foreigners entertained the Great Lord with [the play] 'How the tsaritsa cut off the head of Holofernes, the tsar' and on organs played . . . foreigners and Artamon Sergeevich Matveev's own people."[63] The entry continues with an enumeration, by rank, of the people who accompanied the tsar, beginning with the highest levels in the Boyar Duma: boyar, *okol'nichii* (lord-in-waiting), *dumnyi dvorianin* (state councillor), and *dumnyi d'iak* (state secretary). The list continues with "all of the privy councillors" (*blizhnie liudi*) and the *stol'niki* and *striapchie* (table attendants and stirrupers, both noble service ranks).[64] If these people are not already on the excursion to Preobrazhenskoe with the tsar, the directive continues, they are to be sent for in Moscow and ordered to come.

The next entry in this series continues by naming the Esther play and includes the same series of ranks, along with a list of royal family members:

> In that same year there was, for the Great Lord at Preobrazhenskoe selo, another comedy, and with the Great Lord was the tsaritsa, the tsarevichi, and the tsarevny. And foreigners and Artamon Sergeevich Matveev's people entertained the Great Lord [with the play] "How Artaxerxes ordered Aman to be hanged, according to the petition of the tsaritsa and according to Mordecai's wisdom." And they played on organs and on violins [*fioly*] and on instruments [*stramenty*] and danced. And accompanying the Great Lord at the comedy were the boyars, the *okol'nichie*, the state councillors and state secretaries, and the privy councillors, and the table attendants and people of all ranks.[65]

The series concludes by mentioning an entertainment without specifying a play topic; this matches Hesse's description of the "Ballet," including the musical instruments that were already at Preobrazhenskoe: "And in that same year at the same Preobrazhenskoe selo, there was for the Great Lord an entertainment before the fast. And foreigners, Germans, and Boyar Artamon Sergeevich Matveev's people entertained the Great Lord on organs and on violins and on instruments and danced, and [entertained] with various kinds of entertainments."⁶⁶ This series of reports indicates the tremendous organizational efforts required to transport the necessary people and equipment, all under the firm control of Matveev's ruling hand. The records also show that many of the high-ranking members of court would have been aware of, and even witnessed, the productions, if they had not already done so.

Some of this exposure may have spilled over into ambassadorial accounts from abroad. The Russian envoy who was sent to the imperial court in Vienna in 1674 was Petr Potemkin, already familiar with theater from his mission to Paris in 1668. On that earlier occasion, we learned about Potemkin's theatrical visits only through the French accounts. In this trip to Vienna, however, this experience was recorded in the official report itself. We do not know if this description was prompted by the ambassador's firsthand acquaintance with the tsar's theater—Potemkin had sufficient rank (as a stol'nik) to have been among the spectators, although we have no evidence indicating that he attended. Nevertheless, one suspects Potemkin knew that the performance he saw in Vienna would be of interest at home; as in the case of Trubetskoi and *Aleksei, Man of God*, the court's interest in theatricals was unmissable.

Potemkin's account of the "komediia" in Vienna includes details of protocol, another reason motivating the inclusion of the event in the official report. Initially, Potemkin was reluctant to attend the performance because the emperor would be there, and the Russian party had not yet had its formal audience. This sticking point was smoothed over by the promise of a private box for the visitors. As encouragement, the Viennese representatives informed the Russians, with some hyperbole, that "no such comedy has been [performed] in Vienna for one hundred years and no such comedy has ever been [performed] in other states." Emperor Leopold offered added inducement by sending the Russian party a printed program or synopsis of the performance; the Russian account describes this as "three printed books, and in these books the content of the comedy is printed, [that is,] what will be happening in it." The opera they attended, on October 24/November 3, 1674, was *Il fuoco eterno* (text by Nicolò Minato, music by Antonio Draghi), produced to celebrate the birth of a daughter to Leopold and his second wife.⁶⁷ The Russians were impressed, as their report indicates and as the Viennese hosts recorded.⁶⁸ The visitors described the performers as "dressed in golden and velvet costumes in the ancient Greek and Roman manner, about two hundred or more people."⁶⁹

The theatrical pattern at the Russian court early the following year, 1675, seems to have been roughly the same as for the previous year. A new comedy was introduced in early February, this time on a secular theme, the well-known story of Tamerlane and Bayezid (*Temir-Aksakovo deistvo*). The earliest payment records, from January 23, 1675, indicate that the play was nearly ready and that it would involve the combined Foreign and Meshchanskaia Quarter companies, a total of sixty-eight players, including a small group of dancers.[70] This would allow the organizers to capitalize on the troupes that were already trained and assembled. Again there was a great deal of transport: theatrical materials, including the organ, were to be brought back from Preobrazhenskoe and taken to the "kamideinye polaty" in Moscow (that is, to the Apothecary theater); the young actors were to be brought from the Foreign and the Meshchanskaia Quarters to the Moscow venue (pp. 41–45); and a bound copy of the play text was prepared (p. 38). We discuss the Tamerlane play in our following chapter, but we note here that this is the last work in which Pastor Gregorii might have been involved. According to a petition by his widow, Gregorii died on February 16, 1675, and the only recorded play performance at this time was on February 11 (p. 45).[71] There may have been other performances around this time (Lent began on February 15), and, at any rate, the play was popular enough to be included in the most ambitious undertaking yet: the assembly of six plays late in 1675.

THE SIX-PLAY FESTIVAL AND THE END (LATE 1675–JANUARY 1676)

The most complex project devised by the tsar's theatrical planners emerged in the fall of 1675, when they decided to mount six different plays in a theatrical extravaganza to take place during what was, by this time, the customary fall season. This plan may have been stimulated by the successful combination of the popular Esther and Judith plays with some "ballet"-like entertainments the previous fall. The success of the Tamerlane play earlier in 1675 probably provided additional motivation. We know *Tamerlane* was successful because it was reprised at this time, so the planners would have been able to start with a solid base of three proven plays. This may be reflected in the payment record for the binding of the plays, which lists them in the following order: *Artakserksovo deistvo*, *Judith*, and *Tamerlane* (that is, the existing plays), and *Georgii* (or *Eorgii*, on the story of St. George and the dragon), *Joseph*, and *Adam and Eve* (the new plays; p. 66).[72] *Tobit* is not listed, and there is no evidence that it was revived—clearly this was Pastor Gregorii's one failure. The surviving payment records refer several times to "the six comedies," for example, in combined requisition lists, so it is clear that all six were conceived as parts of a single performance event.

Planning for this monumental effort was intense, with work on all fronts already under way in October, when improvements were ordered for the Preobrazhenskoe site (p. 48). There is an increase in the numbers of Meshchanskaia Quarter actors, from fifty the previous fall to seventy a year later.[73] As before, the actors from both groups were supplemented with additional personnel. In addition to teachers, we have seen how Vasilii Meshalkin, the clerk from the Vladimirskaia Department, was involved in the theatrical productions already in 1673 (p. 26). Now, for these multiple plays, employees from the Ambassadorial Chancery and the Galitskaia Department were pulled in. (The Galitskaia Department is another of the tax collection offices.) The intense rehearsals also required additional space, which Matveev provided by reaching into resources available through the Ambassadorial Chancery. An order from October 28, 1675, provides for a venue "at the diplomatic residence [Posol'skii dvor] on Pokrovka Street, which was [formerly] the residence of the foreigner David Mikolaev," and many of the subsequent payment records show that the space was heavily used (p. 50).[74] This is where the unfortunate musician Vasilii Repskii claimed he was "held in chains" at Matveev's order, and artists and carpenters working on sets and props also used this venue (pp. 50–51, 64–65).[75] All performances, however, seem to have been at Preobrazhenskoe (for example, pp. 63–64, 66).

The first title in the book-binding payment was the court's longest-running play, *Artakserksovo deistvo*. The records for this fall 1675 performance show roughly the same number of actors as in the first production, sixty-three, and indeed, some of the same young actors are still participating.[76] "Ivan An'gler" and "Ivan Berner" are listed in a petition requesting payment for 1675 (pp. 60–61)—both actors are in the cast list attributed to Rinhuber. Another familiar name appears in these payment records: "Lavrentei dokhtur" is paid for teaching the "German children," and he carried out his teaching duties at the new space at the Pokrovka Street residence (p. 51). Sergei Bogoiavlenskii suggests that this is Lavrentii Blumentrost, who had performed in the first court play; he was the son of the elder Dr. Laurentius Blumentrost, the tsar's physician (p. xii). We suggest, however, that this reference is to Laurentius Rinhuber. The younger Blumentrost was not yet a doctor in 1675, unlike Rinhuber, who was not only a doctor but was in Russia at this very time, serving as physician and translator for the imperial mission headed by H. F. von Bottoni.[77] Rinhuber (like the younger Blumentrost) would certainly have been familiar with the "German children," for he had coached this group intensively before the 1672 premiere of *Artakserksovo deistvo*.[78] There are no references in the published records to performers or props required for *Judith*, but because this play was bound at the same time as the others and because the same group from the Foreign Quarter was still performing *Artakserksovo deistvo*, it seems safe to suggest that, similarly, some of the *Judith* actors from the Meshchanskaia Quarter would have presented this play again in late 1675.

For these fall 1675 productions, the Tamerlane play and two of the new plays, on the Joseph and St. George stories, were assigned to a group of seventy young actors from the Meshchanskaia Quarter (p. 69). Their teacher was Ivan Feodorov Volosheninov, who had worked with the young actors from the Meshchanskaia Quarter previously and who was given firewood for its school during rehearsals in October; the next month, he requested payment for teaching seventy students at the overflow residence associated with the Ambassadorial Chancery (the Posol'skii dvor venue mentioned previously). Again, we see an expanding pool of resources to aid in these productions, including an employee from the Smolensk Chancery brought in to help (pp. xii, 51, 61–62). The *Tamerlane* encore required renewal of the stage weaponry, which had clearly gotten a workout by the young actors; artists working at the Posol'skii dvor space were paid for their work on these props (p. 54).[79]

The play about St. George and the dragon does not survive, but there are many references to the necessary props; the dramatic requirements would have been familiar as the imagery had long been associated with the Russian ruling dynasties and their lands. There were payments to tinsmiths who were refashioning older tinplate helmets and armor to form the dragon ("zmei"), straps were needed to attach the snout and the tail, and the unnamed actor who was to portray George required red morocco boots. Included in these requests were fifty candlesticks, which may have been used to produce a lighting effect (pp. 51–52). The new play on the Old Testament story of Joseph fared somewhat better, for it survives, although incompletely. This play is also linked to the group of seventy Meshchanskaia Quarter performers, with the participation of ten people associated with other government offices: Mikhail Belianinov (from the Ambassadorial Chancery) and Kuz'ma Zhuravlev (from the Galitskaia Department) with their cohorts (pp. 51, 61). The records covering the preparations and props for this play may fill in some of the gaps in the surviving text. For example, the Joseph play required the sacks that the twelve Israelite brothers were supposed to fill and take back from Egypt (pp. 52–53). As scholars have pointed out, this scene from the biblical story does not appear in the surviving play text, suggesting perhaps as much as an additional three acts that are now lost (to add to the surviving two acts).[80]

The Adam and Eve play, as it is preserved in two identically incomplete copies, is five acts long (the text breaks off in the fifth act). The scholar O. A. Derzhavina characterizes this work as a cross between a biblical mystery play and a morality play, with a fairly abrupt shift from one dramatic concept to the other, beginning in act 4, scene 2, which has a complete change of cast. As Derzhavina points out, the play is relatively static, with inner-focused action as opposed to, say, the rip-roaring battle scene of the Tamerlane play.[81] (The serpent is one of the main speaking roles, and as Derzhavina remarks, it required quite a lot of talking to convince Eve to take the apple.) Although there is no indication of comic action, which would seem out of place for this topic, the play does feature singing, especially by the angels, integrated naturally into the storyline. In a perfect moment of intertheater, one song in this play is introduced with a spoken declamation by Adam, lamenting Eve's taking of the forbidden fruit (act 2, scene 2). This expression would have seemed natural to the audience through the many settings of "Adam's Lament" (*Plach Adama*), a repentance verse with a rich textual, musical, and visual history in Russia.[82] In the play, this soliloquy is followed immediately by a text headed: "Here they sing a song." The sung text, however, is not the traditional Russian verse but a very close Russian translation of the first strophe of the Lutheran hymn "Durch Adams Fall." We do not know which group of actors performed this play; for the German Foreign Quarter boys, the text would certainly have recalled the familiar church hymn. Indeed, the syllabic, homophonic Lutheran hymn style would have meshed comfortably with the syllabic, homophonic kant style that was increasingly popular in Russia (influenced, as its name suggests, by Western singing practices).

The props for the Adam and Eve play are also suggestive. There were extensive preparations, most of all for the six "heavenly trees" ("raiskie dreva"). Although decorated trees were traditional for the Russian Palm Sunday procession, the six trees for the play seem to have been especially ornate. Wax apples were purchased, green paint and scissors helped create the leaves, and special transport was arranged, in addition to preparations for costumes, including wings for the angels (pp. 49, 50, 52, 54). The play also required silver sheets for a cross or a crucifix ("krest"; p. 55). This may have been a small item held by one of the characters.[83] Based on a slightly later account of the tsar's theater, however, it is possible that this "krest" might have been part of a lost Passion scene that was performed or perhaps revealed in a fashion similar to the tableaux vivants of the initial "ballets."[84] We return to this account in our next section.

For the productions in the fall of 1675, the theatrical organizers relied on someone new to the project: Mikolai Lima, consistently identified as an engineer ("inzhener"). In early November 1675, Lima was part of a group of ten performers who were supplied with costumes and weapons, for which he was responsible. The group was outfitted with armor and helmets, so presumably they appeared as soldiers, although they are not associated with any named play or with either of the two large groups of performers (pp. 57–58, 66). When Lima petitioned later for reimbursement for some transportation expenses, he said that he was at Preobrazhenskoe for the comedy from November 9 to 11; these dates correspond to other records indicating the series of performances at this location (p. 66). One additional support role is an interpreter from the Ambassadorial Chancery, who was paid for working at rehearsals, suggesting that not everyone was speaking the same language even at this relatively late date in the theater's history.[85]

In the account of the imperial mission to Moscow headed by Bottoni—the mission for which Rinhuber served as physician—Adolphus Lyseck referred to these fall 1675 performances, highlighting the Russian interest in a servant in the imperial party who performed magic tricks:[86]

> A few days after our departure [from Moscow on October 26, 1675, o.s.] German players were going to present a comedy for the tsar, which, as they said, would be highly pleasing to the tsar, if only one of our servants would take part. This servant was a conjuror [*gesticulator*], who, with his amusing and illusory tricks, had not only struck with amazement many in the public, especially among the Russians, but had also made them [the Russians] declare unanimously that he was an artist with devilish powers and a sorcerer. He had even brought them to believe that the objects conjured by his tricks—such as knives, garlands, and money—were not real, although we

tried to encourage their doubts and convince them that they were duped by the speed with which he performed his tricks; rather they crossed themselves every now and then. The Germans and a few prominent Russians asked the ambassadors to let him stay in Moscow, so he could show his talents to the tsar and tsaritsa. Their wishes, however, were not fulfilled. Word of our departure got back to the grand prince, and he immediately dispatched his military commander Menzies, a former envoy to the Roman emperor and to the pope, after us, along with a translator, in order to bring back [to Moscow] our above-mentioned servant [the *gesticulator*].

Lyseck then describes the servant's decision to return to Moscow, where he "performed his tricks at their own palace twice, amazing the tsar and the tsaritsa." The entertainer eventually rejoined his party empty-handed, "having squandered everything he had received as a gift from the tsar."[87]

Koch verifies Lyseck's tale:

> [Moscow, November 2, 1675] On the next day after their departure, Col. Minesius [Menzies] and the translator Meysner were sent after them by Mr. Ertemon [Artamon Matveev], and [they asked that] a *Taschen Spieler* [conjuror, magician] who worked as a servant [in their party] should be left here for 14 days in order to perform for His Tsarish Majesty, which Herr Bottoni approved. This aforementioned *Taschen Spieler*, and also another servant, who is a musician, were sent back [to Moscow]. Next Saturday there will be a comedy performed by the youngsters for His Tsarish Majesty, at which the *Taschen Spieler* will also do his tricks.[88]

Amid all this productive activity, the numbers of foreign instrumentalists continued to decline. In September 1675, two of the three remaining musicians—Jacob Philips and Gottfried Berge—ran away. They were not discovered, in spite of a search (pp. 47–48). They were, however, quickly replaced by two musicians who had accompanied the same embassy in which the *gesticulator* had been found.[89] The sole remaining instrumentalist from the initial batch of hires, back in 1672, was Christopher Ackermann, who was paid through the end of 1675, and then sent away in February 1676, soon after the theater was closed down.[90]

The success of this fall 1675 event is demonstrated by the plans for two new plays in January 1676. Previous discussions have focused on their storylines, one based on the familiar account of David and Goliath and the other based on something apparently new: the mythical tale of Bacchus and Venus. Here, we emphasize how these two final works fit within the by now substantial theatrical traditions that had been built up over the previous four years.

Planning must have begun soon after the November festival, for by January, the process was already being carried out in full force, fitting into the pre-Lenten theatrical seasons we have observed. The organized troupes of performers remained basically in place, with the largest apparently drawn from the Meshchanskaia Quarter troupe, which had sixty members. Each of the two new plays had forty or fifty characters, with rehearsals in the Meshchanskaia Quarter, suggesting that the previous additional preparation and rehearsal location was temporary, necessary for the extraordinary requirements of the multiple fall productions (pp. xiv–xv, 69). Matveev continued to draw on other personnel from chanceries at his disposal.[91]

Another reappearing participant is "inzhener" Mikolai Lima, who had apparently successfully completed his previous theatrical tasks, for he is now in charge of twenty Meshchanskaia Quarter actors, a doubling of his earlier responsibility. The group of twenty was headed by Timoshka Blisa, who was among the actors in the fall performances (pp. 60, 67). Lima is named specifically as a dance teacher for the January plays. We do not know in which play Lima and his charges appeared, although because they were equipped with prop weaponry, they probably performed some choreographed fight scenes.[92] Another familiar face is Hasenkroeg, whose involvement thus spanned the entire history of the tsar's theatrical entertainments (p. 74).

One of the new people participating in January 1676, as a teacher, was Stepan Chizhinskii. The previous organizer, Hüfner, disappears from the theatrical records. Chizhinskii would have brought a range of new literary and educational experiences to add to those so consistently drawn from Moscow's German-Lutheran Foreign Quarter. He had served in the cavalry of the Polish crown hetman Stanisław Potocki in the 1660s and later taught Latin at the Kievan Academy; he then moved to Smolensk, where he taught (again, Latin) in the very highly connected Golitsyn family, which is apparently how he came to Matveev's attention. Chizhinskii was in charge of the two new plays; some scholars suggest that he was the playwright as well (pp. xiv, 71).[93] The presence of someone with Chizhinskii's background might help explain the selection of the Latin myth involving Bacchus, Venus, and Cupid. His presence was not a necessary precondition for such a topic—after all, the court theater got its start back in February 1672 in the mythological world, with Orpheus and Mercury appearing before the royal family, and the Judith play also has references to Mercury, Venus, and Mars. Nevertheless, Chizhinskii's participation would have been a good fit.[94]

The two stories have connections with previous productions as well as with each other. The character and prop lists are, quite simply, delightful. There were ten girls (played, of course, by the young men) in addition to four actors who were costumed as bears. Two characters called musicians presumably made music on stage. In addition to ten senators and ten drunks, there were roles for "three people, drunks, lying down," apparently passed out on the stage (p. 72, for "3 chelovekom p'ianitsam lezhashchim"). Both new plays required some special props: oversized figures, in particular, big heads. Goliath, of course, is a giant, but Bacchus, enhanced by a wine cask slung over his shoulder, was also oversized, and several other large figures were constructed for these two plays. Goliath required large armor (for which tinplate was purchased), hair, and a beard; he had a large tin helmet and large wooden legs and held a wooden lance (the large sizes meticulously specified in the requisitions lists; pp. 71–73).[95] Bacchus's big head also required hair and a beard, and he had two tubes running from his head to the wine barrel perched on his shoulder. Other large heads were constructed as well, including two for the "bordachnik" (pp. 72–74);[96] clay models or forms were used, and a team of four artists painted these props. The painters also worked on fifty large bunches of grapes for Bacchus and on the twenty lances that had been constructed for the soldiers in the David and Goliath play (pp. 74–75). Just as the mythological characters were not wholly unknown on the tsar's stage, so were the oversize prop-characters not entirely new: the St. George play had required a large dragon equipped with a snout and a tail. The audience may thus have been primed for such special effects.

Was all this planning worth it—did the tsar see these final plays? Aleksei Mikhailovich died on January 29, 1676. As several foreign observers noted, the tsar's final illness was sudden; he was only forty-five years old. Gjøe wrote on January 26 that he had heard the tsar was dangerously ill but that it was a great secret; in a report written on February 3, shortly after the tsar's death, Gjøe said that he had died after a weeklong illness.[97] Balthazar Coyett's account of the embassy from the Dutch Republic headed by Koenraad van Klenk also stressed the suddenness of the tsar's illness and death, corresponding to the shockingly rapid time frame indicated by Gjøe. The Dutch ambassador made his entrance into the capital on January 11 and had two audiences with Tsar Aleksei, on January 17 and again on January 19. It was only after that second audience that the Dutch visitors reported the tsar's illness.[98] It was all the more surprising because at the second audience the tsar appeared fit and healthy, and the visitors suspected nothing unusual. In fact, on the next day, the tsar had requested that a young page from the ambassador's suite be sent to court for a musical performance.[99] Furthermore, Coyett reports that the tsar enjoyed several theatrical plays that were performed for him: "Still on the next day [January 20], he asked to have sent to him the ambassador's young page, who could play very well on various instruments, and in the presence of the tsaritsa and the aristocrats, the tsar showed his pleasure in the boy's performance, as well as in some [theatrical] plays [*in eenige spelen*] that were performed in his presence."[100] The entertainment described by the Dutch observers was, as usual, a mixture of the planned (theatrical plays) and the opportunistic (performances by the talented young page).

The dates in the Dutch account, indicating that the plays were performed around January 20, fit with Russian payment records. A large group of fifteen tailors was paid for their work on costumes for the two comedies, given food wages for January 15 through 22, and an additional group of four tailors was paid for being at the comedy hall for two (unspecified) days. Bogoiavlenskii suggests that the most likely performance dates would have been January 23 and 24, presumably following payment for work on the costumes.[101] It is difficult to be precise, but the time frame is obviously quite constrained. The performances must have taken place during that penultimate week of January 1676, the last week during which the tsar enjoyed his health.

Tsar Aleksei's death prompted complex reactions among the ruling families—the main focus, in the first few months, was the nearly unanimous resentment of Matveev, as Paul Bushkovitch, relying on the insightful reports by Gjøe, has explained. Not surprisingly, the theater was an early casualty. The link between the theater and its impresario is clear in Gjøe's report from February 23, less than a month after the tsar's death and before his successor's coronation (again distinguishing between comedies and ballets): "it is said that the state will be ordered here according to the ancient custom, that is to say, that the plays and ballets will cease forever.... It is the old boyars who are pressing for the abolition of all these things, and after Easter it will all explode."[102] Apparently, the required attendance at theatrical performances had not convinced the traditionally minded boyars of their value. The theater was an easy and obvious target around which the generalized anti-Matveev factions coalesced.

Matveev began to lose his numerous government positions quickly, although he remained in charge of the Ambassadorial Chancery for several months, until early July 1676. His fall can be tracked through the fate of the theater. Payments for work done for the two January plays were issued, under Matveev's name, through June (June 22 and 28; pp. 69, 75). He lost his post at the Ambassadorial Chancery on July 2, and almost immediately we see two theater-related charges leveled against him—charges that would likely have been impossible only weeks before. The first, on July 10, was by Vasilii Repskii, the young musician forced to play music "in chains" for the comedies. The second was by theater stalwart Hasenkroeg, who on July 20 petitioned to be paid for the organ Matveev had taken from his home to use in the productions. Finally, in December 1676, the Apothecary theater was ordered to be cleared out, and everything—musical instruments (or specifically, the organ), sets, and all the comedy supplies—was to be transferred to the home belonging formerly to Nikita Ivanovich Romanov, an appropriate place, as this was where organist Simon Gutovskii's workshop had been located.[103]

Another reason the theater was so completely shut down after the tsar's death concerns its finances and the closely related issue of staffing, which were entirely reliant on multiple funding sources juggled dexterously by Matveev. Initially, the theatrical productions were supported through the tax collection departments, beginning with the Vladimirskaia Department, from which the initial theatrical expenses were drawn, expanding to include the other main tax collection offices (pp. 8–10). Matveev also drew directly from resources of the Ambassadorial Chancery (p. 14). Still other income sources were used, for example, Gregorii and the foreign musicians received payments in kind from the Siberian Chancery (pp. 23, 27, 35), and in 1674, Matveev also used funds from the Apothecary Chancery to pay theatrical expenses (e.g., pp. 37–38, 45, 56). A year or so later, in the fall of 1675, Matveev was relying heavily on funding from the Ambassadorial Chancery, and some theatrical payments were signed by secretaries associated with this office, with Matveev giving the final approval.[104] Finally, as we have traced throughout, Matveev also brought in staff from several other departments, an ever-widening circle of money and people flowing into the theatrical coffers. But because the Ambassadorial Chancery itself was dependent on funds from the other financial departments, the theater's ad hoc funding required constant shifting to avoid what might be called, in present-day terms, cash-flow problems. With no other funding sources to draw from or to supplement payments (for example, monies provided by wealthy families or revenues from the sale of tickets or boxes, as in the West), Matveev's loss of influence and offices after the tsar's death brought the entire financial apparatus constructed for the theater to a grinding halt.

Although the new tsar, Fedor Alekseevich, had seen theatrical performances along with his family, beginning with the February 1672 "ballet," we do not know his personal opinion of such entertainments. Fedor's tutor was the court poet Simeon Polotskii, who commemorated his pupil's accession to the throne by comparing him to the "great tsar Artakserks," an allusion that could not help but recall the most popular and long-running play of his father's theater.[105] The closing of the theater seems, in the view of Heinz Ellersieck, to have been part of the general anti-Matveev reaction rather than "any particular anti-western attitude" on the part of the new ruler.[106]

The ongoing ramifications of the plays and the hostility they engendered in certain quarters are reflected in an unusual description of Tsar Aleksei's death, in which the plays are actually considered a *cause* of his unexpected demise. This description does not seem to apply to the January 1676 productions but, with its references to reenactments of biblical creation accounts, might possibly refer to the fall 1675 performances, which included the Adam and Eve play. It appears in a report apparently written shortly after the tsar's death by a member of the traditionalist Old Believer religious community and sent to the heart and soul of this movement, Archpriest Avvakum, who was in exile in Pustozersk. In this anonymous account, the tsar's death is linked explicitly to the "utterly shocking" entertainments in which the court indulged:

> [And before he was gripped by illness, the tsar] entertained himself with all manner of amusements and plays. Utterly shocking were the plays they performed—like those about the creation of the world, the Flood, the events before and during the life of Christ, His miracles, or signs of them. And all this was against the letter [i.e., Holy Scripture]. This is what was performed in these plays—the crucifixion of Christ, his burial, his descent into Hades, and his resurrection and ascension into Heaven. And even the non-Orthodox were surprised by these plays and said, "There are in our countries such plays, called comedies, but not among very many of the confessions."[107]

It is this account, explicitly describing a crucifixion scene, that raises questions about the purpose of the cross listed in the requisitions for the play *Adam and Eve*.

Whatever their precise points of reference, the Old Believer reactions underscore the powerful forces at work against the theater and all that it represented. Tsar Aleksei's comedies could not survive the loss of their prime audience member and their prime promoter. The combination of the tsar's death and Matveev's subsequent fall quite literally brought down the house.

INTERTHEATRICAL CONTINUITIES

Many historians have emphasized the links between the Russian court theater and the theatrical history of the Continent, particularly in northern Europe, which was so heavily influenced by the traveling English comedians beginning in the late sixteenth century. Earlier Russian scholars, including N. S. Tikhonravov, P. O. Morozov, and A. N. Veselovskii, wrote substantive summaries of these connections, clearly setting a broad contextual framework for the Russian court theater. Their work echoes in later studies, for example the important essays accompanying the publication of the play texts (in the *Ranniaia russkaia dramaturgiia* volumes). Recent Western scholarship focusing on the impact of the traveling English companies (as well as their imitators and competitors) throughout Europe only strengthens this context.

Character types such as Pickleherring (named in the "ballets" of 1672 and in the Tamerlane play) and similar comic personas (Susakim in *Judith*, Telpel in *Tamerlane*, and the interscenia figures layered into the Esther play) all represent iterations on a continuum, which the concept of intertheater urges us to consider carefully. The Russian experience parallels descriptions of early Continental encounters with English performance traditions, which also emphasized comic physicality and rambunctious dumb-shows as well as dance and music. The English traveler Fynes Moryson disparaged the crudities of the English acting troupe he saw at the Frankfurt fair, probably in 1592, comparing this performance to his theatrical experiences at home: "the serious parts [of the plays] are dully penned, and worse acted," he complained, "and the mirth they make is ridiculous," yet in spite of this, the German audience "flocked wonderfully to see theire gesture and action." A German account from the 1592 fair gives a characteristically opposite view. The Nüremberg merchant Balthasar Paumgartner praised the music, costumes, and acrobatic feats, "the like of which I have never before heard or seen."[108] Nearly seventy-five years later, the roles are reversed. The now theatrically savvy Germans could look with tolerant amusement on the proceedings in Moscow, which were received enthusiastically by the inexperienced Russians. As Rautenfels said, anywhere outside of Moscow the performance would have been offered with apologies, but "to the Russians it appeared unique and artistic."

The shocked narrative in the Old Believer account quoted previously expands this continuity through details of the staging witnessed, or at least alleged, in the Russian productions. The horrified description of the goings-on at the tsar's court continues: "How strange and frightening it is to hear that a simple peasant in Christ's image is nailed to a cross, a crown of thorns is put on his head, and a bladder with blood is hidden under his armpit so that he bleeds between the ribs when stabbed. Moreover, instead of the image of the Virgin, a foreign damsel with loose hair weeps; and instead of John the Theologian being summoned, the body of Christ is handed over to a young beardless man."[109]

There is no evidence of any female participation in the Russian court theater, so (if this description does reflect the court productions) the "foreign damsel" might be taken as a backhand tribute to the skills of the youthful male actors. The "young beardless man" might describe just about any of the student-actors who performed for the tsar. The bloody stage effects—unknown in any other account—might indeed have been reproduced from theatrical knowledge among the Foreign Quarter community, drawing on experiences from their home countries. Blood and gore were staples of Dutch productions, in particular, and the very effect mentioned in this passage is echoed closely in a later description of over-the-top Dutch theatrical realism. As the historian Louis Riccoboni, writing in the second quarter of the eighteenth century, remarked: "In the old [Dutch] tragedies they represented the action on stage as it had happened.... [In one play] the Hero stabs himself and falls dead after having inundated the scene with all the blood contained in a bladder which he hides in his armpit."[110]

Over the course of the Russian theatrical experience, the planners labored consistently to build up a core of participants: teachers, actors, suppliers, musicians, and so forth. They were, in effect, building what amounted to a repertory company, concentrated in the Foreign Quarter and backed financially and organizationally by Matveev's authority across a range of governmental institutions. The origins of this company are in the initial "ballet" performances of early 1672, and some of the most valuable information provided by the foreign reports is their testimony showing how consistently such "ballets" were featured along with the full-length plays, which represented the second stage of the court's theatrical development. This consistently goal-oriented focus of what we are characterizing as a repertory company encourages us to look at the plays in new ways, as part of this same organizational impulse. Although previous scholars have proposed holistic approaches in analyzing the plays as a group, the clarifications provided by our detailed sources allow for a different set of observations.[111]

In the first place, keeping in mind the importance of the "ballets" throughout the whole course of the court theater, we can form a better idea of how this type of entertainment was integrated into the plays ever more successfully. The Russian planners were making conscious decisions in response to the reactions of their exalted audience, demonstrating a willingness to experiment and refine their options. This may help us understand, in very general terms, why some of the plays seemed to be so popular and why others, particularly *Tobit*, were not. When embarking on *Artakserksovo deistvo*, the first full-length play, the planners faced a new set of problems: how to retain the comic elements, which had apparently been conceived of, music-hall style, as a series of separate "acts," but integrate them into a new play with its own storyline and characters. The solution was to divide the comic turns into short scenes that were positioned between the acts. This approach would have seemed natural to Gregorii and Rinhuber, drawing on their presumed theatrical exposure in the West, as spectators, students, or teachers, where such comic interludes were the norm. We do not know if this separation of elements was maintained throughout the play's long run.[112] What we can observe is that later plays, in particular *Judith* and *Tamerlane*, offered a different kind of layout in which the comic elements were more fully and, apparently, deliberately merged into the play texts themselves; presumably, these plays did not feature—they did not need to feature—the separate interscenia of *Artakserksovo deistvo*. Because we know that *Judith* was the third (not the second) play, we can see that this integrated approach was selected for the next two plays in a row. Even if we suppose that some separate interscenia were written for *Judith* and *Tamerlane* and that they are simply lost now (not an unreasonable assumption), it is still evident that the construction of these two plays is different from that of the first play, with the comedy, so to speak, built in and written out.

Judith illustrates this approach. Its comedy, especially by the character Susakim, would have been familiar to the players and playwrights as well as to the Russian audience. Susakim is a soldier, and he appears consistently with other soldiers. (Soldiers had been introduced at least from the May 1672 event, with its "Peace and War" scenario, and there is a "Soldat" in the *Artakserksovo deistvo* interscenia, as well as a character called Thraso, a common soldier name.) In a few scenes, Susakim participates in the main action of the drama—his character is thus more fully integrated into the larger play than the hangman in *Artakserksovo deistvo*, who does, briefly and apparently uniquely, breach the interscenia-main plot divide.[113] Susakim is obsessed with food, sausages in particular, and he is rowdy and rambunctious, the latter very much in line with the popular comic action of the "ballets" and the *Artakserksovo deistvo* interscenia. Pickleherring and the related iterations on Western stages were similarly preoccupied incessantly with food, especially sausages, blatantly suggestive.[114] At the end of act 6, threatened with execution, Susakim delivers a series of farewells to life (and food and drink), interrupted with increasing irritation by his "executioners." He is finally beheaded with a foxtail, another link with the Pickleherring persona and an action that prefigures Holofernes's fate in the next act.[115] Coming out of his daze, Susakim attempts to locate his head, searching the stage and imploring the audience to help him find it—such direct address is characteristic of Pickleherring and other Western comics.[116] Susakim is not the only bawdy character in the play. Judith's maid, Abra, also delivers some snappy comments. At the drama's climactic moment, when Holofernes passes out on his bed, Abra asks Judith, brightly, "What would you like, my dear mistress? Do you want to be undressed?" And after the beheading (the real one this time), Abra functions as a kind of female Susakim, wondering what Holofernes will do when he discovers that his head is gone.[117]

Judith thus retained some of the comedy of the Esther play, unified more thoroughly by embedding these actions into the main story. We will focus on the Tamerlane play in our next chapter, but at this point, it is worth noting that although quite different in length and source material, *Judith* and *Tamerlane* show the same overall approach to the integration of the comic elements. The comedy was probably more pronounced in *Tamerlane* because it is shorter (three acts versus five in *Judith*), but the comic scenes are positioned in roughly the same way: each play has two longish comic interludes that include songs.[118] Given the focus on and integration of the comedy in these two later plays, it appears that *Tobit* somehow did not easily provide for such comic or musical moments—at any rate, the trend in the two following, and popular, plays indicates that these elements were priorities.

Of course it would be a mistake to assume that this speculative trend in structuring the court plays applied to all of them. Indeed the surviving texts for *Adam and Eve* and *Joseph* offer what appear to be contrasting models. For *Adam and Eve*, we would not presume lost comic actions—it is impossible to imagine Pickleherring bouncing through the Garden of Eden or, indeed, at any point in this narrative. Singing is an important focus in this play, particularly in the first (biblical) portions. For *Joseph*, there are no surviving comic scenes; moreover, there are difficulties in determining exactly how long the play was meant to be and, consequently, how any comic or musical elements might have functioned overall. However, since *Adam and Eve* and *Joseph* were part of the six-play festival and thus were presented within a very rich theatrical environment, it may be that their individual comic or musical components would not have been so important.[119]

Although there are no surviving texts for the two 1676 plays, which were based on the mythological story of Bacchus and Venus and the biblical story of David and Goliath, we can see that they fit into the previous patterns. In addition to being plot- or story-based, these last two plays indicate that the "ballet" elements (comedy and music) were fully and prominently incorporated, as shown by the necessary characters. They also had an official dance instructor in "inzhener" Lima, and they provided the same kinds of elaborate props that we saw for the six plays produced the previous fall. One wonders if this continuing merging with the "ballet" features contributed to the theater's downfall after Tsar Aleksei's death, that is, the continuing, even increasing, focus on such racy antics may have made it that much easier to shut the whole thing down, especially as many of the traditionalists did not like the endeavor in the first place.

This wider view also suggests a framework for two additional plays: Simeon Polotskii's settings of the Prodigal Son story and of Nebuchadnezzar and the three boys in the fiery furnace. In writing his own plays, Simeon showed his awareness and appreciation of the court's theatrical interests, also drawing on the long-standing performative traditions of declamations and liturgical drama. His Nebuchadnezzar play, the shorter of the two, illustrates what historian Ronald Vroon calls the "interfacing of the liturgical and non-liturgical" that is so characteristic of declamations.[120] Simeon's version is based on the same biblical story that had been rendered annually in Russia as a liturgical drama, performed (at least in some locales) until the early 1660s—so, although it was not being presented during the time of Tsar Aleksei's theater, it was a familiar story, long associated with performed realizations.[121] Simeon's play setting reflects the tradition and structure of declamations: it is relatively short (compared to the surviving court plays), written in rhymed couplets with opportunities for the three boys to recite serially, and with directions specifying the appropriate liturgical text, including cues to the Old Testament account in the book of Daniel, where the story appears. But his setting also explicitly calls for singing, instruments, and dance.[122]

Simeon's other play, a treatment of the Prodigal Son story, is longer and more elaborate, with many characters and with scenic settings that are divided into numbered parts, each of which is marked by a break. In the text of this play as it is transmitted in the *Rifmologion* (Rhyme book, Simeon's own massive compilation of his writings), directorial annotations are added, apparently in Simeon's own hand, to specify action that is to occur during these breaks. A typical example, marking the end of part 1, is: "The singers sing, and there is an Intermedium" (the last word written in Latin letters).[123]

We have so far discovered no evidence indicating that either of Simeon's plays were performed at the court theater. Indeed, the "ballet" origins of the theatrical project made it natural for Matveev and the Foreign Quarter planners to take the lead in providing such entertainment, as indicated by all of the source material we have examined, Russian or foreign. The published theatrical payment records include a reference to the binding of a "comedy on Tsar Nebuchadnezzar," in February 1674.[124] We suggest that this refers to the court play on the Judith story and not to Simeon's version. The binding order occurs exactly when initial preparations for the Judith play were under way, in February 1674, and the character Nebuchadnezzar features prominently in the play's opening acts. The court play is referred to in several ways, as either the Judith or the Holofernes comedy, so this reference to Nebuchadnezzar would represent another such variant.[125] Simeon's play and the court Judith play were both published for the first time in the encyclopedic source compilation *Drevniaia rossiiskaia vivliofika* (Ancient Russian library, 1789). In this publication, both plays are identified by the Nebuchadnezzar character; the (shortened) title of the court play is given as

Komediia Navukhodonosor (Comedy about Nebuchadnezzar), thus another example of the character Nebuchadnezzar being invoked to refer to this play.[126] This book-binding reference is thus a very slender thread on which to propose a performance (or even the composition) of Simeon's play at this early date. Indeed, decoupling Simeon's plays from the court theater offers a wider possible chronological range for their creation.[127]

Nevertheless, Simeon's plays were certainly part of the same impulse that produced the dramas at the court theater, and his earlier declamations, offered by other trained squadrons of young performers in the 1660s, were an important model for the theater and its audience. Thus, as speculative as all this may be, taking a broader view of the relationships among the court theater's plays, on the one hand, and Simeon's separate efforts, on the other, encourages us to see the theater as a continuum within Russia itself and within the larger history of Western performative culture. Tsar Aleksei's theater was a process, not an anomaly, and trying, even if admittedly incompletely, to recognize the planners' continuing efforts at refinement brings a welcome and vivid dynamism to a consideration of late seventeenth-century Russian cultural history.

Before appraising the aftermath of Tsar Aleksei's theatrical experience, we will focus on a single play, on the story of Tamerlane, in order to appreciate how these strands of influence and experience came together on the Moscow stage. Just as the history of the court theater itself cannot be told without the aid of foreign sources, so *Tamerlane* is enriched by considering its foreign contexts.

NOTES

1. The controversies spanned the 1660s; see Lahana, "Novaia nemetskaia sloboda," esp. 107–108; Tsvetaev, "Pamiatniki," 1–41. Gregorii had been accused of a disrespectful reference to the tsar but the play-writing commission shows (as does the resolution of other problems) that all had been forgiven.

2. Bogoiavlenskii, "Moskovskii teatr," 8; throughout the remainder of this chapter, references to Bogoiavlenskii will be placed in the text identified with page numbers only. The departments (*cheti* or *chetverti*) mentioned in this series of documents were the offices responsible for collecting taxes (Liseitsev, Rogozhin, and Eskin, *Prikazy*, esp. 227–238; P. Brown, "Muscovite Government Bureaus"). As we will see, Matveev drew on an ever-widening group of offices for theatrical funding, a standard financial approach; see Mordison, *Istoriia*, 22–23; Griffin, "Production," 59, 67–68.

3. Gregorii was paid for his work or for supplies through the summer and fall (Bogoiavlenskii, "Moskovskii teatr," 11, 14–15); payments begin in June to foreign artists, including Engels and Johann Wander, and in August to four Russian artists (pp. 15–16). Engels was

from Hamburg, documented as a "perspective painter" in Copenhagen (Amburger, "Die Mitwirkenden," 305, and the Amburger-Datenbank, s.v. "Inglis/Engels, Peter"). He can be traced in Moscow from 1662, first as a trader and later as an artist ("zhivopisets"; *Sobranie gosudarstvennykh gramot* 4:249–251, No. 69); see also *Slovar' russkikh ikonopistsev*, s.v. "Engel's, Petr Gavrilov" and "Semenov, Ivan." Engels was the brother-in-law of another foreign theatrical participant, Georg Hüfner; see later in this chapter.

4. Bogoiavlenskii, "Moskovskii teatr," 12, 14; in both records, Hasenkroeg was paid "na stroen'ia" (for the construction or creation) of costumes. The fabric was deluxe, and a foreign tailor (or fabric cutter) assisted (Bogoiavlenskii, "Moskovskii teatr," vii–viii, 15).

5. Hasenkroeg says that the organ was spoiled during transport to the theatrical venues, claiming he would have been able to sell it to the Persians for the 1,200-ruble price; the Russians had given organs as gifts to the Persians twice before (Roizman, *Organ*, 71–75, with comparative prices for organs on p. 85). We do not know if Hasenkroeg already owned the organ or if he procured it with the court's new theatrical interests in mind; Roizman, *Organ*, 90–91, suggests that Hasenkroeg might have purchased it in Arkhangel'sk in the summer of 1672. The court organ builder Simon Gutovskii was involved in moving the instrument between theatrical venues but was apparently not involved in its initial procurement, and there must have been no suitable instruments at court.

6. The word *komediia* was familiar from earlier diplomatic reports and kuranty references but it was not applied to the February and May entertainments, which were consistently called "ballets" in the foreign accounts (although see chap. 3 for one exceptional use of *komediia* to indicate these initial productions).

7. Western traditions of the Esther story are summarized in Ardolino, "Hans and Hammon," 148–156; Watanabe-O'Kelly, "Early Modern Period," esp. 102–109; Schwartz, *Esther*. Swoboda, "Old Testament 'Apocrypha,'" esp. 429–430n1, outlines the complex situation occupied by the book of Esther in the various confessions.

8. Robinson, "Pervyi russkii teatr," 13–14; *RRD* 1:70–71. See also Martin, "Muscovite Esther"; Crummey, "Court Spectacles," esp. 139–140.

9. On the surviving manuscripts, see *RRD* 1:461–464. There are two (largely) complete seventeenth-century texts, one in Russian (Kudriavtsev, *"Artakserksovo deistvo,"* and later published in *RRD* 1), the other a bilingual Russian-German source (Mazon and Cocron, "La Comédie," and also in *RRD* 1); one act missing in the bilingual source survives separately (Günther, "Das Weimarer Bruchstück"). An English translation is in Louria, "Comedy." Mazon and Cocron, "La Comédie," 54, lists a fourth scene in act 7, described as "Mardoch. in solio, cum Judaeis." There is no such scene in any surviving source; this may refer to scene 1 of this act. The final strophic choral number in act 7, scene 3 seems to wind up the play nicely.

10. The Hebrew texts appear in act 4, scenes 3 and 4; see the discussion in Jensen, *Musical Cultures*, 192–195. In 1661, Gregorii began his studies in Jena, where he was awarded the degree of *magister* later that year (Koch, "Die Sachsenkirche," 277). Although the exact program of his study is unknown, Hebrew was, as in many Lutheran universities, part of the curriculum at Jena, where it had been offered for over a century (Burnett, *Christian Hebraism*, 30).

11. Mazon and Cocron, "La Comédie," 55, lists Snikkert (or Schnikkert) in the interscenia roles of Thraso and Muischelow; Thraso is a common soldier name, probably taken from Terence's *The Eunuch*, which was widely known in Germany in translation (J. Stone, "Pastor," 240; Schade, *Studies*, esp. 48–49). In the play itself, Snikkert took the role of Hatach. An additional soldier character in the interscenia was played by Klifman, who also performed the major role of Haman in the play. (We note that these were Foreign Quarter youth, not

professional actors, as in Pivovarova, *Istoriia*, 16.) Mazon and Cocron, "La Comédie," 55n1, suggest that the handwriting in the outline is Rinhuber's.

12. Von Staden's musicians had not yet arrived but we know, from the "ballets," that the Foreign Quarter could supply some instrumentalists; given the royal family's earlier delight in accompanied songs, it seems likely that instruments would have been acquired for the premiere.

13. The annotations appear only in the bilingual Lyon source but the Russian-language play text includes the character names (Elena is renamed Gelenka). The word *mops* means a pug dog, and J. Stone, "Pastor," 240n78, points out that another interscenium character, Muischelow, can also refer to a dog. *Mop* or *mope*, in English, can also indicate a fool or clown (*OED*); see also Hilton, "Pickelhering," 135. On the role of Mops in the Russian play, see, for example, *RRD* 1:44, 102 (the listing of characters); J. Stone, "Pastor," 240. Kaplun, "Rekonstruktsiia intermedii," does not seem to be aware of these descriptive Latin annotations.

14. *RRD* 1:102.

15. The Hans Knapkäse character is summarized briefly in Cohn, *Shakespeare in Germany*, cix; Garvin, *Development*, 28; text in *Spieltexte*, 68–69.

16. Rinhuber's early time in Russia is in Dumschat, *Ausländische Mediziner*, 167, 666–667; Brikner, "Lavrentii Ringuber," 399–400; Pierling, *Saxe et Moscou*, 15–16. The Foreign Quarter, as we have seen repeatedly, was very tightly knit; Rinhuber, *Relation*, 242–243, writing in 1684, mentions that "Herr Cristof van Koken"—our reliable Moscow informant Koch, who by then had been ennobled as "von Kochen"—was a good friend, and Rinhuber knew many of the other foreigners there.

17. The departure date is given in *PDS* 4:946 (in the context of the Menzies mission), and Charykov, *Posol'stvo v Rim*, 29. On the mission, see Dukes, "Paul Menzies"; Kazakova, "A. A. Vinius."

18. On the Dresden stay, see *PDS* 4:972–976. Duke Ernst's donation to Gregorii is in Koch, "Die Sachsenkirche," 284–292, esp. 289. The donations were known to the Russian government, for they appeared in one of the petitions generated by the Foreign Quarter controversy noted earlier; Tsvetaev, "Pamiatniki," 31–32. Dates in this correspondence reflect old style.

19. Rinhuber, *Relation*, 29–30 (the letter is in FB Gotha, Chart. A 102, fols. 7r–11r, preserved in a copyist's hand). A partial Russian translation is in Brikner, "Lavrentii Ringuber," 400–401; a partial English translation is in J. Stone, "Pastor," 229n59. We thank Hans Helander and Winfried Schumacher for their advice on this translation from Latin.

20. Rinhuber, *Relation*, 51. After reaching their ultimate goal, Rome, in August, Rinhuber fell ill on the return trip back through Vienna and Dresden (Pierling, *Saxe et Moscou*, 24–25, hints that this illness was a matter of convenience), and his recovery allowed him more time to communicate with the duke. He was not with the rest of the party when they saw a comedy at Küstrin (Kosztryn) on January 4, 1674 (*PDS* 4:1067–1068), as they continued back to Russia.

21. See Pierling, *Saxe et Moscou*, 127–128, on the sources preserving this autobiographical account; on p. 129, Rinhuber characterizes Matveev as *polytropus*, suggesting an Odysseus-like slipperiness.

22. *PDS* 4:800 (the order is repeated here and on cols. 801–802); see also Charykov, *Posol'stvo v Rim*, 28–29, in the context of the theater.

23. They report their hiring failures in *PDS* 4:1074–1075.

24. Charles Cottrell, the master of ceremonies in London, reported that he took Vinius "to see the Town, our Comedies, and such other things as were remarkable"; quoted in Vinogradoff, "Russian Missions to London," 54.

25. The tsar's activities are in *Vykhody*, 562. Koch's report is in RAS, Livonica II, vol. 180: "Vorgangen sonabend wahr ich bey dem Herrn Artemon zum AbendEßen, da frug Er mier ob ich keine nachricht von Schwedische Gesanten Hette.... Den andern Tag darauf sahe er mier bey die Commedia." If we interpret Koch's "last Saturday" as referring to the Saturday a week earlier (October 19), then the performance "on the following day" would be on October 20—still an encore after the October 17 premiere. This seems less likely; although the *Vykhody* are incomplete, they can serve as a general guide, particularly when bolstered by additional evidence—they do not indicate the tsar's presence at Preobrazhenskoe at that time.

26. *Vykhody*, 563.

27. Kholodov, *Teatr i zriteli*, 33–35, citing *DR* 3:908 (November 2).

28. RAC, TKUA Rusland 73–93, Mons [Mogens] Gjøe to Conrad Biermann, Moscow, November 19, 1672: "Depuis qu'ils sont revenu du peur que les turqs les faisoit la plus grande occupation de ce premier Ministre est, à faire jouer des commoedies, jusques à s'exposer au Theatre, pour faire tenir ordre aux enfants qui jouent." (See also Forsten, "Datskie diplomaty," 119n3; Bushkovitch, "Cultural Change," 99 and n. 19.) On Biermann (1629–1698, ennobled as von Ehrenschild), see Heiberg, *Dansk biografisk lexikon*, s.v. "v. Ehrenschild, Conrad Biermann."

29. *Vykhody*, 563 (November 5 and 8, with his departure on November 14).

30. In the following series of entries from January 1673, we give the ordering and the (slightly fuller) wording in Kalachev, "Materialy," here on p. 16; we continue to give parenthetical page numbers to Bogoiavlenskii, "Moskovskii teatr," in the text. Kalachev's ordering seems to better reflect the chronology.

31. Kalachev, "Materialy," 16–17. Bogoiavlenskii, "Moskovskii teatr," v–vi, n. 1, gives a later petition by Hüfner, outlining his arrival, from Smolensk, in Moscow's Foreign Quarter, where he was to teach Latin and German to the foreign youngsters. This petition, oddly, underestimates his work in the theater, noting that he participated in the years 7183 and 7184 (September 1674 through the tsar's death in January 1676); the signature noted in the record cited here indicates that his role began earlier, in 1673. It is this petition in which Peter Engels is listed as Hüfner's brother-in-law. Later, in January 1675, Hüfner signed for requisitions, adding that he did not read Russian very well (Bogoiavlenskii, "Moskovskii teatr," 45); as Bogoiavlenskii remarks, because Hüfner ended up, in 1679, as a translator for the Ambassadorial Chancery, his Russian skills presumably improved.

32. Kalachev, "Materialy," 22.

33. Kalachev, "Materialy," 17–19.

34. Kalachev, "Materialy," 19.

35. Kalachev, "Materialy," 21–22.

36. Bogoiavlenskii, "Moskovskii teatr," viii–ix, does not believe a performance took place.

37. Bogoiavlenskii, "Moskovskii teatr," 24 (indicating that the audience took place on April 7); in *Dneval'nye zapiski*, 300, the audience is under April 6. The group stayed in a residence (the "Posol'skii dvor"), associated with Matveev's Ambassadorial Chancery and apparently located on Il'inka Street, right next to the Kremlin (see the seventeenth-century map in RGADA, f. 210, Moskovskii stol, stlb. 482, fols. 38–39; available online at http://rgada.info/geos2/zapros.php?nomer=23).

38. "Sa Majeste Zarienne tesmoigna un si grand regret de ce sinistre accident qu'il en pleura et remist la comedie et le ballet qui se devroit jouer le mesme soir" (RAC, TKUA Rusland 73–93; see also Bushkovitch, "Cultural Change," 99n19; Shcherbachev, "Iz donesenii," 35–36). The tsar's visit in the hospital or sickroom is in *Vykhody*, 575 (May 25). Based on the (incomplete) entries in this source, the tsar did not return to Preobrazhenskoe at least through the summer.

39. On the salaries, see Demidova, *Sluzhilaia biurokratiia*, esp. 124–141, but see Hellie, *Economy*, chap. 20, esp. p. 438, on the possible impact of the declining cost of rye over the century.

40. The city is now part of Ukraine. On the origins of the Meshchanskaia sloboda (and Volosheninov), see Bogoiavlenskii, *Nauchnoe nasledie*, esp. 15–18, 43.

41. The year is specified more clearly in Bessonov, "Zapisnoi raskhodnyi stolbets," 6.

42. Luther's preface to the book of Tobias is quoted in Fitzmyer, *Christological Catechism*, 31; dramatic settings are summarized in Watanabe-O'Kelly, "Early Modern Period," 103–104, 106. The neo-Latin tradition of school drama, for example by Schonaeus, also included settings of the Tobias story (as well as of Judith and Joseph, both of which were dramatized for the Russian court); see Verweij, "*Terentius Christianus* at Work." Swoboda, "Old Testament 'Apocrypha,'" notes the Apocryphal status (in the Protestant tradition) of the first three court plays, which were regarded as canonical in the Orthodox tradition. Of the three biblical stories mentioned by Luther as appropriate for theatrical renditions—Susanna, Judith, and Tobias—only Susanna was not set for the Russian court.

43. RAS, Diplomatica Muscovitica, vol. 83: "mit Jagen Comedien spielen und Balletten tantzen belustiget." The tsar's stay at Preobrazhenskoe is in *DR* 3:908. Eberschildt was in Moscow as the Swedish resident in 1662–1665 and 1667–1669 and as an envoy in 1671 and 1672–1674; Jensen and Maier, "Orpheus," 163.

44. Tikhonravov, *Russkie dramaticheskie proizvedeniia* 1:xliii also proposed *Tobit* as the second court play, produced in November 1673.

45. This distinction also supports the possibility of "ballet" performances back in late January of this same year.

46. The Tobit play is mentioned in a petition by the foreigner Iagan Paltser (Johann Pfalzer or Pfälzer?); Bogoiavlenskii, "Moskovskii teatr," 59. In his request for payment, Paltser mentions his participation in *Artakserksovo deistvo* and in the Judith and Tobit comedies; he says that he taught the young actors of *Judith* and *Tobit* in the year 7181 (the period from September 1672 through August 1673) and 7182 (September 1673 through August 1674). This time frame is thus consistent with references to performances of *Tobit* in October-November 1673 and, as we discuss later, to *Judith* in February 1674.

47. A comprehensive survey of Judith treatments is in Günther, "Das Moskauer Judithdrama," 171–195, 198–200; Günther believes the Russian play was originally written in German (p. 196; he provides a German translation on pp. 42–133). See also the discussion, with some short excerpts translated into English, in Swoboda, "Old Testament 'Apocrypha,'" 443–448, and W. Brown, *History*, 147–148. *RRD* 1:36–40 emphasizes the strong emotional shifts in the court plays.

48. Günther, "Das Moskauer Judithdrama," 166–168, discusses musical elements; Swoboda, "Old Testament 'Apocrypha,'" 446–447, translates several strophes of the final ensemble. This concluding song is set to a text based closely on the biblical song of praise in Judith 16 (*Oxford annotated Bible*, 94–95, and cf. *RRD* 1:456–458).

49. The people being transported are "Simon Arganista" (Simon Gutovskii) and his fellows, the "igretsy" (players) including Hasenkroeg and his associates, and the muzykanty.

50. *Nordischer Mercurius* ("Extraordinaires Relationes aus allerley Orten," Moscow, March 13, 1674), reporting the fire on February 25: "Dero Gemüthe in etwas darübe [*sic*] zu recriiren/ haben selbige einige Nächten darauff durch theils Teutschen Balleten/ Tantzen und von selbiger Nation Commedien spielen auch des Tages/ Leoparden/ Bähren und Wolff-Hetzen anstellen lassen."

51. *RRD* 1:475 suggests that *Judith* premiered the previous year, in February 1673, and that the February 1674 date reflects a repeat performance (although noting that other

scholars have suggested the later premiere date we propose here). In addition to the Paltser petition previously cited, another account, anonymous and dated 1686, is also consistent with our date for *Judith*. It reports that: "In the years 7181, 7182, and 7183 [i.e., September 1672 through August 1675] in Moscow at Preobrazhenskoe selo there was made a comedy" based on biblical writings (*RRD* 1:479). It then describes the Judith play and, more briefly, the Esther play. Here again, the dates provide no reason to propose an early performance period for *Judith*; as in Paltser's petition, the chronology fits the ordering in the published payment records. Perhaps the survival of a complete manuscript for *Judith*, as opposed to the disappearance of *Tobit*, encouraged scholars to propose the early date for the Judith play.

52. The cast list is in RGADA, f. 139, op. 1, No. 32. Luka (Luchka) Stepanov (playing the role of Iosiia) and Nikolai Ivanov (playing Korei) appear among the twenty-six Meshchanskaia Quarter actors from the summer of 1673 (Bogoiavlenskii, "Moskovskii teatr," 26–27) but the names are very common. Oddly enough, the characters Judith and Nebuchadnezzar (the latter opens the play) are at the very end of the list, with no actors' names attached. The instructor was Ivan Volosheninov, of the Meshchanskaia Quarter (Bogoiavlenskii, "Moskovskii teatr," 51, 61), although we have no evidence to attribute the cast list to him.

53. Waldonn's death is in RGADA, f. 150, op. 1, 1672, No. 1, fol. 132.

54. Sazonova, "Teatral'naia programma," esp. 136–137; Kholodov, *Teatr i zriteli*, 45, on Trubetskoi's likely attendance at the October premiere of *Artakserksovo deistvo*. *Aleksei* is preserved in a manuscript text and in an abbreviated program printed in Kiev (February 1674), most likely for the intended performance the previous year by students at the Academy. The play text is in Tikhonravov, *Russkie dramaticheskie proizvedeniia* 1:3–75.

55. Another event at court seems to reflect the entertainments cultivated so vigorously that fall. On October 21, 1674, the tsar gathered his advisers (including his confessor, Archpriest Andrei Savinovich, but not Matveev) for an informal gathering at the Poteshnye khoromy, where they were entertained by a variety of musical instruments: a foreigner played the organ, and surny, trumpets, and percussion sounded out (*DR* 3:1080–1081).

56. RAC, TKUA Rusland 73–93: "Sa Mayesté Zarique avec la cour continue encore son sejour hors d'icy à une maison appellée Pria Brazenza, ou elle passe son temps à voir les Balets et comedies, que les Estrangers s'ingenuent à contrefaire le mieux qu'ils peuvent pour la divertir"; also summarized in Bushkovitch, "Cultural Change," 99n19.

57. *Dneval'nye zapiski*, 314. *Vykhody*, 587, dates the family's departure from Moscow to Preobrazhenskoe on October 25; as we see in our discussion, they stayed there (or in the immediate environs) for many days.

58. This is the Nativity, or Philipian, fast—again, the theatrical performances fit into the liturgical calendar (see, for example, Kholodov, *Teatr i zriteli*, 34–35). Performances of the liturgical drama *The Play of the Furnace* had been tied to the Sunday of the Forefathers (generally two Sundays before Christmas), so although this drama was no longer being performed, there was a tradition of performed representations around Advent.

59. RAS, Livonica II, vol. 181, Koch to "Herrn Willm de Friehs" in Amsterdam, headed "Moskau den 17. November Anno 1674." The report continues: "Ihr Zaars Maytt. und der gantze Hoff, befinden sich noch zu Prijobrazenska, da selbsten Sie sich dieser Tagen und vor der eingetroffenen fastern, Comoedien spielen und Balletten tantzen laßen, worauß sie solchen guten Genügen geschöpffet, den order gegeben werden solle, einen guten Tantzmeister und Comoedianten herein zu verschreiben, welche[r] die Knaben weiter perfectioniren und unterrichten solle, in ob erwehnte Baletten ist unteranderm auch ein Liefflandisch undt Zwar Ehstnisch pawertantz repræsentiret worden."

60. Hesse to Joachim Scultetus, from Moscow, published in Hirsch, "Brandenburg," 292–293. Hesse accompanied Scultetus to Russia in 1673 and remained there to study Russian.

61. Bogoiavlenskii, "Moskovskii teatr," 37–40 (the records are not in chronological order on these pages). The players are listed on p. 37, and the cast list is in Mazon and Cocron, "La Comédie," 55.

62. These entries are discussed in Kholodov, *Teatr i zriteli*, 33–35; he suggests that they were recorded slightly after the fact. They are all entered following a reference dated December 8 (*DR* 3:1130–1132), but they give no month or date, noting simply "in that same year" ("togo zh godu"), which is uncharacteristic; at the end of this series, the next specific date is December 9 (*DR* 3:1132). The *Vykhody*, 587, are incomplete but the entry for November 8 puts the tsar at Preobrazhenskoe (and at another nearby location, the village of Pokrovskoe); after a gap, entries resume on November 21, when the tsar is at Preobrazhenskoe.

63. *DR* 3:1131 (ellipses in the published source).

64. Translations from Hughes, *Sophia*, xii (although she renders *striapchii* as *crown agent*). The *stirruper*, like *table attendant*, is a ceremonial title preserving a relic of previous duties; see P. Brown, "How Muscovy Governed," esp. 506; Crummey, *Aristocrats*, 21–22.

65. *DR* 3:1131–1132.

66. *DR* 3:1132.

67. *PDS* 4:1190–1191. The opera had three acts, so perhaps the description refers to three separate sections covering the action. The mission returned to Moscow in March 1675; the fate of these "books" is unknown.

68. *PDS* 4:1192; the Viennese account is in HHStA, Zeremonialakten, "Ankunft und Audienzen der russichen Gesandtschaft in Wien" (November 3, 1674; this corresponds to the October 24 date given in the Russian account), fol. 4v: "Sonst aber Sÿe gleich des andern Tags nach Ihrer ankhunfft, zu einer beÿ Hoff gehaltenen Comoedia eingeladen worden, und derselben beÿgewohnt, darüber Sÿe grosstes Wollgefallen erzeigt. Im übrigen hat die StadtGuardia beÿ dieser Audienz mit 3. fähndl auff dem Burgplatz auffgewarth." The work is discussed in Goloubeva, *Glorification of Leopold I*, 112–113, and Noe, *Nicolò Minato*, 81–83 (he does not include this third performance).

69. *PDS* 4:1192. Another impressive element was the extraordinary guard posted at the theater, due to the presence of the royal family (as mentioned in the Vienna account); this appears in several newspaper reports, including the *Nordischer Mercurius* ("Die 37. Extraordinarie Relation Von Allerley Orten," 1674, fol. 290) and the Paris *Gazette* (December 1, 1674, dateline Vienna, November 9).

70. Koch had indicated the previous fall that the organizers were looking for a dance teacher; no name is given at this point, however.

71. Performance date in *DR* 3:1224; no play is named but the context in the theatrical payment records makes it certain that this is the new comedy on the Tamerlane story; see chapter 5 of this volume.

72. The only surviving seventeenth-century copies of *Joseph* and *Adam and Eve* belong to a collection of manuscripts acquired by the scholar J. G. Sparwenfeld, now kept in the city library of Västerås, Sweden (SBV, Codex AD 10; see Dahl, *Codex AD 10*, esp. 114–125); both plays are preserved only partially. The Sparwenfeld manuscripts were apparently made around 1685. In the nineteenth century, both plays were copied directly from the Sparwenfeld sources at the initiative of Count J. P. van Suchtelen (now in RNB, F.XIV.6), and published by Tikhonravov, *Russkie dramaticheskie proizvedeniia* 1:243–269 (*Adam and Eve*) and 270–295 (*Joseph*). Three theses relating to the seventeenth-century texts were written at

Uppsala University: Borg, "En komedi"; Pontoppidan-Sjövall, "En Josef-komedi" (both in the 1940s); and Watson, "Žalobnaja komedija" (2005).

73. Bogoiavlenskii, "Moskovskii teatr," 37 (fall 1674), a group headed by Ivashka Ivanov; for 1675 (pp. 59–63), they numbered seventy, also including one Ivashka Ivanov, the ultimate in generic Russian names (although the name appears in 1674 and 1675 as the group leader). These 1675 listings also include Timoshka Blisev, a less generic name appearing a few months later (January 1676), so in this case, it seems less risky to assume that the same person appeared in both performance settings.

74. This location is on the seventeenth-century map in RGADA, f. 210, Moskovskii stol, stlb. 482, fols. 38–39 (available online); see also Kochegarov, "K istorii," 21. David (or Davyd) Mikolaev was a well-known Dutch merchant, mentioned frequently in the Russian sources (for example, *Vesti-Kuranty* III:87 and passim).

75. Starikova, "K istorii," esp. 57. Repskii's name does not appear in the documents published by Bogoiavlenskii. Another "diplomatic" connection is the reference to the pod'iachii Mikhail Belianinov and nine additional participants from the Ambassadorial Chancery, mentioned in the context of these rehearsals (p. 51); Belianinov is named in connection with the Joseph comedy (see later in our discussion). There is another familiar name, Peter Sievers, who was involved in ordering theatrical goods; he had taken part in the February 1672 "ballet" (Bogoiavlenskii, "Moskovskii teatr," 53, 55–56, 61).

76. The total number of 133 (63 from the Foreign Quarter group and 70 from the Meshchanskaia Quarter group) is verified in a payment request for the bulk purchase of red and green stockings for the players (Bogoiavlenskii, "Moskovskii teatr," 52).

77. On the younger Blumentrost's medical career, see Dumschat, *Ausländische Mediziner*, 572; he was sent abroad to study medicine only in 1680, and he later worked with his father. Rinhuber was appointed as a doctor at Moscow's Apothecary in late 1675 (Dumschat, *Ausländische Mediziner*, 667).

78. This may help explain Rinhuber's reference to the court plays in his memoirs—if he had been involved with the court theater again in 1675, we understand why he mentioned it in this later writing, from around 1679.

79. The artists (*zhivopistsy*) were headed by Andrei Avvakumov (or Abakumov), who may be identified with another known artist at court (see *Slovar' russkikh ikonopistsev*, s.v. "Abakumov, Andrei"); he appears at several points in the payment records (Bogoiavlenskii, "Moskovskii teatr," 15 (as "Abakumov"), 51, 53, 65–66). He and the other artists also worked on props for *Joseph*.

80. *RRD* 2:20–21; *Slovar' knizhnikov* 2:328.

81. Derzhavina, "U istokov," esp. 100, 102. The cast changes from biblical figures (Adam, Eve, angels, etc.) to the school drama or mystery play characters (Truth, Peace, and others, including also God the Father and God the Son).

82. *RRD* 2:124–126; this passage is identified in Günther, "Neue deutsche Quellen," 671–672. See also Jensen, *Musical Cultures*, 200–202, with a summary of the extensive literature about "Adam's Lament" on p. 252n6.

83. *RRD* 2:310; Derzhavina, "U istokov," 103.

84. Shamin, "O nesushchestvovavshikh teatral'nykh postanovkakh," 477.

85. The translator, Ivan Enak or Enakov, had had earlier contact with the theater, when he was sent by Matveev to request the use of a private house for rehearsals; Bogoiavlenskii, "Moskovskii teatr," 46, 63. On Enak, see also Beliakov, *Sluzhashchie*, 300. There is no evidence that Lima was associated with any earlier productions, specifically, with the earlier "ballets" (as in Pivovarova, *Istoriia*, 16).

86. The mission is described briefly in Bantysh-Kamenskii, *Obzor* 1:25–26; Brikner, "Lavrentii Ringuber," 408. The Russian account is in *PDS* 5:1–406.

87. Lyseck, *Relatio*, 118–119; a Russian translation is in [Lyseck], "Skazanie Adol'fa Lizeka," 391–392, where *gesticulator* is rendered as "rope walker" (*balanser*). The meaning seems to be similar to *Taschenspieler* used in the Koch account cited later in our discussion, that is, a conjuror or trickster. Our translation is based on the Latin original (the Russian translation is inaccurate in this section); our thanks to Hans Helander, Winfried Schumacher, and Marianne Wifstrand Schiebe for their help on this difficult passage.

88. RAS, Livonica II, vol. 181: "den andern Tag nach ihrer Abreise, wart Oberster Minesius und Translator Meysner von den H. Ertemon ihnen nachgesant und einen Taschen Spieler der vor Laquay dienete auff 14 Tagen vor ihrer Zar. Maytt. zu spielen, alhier zu laßen, welches H. Bottoni bewilligt, den erwenthen Taschen Spieler und noch ein Laquey, der ein Musicant ist, wieder zu rücke gesant; zu künfftigen Sonabend soll eine Commedie von Knaben vor I. Z. Mt. gespielet werden, alß den der Taschen Spieler seine poßen auch machen soll." "Next Saturday" could mean either the Saturday after he wrote this (November 6), or the following Saturday (November 13); there were performances over this entire period.

89. The replacements, Jan (Janus) Branten (Kraltsen) and Maksimilian Markus (Kreiken), appear in Russian documents beginning in November 1675 (Bogoiavlenskii, "Moskovskii teatr," 62–63).

90. Ackermann's dispatch home, on February 25, 1676, is in RGADA, f. 150, op. 1, 1672, No. 1, fol. 170.

91. Bogoiavlenskii, "Moskovskii teatr," 70 (two experienced participants, Zhuravlev, from the Galitskaia Department, and Meshalkin, from the Vladimirskaia Department; a third employee, Ivan Vladislavlev, from the Ambassadorial Chancery, who headed a group of nine, also participated; on Vladislavlev, see Demidova, *Sluzhilaia biurokratiia: Spravochnik*, 115).

92. The prop weaponry for the Goliath play is in Bogoiavlenskii, "Moskovskii teatr," 75; it includes, among the spears or lances and three broadswords, a reference to "8 boletov." Although Bogoiavlenskii (p. xv) appears to equate this with the dancers (thus, as *balety*), we are not convinced; the term may be a misreading for *bulat*, a sword.

93. See *Slovar' knizhnikov* 4:229–232; a brief biographical summary is in Lukichev, "S. F. Chizhinskii."

94. The *Judith* references are in *RRD* 1:448; these figures are highlighted in Kaplun, "Personozhi-shuty," 64. Sazonova, *Literaturnaia kul'tura*, 138–145, esp. 144, notes that Venus, Cupid, and Bacchus do not appear in Simeon Polotskii's Moscow work, although other mythological figures do. Chizhinskii, of course, would not have been the only possible source for such knowledge; see chapter 3 in this volume, for example, on Spafarii.

95. [Coyett], *Posol'stvo*, 113 (Dutch text)/404 (Russian translation), mentions seeing a depiction of the David and Goliath story decorating the walls at his reception at the tsar's court. A brief description, in English, of the decorations at the Faceted Palace is in Bushkovitch, *Peter the Great*, 18–19.

96. The word *bordachnik* has an alcoholic flavor about it, deriving from *barda*, which refers to the dregs remaining after the distillation process (Dal', *Tolkovyi slovar'*, s.v. "barda").

97. Both reports are in RAC, TKUA Rusland 73–93; the February report is published in Shcherbachev, "Iz donesenii," 38–40.

98. The dates here are according to the old style, although the published account gives dates in the new style. The first audience (January 17/27) is in [Coyett], *Posol'stvo*, 109/399; the second audience (January 19/29) is on pp. 123/415.

99. On the tsar's health, see [Coyett], *Posol'stvo*, 136–137/430; on other performances by the young page, see pp. 129–130/422. The young page was Solomon Verbeek, described as someone who "zeer wel op Staafjes kon spelen" (pp. 31/303). Some form of the word *staafspel*—a set of chimes or a small carillon (Bouterse, "Van Bolhuis Auction," 21)—is used throughout, as Solomon's skill attracted attention during the party's journey from Arkhangel'sk to Moscow, and then, as described here, at the court itself ([Coyett], *Posol'stvo*, 70–71/353; 78–79/362; 80/364; 88/374; 123/415).

100. [Coyett], *Posol'stvo*, 136–137/430; Solomon gave another performance, after the tsar's death, for the family of Prince Iu. A. Dolgorukii (pp. 213/517–518).

101. Bogoiavlenskii, "Moskovskii teatr," xvi (his suggested performance dates, implying that the larger group of tailors was paid for their preparatory work, January 15 through 22, and that the smaller group was paid for the time they were actually at the performance, on the two days, i.e., January 23 and 24); the tailors' petition is on p. 75.

102. Quoted and translated in Bushkovitch, *Peter the Great*, 87 (we rely here on his discussion on pp. 79–89); cf. Bushkovitch, "Cultural Change," 99. The source is RAC, TKUA Rusland 73–93.

103. Zamyslovskii, *Tsarstvovanie Fedora Alekseevicha*, Prilozheniia iv, No. 2 (IRLI, f. 166, op. 6, No. 53; we thank Kirill Khudin for information on this source). The order calls for the "organy, i prekspektivy [sic], i vsiakie komidiinye pripasy" to be moved; the term *organy* here may refer to an actual organ (Hasenkroeg's, presumably) or to musical instruments in general. Roizman, *Organ*, 75, notes the location of Gutovskii's workshop.

104. For example, the d'iaki Bobinin (Bogoiavlenskii, "Moskovskii teatr," 48, 59, 63) and Ukraintsev (pp. 54, 56, 59).

105. In *Gusl' dobroglasnaia* (The beautiful-sounding psaltery); see *RRD* 1:79–80; Kudriavtsev, *"Artakserksovo deistvo,"* 39. On Fedor's library, see Waugh, "Library," 307–308; his musical manuscripts are described in Protopopov, "Notnaia biblioteka."

106. Ellersieck, "Russia under Aleksei Mikhailovich," 273.

107. Translation (slightly modified) from Uspensky, "Schism," 127; the Old Believer account is discussed in Bubnov and Demkova, "Vnov' naidennoe poslanie," with this passage on p. 143. A survey of Avvakum's life and writings is in Morris, *DLB* 150, s.v. "Archpriest Avvakum (Petrovich)."

108. The widely cited Moryson and Paumgartner accounts are quoted from Katri(t)zky, "Pickelhering and Hamlet," 113, 117.

109. Uspensky, "Schism," 127.

110. Quoted in Brandt and Hogendoorn, *German and Dutch Theatre*, 421 (from the 1740 edition).

111. *RRD* 1:29–41, for example, considers the plays broadly, looking at their overall thematic concerns and structural continuities: formal rejoicing at the conclusions of plays and the overall sense of harmonious endings, the care exhibited by the ruler for the ruled, the importance of dress and feasts, the juxtaposition of dramatic elements, and so forth.

112. We do know that Klifman, who played the role of Haman in the premiere and in the fall of 1674, also played one of the roles in the interscenia at the premiere (as the soldier). However, we cannot conclude that the interscenia roles or subjects necessarily continued in this later performance. The Western traditions of comic insertions are on display in the 1620 German collection of English plays referred to previously. For example, in the German version of the Esther play, the extended comic actions of Hans Knapkäse and his wife generally appear between acts. This collection also has a series of separate Pickleherring actions. (We note, however, that overall the text and cast requirements for the 1620 German play are quite

different from those for the Russian play; see our forthcoming "Authorship, Influence, and Intertheater: The Origins of Gregorii's *Artakserksovo deistvo*.")

113. Susakim appears in act 1, scene 2 (with other soldiers of Nebuchadnezzar; this is the comic interlude of the first act); act 2, scene 3 (more horseplay among the same soldiers); act 3, scene 2 (other soldiers, urged on by Holofernes); act 3, scene 4 (the main action of the play, with some noncomic characters, as in act 3, scene 2; they take Achior away at Holofernes's order, and the mezhdosenie lament occurs immediately after this low point); act 5, scene 2 (including the drinking song with the soldiers; the Israelite soldier Vaneia interrupts); act 5, scene 4 (they haul him away and threaten him); and act 6, scene 5 (Susakim reflects on his adventures; his temporary decapitation).

114. Many earlier scholars discussed the Susakim character in the context of Western stage clowns; see Tikhonravov, *Russkie dramaticheskie proizvedeniia* 1:esp. xx–xxii; Morozov, *Ocherki*, 167–169; Findeizen, *Ocherki* 1:xxxi, n. 389. Western studies include Günther, "Das Moskauer Judithdrama," esp. 155–157, and J. Alexander, "Will Kemp," 470 and n. 37, citing Wesselofsky, *Deutsche Einflüsse*. The food connections in general are widely discussed, for example, J. Alexander, "Ridentum dicere verum," 754; the same author's "Language"; Katritzky, "A Plague o' These Pickle Herring."

115. Morozov, *Ocherki*, 169, also notes the foxtail association with the Western Hanswurst character, and J. Alexander, "Ridentum dicere verum," 759, mentions the use of a *Fuchsschwanz* in connection with the related character Jean Potage. Stříbrný, *Shakespeare and Eastern Europe*, 18, cites a 1621 illustration in which Pickleherring wears a cap "decorated with a fox brush as a sign of his cunning" (reproduced on p. xiv; see also Asper, *Hanswurst*, image 1). The double meaning of *Fuchsschwanz* ("foxtail" and "a type of a saw that is shaped like a foxtail") may have been intentional, as such wordplay is strongly associated with the Pickleherring character (for example, J. Alexander, "Language").

116. For example, in a German-language setting of *Romeo and Juliet*, probably from the 1620s, the character "Pickl Häring" appears throughout, addressing the audience directly at the end of act 1 (Cohn, *Shakespeare in Germany*, 330, cxxiii–cxxiv); see also Lande, *Persistence of Folly*, esp. chap. 3. W. Brown, *History*, 148, translates the monologue in which Susakim wonders if he is still alive, even calling Susakim the play's Pickleherring.

117. *RRD* 1:43, 450–451; Morozov, *Ocherki*, 169.

118. Although it reflects different performance traditions, the play *Aleksei, Man of God* has the same structure, with two comic scenes written into the drama, labeled "Intermedium, ili smekh" (literally, "laughter") in the printed program; Sazonova, "Teatral'naia programma," 147.

119. Of course, separate interscenia might have been lost precisely because they were separate. After all, we would not have known much about the structure of *Artakserksovo deistvo* without the annotations in the Lyon source.

120. Vroon, "From Liturgy to Literature," 124; on the liturgical use of such texts (a question far beyond the bounds of the present study), see, for example, Sazonova, "Pravoslavnaia liturgiia." Declamations could be quite elaborate, such as those performed at Izmailovo during Fedor's reign; see Topychkanov, *Povsednevnaia zhizn'*.

121. The reference by the Carlisle mission to a performance in Vologda in the 1660s is quite late, as noted in chapter 2 of this volume. The production's heyday was through the 1640s; see the summary and bibliography in Stennikova, "Tserkovno-teatralizovannye deistva," chap. 2.

122. The play was first published in *DRV* 8:158–169 (all references are to the second edition unless otherwise noted); the epilogue labels the work as a "comic action," in the broader sense of the term *komediia* we have seen throughout: "komidiinoe sie delo nashe" (p. 168; the

text preserved in Simeon's own *Rifmologion* (Rhyme book) collection is published in *RRD* 2:161–171, here 171.

123. "Певцы поют, и будет Intermedium" (*RRD* 2:144). The publication of *Prodigal Son* in vol. 8 of *DRV* (second edition) includes the "directorial" annotations, whereas they are lacking in the text of the play copied for Johan Gabriel Sparwenfeld during his stay in Russia in the mid-1680s (the source is discussed previously in this chapter; on Sparwenfeld's access to the material, see chap. 6 of this volume). Presumably a missing protograph included these annotations. For a discussion of these complex source relationships, see *RRD* 2:esp. 313–318, which classifies the sources for Simeon's *Prodigal Son* into two basic textual groups.

124. Bogoiavlenskii, "Moskovskii teatr," 37, payment to the same foreigner who had bound the other play books (pp. 38, 66).

125. See the variants in Bogoiavlenskii, "Moskovskii teatr," 37, 66; *DR* 3:1131.

126. These two play texts, in addition to Simeon's *Prodigal Son*, appear in vol. 8 of the second, greatly enlarged, edition of *DRV* (1789), where the title is on p. 187; see further in chapter 6.

127. Certainly, as a highly influential teacher and writer, Simeon would have been aware of the court's interest in the theatrical productions. However, the only link between Simeon and Tsar Aleksei's court theater appears to be Simeon's contact with Vasilii Repskii (the unwilling instrumentalist), although their direct interaction was from an earlier time, before the establishment of the court theater, when Repskii was assigned to study with Simeon. Nevertheless, Simeon's testimony in Repskii's later case against Matveev (after Tsar Aleksei's death) suggests he would have known about Repskii's sad theatrical experiences.

5

The Play of Tamerlane

When Tsar Aleksei Mikhailovich sat down on February 11, 1675, to watch the newest offering in his theater, he might have anticipated something special. The subject matter would probably not have been a complete surprise, as it seems unlikely that the very different theme of this newest play would have been undertaken without some consultation with the prime audience member. The play was on the epic story of the confrontation between the Central Asian ruler Tamerlane (called Temir-Aksak in the Russian play) and the Ottoman sultan Bayezid I (Baiazet in the play), near Ankara in 1402, during which Tamerlane humiliated his defeated foe by placing him in a cage and parading him throughout the countryside, as some accounts describe. The Russian play was called *Temir-Aksakovo deistvo*, the Play of Tamerlane.[1]

Tamerlane was the first of the full-length Russian court plays that was not based on a biblical theme. The departure in subject matter apparently met with approval, as another secular play, on Bacchus and Venus, was in production a year later, in January 1676. It was also the first Russian play to have a clear context in contemporary events. True, the first play, *Artakserksovo deistvo*, had obvious parallels to the domestic situation at the Russian court, with its portrayal of a new and young wife, a wise adviser, and a king willing to take advice but fully and forcefully in charge. But *Tamerlane* was different, for it reflected ongoing political and military concerns of the Russian court. Throughout the early 1670s, the Orthodox tsar had been looked on to defend the Christian populace in the continuing conflicts with the Muslim forces of the Turks and Tatars. As we have seen in previous chapters, the shadow of this struggle had hovered consistently over the theater. So, although we cannot point to a specific event that triggered this choice of topic, it reflected ongoing encounters that were transmitted widely in news summaries and other sources and were of continuing concern at the highest levels of the tsar's government.[2]

The Tamerlane play offers a wealth of material regarding intercultural theatrical traditions, tapping into rich streams of Russian and Western renditions of the story in images, literary and historical writing, and staged performances. The historian A. T. Parfenov made insightful observations about the use of borrowed source material in this play. A close examination of how the story fits into its late seventeenth-century Russian context—how it was transmitted, how the playwrights knew about it, and how they rendered the events and characters—helps identify the borrowed sources more precisely and indicates how they reflect the drama's creative milieu. Taking a wider view of the Tamerlane story as a play topic also leads to some tentative conclusions about the work's ties to the repertoire of the traveling players on the Continent. Such influence is particularly prominent in *Tamerlane*, as the play employs two typical German comic characters: Pickleherring (Pikel'gering) and Tölpel (Telpel), who are named in the text and perform their characteristically disruptive roles with gusto. Before considering the play through these overlapping contextual layers, we begin with a short synopsis and a discussion of the preparations for its premiere.

Like the other surviving plays for the court theater, *Temir-Aksakovo deistvo* begins with a prologue addressed directly to the tsar and expressing grateful praise and humility. This prologue focuses on the range of emotions the play evokes—piety, sadness, comedy—and the useful things one might learn from such a presentation, which recalls important happenings from the past. By praising historians' portrayals of these events, the prologue anticipates the play's emphasis on history and the learned historian and then concludes by reassuring the audience that everything will come out as it should: evil is vanquished and good prevails.[3]

Act 1, scene 1, is a kind of supplementary prologue that opens, literally, with a bang: Mars appears on stage to set the proper military mood with a short, raging statement (he is directed to speak "with fury"), and the scene ends with a "great fanfare" of trumpets.[4] The main action begins in the second scene, when we meet Tamerlane, just awakening from a disturbing dream. He describes it in detail and asks for an interpretation; Aksalla, his trusted adviser, tells him that it must portend a victory. Immediately thereafter, a messenger enters with a plea from the Byzantine emperor Paleologue, asking for help in defending Constantinople from the armies of the Ottoman sultan Baiazet. The meaning of the dream is clear, and Tamerlane dispatches a cease-and-desist message to the sultan.

Scene 3 switches to Baiazet's camp, where we hear, not for the last time, the leader's exaggerated views of himself and his power, echoed by his entourage. They receive Tamerlane's memo, react furiously, and send their own messengers to communicate this displeasure to the opposing camp. Scene 4 shows the sultan's messengers in Tamerlane's headquarters, where they are treated with respect; the leader resolves to call up the troops.

The final scene in act 1 is a long comic excursus that is related, in its characters and setting, to the main action of the play. Two of Tamerlane's soldiers, with the obviously Western names Leonardius and Valerio, intercept a man going to Constantinople with what he claims is food and drink. The soldiers challenge him, taking the "food," which they discover to be money. The messenger admits that he has been sent to deliver a note from Baiazet, ordering Emperor Paleologue to be killed. The soldiers react—naturally enough in such a scenario—by chopping off the traveler's head. As they discuss this turn of events, Pickleherring appears and steals (or consumes) everything, frightening the soldiers. The scene ends in a general melee.

Act 2 resumes the back-and-forth between the two opposing camps as they plan their attacks, opening with Tamerlane's reckoning of his forces. It is interrupted, in scene 2, by another soldier-themed comic interlude: Tamerlane's men, who have been paid in advance (another mark of an honorable leader), are eager to spend their money on a feast. A drinking song is performed by a cup-wielding soldier (no notated music survives, nor is there any indication that there ever was any; the rhyming text, however, is labeled "song"). The revelry is interrupted by another obviously Western comic character, Telpel, who appears immediately after the song. He asks the soldiers if he might join their ranks and they answer with a series of mocking questions, to which he responds fully in character, with ignorant and foolish answers. The predictable result is more physical violence. When the main action resumes, Tamerlane is reviewing his troops and ascertaining the whereabouts of the enemy forces (scene 3),[5] Baiazet is reveling in his upcoming victory (scene 4), and Tamerlane, in an exchange with the captured Pasha (Baiazet's messenger and brother), warns that he is sent by God to humble the proud. Tamerlane supplies Pasha with a horse and sends him back, respectfully, to the opposing camp.

The third and final act begins in Baiazet's camp, as he receives Pasha with his message from Tamerlane, realizes the strength of his opponent, and reacts in fear. Meanwhile, Tamerlane, on his knees in prayer, prepares for the battle. The battle scene itself takes place onstage in the second scene, with a frenzy of shouted turmoil from the young, presumably very enthusiastic, male actors, from which it emerges that Baiazet is captured and taken to Tamerlane as a prisoner. In their first face-to-face exchange, Tamerlane asks what Baiazet would have done had the situation been reversed. The captive replies that if he had taken Tamerlane prisoner, he would have thrown him into a cage and paraded him around in it, and he would have fed him with scraps from his table and used him as a mounting block. Fine, replies Tamerlane, it will be as you say.

In the final scene (act 3, scene 3), we see the realization of this punishment. Baiazet appears onstage in his cage, and his humiliation is enhanced by the involvement of his wife, Milka, who is ordered to entertain Tamerlane and his men at their victory banquet. Baiazet, in torment, kills himself by bashing his head against the bars of the cage. Tamerlane intones the concluding moral: this is what happens in the face of overweening pride. The play concludes with a jubilation, thanking God and offering a final praise of the tsar.

The play, although short and compact, was thus fairly elaborate. There were more than a dozen characters representing the two main camps, along with almost the same number of characters for the two comic scenes, and probably around the same number of extras for the battle scene and to fill out some of the other action. (Some of these roles, of course, may have been doubled.) As in the longer Judith play that directly preceded it, the comic scenes in Tamerlane were loosely integrated into the main storyline, although they would have seemed more prominent given its shorter length.[6]

It is difficult to establish exactly when planning for this play began or even who the author was. The surviving payment records begin in late January 1675 and indicate that a great deal of work had been accomplished by that point. Pastor Gregorii, author of the earlier court plays, died on February 16, 1675, about a week after the first recorded performance, but his role in the preparations or in this performance is unknown. The play is generally attributed to Georg Hüfner, who had worked with Gregorii previously and who was the point-person for theatrical planning throughout the remainder of 1675.[7] At the premiere, the court record says that the comedy was also given with "various performances" by "foreigners" and "Matveev's people."[8]

Hüfner signed a detailed listing of the costumes, props, and other items needed for the Tamerlane play that was issued between January 23 and 25, 1675 (pp. 41–45).[9] Although the production used less costly fabrics than for the Esther play (p. xi), the preparations were nevertheless impressive. Fabrics with glittering thread were ordered for the leaders' attire and richly colored cloth was required for other costumes, including a beautiful skirt for Baiazet's wife, along with decorative ribbons, lace, stockings, hats, buttons, and thread in an array of colors and styles. The young actors wielded suitable prop weaponry, including shields and swords ornamented with silver and gold, in addition to pennants, sabers, bows, and arrows. Black and white sheepskin was purchased, presumably to construct appropriate beards and wigs. There was food for the banquet, drinking glasses to hold aloft, and a variety of prop missives to pass back and forth. The most famous prop of all, Baiazet's cage (*kletka*), was listed, along with other supplies: candles, nails, paint, and frames (*ramy*) for the organ, all of which was transported to Moscow (thus to the Apothecary venue). There were dancers in at least one of the comic scenes and perhaps for the final banquet. Hüfner signed for multicolored clothing for them: tunics, trousers, stockings, and hats (pp. 44–45).

Following this performance in February 1675, the next documented production of *Tamerlane* was in the six-play festival held in the fall of that year. One detail speaks to the activities of the actors over this initial period: Matveev had requisitioned for rehearsals a house in the Foreign Quarter owned by a Danish merchant identified as "Vinont Liudden," who then in April petitioned for damages, claiming that the young people "ruined the stove, and the window frames were completely destroyed" (pp. 45–47).[10] It is hard to resist the notion that the damage occurred during overenthusiastic rehearsals of the battle scene (although the brawls concluding the comic interludes would also be good candidates for such destruction). This was the second rehearsal space to have suffered this fate: the school in Gregorii's house in the Foreign Quarter, especially the windows, had also been damaged by the youngsters (pp. xi, 28). For the six-play festival in November and early December 1675, some repairs were required for the *Tamerlane* production, including for the wooden weaponry, which was evidently well used (p. 54). The fall rehearsals for *Tamerlane* were at the Posol'skii dvor venue associated with the Ambassadorial Chancery, where seventy players prepared *Tamerlane*, *Joseph*, and the lost George (Eorgiev) play.

LITERARY LANDSCAPES FOR THE RUSSIAN *TAMERLANE*

Two in-depth articles have been written about the court Tamerlane play, taking what appear to be completely opposing views of the work and its origins.[11] The earliest is by A. S. Bulgakov (1928), whose point of departure seems perfectly logical—even obvious—to anyone with only a passing knowledge of theater. In the Russian play, Baiazet brains himself against the bars of his cage in his desperation and humiliation; the same action is in Christopher Marlowe's *Tamburlaine the Great Part 1*. And, although Bulgakov does not emphasize this, Baiazet's gruesome end does not appear in other seventeenth-century plays on this theme. Thus, in addition to careful discussions of the scenic action, Bulgakov's efforts are devoted to finding similarities between the Russian play and Marlowe's. The later study of the Russian play, by A. T. Parfenov (1969), takes a very different approach, although one that is also based on contemporary Western models.[12] Parfenov, with real insight, took seriously the reference in the prologue to the learned historian. He thus considers published historical works that the Moscow playwrights might have used, focusing on Jean Du Bec's *Histoire du grand empereur Tamerlan* (1595), which circulated widely throughout the seventeenth century in multiple translations and editions. Parfenov also looks at Russian chronicles and their treatment of the historical Tamerlane. His insights, particularly about Du Bec's history, were persuasive and his use of the Western historical tradition was impressive. Yet there is still more to be uncovered about the source history of the Russian *Tamerlane*. Only by combining the contributions of both scholars can we unfold the multiple contexts of this play, starting with an examination of Parfenov's approach and then taking up Bulgakov's more speculative focus on Marlowe.

As Parfenov observed, the Russian chronicle tradition relating to Tamerlane is largely focused on the miracle-working icon of the Vladimir Mother of God, which caused the invader to turn away from a planned assault on Russia in 1395. The heading in the sixteenth-century Nikon Chronicle says it all: "a tale of a most glorious miracle worked by the icon of the Most Holy Theotokos, which is called 'Vladimir' ... which was brought from the town of Vladimir to the God-loving town of Moscow [threatened with an] invasion of the impious tsar Temir Aksak."[13] Tamerlane's later encounter with the Ottoman sultan Bayezid, in 1402 near Ankara, receives less attention in the Russian sources, although their battle and Bayezid's confinement in the cage are depicted in a sixteenth-century illustrated chronicle (fig. 5.1). However, as Parfenov notes, the treatment of the Tamerlane figure in the court play is very different from that in the chronicle accounts: in the play, Tamerlane, who in fact was Muslim, is not just a hero but a wholly Christian hero, coming to the rescue of Emperor Paleologue to save Constantinople from the Ottoman threat. How and why, Parfenov asks, does this change in the interpretation of the historical Tamerlane take place?

This question leads Parfenov to a consideration of Western histories of Tamerlane, where one can trace this transformation. This changing image might be observed, surprisingly, in the title page of the first published edition of Marlowe's play (1590), in which the character is hardly depicted as a humble Christian hero. Here, as literary historian Kirk Melnikoff emphasizes, publisher Richard Jones describes Tamburlaine as "a most puissant and mightye Monarque." Melnikoff concludes that "Jones's marketing of Marlowe's plays ... should be seen not simply as a consequence of Tamburlaine's revised reputation at the end of the sixteenth century but also, given [the play's] popularity, as ultimately a contributing element [to this revision]."[14] One of the earliest Western sources to present this positive, even heroic, view of Tamerlane is the long narrative history by the cleric and historian Jean Du Bec (d. 1610), first published in Rouen in 1595 and quickly reissued and translated into several languages; the work ultimately appeared in over a dozen editions before the composition of the Russian play, in the original French as well as in English, German, and Dutch translations. Du Bec's approach to Tamerlane was taken up widely. A London procession written by Thomas Middleton, "The Triumphs of Integrity" (1623), featured a series of constructions honoring heroes who had risen from humble beginnings, culminating with "the great victor Tamburlain."[15] The image of the noble Tamerlane and the caged Bayezid was invoked in the so-called Great Wedding of 1634, joining the Danish and Saxon houses, which displayed prominently this heroic, even Christianized, view of Tamerlane. Mara Wade cites Du Bec's work as influencing the European-wide view of Tamerlane,

FIG. 5.1

Bayezid in his cage, *Litsevoi letopisnyi svod* (BAN, 31.7.30–2, fol. 530, used by permission)

noting that in the Danish wedding, the role of Tamerlane was taken by the younger, and obviously Christian, brother of the groom.[16]

Parfenov's focus is on Du Bec's work, and his strongest and most startling example of this author's influence on the Russian play is the dialogue between Pasha, who has been detained in the enemy camp, and Tamerlane (act 2, scene 5). Both Du Bec and the play lay out a long exchange in which Tamerlane asks his captive why Baiazet shows such great contempt for his (Tamerlane's) forces, warning that Baiazet's unwarranted pride will be punished. Pasha replies that Baiazet himself, the "sun of the earth," was astonished at Tamerlane's audacity in challenging him. Tamerlane replies that he is "sent from heaven to punish his [Baiazet's] rashness" and to teach him that God vanquishes the proud and raises the lowly. He then asks if Baiazet really intends to do battle. Pasha answers honestly that he does indeed intend to do so and asks permission, again honorably, to rejoin his master in this effort. Tamerlane responds with equal respect, allowing Pasha to return and even providing him with a good horse to transport him back. He tells Pasha to warn his master of the impending fight, saying that he will be found on the battlefield under a green standard.

As Parfenov showed, the Russian play presents a nearly word-for-word translation from Du Bec's book. Unfortunately, in Parfenov's article the passage quoted from Du Bec is almost invisible due to a confusing layout, and Parfenov mixes these close borrowings with other, far less persuasively related, passages.[17] It is worth presenting the entire section clearly. Initially, the textual overlap is general, not word for word, but as the exchange continues, the quotations become quite close, as Parfenov observed, especially in the first block of text, presented here as example 1. In this series of exchanges, the Russian play dispenses with the verbal cues in Du Bec identifying the different speakers, unnecessary in a performed drama; otherwise, the 1597 English translation of Du Bec given in example 1 functions quite well as a "translation" of the Russian play text. The passage begins with Pasha defending his lord, Baiazet:

EXAMPLE 1 PASHA-TAMERLANE EXCHANGE (ACT 2, SCENE 5)[18]

Pasha

Господарь мой, иже солнцем всего мира есть, никоего терпети может себя товарыща. Но удивляюся безумию твоему, что так от далеких мест пришел еси госдподарю моему помешку чинити во благополучие его, еже самое небо ему не возбраняет. Тебе же невозможно есть силы его сопротивлятися, понеже вся вселенная ему усмиряется; токмо ты един хощешь ему супротивник быти, о безумне!

The other [Pasha] answered, that his Lord was the Son[19] of the earth, that he could not indure a companion, that hee surely was astonished, how he from so far had enterprised so dangerous a journey, to hinder the fortune of his Lord, in whose favour the heavens did bend themselves, because they were not able to withstand him, that all the round world did subject themselves unto him, and that hee committed great folly in going about to resist the same.

Tamerlane

Аз же из неба послан, да дерзость его усмирю и научю, яко Господь Бог гордых казнит, его же сила есть гордых низложити, смиренных же возвышати. Уже меня ради принужден Костянтинополя отступитися, и ты сам узнал, что подъездные райтаровя моя над тобою учинити. Или еще надеешься, что государь твой возможет ми бой на поли поставити?

The Emperour answered, I am sent from heaven for to punish his rashnesse, and to teach him that the proud are punished of God, whose principall action is to cast downe high things, & to raise up the lowly: at the least yet I have already constrained thy maister to raise his siege from before *Constantinople*. And moreover, thou hast already felt (although I lament thy mishap) what the valour of my Parthian horse is against thy Turkish. Doest thou think (changing of his speech) that thy master doth come to bid me battaile?

Pasha

Ей, истинно. Но молю вас, да мя паки к государю моему отпустите, яко да увижу ваши великие дела.

The Passa answered, yea, assuring you that there is nothing hee more desireth: and I beseech you that I may acknowledge your greatnesse in giving me leave to assist my Lord at this Battaile.

Tamerlane

Добро; позваляю на то. Иди к государю своему, извещая ему, яко мене видел еси; а во утрешний день и сам мене на бою увидит на том месте, где великое зеленое знамя мое поставлено имать быти.

The Emperor said unto him; I give thee leave, go and tell thy Lord that thou hast seene me, and that I will fight on horseback in the place where he shal see a greene ensigne.

The Moscow playwrights made a good choice in using Du Bec for, as example 1 shows, his narrative is full of vivid dialogue, a ready-made play, as it were, that required little rewriting. The "greene ensigne" mentioned in the exchange is a clear marker (if additional evidence were necessary) of the play's reliance on Du Bec's text. The image does not appear in other historical sources, as far as we are aware.[20]

There is another passage in the Russian play lifted directly from Du Bec, a passage confirming that, whatever other sources the Moscow playwrights might have consulted, they certainly had a copy of Du Bec at hand. Parfenov did not identify this borrowing, perhaps because of his focus on identifying a Russian source for the play (the chronicle account, as described in the following discussion), or perhaps because the passage appears in Du Bec's work slightly before the main Tamerlane-Bayezid encounter, so he simply did not see it. Whatever the case, Parfenov's identification of Russian chronicle sources for Tamerlane's dream was not convincing, certainly lacking the specificity of the quotations in example 1.

Parfenov relies on the account of Tamerlane's vision as presented in the Nikon Chronicle, under the year 1395 (the chronicle itself was compiled in the mid-sixteenth century). The passage presents an extremely negative, and entirely traditional, view of Tamerlane, emphasizing his lameness (which is stressed in the play as well) and labeling him in no uncertain terms as a dangerous and violent man. After enumerating his conquests, the chronicle account gets to the heart of the matter, describing Tamerlane's approach to Russian territories, which, in turn, brought the Russian Grand Prince Vasilii Dmitrievich to defend his lands. In consultation with the Russian metropolitan, they called for the icon of the Vladimir Mother of God to be brought as protection. This is when Tamerlane's dream-vision in the chronicle occurs: after falling asleep, he saw "a woman in purple robes with many warriors, threatening him fiercely" and blocking his way forward. Tamerlane awakened, trembling, and promptly ordered his forces to retreat.²¹ The Russian audience could have been familiar with a dream associated with Tamerlane, although it is not clear how the German playwrights might have learned about this tradition—perhaps conveyed by one of the Russians in charge. There is, however, a far more direct source.

Again we turn to Du Bec's work, which does indeed include a vision scene for Tamerlane, marked (in the English translation of 1597) with the rubric "Tamerlan his dreame." This is clearly the source for the Russian play's dream sequence. Like the Tamerlane-Pasha exchange, it is used in places nearly word for word as Tamerlane recounts his dream to his followers (a first-person account, by Tamerlane, in the Russian play; a third-person narrative in Du Bec). The English publication from 1597 again provides a viable "translation" of the Russian text in example 2.

EXAMPLE 2   TAMERLANE'S DREAM (ACT 1, SCENE 2)²²

А видел во сне я то, будто многие честные храбрые люди, которые мне обще руку дали и о помочи просили, чтоб я их от некоторых варвар, которые их многим мучением отягчают; исповедаваю вам так, что я никогда таких дородных и честных людей не видал есмь.

that he did see as he thought, a great multitude of reverent men, who put forth their hands unto him, requiring his succour against the violence of certaine tyrants, who did afflict them with sundry kindes of tormentes: he sayd, that he did never see more reverent countenances

Du Bec drops the dream immediately after recounting it ("no body was able to give him the interpretation thereof, and him selfe thought no more of the same"); the Moscow playwrights, however, incorporate it directly into the dramatic action. In the Russian play, immediately after this dream, as Tamerlane and his comrades are pondering its meaning, a messenger enters to announce Baiazet's threat, and Aksalla (Tamerlane's main adviser) exclaims that this must be what the dream foretold. The Moscow playwrights thus demonstrate nice dramatic instincts: this passage gives the audience a good introduction to the character Tamerlane, for this is how he is first seen onstage, and the dream narrative is smoothly woven into the following action.

Since Du Bec was clearly a source for this play, how might the Moscow playwrights have found a copy? The book was readily available in multiple publications and translations and might easily have been owned already by someone in Moscow's Foreign Quarter; given the short preparation period, a special order from abroad does not seem possible. There were many editions of Du Bec issued over the course of the seventeenth century. Although we have been quoting from the English translation of 1597, we certainly do not suggest that this is the version the German playwrights in Moscow would have relied on. A third passage from the play allows us to identify precisely the playwrights' source: a Dutch translation published three times before the Moscow play was written, in 1613, 1638, and 1647, as *Historie van t'leven ende de daden van den Grooten Tamerlanes*. The identification of this particular translation of Du Bec's work allows us to explore how this passage sheds light not just on historical writings about the Tamerlane-Bayezid confrontation, but also on Moscow's Foreign Quarter community, the milieu from which all the court plays originated.

The actions discussed here appear at the climax of the play, the first one-on-one confrontation between the protagonists, which occurs immediately after the battle and Baiazet's capture (act 3, scene 2). This encounter reflects identifiable historical traditions. As Linda McJannet has written, this face-to-face confrontation is one of the places in which the approach of Eastern (especially Turkish) sources diverges from the story as presented in Western sources. Bayezid is not spared his sufferings in any of the accounts, but they are framed somewhat differently in the two traditions. According to McJannet, Du Bec's presentation falls somewhere in the middle, for he relies on narrative approaches characteristic of the Eastern tradition, which are garbled—at least, in the French original and in the published English and German translations.[23] The presentation of this encounter in the Russian play is clearer than in Du Bec's original text, and it is at precisely this point that the Dutch Du Bec can be identified unambiguously as the play's source, for it, too, uniquely diverges from the other published Du Bec versions and inserts additional material.

In Du Bec's original publication (and in the translations we have been considering), Tamerlane begins this encounter by observing that he holds Bayezid's life in his hands, to which Bayezid replies contemptuously that death at Tamerlane's hands would be happiness. The exchange continues as a series of questions and answers. Tamerlane asks why Bayezid subjugated the Greek emperor, Paleologue; Bayezid answers, "The desire of glorie and rule." Du Bec's Tamerlane then asks why Bayezid had been so cruel, to which the prisoner answers: "To give the greater terrour to my enemies." In Du Bec's setting, Tamerlane concludes, somewhat confusingly, "So shalt thou receive the like reward." The statement is unclear because the final question in this series is lacking: what would Bayezid have done if he had captured Tamerlane? As McJannet observes, in Du Bec's text, "it is as if the set-up (the final question and Bayazid's answer) has slipped out of the narrative, but the punch line (Timūr's [Tamerlane's] order) has been preserved."[24]

In the Russian play, Tamerlane indeed asks the crucial question (see example 3). The Russian play and the Dutch Du Bec are the only versions that include this exchange, in effect, providing the set-up for the punch line that is lacking in the other versions. Thus, the sequence develops logically: Tamerlane first threatens Baiazet with punishment and then asks his captive what kind of punishment would be appropriate if their places were reversed. The correspondence with the Dutch is not literal. Example 3 begins at the point where the Dutch text diverges from all other versions of Du Bec.

EXAMPLE 3 CONFRONTATION BETWEEN TAMERLANE AND BAIAZET (ACT 3, SCENE 2)[25]

Tamerlane

Ныне убо ты, со всем своим государством в равенстве, возмездие получишь.

(Now you and your whole realm equally will receive punishment.)

Daerom sult ghy oock met deselve munte betaelt werden, seyde den Keyser.

Tamerlane

Но слушай ты, безмочный Баазет, скажи ты мне: егда бы я в руках твоих был, какую бы ты мне честь сотворил?

(But listen, powerless Baiazet, and tell me: if I were in your hands, what fate [honor] would you have devised for me?)

Indien ghy my gevanghen hadt ghekregen, wat wout ghy my gedaen hebben?[26]

Baiazet

Занеже ты хром и ходить не можешь, тогдаб я тебе к чести повелел зделать железную клетку и в тое бы тебя всадить велел и чрез все государство пред собою вести,

(Because you are lame and cannot walk, I would order an iron cage to be made for you in your honor, and would have you placed in it, to be carried before me throughout the whole realm)

Bajazet antwoorde: Ick woude in een Ysere getralijde Koye besloten hebben, ende soude u alsoo tot een Schouspel en spot door het gantsche Lant ghevoert hebben.

As Baiazet, in the Russian play, continues with his ill-considered threats, he lists the humiliations long familiar in Western writings, in addition to the cage: feeding the captive with scraps from the table and using him as a mounting block. The Russian play presents these additional punishments as possible future action—what Baiazet would do—whereas the Dutch Du Bec translation offers them in a narrative describing what Tamerlane actually did. The Russian text omits several lines of the Dutch translation, as indicated by square brackets in example 4, which takes up directly from the Russian text in example 3. These omitted passages explain that Tamerlane has decided to accept the cage idea, so these lines are unnecessary in the spoken drama, which jumps directly to the action items.

EXAMPLE 4   CONFRONTATION BETWEEN TAMERLANE AND BAIAZET, CONTINUED (ACT 3, SCENE 2)[27]

Baiazet (continued)

а пропитание твое бы было с стола моего равно псом - укрухи хлебны. И егда бы аз куды выехать похотел, и тогда бы ты имел быть подножие мое.

(and your feeding would be from my table, like a dog, with dry bread crumbs. And if I wanted to ride out somewhere, then you would serve as my mounting block.)

[Tamerlanes heeft Bajazetem ... in eene Ysere Koye doen besluyten ...] hem voedende met de kruymen ofte brocken die van zijn Tafel vielen/ welcke men hem als eenen Hont toe worp. Wanneer Tamerlanes dan te Peerde ofte op zijn Koetse wilde klimmen [...] ghebruyckte hem alsdan tot een Voetbanck.

Finally, Tamerlane states that his captive's fate has been brought on by his own words, fully deserved due to his overweening pride. These concluding sentiments are similar to those expressed in Du Bec, although they do not appear to be drawn directly from the Dutch text.

How and why did the Dutch translation include this complete series of questions and answers, lacking in the other Du Bec versions? All of the Dutch text quoted in examples 3 and 4 appears in an addendum (*Byvoeghsel*) to the Dutch Du Bec.[28] Next to this supplement, in the margin, is a listing of the sources from which this additional information is drawn. The Dutch translator/editor clearly did his homework, for he uses well-known histories, all of which were available by the time of the earliest Dutch translation of Du Bec (1613) and were considered as authoritative enhancements to the original.[29] The list of sources and the addendum itself is the same in all three Dutch editions (1613, 1638, 1647).[30] Examining the sources used in this addendum helps us identify the editor himself.

One of the marginal references, cited as "Histor. turc. tom 1. lib. 1. pag. 14," indicated perhaps the most authoritative and influential late sixteenth-century Western source about the Ottomans, the heavily annotated translation of a long Turkish chronicle by Joannes Leunclavius (Lewenklaw); in the addendum, this work is cited in its revised German version (1590, 1595).[31] Lewenklaw's publication, although not reprinted in the seventeenth century, was known widely; it was cited by another of the sources consulted by the Dutch editor of Du Bec, the *Apophthegmata Christiana* by the Dutch theologian Willem Baudartius (1565–1640), first published in 1605.[32] Baudartius provides the clear source for the Dutch Du Bec in the question-answer series we are examining, illustrating how the Dutch editor pivoted away from Du Bec's original text to incorporate this vivid series of confrontations.

Another of the important Western sources transmitting the Tamerlane-Bayezid encounter, the account by the Spanish historian Pedro Mexía (d. 1551), allows us to identify the Dutch editor of Du Bec. Mexía's *Silva de varia lección* first appeared in 1540 and was widely published in translation, appearing in editions and anthologies throughout the century.[33] The annotations in the Byvoeghsel show that the Dutch editor of Du Bec relied on two versions of Mexía's text: a Dutch-language edition from 1607 and a compilation by Antoine Du Verdier.[34] It is the latter that allows us to identify the author of our Dutch Du Bec addendum. A Dutch-language edition of volume 2 of Du Verdier's work, *Het tweede deel Petri Messiae, dat is De verscheyden lessen Antony du Verdier*, was issued in the same place and year as the Dutch Du Bec appeared: Rotterdam, 1613. On the title page, the Du Verdier translator is given as "I. L. B." and the publisher is identified as "Ian Leendersz[oon] Berewout." The Dutch translator of Du Bec was also "I. L. B."—it seems reasonable to assume that they were one and the same person.[35] Although there were many editions of Mexía/Du Verdier, Berewout would most likely have consulted his own translation; indeed, the Byvoeghsel itself probably resulted from Berewout's familiarity with these sources. When he realized that Du Bec's rendition of the Tamerlane-Bayezid encounter omitted some of this material, he was able easily to insert it from one of his own translations into another, from Du Verdier to Du Bec.

The information in the Byvoeghsel thus identifies the specific version of Du Bec used by the Moscow playwrights, and it accounts for the differences between the Dutch translation of Du Bec, on the one hand, and the original French text and the additional translations, on the other. This knowledge helps explain some aspects of the play's final scene (act 3, scene 3), the celebratory banquet Tamerlane had called for at the end of the previous scene. A new character is introduced in this final scene: Baiazet's wife. In the Russian play, her name is mentioned only once, as "Milka." The name Milcah is biblical, derived from the Hebrew word for "queen."[36] This name is not otherwise known in the histories of Tamerlane, and its origins for the Russian play are unclear (although we recall the transliterated Hebrew in the Esther play). The addendum in the Dutch Du Bec mentions a wife but gives her no name; other Du Bec sources, as far as we are aware, omit the wife entirely.

As in other historical treatments, in the Russian play the inclusion of Baiazet's wife in his debasement makes the punishment all the more anguishing—as one contemporary writer remarked, the imprisonment of his wife results in "the doubling of his greefe."[37] In both Eastern and Western historical traditions, Bayezid's wife (named or unnamed) is described as either captured or captured and then further tormented by being forced to wait on Tamerlane's men as a servant.[38] It is in the Western sources that her humiliations are listed in detail; they appear in the addendum of the Dutch Du Bec and are enumerated particularly vividly in the Du Verdier publication.[39] As in other Western sources, in Du Verdier, Bayezid's wife is described as being half-naked (her clothes were cut off from below the navel) and forced to serve food to Tamerlane's men. These actions are depicted with particular force in another influential Western source, by Petrus Perondinus (1553), also relying on Mexía (and others); as Perondinus writes, "before Bayazed's own eyes, Tamerlane forced her, clad insultingly only in sandals and an extremely short military cloak, to serve drinks to the Scythian chieftains as they reclined, obscenely naked."[40] A sixteenth-century German image portrays with precision the degradations undergone by both husband and wife, with a reference to Perondinus at the end of the text (fig. 5.2).

Parfenov's insightful observations about the connections between Du Bec's history and the Russian play opened the door to a more comprehensive analysis of both works and revealed Du Bec to be the source material for two important scenes: the opening dream and the exchange between Pasha and Tamerlane. As far as we know, among historical accounts of Tamerlane, the dream sequence is recounted only in Du Bec. Much of the action in the final scenes of the play appears only in the addendum of the Dutch translation of Du Bec, which explicitly draws on a variety of source material representing an amalgamation of Eastern and Western traditions (as does Du Bec's work itself, although his Eastern sources are not known).

Du Bec's history had another advantage from the perspective of the tsar's playwrights, for its point of view was consistent with the one they had been offering in other plays, in which rulers were depicted as wise and decisive, yet humble and God-fearing. In *Tamerlane*, the protagonist was portrayed not as a vengeful conqueror but as a temperate hero, treating his opponents honorably (in the case of Pasha) and dispensing the punishment the vanquished foe himself had stipulated. Indeed, the characterization of Tamerlane in the Russian play goes beyond the presentation of a hero—it portrays, as Parfenov observed, a devout Christian prince, shown praying to God before the battle and delivering only just retribution to the proud and defeated Baiazet.[41] The historian Anders Ingram characterized Du Bec's Tamerlane as "a crypto-Christian 'Parthian,' who is described as an idealized Renaissance prince"—a criticism of Du Bec's approach but perfectly apt for the Russian court play. Finally, as we have seen throughout these examples, Du Bec's account was ready-made for a theatrical setting, full of vivid scenes and

FIG. 5.2

Bayezid's humiliations, sixteenth century (Wikimedia Commons)

sharp verbal exchanges.[42] All three editions of the Dutch text use different typefaces for the speech or dialogue sections and for the reported texts, so in a sense, the published book itself looks something like a play already. Given what appears to be the rapid composition of the Russian play, it is relevant that the quoted material is distributed in each of the three acts, forming a textual foundation for building the rest of the work quickly and efficiently. When this "ready-to-perform" published material is combined with the two lengthy comic scenes (in acts 1 and 2), we can see that it would have been possible to put the play together in a very short time.

The Dutch version of Du Bec's book was so widely available in the three separate publications that it is not a stretch to propose that someone in Moscow's foreign community owned the book already and made it available to the playwrights. The subject was certainly apt, given the court's political concerns. Did the Foreign Quarter playwrights decide on this particular story because someone already had a copy of Du Bec? Or did the court request this topic for the theater and thereby set off a scramble for appropriate source material among the Foreign Quarter's readers?

One of the most likely sources for a copy of the Dutch Du Bec in Moscow was Andrei Andreevich Vinius (1641–1717). Vinius had been raised in Russia and was fluent in Dutch and Russian (probably also in German). In 1664 these linguistic skills led to his assignment to the Ambassadorial Chancery, where his tasks included the translation of foreign newspapers (kuranty), which would have kept him up to date on the government's concerns about the Ottoman Turks. Although we have no direct proof that Vinius owned the Dutch translation of Du Bec, he did possess two of the books that were used in the addendum: Baudartius and a Dutch version of Mexía's text, *De Verscheyden lessen Petri Messiae* (1595).[43] Vinius also worked as a translator for the 1664 Dutch embassy of Jacob Boreel, which included among its members a distant relative, Nicolaas Witsen.[44] Witsen and Vinius maintained ties for many years, and Witsen was, according to Vinius himself, a source for some of the books in his large collection.[45] Furthermore, Vinius had been involved in the early stages of the tsar's theater: he was paid, in September 1672, for six hundred leaves (or sheets; *listy*) of gold that were used for ornamenting the costumes (pp. viii, 12). Vinius was among the three messengers dispatched just after the court theater's premiere in October 1672, in response to the Turkish military threats earlier that year. He was sent to London, where he arrived in February 1673 after a difficult trip that included a stop in the

Dutch Republic. He was back in Moscow by early 1674, thus about a year before the premiere of the Tamerlane play.[46] The second (and final) reference to Vinius in connection with the tsar's theater comes from November 1675, during preparations for the six-play festival, when he assisted by acquiring paper (pp. 55–56).[47] There are many ways through which Vinius (or someone else) in Moscow's Foreign Quarter might have acquired Du Bec's book, but whatever its exact route, the Russian play text shows that a Dutch edition was in Moscow when the playwrights embarked on their assignment.

The Foreign Quarter playwrights' skillful use of Du Bec as an inspiration for the dramatic setting—for example, the integration of Tamerlane's dream, taken from a separate section of Du Bec's account and placed seamlessly as the introduction of the title character—shows their previous experience with theater, either through the earlier plays for Moscow or previously, in their homelands (or both). These editorial skills give us reason to expand our inquiries beyond the obvious use of the Dutch Du Bec, moving more directly into the realm of theater as a source of inspiration for this play.

INTERTHEATER, REDUX

Whereas Parfenov touches briefly on Western theatrical traditions as a context for the Russian Tamerlane play, this is the prime focus of Bulgakov's study. The clearest examples are in the Russian play's comic scenes, which Bulgakov (and earlier scholars) naturally situate in the context of theatrical, rather than historical, traditions.[48] The play's comic actions follow the manic path laid out by Susakim in *Judith*, by Pickleherring in the early 1672 "ballets," and by the soldiers in *Judith* and presumably also those in the *Artakserksovo deistvo* interscenia. Also as in *Judith*, the comic scenes, however discursive, are related to the main action. Even the song text given in *Tamerlane* is quite similar to that in *Judith*—both are drinking songs performed by celebrating soldiers facing their upcoming battle.[49] It is immediately after this drunken interlude that the foolish character Telpel appears—the German word *Tölpel* means "dunce" or "dolt" and would further have been familiar, to the playwrights at least, as the well-known name of Martin Luther's dog.[50] In the play's brief concluding statement, the authors acknowledged their haste, describing the play as short (or small) and quickly written. There are other fingerprints pointing to their rushed efforts, for example the inconsistencies in the spellings of the characters' names.⁵¹ The comic scenes, like the reliance on Du Bec, would have come in handy under these circumstances as the situations (soldiers, drinking songs, comic mayhem) are both stereotyped and flexible—roles for Pickleherring and Telpel could, almost literally, write themselves. Even better, they were tried-and-tested surefire successes for the royal audience.

But Bulgakov makes more specific claims for the links between the Russian Tamerlane play and Western theatrical practices. He gives a scene-by-scene summary of the Russian play, seeking similarities or direct models in acts 3 through 5 of Christopher Marlowe's *Tamburlaine the Great Part 1* (*1 Tamburlaine*), in which the encounter with Bayezid takes place.⁵² Many of Bulgakov's observations reflect the fact that both plays are set in the same historical moment, with references to Bayezid's siege of Constantinople, an overlap in subject too general to suggest specific influence from the earlier play on the Russian setting. In a few other cases, Bulgakov points to what he believes are identifiable linguistic influences from Marlowe on the Russian playwrights. For example, he highlights the encounter between Tamerlane and Pasha discussed previously (act 2, scene 5), which he compares to the text of Marlowe's *1 Tamburlaine*, act 3, scene 3. Bulgakov is struck by the similarities in Tamerlane's thundering language, some of the most famous in Marlowe's play:⁵³

> I that am term'd the Scourge and Wrath of God,
> The only fear and terror of the world

The character is similarly boastful, as we saw in our discussion, in the same encounter in the Russian play. Bulgakov points to this passage: "Аз же из неба послан, да дерзость его усмирю и научю, яко Господь Бог гордых казнит, его же сила есть гордых низложити, смиренных же возвышати."⁵⁴ We can supply an English equivalent that is roughly contemporary to Marlowe, ironically, because this is a passage that the Moscow playwrights took directly from Du Bec (see example 1): "I am sent from heaven for to punish his rashnesse, and to teach him that the proud are punished of God, whose principall action is to cast downe high things, & to raise up the lowly."

Here, as in other such passages Bulgakov cites, the proposed textual relationships between Marlowe and Moscow are, in truth, unconvincing. In fact, Bulgakov and Parfenov use the same approach, although with different aims. Both quote isolated words or short phrases in the Russian play that contain formulations similar to readings in the proposed foreign models. In Parfenov's case, this fragmentation sometimes makes it more difficult to appreciate his identification of significant literal reproduction from Du Bec to the Moscow play; in Bulgakov's case, such repetition of individual words feels largely coincidental and does not suggest persuasively that one play was the source for the other.

Yet Bulgakov identifies some additional parallels in the actions of the two plays that are more compelling.[55] In the last scene of the Russian play, Baiazet's wife is brought in at Tamerlane's request. Tamerlane addresses her mockingly, referring to the cage: "So, great tsaritsa, how do you like your tsar's palace?" ("Яко, великая царица, полюбилась тебе полата сия царя твоего?"). One of Tamerlane's men remarks that she is a good singer ("Ей, она умеет изрядно пети")[56] and then continues by observing that "she should be in this cage," making a comparison to her husband ("угодно6, она и в клетке сей"). Baiazet reacts in horror, lamenting the day he was born and grieving over the humiliation suffered by his beloved wife.

The next bit of stage action is somewhat open to interpretation, although however we read these lines, the references are to singing as entertainment for the captors. First, one of Tamerlane's men applauds the musical efforts, saying "An excellent song! Sing again" ("Сие бо урядная песнь! Пой еще"). This could refer to either the wife's command performance (she has already been called a good singer) or Baiazet's agonized (spoken) outburst—at any rate, the imagery invoking music and singing continues. Tamerlane responds by saying:

> Ни, ни! Птицы, которые сперва в клетку всажены бывают. Аще ли бы наумильнийшии пели, тогда в три дни гласу своего не окажут. Аз надеюсь, что в те дни лутчюю песнь о смиренстве пети будет.

> No, no! Birds first have to be placed in a cage. But if they should sing very well, then they can rest their voices for three days. I hope that after that time, a better song about humility will be sung.

It is this mockery that finally does Baiazet in. He cries that he can no longer live and has no means to kill himself other than the iron bars of his cage, against which he will smash his head, which he proceeds to do ("Нет ли инаго средствия меня умертвити, тогда имеет сие железо главу мою сокрушить"). Tamerlane, apparently unfazed, remarks that it would be better to be hanged. Baiazet's wife reacts strongly, in her only spoken lines of the play (and the only written reference to her name), a series of disjointed and frenzied exclamations: "Alas! Dead! Alas! Alas!" ("Увы! Ужь умре! Увы! Увы!"). Tamerlane orders the "crazed wife" to be removed, saying that it was Baiazet's own decision to kill himself—he did the deed himself. Aksalla remarks, unhelpfully (although underscoring the on-stage action), that Baiazet smashed his head and that one can see his brains.[57] This leads into Tamerlane's final speech, about the logical consequences of pride, and the concluding address to the royal audience.

This gory suicide does not occur in most editions of Du Bec (including the French original); in all of these, Bayezid dies in captivity in Samarkand, where Tamerlane had taken him. It does appear in the Dutch addendum to Du Bec, where Bayezid is described as "smashing his head against the iron bars of the cage until he ended his unhappy life." This is another place in which, in the addendum, the Dutch translator seems to be relying on several sources: Lewenklaw, Baudartius, and Du Verdier all mention the suicide by braining.[58]

However, Aksalla's remark about the visible gore goes beyond even the violent end described in the Dutch translation of Du Bec, and none of the source materials we have been considering includes the musical imagery used in the Russian play. Both elements—singing and brains strewn across the stage—have counterparts in Marlowe's *Tamburlaine*. In the same dramatic situation, in which the captives are displayed for the pleasure of their conquerors, Marlowe also makes reference to musical entertainment (as Bulgakov observes). In Marlowe's play, Tamburlaine addresses his wife, Zenocrate, suggesting that the prisoners might provide some amusement: "How now, Zenocrate, doth not the Turk and his wife make a goodly show at a banquet?" She dutifully answers yes, and Theridamas (a Persian lord in Tamburlaine's suite) says: "Methinks 'tis a great deal better than a consort of music." Tamburlaine takes up the idea: "Yet music would do well to cheer up Zenocrate. Pray thee tell, why art thou so sad? if thou wilt have a song, the Turk shall strain his voice."[59]

In Marlowe, Bayezid's wife, Zabina, shares her husband's fate to a much greater degree than in either the Russian play or the historical accounts. Not only does she witness the spectacle of her husband in the cage, as in the Russian play, but she actually sees him being fed and used as a footstool (here, a proxy for the mounting block). Even more extreme is her reaction after Bayezid kills himself against the bars of his cage. As in Aksalla's remarks in the Russian play, Marlowe's Zabina is left to react in horror: "What do mine eyes behold?" she cries, "my husband dead! His skull all riven in twain! his brains dash'd out." Zabina, like Milka in the Russian play, dissolves into a series of hysterical utterances, and finally she, like her husband (and unlike the Russian Milka), runs against the cage and brains herself.[60] The excessive gore seems to come, in Marlowe's play, from Perondinus, where the captive, after watching his wife being forced to serve Tamerlane's men, "was pierced through by rage, seized by grief, and overwhelmed with insult; he begged for death, and, when in his right mind, made an inexorably determined vow to take his own life. By repeated blows against the iron bars of his cage he smashed his head so that it broke open and the brains spilled out, and so brought about his unhappy, mournful fate."[61]

In the bloody suicides and the musical imagery, then, the two plays show some similarities. In light of these shared approaches, which seem to reflect the demands of staged performance and not simply overlaps in plotlines, we ask a further question: although Bulgakov may have been a bit off track in claiming clear borrowings in the Russian play from Marlowe's *Tamburlaine*, was he nevertheless correct in suggesting that such theatrical parallels might be worth pursuing? In other words, could there be such a thing as a Marlowe-Moscow axis?[62] Such questions are at the heart of both Bulgakov's and Parfenov's studies: the former assumed such a relationship, the latter strove to counter this assumption by offering other explanations, with a particular emphasis on the Russian chronicle tradition. Both made important contributions; neither was wholly satisfactory.

The following exploration of the possibility of links between Marlowe's *Tamburlaine* and Moscow's *Tamerlane* is necessarily, and admittedly, speculative, especially given the tangled historico-theatrical traditions that both plays relied on. Indeed, in his writing on intertheater, Anston Bosman assumes the inevitability of a speculative approach, noting that so far "the archive has yielded only traces of the ephemeral performances, but there are already signal instances where original texts, memorial reconstructions, and subsequent translations can be collated to map out the theater's range of performable possibilities."[63] It is not enough, however, to assume that traveling English players must have carried *Tamburlaine* abroad, for in all of the references to the dozens of plays known to have been brought to the Continent by English actors or created there by these players or their German and Dutch followers, Marlowe's *Tamburlaine* is conspicuously absent. Other Marlowe plays were given during this period but no one has identified a performance of his *Tamburlaine* setting.

As we have seen throughout, there are clear links between the products of Moscow's Foreign Quarter writers and the theatrical traditions of the West. There is, for example, enormous overlap in themes and sources: all of the play subjects performed for Tsar Aleksei would have been familiar fare at any of the courts or cities visited by the traveling players on the Continent. Without much exaggeration, one might say that any of the Russian plays, if they appeared in German, would have been unremarkable in the famous 1620 print, *Engelische Comedien und Tragedien*, that preserves repertoire typical of this early period (including Pickleherring actions).[64] Even the stark black-and-white portrayal of the protagonists in the Russian plays echoes what German audiences would likely have witnessed in performances by English players abroad. As Simon Williams remarks, characterizing the overall reductions in character development and scenic complexity in English plays given for Continental audiences: "Such simplifications and omissions make the conflict melodramatic, asking for a simple response from the audience, sympathy for the good, persecuted characters, antipathy towards the evil."[65] Such melodramatic compression is reflected not only in the concise Tamerlane play but is embedded in the basic dramatic structure of all the plays created for the tsar's theater.

Another example suggests even more direct influence. As we have noted, the drinking song in the Russian *Tamerlane* (act 2, scene 2) is similar to the drinking song in *Judith*. Its language, however, suggests much wider crossover appeal. In *Tamerlane*, the song ends with a line of nonsense syllables: "Sa sa sa sa sa sa sa sa." This has no obvious meaning in Russian but is a common refrain in English plays of the late sixteenth and early seventeenth centuries, and thus it might have been a natural response (admittedly several steps removed) by the playwrights to fill out the syllabic scheme of the song.[66]

How, then, might we proceed to map these "performable possibilities"? In the following section, we consider some scenarios by means of which Marlowe's play might have traveled to Moscow, in ways both (somewhat) direct and indirect.

The Admiral's Men and the (More-or-Less) Direct Routes of Contact

In this scenario we consider the most straightforward implications of Bulgakov's suggestion that Marlowe's *Tamburlaine* crossed to the Continent through the travels of actors associated with the English company called the

Admiral's Men.[67] It was this company that originally performed *Tamburlaine* and revived it in the mid-1590s. Several members of the Admiral's Men did indeed go to the Continent, where they formed the nucleus of itinerant acting troupes, bringing their repertoire and theatrical traditions with them. Bulgakov thus implies that Marlowe's *Tamburlaine*, which he sees as a source (actually, *the* source) for the Moscow play, was initially brought by its original players to the Continent and subsequently circulated there, eventually becoming known, in some fashion, to the German playwrights in Moscow.

Addressing this hypothesis requires delving into the activities of a very busy group of English actors. There were two early opportunities for the play to make an impact: the first performances in London and in the countryside, in the late 1580s, which apparently generated the initial publication of the text (1590), and the later show-stopping performances by actor Edward Alleyn in the title role, during the Rose Theater's 1594–1595 season. At both of these points, there are several paths by which knowledge of *Tamburlaine* might have traveled abroad.

1 Tamburlaine most likely premiered at some point in the winter months of very late 1586–1587 and the second part of the play (*2 Tamburlaine*) in the fall of 1587.[68] Both parts were published in London by Richard Jones, who registered them with the Stationer's Office in August 1590.[69] The Admiral's Men were associated with the play and the playwright early on, for example in the 1590 publication, which refers to this company by name. It was thus apparently to this group that Marlowe initially sold his play—the company was already drawing attention through Alleyn's performances in the mid-1580s, and Marlowe may have met the actors during one of their trips to London.[70]

The first clearly documented performances of the plays, however, are from several years later, in 1594–1595, with Edward Alleyn (1566–1626) in the role of Tamburlaine. The strong run over this season is recorded in the important diary kept by Philip Henslowe (d. 1616), the manager of the Rose Theater in London, where Alleyn and the Admiral's Men performed. Henslowe recorded seven performances of *1 Tamburlaine* between late August and late November 1594, and then a series of alternating, usually sequential, performances of both parts of *Tamburlaine*, running from December 1594 through November 1595. The plays had been published again before this run, with a second edition in 1593.[71] Apart from these, no other London performances are documented. Thus, in order to map out the play's possible dissemination routes abroad, we must determine who might have known about the plays between the earlier (prepublication) performances in the late 1580s and this run in 1594–1595, and then who might have known about them (especially 1 Tamburlaine, which seems to have been the more popular part) after that time.[72]

These are the questions that require delving into the travels of the busy groups of players. In January 1589, actors Robert Browne and Richard Jones, both of whom had long been associated with the Admiral's Men, were involved in a sale of theatrical properties (including "playe bookes") to Alleyn and his brother.[73] By October 1590, Browne was on the Continent, in Leiden, where he, together with other unidentified performers, offered the "diverse comedies and histories" that were mentioned in our previous chapter. These would certainly have included actions familiar from the Admiral's repertoire that Browne had been performing over the past several years (indeed, material he apparently had some ownership in), so this would be a possible window for *Tamburlaine*, in some unknown form, to cross to the Continent at this early date. Because *Tamburlaine* was registered at the Stationer's Office in mid-August in that same year, 1590, it is conceivable that Browne took the published text (which must already have been known to him) on his trip abroad.

At this same time in London, around 1592, Edward Alleyn joined Lord Strange's theatrical company, where he remained for a year, performing widely, including at court.[74] Other members of the Admiral's Men were touring the English countryside. As theater historian Andrew Gurr proposes, the fact that neither the Tamburlaine plays nor another of Marlowe's plays, *Faustus*, were recorded as being performed by Strange's company "is a powerful argument that they were out of London through these years, and the obvious place for them was with the traveling Admiral's Men."[75]

Actor Robert Browne returned to London from the Continent briefly during this time but already in February 1592, Browne and three other actors (Richard Jones, mentioned previously in connection with the sale of theatrical properties, Thomas Sackville, and John Bradstreet) were given permission to go to the Continent. Their travel pass was signed by the Lord High Admiral, and it is generally accepted that all four were associated with the Admiral's Men.[76] They traveled widely, documented in Arnhem, Wolfenbüttel, and Frankfurt.[77] A snapshot of a Frankfurt performance, which took place during the large August fair, probably in 1592, shows that the audience received them enthusiastically. These are the performances recorded in the well-known description by the English traveler Fynes Moryson, who gives them a fairly negative review, although he does mention that the troupe performed "peeces and Patches of English playes." In other words, Moryson recognized excerpts or renderings of plays that were familiar to him—and, of course, familiar to the players, repertoire they brought with them on this and, perhaps, also on the earlier trip to the Continent. Alleyn and Henslowe, back in London, kept in touch with the contingent abroad.[78]

Robert Browne returned to London briefly, staying until at least March 1594, and he is documented back on the Continent in early 1595, at the court of Hesse-Cassel.[79] During this period, between mid-1592 and mid-1594, London experienced a devastating plague epidemic, causing the closure of the city's theaters for almost the entire time.[80] In May 1594, after the danger had subsided and the theaters were reopened, the theatrical "duopoly" of the Lord Admiral's Men at the Rose Theater (including Alleyn) and the Lord Chamberlain's Men (Shakespeare's company) at the Theatre was established.[81]

The main import, for our purposes, of all these comings and goings among the London theater folk is this: *Tamburlaine* was associated with the Admiral's Men from the beginning, around 1586–1587. From 1590 on, there was a continual flow from the Admiral's Men to the Continent and back (through the travels of Browne, Jones, and others). In London, beginning in August 1594 at the Rose Theater's first full (postplague) Admiral's Men season, Alleyn began his long and successful string of performances in *Tamburlaine*. Browne continued to travel back and forth, and after he returned to the Continent (by early 1595), there are references to Marlowe plays (especially *Faustus*) being performed there, although none specifically to *Tamburlaine*. Marlowe's works were popular in the new environment, and there were clearly actors (Browne, Jones, Sackville, and Bradstreet, at the least) who would have been familiar with *Tamburlaine* and may even have performed it themselves previously.[82] It is possible that they had the published play with them as early as the initial, 1590, trip abroad.

Was *Tamburlaine* repeated in London later in the 1590s, after the towering performances by Alleyn in the 1594–1595 season? That is, in our context, were there continuing opportunities for actors to have become acquainted with this play and subsequently to have taken this performance experience to the Continent? It is difficult to answer this question of *Tamburlaine* revivals, partially because of the changed nature of Henslowe's diary, which morphed into an accounting of the business rather than a record of performances.[83] The strongest evidence for the long life of *Tamburlaine* is the simplest: the multiple publications of its text, which continued, after the two initial publications (1590, 1593), with two later editions (1597, 1605–1606).

Even if it was not produced in London after the initial run in the mid-1590s, the play itself, and Alleyn's striking performance of the main character, lived on. There are scattered references to the play or its subject throughout the decade, with mention of a staged version of the character in a 1597 satire by Joseph Hall.[84] This is the last known reference specifically to the play (as opposed to more general references to the figure of Tamerlane) for several years and, probably not coincidentally, it is at about this time that Alleyn stepped back from his acting career to focus on his entrepreneurial concerns with Henslow.[85] Alleyn briefly returned to the stage to support the new theater they had formed together, the Fortune, and even before this, he had performed regularly at court entertainments at the request of the queen. It is generally assumed that Alleyn would have brought back some of his best known roles at this time, although there seems to be no specific evidence of this.[86] It is around the time of Alleyn's retirement that the Henslowe papers list the company's *Tamburlaine* costumes and props, including rich costumes for the title role as well as the indispensable cage (1598).[87]

Memories of Alleyn in the role of Tamburlaine continued after his death (1626). In a new publication of Marlowe's *The Jew of Malta* (1633), Thomas Heywood praised Alleyn's performances, particularly as Tamburlaine.[88] A decade later, in Abraham Cowley's play *The Guardian* (1642), one character defuses another by saying: "for though you should roar like *Tamerlin* at the Bull [Theater], 'twould do no good with me." The Red Bull Theater had a reputation for such full-throated, popular productions, although no specifics are known of a revival—the imagery, at any rate, was obviously comprehensible.[89] Another decade later, in 1654, the writer Edmund Gayton remarked that players, responding to audience requests, performed "sometimes *Tamerlane*, sometimes *Jugurth*, some times the *Jew* of *Malta*, and some times parts of all these."[90] The remark recalls the "peeces and Patches" offered by the English players at the Frankfurt fair over fifty years earlier.

So, all things considered, there were many opportunities for actors to become acquainted with Marlowe's *Tamburlaine* and take this knowledge abroad. In spite of the uncertainties, such a (hypothetical) route bringing some experience of *Tamburlaine* from England to the Continent via the Admiral's network of traveling players seems to be viable. But how else might these stage actions and characters have circulated on the Continent?

Moryson's "Peeces and Patches" and an Even Less Direct Route

Bosman's writing on intertheater suggests another route by which something of Marlowe's *Tamburlaine* might have made its way to the Continent and thus possibly impacted the Moscow play. As Bosman writes: "We cannot say, for example, whether a given play would have begun its continental run as a printed edition, prompt-book, touring abridgement or memorial reconstruction, but we can be sure that any script would have been transformed in the staging process, and that this transformation would have intensified as the company traveled on." Orlene Murad emphasizes such transformations in her discussion of Continental versions of English plays, which "were not translations of English plays, but German versions of what the [English] Comedians had previously presented in English." She characterizes the texts as "a Thespian stew in which bits and pieces from here and everywhere tended to be thrown together."[91] As Simon Williams points out, Marlowe's plays were especially well suited for such treatment: "when the Comedians came over to Germany they were not at all concerned to give a faithful representation of the plays as they might have been seen in London. In fact Shakespeare's plays were probably of less use to them than, for example, those of Marlowe or Kyd, as these incorporated sensational situations and gory events more consistently than Shakespeare's."[92]

A reliance on such sensational extracts would have been especially effective for *Tamburlaine*. The spectacular scene of the braining of Bayezid (and his wife) is discrete and separable as well as extremely memorable. Indeed, with the numerous multimedia portrayals of Bayezid in his cage (brains intact), no additional context would have been needed to sketch out the setting. This abundant surrounding context would have served perfectly a group of players performing in a country and in a language not their own (or, in the case of Frankfurt, in a language not their audience's). It was the ideal shorthand reference.[93]

Thomas Dekker's play *Old Fortunatus* suggests another way in which the Tamerlane theme might have been kept alive for audiences, especially through the character of Bayezid.[94] There are several versions of *Fortunatus*.

The play, in an unknown form, was in the Admiral's repertoire in the mid-1590s, for it is mentioned in Henslowe's diary, with performances noted in February, April, and May 1596. Henslowe gives no author but scholars are comfortable in concluding that this version was by Dekker, an Admiral's Men's playwright. In November 1599, Dekker was paid by Henslowe for *The Whole History of Fortunatus*; immediately thereafter, the playwright was paid again to "alter" the *Whole History* for the Christmas (1599) performance at Elizabeth's court. This version was published in 1600 and includes a piteous portrayal of Bayezid, who is among four fallen kings used as stairs for the character Fortuna to ascend to her throne.[95]

Fortunatus was offered widely on the Continent by the traveling English actors, with performances recorded in Kassel in 1606–1607, Graz in 1608, and Dresden in 1626; furthermore, it was one of the plays published in the 1620 *Engelische Comedien und Tragedien* collection, so its connection with the English players and its popularity in German lands is clear.[96] The role of the Bayezid character is less clear, for the published German version does not include him. Theater historian June Schlueter suggests that the German publication was based not on the published 1600 English version for court, which does include Bayezid, but rather on the earlier *Whole History*, which Dekker had revised in 1599 (and then revised again almost immediately for the Christmas performance). Her hypothesis thus suggests that this lost *Whole History* also did not include the Bayezid scene.[97]

With respect to the Bayezid character in *Fortunatus*, however, there are some compelling connections with Marlowe's *Tamburlaine*. Productions of these two plays—*Tamburlaine* and the first, anonymous, *Fortunatus*—followed each other in quick succession, with the last performances of *Tamburlaine* in November 1595 and the first performance of *Fortunatus* in February 1596, both at the Rose Theater by the Admiral's Men. The references in *Fortunatus* to Bayezid seem clearly to point to the Marlowe play, which had been tearing through the Rose's stage for the entire preceding season. In Dekker's text (from the published version issued in 1600), Fortune is displaying four deposed kings as proof of her power: "Behold these foure chain'd like Tartarian slaves, / These I created Emperours and Kings, / And these are now my basest underlings." The third king is Bayezid, about whom Fortune says:

> Here stands the verie soule of miserie
> Poore Baiazet old Turkish Emperour,
> And once the greatest Monarch in the East;

> Fortune her selfe is sad to view thy fall,
> And grieves to see thee glad to licke up crommes [crumbs]
> At the proud feete of that great Scithian swaine,
> Fortunes best minion, warlike Tamberlaine:
> Yet must thou in a cage of Iron be drawne
> In triumph at his heeles, and there in griefe
> Dash out thy braines.[98]

To which Bayezid, labeled only as the third king, replies: "Oh miserable me."

All of the agonies mentioned in this short passage—eating crumbs, the cage, and the dashing out of his brains—were actions seen only recently, and many times, on the very same stage in Marlowe's play. And, as a practical bonus, the company would already have had the prop cage. The reference to Bayezid would thus be especially appropriate for the early (1596) version of *Fortunatus*, and, because this scene was so readily recognizable in a convenient shorthand reference, it seems reasonable to suggest that it also appeared in some of the Continental performances. This is especially true given the wide-ranging travels of actor Robert Browne—familiar from our previous discussion—who was joined in Lille in 1603 by another English actor, John Green. The two traveled together for several years, until Browne returned to England and Green took over the leadership of the group.[99] It was Green's troupe that played *Fortunatus* in Graz in February 1608; the repertoire he performed there, and elsewhere on the Continent, was heavily indebted to the Henslowe-Rose Theater-Admiral's Men axis that was also part of Browne's background.[100] *Fortunatus*, then, might have provided an image of the Bayezid character, and his tragic end, to German audiences—another route by which the theatrical possibilities of a Bayezid portrayal might have filtered through, eventually, to the German playwrights in Moscow.

Other Tamerlanes on Stage

In addition to the indirect routes taking *Tamburlaine* to the Continent, there are other plays that might have been influential for the Moscow setting. These plays are not based on Marlowe's version and do not include the bloody braining scene, but they do indicate that the two main characters—and that iconic cage—were widely known on seventeenth-century stages. The most important is by the Dutch playwright Johann Serwouters, *Den grooten Tamerlan, met de doodt van Bayaset de I, Turks keizer* (Amsterdam,

FIG. 5.3

Serwouters, *Den grooten Tamerlan* (Amsterdam, 1661; Google Books)

1657, with a second edition in 1661; see fig. 5.3). Serwouters's play was based on a Spanish setting by Luis Vélez de Guevara, *La nueva ira de Dios y Gran Tamorlán de Persia*.[101] Plays by the great Spanish playwrights Lope de Vega, Calderón, and, to a lesser extent, Vélez de Guevara were extremely influential in the formation of Dutch theater and made up a substantial part of the repertoire of both the primary Dutch playhouse, Amsterdam's Schouwburg, and the traveling acting companies, including the Dutch and mixed Dutch-English troupes that toured throughout northern Europe. Serwouters wrote his Tamerlane play while he was a regent of the Schouwburg, a position he

FIG. 5.4

Lonicer, *Chronicorum Turcicorum* ... (Frankfurt, 1578; Google Books)

held from 1655 to 1663.[102] Although his play is not an exact translation of the Spanish original, the two settings show a large overlap in characters and have the same main action.[103] The title page of the Serwouters play (fig. 5.3) also reinforces the power of visual imagery in telling the Tamerlane-Bayezid story; it resembles one of the important sixteenth-century illustrated histories of Tamerlane, by Philip Lonicer (fig. 5.4).

The Dutch and Spanish plays are quite different from Marlowe's *Tamburlaine* and also from the Russian play: they tell a convoluted love story in which, although we do see Bayezid in a cage, Tamerlane's life is ended by poison and Bayezid dies by stabbing himself. However, as a model for a staged rendition of the encounter between Tamerlane and Bayezid, complete with cage and audience-pleasing gore, Serwouters's play is quite relevant, for it traveled far and wide, particularly throughout German territories, and is exactly the type of performance that our German playwrights and others living in Moscow's Foreign Quarter might have seen in their home countries.

The troupe headed by the Dutch actor Jan Baptist van Fornenbergh (1624–1696/97) performed Serwouters's *Tamerlan* in Hamburg in June

1667.[104] Their production was described by a Swedish traveler, the writer, medical doctor, and scientist Urban Hjärne, who praised the performance for its realism and, notably, for Tamerlane's horse appearing on stage. Because Hjärne was able to summarize this (and another play he saw at this time) accurately, the troupe must have performed it in a language that was comprehensible to him and to the Hamburg audience. In his diary he writes:

> but when I came to the market place, I saw a house which they use to play comedies. I paid 8 solidi and entered. I finally found a place in the upper part [of the theater], from where I could see the whole comedy, which started with a delay. The story was about Tamerlan, who is defeating Baiazeth. It was really remarkable, in what a realistic way Turks and Tartars were presented. Above all Tamerlan himself, with a red spot on his face. Then there was a woman called Maëcha, who was dressed as a jester; Tamerlan's horse on the stage; the defeat of Baiazeth; Tamerlan is poisoned.[105]

Serwouters's Tamerlane play was widely associated with the extremes of Dutch theatricality. In describing Dutch staging practices, the eighteenth-century theater historian Riccoboni (cited in chap. 4) mentions that "in *Tamerlan* that prince appears on a horse with Bajazet."[106] We recall the stage direction in the Russian play indicating that Tamerlane is to enter on a horse for the concluding scene.

Van Fornenbergh was an actor wholly representative of his generation, with ties to the English players who traveled on the Continent in the first part of the century. In 1645, he associated himself with the English actor John Payne; they called themselves "Engelse komedianten." In March 1646 another Englishman, William Roe, and several other Dutch players joined the group. This collaboration was brief, for the two Englishmen had disappeared by the summer of 1646, and from spring 1647, the new troupe headed by Fornenbergh traveled widely throughout the Netherlands (including the southern, "Spanish," Netherlands) as "Oprechte Nederduytsche commedianten" (genuine Low German, i.e., Dutch, comedians).[107] In the 1650s Fornenbergh's troupe traveled to German-speaking territories and made its first visit to Sweden in 1653, where the players performed at Nyköping Castle (this excursion recalls the Swedish commercial opportunities pioneered by Simon Dannenfels nearly thirty years earlier).[108] It was on the return from their second Swedish visit, in 1667, that Hjärne caught the troupe's performance in Hamburg, where they had played previously—it is worth recalling that many of the merchant-performers in the February (and probably May)

1672 "ballets" in Moscow were from Hamburg and some, for example Dirck Hasenkroeg, had Dutch roots. The busy mercantile atmosphere of Hamburg was a natural destination for traveling acting companies. In later years, the troupe continued to tour throughout the Netherlands, and in 1660, van Fornenbergh founded The Hague's first public theater.[109]

Another popular and well-traveled company was that headed by Carl Andreas Paulsen and later by Johannes Velten. This is the troupe the tsar's agent, Colonel Nicolaus von Staden, had tried to engage in the summer of 1672, when he was in Riga looking for acting companies. Riga was a good place to look, as it, too, was a destination point for the mixed groups of English, German, and Dutch "English comedians," including the Paulsen-Velten company as well as van Fornenbergh's (the latter troupe performed in Riga in February–March 1666).[110] The Paulsen company traveled throughout northern and central German-speaking lands in 1665, including a swing through college towns, among them, Jena. Pastor Gregorii had been schooled in Jena a few years earlier, in 1661, so although we cannot track any direct contact, it is at least a reasonable place for a student to come into contact with traveling theatrical troupes.[111] After his time in Jena, Gregorii was ordained in Dresden (April 1662). Dresden had long been a center for the "English comedians," and indeed, just a few years later, in the 1670s, the Velten troupe had extended contacts there.[112] Again, Gregorii was in the right place at almost the right time to have been exposed to the traditions of the traveling companies (in addition, of course, to the school dramas that would have formed part of his instruction in his student days). Many of the plays in the Velten repertoire have been identified, and although there are no known settings of the Serwouters Tamerlane play, they did perform several settings of Spanish plays as early as 1669.[113]

The network of connections surrounding the Tamerlane story is thus compelling (if not, admittedly, entirely nailed down with precision). In combination, all of these influences and sources—histories, plays, pageants, visual images, links between acting traditions, and all the rest—provide us with enough raw material to account readily for the Moscow Tamerlane play. The German playwrights in Moscow were familiar with popular contemporary historical treatments of the story (obviously, because they quote them directly from the Dutch translation of Du Bec's book), and it is even possible that someone in Moscow's Foreign Quarter had seen or heard about the Dutch theatrical setting of the story, however distant its plot from the Moscow version. Although we are certainly not proposing Marlowe's play as a model for the Russian version, even indirectly, we do not discount entirely any knowledge of his *Tamburlaine* (or "peeces and Patches" of it) on the Continent, because there were so many means and configurations through which such knowledge might have been transmitted. Like the tsar's court theater as a whole, there are many nodes of convergence that produced the Russian Tamerlane play. The Tamerlane theme resonated deeply in the West and in Russia; the resulting Russian play reveals the ties joining the amateur playwrights in Moscow to the traditions of Western theater with which they were obviously familiar, and, in this context, the play tells us a great deal about the theatrical exposures and assumptions of contemporary audiences, particularly in German and Dutch traditions.

Furthermore, although speculative, this exploration may help specialists look at new kinds of sources in new kinds of ways. Historians of western European theater might fruitfully incorporate knowledge of the Moscow court plays of the 1670s into their surveys—these plays, too, are part of the continuum, with pertinent and revealing relationships to European theatrical history as a whole.[114] And in the spirit of intertheater, the ties we have proposed in this chapter may stimulate new thinking about how Marlowe's *Tamburlaine* might have echoed through the performances of the English players and their German descendants over the course of the seventeenth century.

Our final chapter takes up this Tamerlane thread again, unspooling it into the early eighteenth century. For although Tsar Aleksei Mikhailovich's death resulted in the closing of his court theater, the Russian experience did not end there. Indeed, in the reconstitution of the Russian theatrical links with the traveling companies, Tamerlane—most likely in Serwouters's version—reappeared in Moscow.

NOTES

1. A note on spelling: we use *Tamerlane* for both the historical figure and the character in the Russian play (acknowledging the historical inaccuracy yet attempting to impose some consistency); we use *Tamburlaine* for the character in Christopher Marlowe's play. We use *Bayezid* for the historical figure and for the Marlowe character (where it is spelled "Bajazeth"); we use *Baiazet* for the character in the Russian play (which displays marvelous orthographic creativity, although this is the most frequent usage). Exceptions occur when we quote published sources.

2. See the brief summary in Waugh, *Great Turkes*, 7–9; a broader survey is in Litavrin, *Osmanskaia imperiia*.

3. This discussion is based on the text in *RRD* 2:59–92 (the source in Tikhonravov, *Russkie dramaticheskie proizvedeniia* 1:204–242, lacks part of the prologue and act 1, scene 1). Other summaries of the play are in Bulgakov, "Komediia," 325–338; Morozov, *Ocherki*, 181–184. On the references to history and the historian, see Parfenov, "K voprosu," 16; *Slovar' knizhnikov* 4:6.

4. A similar opening trumpet fanfare, in this case revealing Mercury, appears in a 1657 school drama from Leipzig; see Bolte, *Das Danziger Theater*, 86n2, referring to J. G. Schoch's *Comoedia vom Studenten-Leben*. Schoch's play is discussed in Lande, *Persistence of Folly*, 71–72.

5. This military review would have echoed recent events at court. *DR* 3:1204–1213, from late January 1675, refers to preparations for such a review at the entry of the Persian embassy from Shah Abbas.

6. Morozov, *Ocherki*, esp. 184, makes the connection to *Judith*.

7. Grigorii's death is in Bogoiavlenskii, "Moskovskii teatr," 45; we continue to cite references from Bogoiavlenskii's work in parentheses in the text, indicating only the page number. Mazon, "'Artakserksovo deistvo' i repertuar pastora Gregori," 361–362, ascribes the play to Gregorii. Russian sources refer to Hüfner as Iakov Givner or Iurii Mikhailovich.

8. *DR* 3:1224 (February 11, 1675): "On this year and date there was a comedy [performed for] the Great Lord, at the fifth hour of the night, and foreigners and Boyar Artamon Sergeevich Matveev's people entertained the Great Lord with all kinds of various performances. And the comedy for the Great Lord went until the third hour before daybreak." Time was reckoned by sunrise and sunset, which results in great seasonal variations (Simonov and Khromov, "Chasy na krugu," esp. 22). The performance began at the fifth hour at night (five hours after sunset, so in February around 10:00 p.m.) and continued until the third hour before sunrise, or around 4:00 a.m., for a total length of roughly six hours. The "various performances" could indicate the supplemental entertainments we have seen, especially in the fall of 1674; it could also refer to the comic actions in this play. At any rate, the "various performances" help account for the overall length. Although the performance given here does not name the play, the payment records show that *Tamerlane* is the comedy in question.

9. See also Bulgakov, "Komediia," 350–354.

10. Liudden's identity is unclear; the spelling is from the Russian source. The Amburger-Datenbank lists a "Willem Luden," from the Netherlands, ca. 1664. An interpreter from the Ambassadorial Chancery, Ivan Enak, contacted Liudden at Matveev's request, and Enak did additional theatrical work later that year (Bogoiavlenskii, "Moskovskii teatr," 63); see chapter 4 of this volume.

11. This discussion is based on Bulgakov, "Komediia," and Parfenov, "K voprosu."

12. Parfenov, "K voprosu," 21–23, acknowledges the general influence of Western plays on the Russian theater but does not see influence specifically from Marlowe. Elsewhere, Parfenov wrote extensively on Marlowe; a recent review of his work is in Zhatkin and Riabova, "Osmyslenie khudozhestvennogo svoeobraziia."

13. *PSRL* 11:158. Translation from Lenhoff, "Temir Aksak's Dream," 45 (insertion in square brackets by Lenhoff). See also the same author's "Tale of Tamerlane."

14. Melnikoff, "Jones's Pen," 206–207. Milwright, "So Despicable," focuses on images of Tamerlane in printed books, also noting other media in which the rulers appeared (esp. pp. 337–338nn2–3). On images of Tamerlane in the 1590 and 1593 editions of Marlowe's play (which were taken from an earlier publication by Jones), see Milwright, "So Despicable," 321.

15. Kaplan, "Middleton's Tamburlaine," 259.

16. Wade, *Triumphus Nuptialis Danicus*, 200 (the wedding included a theatrical component involving formal court presentations and itinerant troupes; see Wade, esp. parts II and IV). Milwright, "So Despicable," surveys imagery, including similar shorthand illustrations of Bayezid in a cage (esp. 324 and 341n55); see also Milwright and Baboula, "Bayezid's Cage," esp. 244. Other images are discussed in Denny, "Images of Turks"; musical associations are in Bowles, "Impact"; Bevilacqua and Pfeifer, "Turquerie," esp. 98–101.

17. For example, Parfenov, "K voprosu," 26–27.

18. *RRD* 2:81–82; Du Bec, *Historie* (1597), 117–118.

19. In other contemporary English translations, this is *Sunne*—surely the meaning intended here, obscured by orthographic inconsistencies; the French original has *Soleil* (Du Bec, *Historie* [1595], 229). We have slightly modernized the spelling in all excerpts from Du Bec, *Historie* (1597).

20. Knolles, *Generall Historie*, 217, relying very closely on Du Bec at this point, also refers to the "greene ensigne." In the Russian play, Tamerlane had already mentioned a green *bunchiuk* (or *bunchuk*), a horsetail mounted on a tall pole as a standard (*RRD* 2:73). This symbol does not appear in Du Bec, but the green color in the play may have been suggested by Du Bec's "greene ensigne." Green clothing was strongly associated with Islam in writings of contemporary Europeans, for example, by the English traveler Fynes Moryson, cited in our previous chapter and also later in our discussion for his remarks on theater; see Chew, *Crescent and the Rose*, 198–199. McJannet, *Sultan Speaks*, 101, notes Du Bec's rejection of the colored tents that are so vivid in Marlowe's play.

21. *PSRL* 11:160; translation from Lenhoff, "Temir Aksak's Dream," 46n19; see also Parfenov, "K voprosu," 19 (citing the version in *PSRL* 11:252).

22. *RRD* 2:61–62; Du Bec, *Historie* (1597), 102.

23. Garbled or not, Du Bec's presentation verifies to a certain extent his claim, on the title page, that the book was "Drawen from the auncient Monuments of the Arabians" (Du Bec, *Historie* [1597]; McJannet, *Sultan Speaks*, 92, 97). This Eastern origin has often been dismissed; one scholar calls Du Bec's history a "fantasist forgery" (Ingram, *Writing the Ottomans*, 71; see also Ellis-Fermor, *Tamburlaine*, 34). Although McJannet acknowledges suspicions regarding Du Bec's authenticity, she points out that he did apparently access Eastern traditions, which then began to circulate via the many publications and translations of his work (*Sultan Speaks*, 97; see also Milwright, "So Despicable," 338n15).

24. McJannet, *Sultan Speaks*, 114. McJannet discusses Eastern sources in this question-answer series on pp. 112–113. The passage is in Du Bec, *Historie* (1597), 125.

25. *RRD* 2:87; Du Bec, *Historie van t'leven* (1647), 179. The Dutch Du Bec diverges from the French original (Du Bec, *Histoire* [1595], 246) and the English translation (Du Bec, *Historie* [1597], 125).

26. This is the beginning of the addendum, which is presented in our following discussion. We omit several lines of explanatory text in the addendum, beginning here with the first direct dialogue of this section.

27. *RRD* 2:87–88; Du Bec, *Historie van t'leven* (1647), 179–180.

28. All three pre-1675 Dutch Du Bec editions include the Byvoeghsel: Rotterdam, 1613 (addendum on p. 201); Haarlem, 1638 (p. 202); Amsterdam, 1647 (p. 179).

29. Du Bec's book itself was recognized as authoritative; by the time of the earliest Dutch translation, in 1613, it had already been published in several French editions as well as the 1597 English translation we have been citing. We have not been able to identify all of the sources noted in these shorthand references in the addendum.

30. We did not make a detailed comparison of these three Dutch editions. They are generally the same, at least in the addendum, although there are some small differences. Changes in the 1638 edition, relative to that of 1613, are generally followed in the 1647 edition. Nevertheless, overall it is clear that all three editions are based on the same translation, first published in 1613.

31. Leunclavius, *Annales sultanorum Othmanidarum* (Frankfurt, 1588, 1596) and the revised German edition, Lewenklaw, *Neuwe Chronica Türckischer Nation* (Frankfurt, 1590, 1595). These are translations of the five-volume history by Sadeddin Mehmed ibn Hasanjan. Although the title reference in the Dutch addendum is in Latin, the page number points to one of the German editions of Lewenklaw (the encounter appears on p. 14 in both German editions). Parfenov, "K voprosu," 28 and n. 37, identified Lewenklaw as a source relevant to the Russian play. Because he did not know about the Dutch translation of Du Bec, however, he did not realize that Lewenklaw's work was known only indirectly to the Moscow playwrights.

32. Baudartius, *Apophthegmata Christiana*, 76, refers to the "Annal. Turc." (i.e., Leunclavius/Lewenklaw); he gives no page number, so it is not clear to which edition he refers. The widespread knowledge of Lewenklaw is indicated in Waugh, "Ioannikii Galiatovs'kyi's Polemics," 912; Nicolae, "Foreign Names," 343. On the publications of Lewenklaw, see Göllner, *Turcica* 2:741 (a listing of the editions) and 3:248.

33. Thomas and Tydeman, *Christopher Marlowe*, 74, note more than thirty Spanish editions by 1600, with many translations. Ocasar Ariza, "Genetic Edition," 179n26, notes seventy-five foreign editions of Mexía's text over roughly a century, in addition to the Spanish publications.

34. For the 1607 text (in the addendum as "Pieter Messias"), the chapter and page references correspond to a Dutch version of Mexía, *De Verscheyden lessen Petri Messiae* (Leiden, 1607). The reference in the addendum to "Anton. du Verdier" (book 2, chap. 30) corresponds to the well-known French bibliographer and anthologist Antoine Du Verdier (1544–1600). There were several editions of *Les Diverses leçons d'Antoine Du Verdier . . . suivans celles de Pierre Messie* issued before the 1613 Dutch addendum was written; this was yet another compilation of Mexía's text, and it includes material that does not appear in *De Verscheyden lessen*.

35. See Blaak, *Literacy in Everyday Life*, 357–358. Stronks, "No Home Grown Products," 229–230n22, identified "I. L. B." with Berewout.

36. *Interpreter's Dictionary* 3:378, s.v. "Milcah." Some historical sources (e.g., Knolles, *Generall Historie*, 221) call her Despina, possibly reflecting Bayezid's marriage to the daughter (Despina or Despina Olivera) of a Serbian leader; Seaton, "Fresh Sources for Marlowe," 393, and, following her, Ellis-Fermor, *Tamburlaine*, 65, suggest that Marlowe's Zabina comes from this Despina.

37. Knolles, *Generall Historie*, 221.

38. The humiliation of Bayezid's wife appears widely in Eastern sources; see McJannet, *Sultan Speaks*, 109–112, and Milwright and Baboula, "Bayezid's Cage."

39. This emphasis does not appear in *De Verscheyden lessen Petri Messiae*, discussed previously.

40. Perondinus, *Magni Tamerlanis Scytharum* (Florence, 1553), quoted from Thomas and Tydeman, *Christopher Marlowe*, 109. Ellis-Fermor, *Tamburlaine*, 31, emphasizes the power of Perondinus's "packed and pregnant Latin" in cementing the story in the Western tradition; Ellis-Fermor cites his text on pp. 300–302. Perondinus is closely quoted in Philip Lonicer, *Chronicorum Turcicorum . . .* (Frankfurt, 1578); neither source gives Bayezid's wife a name. Parfenov, "K voprosu," 29, juxtaposes passages from both Perondinus and Lonicer with the

Russian play text; however, these passages are aligned with the "what would you have done" section of the play, although neither Lonicer nor Perondinus (from whom Lonicer draws closely) includes this exchange.

41. This characterization might account for Tamerlane's remark after Baiazet's horrific death, saying that hanging would have been better—perhaps intended as a more compassionate end to his life.

42. Ingram, *Writing the Ottomans*, 71. The playworthiness of the Eastern sources and their translations is noted in McJannet, *Sultan Speaks*, 93, 106.

43. Savel'eva, *Knigi*, items 22 and 178 (although it is not always clear exactly when specific titles came into Vinius's possession); item 177 is another Dutch translation of Mexía. Iurkin, *Andrei Andreevich Vinius*, chaps. 1 and 2, details the backgrounds of Vinius and his father, who had also worked in Russia; there is a summary in Boterbloem, *Moderniser of Russia*, esp. 36–44, 54–60. On Vinius's work with the kuranty, see *Vesti-Kuranty* VII, where signed translations are on pp. 207, 213, 226; Waugh and Maier, "Muscovy," esp. 92–94.

44. Witsen came to Russia just after finishing his university education, in Leiden, where he studied with the renowned Arabist Jacob Golius, with whom he became close (Vitsen, *Puteshestvie v Moskoviiu*, 5). Golius, in 1636, wrote a Latin preface to the Arabic history of Tamerlane by Ahmad ibn Muhammed ibn Arabshah—Golius, then, would have had good reason to know about Du Bec's history, which also claimed to be based on Arabic sources (McJannet, *Sultan Speaks*, 96–97); perhaps he passed this knowledge on to his student, Witsen. On the early stages of the Witsen-Vinius relationship, see Iurkin, *Andrei Andreevich Vinius*, esp. 87–88, 390–391; Iurkin outlines the familial ties, through Vinius's mother, on p. 29.

45. Iurkin, *Andrei Andreevich Vinius*, esp. 439–441, discusses the many routes by which Vinius would have been able to acquire books, including through Witsen; see also Savel'eva, *Knigi*, esp. 10–11.

46. Kazakova, "A. A. Vinius," emphasizes the Turkish threat in the context of these missions, so if Vinius had seen Du Bec's book on his travels, it might have caught his attention—we do not, however, have any specific knowledge of book acquisitions on this trip, nor is it clear for how long Vinius stayed in Holland. He had traveled, via Danzig (early January 1673) and Hamburg, to Amsterdam and The Hague before embarking on a mail ship to England on February 23 (Kazakova, "A. A. Vinius," 353; Kozlovskii, *Pervye pochty* 1:188). Iurkin, *Andrei Andreevich Vinius*, 99n17, estimates that Vinius was in Holland for roughly ten days; see p. 100 on his return in early 1674.

47. The order also mentioned Emel'ian Ukraintsev, one of the three emissaries dispatched to the West at the same time as Vinius. Ukraintsev later became Vinius's brother-in-law (Iurkin, *Andrei Andreevich Vinius*, 500).

48. Morozov, *Ocherki*, 184–186; Tikhonravov, *Russkie dramaticheskie proizvedeniia* 1:esp. xxiii–xxiv.

49. Morozov, *Ocherki*, 184–186, compares the comic scenes and the songs. In *Judith*, the drinking song is performed serially by three characters in separate strophes; there is only a single strophe in the *Tamerlane* song.

50. Kleimola, "Hunting for Dogs," 481, reports that the only known dog names in Muscovite sources are for dogs given as diplomatic gifts taken to Persia in 1597–1598; they were named "Smerd" (stinker) and "Durak" (dummy), so our theatrical association, "Tölpel," seems consistent.

51. *RRD* 2:92; Bulgakov, "Komediia," 338–339. Parfenov, "K voprosu," 19–20, notes that some spellings differ by act. Probably several copyists were involved in the process, especially if they were working under time pressure.

52. The publisher of Marlowe's play excised the comic interludes, so no direct comparison is possible (yet the excision of such material at least indicates that it existed). Although much of this comic action would have been stereotyped (as in the Russian play), we do not know if there were any specific comic characters associated with Marlowe's *Tamburlaine*. See Melnikoff, "Jones's Pen"; Gill, "Such Conceits," 55.

53. Ellis-Fermor, *Tamburlaine*, 126–127.

54. Others noted this striking passage and its relationship to Marlowe, e.g., Morozov, *Ocherki*, 183.

55. Bulgakov, "Komediia," esp. 336–338.

56. *RRD* 2:88; text in this line appears only in one of the two seventeenth-century sources of the play (described in *RRD* 2:293). The entire sequence under discussion here appears in *RRD* 2:88–91.

57. *RRD* 2:91: "Ей, голову всю сокрушил и мозг видеть" (with a variant reading as "мозг видит"). We thank one of our anonymous readers for pointing out that a very similar formulation (as "мозг выдет") appears in legal documents of the time.

58. Du Bec, *Historie van t'leven* (1647), 181: "zo heeft hy sijn Hooft soo lange tegen de Ysere Tralien der Koye geslagen/ dat hy zijn ongelukich leven ge-eyndicht heeft." Lewenklaw, however, may not be the source for the Dutch Du Bec. This suicide is in one of Lewenklaw's lengthy addenda; in both editions of the *Neuwe Chronica* (1590 and 1595), it appears in n. 65, p. 233, which is not referenced in the Dutch Du Bec Byvoeghsel. Du Verdier and/or Baudartius seem the most likely sources.

59. Act 4, scene 4; quoted from Ellis-Fermor, *Tamburlaine*, 152. See Bulgakov, "Komediia," 336.

60. Act 5, scene 2; Ellis-Fermor, *Tamburlaine*, 170.

61. Quoted from Thomas and Tydeman, *Christopher Marlowe*, 109.

62. Some have pointed to the reverse, a "Moscow to Marlowe" impact, although quite different from our point here. See, for example, Dimmock, *New Turkes*, esp. 136–137, where the author describes the precise "geographical scope, relished and scrutinized in both parts of *Tamburlaine*," which represents exactly what the "officially sanctioned Muscovy and Levant companies sought to exploit"; *Tamburlaine*, in this context, represents "a relentless catalogue of goods and trading locations reminiscent of the reports of [Anthony] Jenkinson and others that begins to open the east to the English mercantile gaze."

63. Bosman, "Renaissance Intertheater," 570.

64. A similar repertoire (including plays on Esther and the Prodigal Son and several Pickleherring entertainments) is outlined in a 1660 petition from a company headed by Christian Buckhäußer (Bockhäuser) to the Lüneburg city council (Kitching, *Europe's Itinerant Players*, 76 and 89n82).

65. Williams, *Shakespeare on the German Stage*, 42 (regarding revisions to *Titus Andronicus*); see also p. 45.

66. *RRD* 2:75; the English context is in West, "Intertheatricality," 157 and n. 12, where he recounts appearances in nearly twenty English plays of the "sa, sa" refrain.

67. Bulgakov, "Komediia," 320n2; other scholars, for example, Morozov, *Ocherki*, 180–181, have made the assumption of direct transmission by traveling English troupes.

68. These dates are based on a November 1587 letter that appears to refer to 2 *Tamburlaine*, so the first part of the play, in which Bayezid appears, must have preceded it (see Gurr, *Shakespeare's Opposites*, 8–10). Levin, "Contemporary Perception," 52, gives a 1588 reference by dramatist Robert Greene that may also suggest early knowledge of the play.

69. Publication information is in Melnikoff, "Jones' Pen," esp. 202; see also Ellis-Fermor, *Tamburlaine*, 1–6, 11–17 (noting that none of the four contemporary publications includes Marlowe's name), 67; Gurr, *Shakespeare's Opposites*, 207–208, 212–213.

70. Gurr, "Great Divide," 34–35. The early (1583) listing of the Admiral's Men is in Chambers, *Elizabethan Stage* 2:224.

71. A tabulation of the performances is in Hutchings, "Turk Phenomenon"; see also Gurr, *Shakespeare's Opposites*, 207–208, 212–213, taken from Henslowe's diary.

72. Gurr, "Great Divide," 35, poses this question clearly, although with a different, and more direct, focus.

73. The sale record is in Brand and Rudin, "Der englische Komödiant," 14–15. Cerasano, *DNB*, s.v. "Alleyn, Edward," suggests that the items were purchased from Jones in order to "furnish their [the Alleyns'] company." Gurr, *Shakespeare's Opposites*, 17, believes that "Jones cannot have sold him [Alleyn] the Marlowe playbooks at this time," suggesting instead that *Tamburlaine* (and *Faustus*) were in the countryside with the traveling Admiral's company, not in London; he proposes that *Tamburlaine* may have come to Alleyn via a similar route, through another associated actor, James Tunstall, and perhaps Jones, who were involved in the old (1580s) Admiral's as well as the new (mid-1590s) company. For our purposes, the variety of connections is sufficient, even if the exact route is uncertain.

74. The exact dates of Alleyn's association are uncertain; see Cerasano, *DNB*, s.v. "Alleyn, Edward"; Gurr, *Shakespeare's Opposites*, 14–15.

75. Gurr, *Shakespearean Playing Companies*, 237 (stated more strongly on p. 70), 235 (possible meeting on tour), 254–255 (travel itineraries); on touring, see also Brand and Rudin, "Der englische Komödiant," 17–18.

76. This passport is discussed in Bosman, "Mobility," esp. 493–500; Schrickx, *Foreign Envoys*, esp. 184–185; Brand and Rudin, "Der englische Komödiant," 18–21, 120–121.

77. Schrickx, *Foreign Envoys*, 186–189 (including a possible visit to Nürnberg in August 1593); Brand and Rudin, "Der englische Komödiant," 24–27.

78. Katri(t)zky, "Pickelhering and Hamlet," 114, 116–117. See also Gurr, *Shakespearean Playing Companies*, 234–235; Schrickx, "English Actors," 159. A lost account by a Württemberg merchant mentions seeing plays by the "very famous Mr. Christopher Marlowe" performed by "Englishmen" at the Frankfurt fair, which would refer to Browne's company (Murad, *English Comedians*, 45 and 80n46). Schrickx, *Foreign Envoys*, 187, reports this as fact (drawing back slightly on p. 195); Brand and Rudin, "Der englische Komödiant," 30, place it "ins Reich der Fabel." Although the information seems plausible enough, given the close ties of the English company in Frankfurt to the Admiral's Men in England, we (regretfully) relegate this to a note.

79. Schrickx, *Foreign Envoys*, 189, 193; Brand and Rudin, "Der englische Komödiant," 40–41.

80. Gurr, *Shakespeare's Opposites*, 2, notes two short periods in which the London theaters functioned during the plague, January 1593 and January 1594, when the cold weather reduced the spread of the disease.

81. Gurr, *Shakespearean Playing Companies*, chap. 4 (the "duopoly"); on p. 70 he suggests that, after Alleyn was established at the Rose, he deliberately collected the scattered company, with the goal of "renew[ing] his former roles in the early Marlowe plays."

82. On the ties to the Rose's repertoire, see Schrickx, *Foreign Envoys*, 195–197, 231; Katri(t)zky, "Pickelhering and Hamlet."

83. Chambers, *Elizabethan Stage* 2:159.

84. Levin, "Contemporary Perception," 53; Gurr, "Who Strutted," 98–99.

85. Gurr, "Who Strutted," 99, observes that references to *Tamburlaine* are related to the times when Alleyn was acting, they disappear when he "retired" and return when he came back to the stage. Cerasano, "Edward Alleyn," 51–52, notes that even though *Tamburlaine* was not revived, this type of role was "often replaced by other plays that were similar in

nature to the earlier 'hits.' Thus, Alleyn's ... influence was felt even when he ceased to perform." On Alleyn as an actor, see also Armstrong, "Shakespeare," and J. Brown, "Marlowe and the Actors." One wonders if Alleyn's "retirement" in 1597 interfered with plans to revive *Tamburlaine*. The work, if it first appeared around 1587, was then revived, after the plague closures, in the 1594–1595 season. As Gurr, *Shakespeare's Opposites*, 55, notes, revivals tended to follow after two or three years. So right around Alleyn's retirement might have been a logical time for a (third) revival of the play. See also Knutson, "*Henslowe's Diary*," on revivals.

86. Chambers, *Elizabethan Stage* 2:173–174, on Alleyn's return to the stage; on later repertoire, Gurr, *Shakespeare's Opposites*, e.g., 5, 55, seems to assume performances of *Tamburlaine* at the Fortune into the seventeenth century.

87. Cerasano, "Edward Alleyn," 52–53, emphasizes how these props demonstrate the centrality of Alleyn's roles (especially Tamburlaine); props and costumes for *Tamburlaine* in an inventory from March 10, 1598, are in [Henslowe], *Henslowe's Diary*, 320–321 (summarized in Gurr, *Shakespeare's Opposites*, 208); the cage, listed in the same inventory although not labeled specifically as belonging to *Tamburlaine*, is in [Henslowe], *Henslowe's Diary*, 319.

88. Cerasano, "Edward Alleyn," 55–56.

89. Levin, "Contemporary Perception," 63 (quoting Cowley's play); on 69n42 he suggests that this refers to an unrecorded revival of *Tamburlaine*. Cowley's *The Guardian* was published in 1650 (Lindsay, *DNB*, s.v. "Cowley, Abraham"). On the Red Bull Theater in the early seventeenth century, see Griffith, *Jacobean Company*; many articles on seventeenth-century actors in *DNB* refer to the down-market character of the Red Bull. R. Bowers, "*Tamburlaine* in Ludlow," notes the coincidence of two boys christened "Tamburlaine" in 1620, suggesting that a touring version of the play made an impact in the town.

90. Gurr, *Shakespeare's Opposites*, 250n109; Bentley, *Jacobean and Caroline Stage* 2:691. Kiefer, "Lost and Found," proposes a familiar context for this remark, linking the play *Jugurth* to Edward Alleyn, the Rose, and the Admiral's Men; see esp. 24–25.

91. Murad, *English Comedians*, 29; Bosman, "History between Theaters," 196.

92. Williams, *Shakespeare on the German Stage*, 33.

93. Other plays allude to this image; see Levin, "Contemporary Perception," esp. 58–59. Berek, "*Tamburlaine*'s Weak Sons," esp. 57–58, 79, emphasizes stage effects recalling those of Marlowe's setting. The 1606 complaint from the Pomeranian town of Loitz, referred to in chapter 1 of this volume, underscores the danger of such language barriers: "Because their comedies are written and presented in an unknown language, it is not known ... what they include and deal with ... and whether it is in accord with the Word of God" (quoted in Limon, *Gentlemen of a Company*, 83).

94. On the Dekker play, see Schlueter, "New Light"; Murad, *English Comedians*, 57–59; F. Bowers, *Dramatic Works of Thomas Dekker* 1:107–110; Hunt, *Thomas Dekker*, 28–35 (esp. 32–33 on Marlowe resonances). Kaplan, "Middleton's Tamburlaine," 259n4, also connects the Tamerlane figure and Dekker.

95. Performances in 1596 in [Henslowe], *Henslowe's Diary*, 34–37. The November revision is summarized in Knutson, "*Henslowe's Diary*," 18n26; Schlueter, "New Light," 120. The 1600 publication is in F. Bowers, *Dramatic Works of Thomas Dekker* 1:105–205.

96. Continental performances in Schlueter, "New Light," 121; 1620 text in *Spieltexte* 1:129–209.

97. Schlueter, however, does not attribute all of the changes appearing in the 1620 German print (relative to the 1600 London print) to this lost 1599 revision.

98. F. Bowers, *Dramatic Works of Thomas Dekker* 1:121–122 (spelling slightly modernized).

99. Chambers, *Elizabethan Stage* 2:280–281; Schlueter, "English Actors in Kassel," esp. 246.

100. Schrickx, *Foreign Envoys*, 230–231; Limon, *Gentlemen of a Company*, 21–22; Murad, *English Comedians*.

101. First published in Valencia, 1642, wrongly attributed to Lope de Vega; see Spencer and Schevill, *Dramatic Works*, 200–204.

102. Álvarez Francés, "Phoenix," 61; graphs 1 and 2 (p. 19) illustrate the popularity of Spanish playwrights as sources for Dutch plays and, specifically, for productions at the Schouwburg; Serwouters's *Tamerlan* was produced at the peak of Spanish source material produced there. See also surveys in Sullivan, *Calderón*, esp. chaps. 2 and 3; Brandt and Hogendoorn, *German and Dutch Theatre*, 337–341.

103. Jean Magnon's *Le Grand Tamerlan et Bajazet* (performed in 1647 at the Hôtel de Bourgogne, published in 1648) does not seem to have influenced the Serwouters play (although see Junkers, *Niederländische Schauspieler*, 237n1)—it is, like Serwouters's version, a romance, but there are almost no overlapping characters (apart from the two protagonists), and the plot is quite different (see plot summaries in Houts, "Two Sources," 9–12; Rouillard, *Turk*, part 4:478–481). Another French drama on the Tamerlane theme was Racine's *Bajazet*, which premiered in 1672, and was reported in the *Mercure galant* (January 1672, pp. 65–90), with a short notice in the *Nordischer Mercurius* (datelined Paris, February 26, 1672). However, there is no evidence that this play was known to the Moscow playwrights.

104. Albach, *Langs kermissen en hoven*, 101; van Fornenbergh was buried, in The Hague, on January 2, 1697 (p. 136). The troupe's repertoire and travels are summarized in Albach's study in Appendixes C and D, pp. 149–154; they performed Serwouters's play again in Ghent in 1675 (pp. 118, 154).

105. Hjärne's diary is in UUL, D 701, where this passage, written in a very difficult hand, reads (fol. 126r-v, June 25, 1667): "sed cum in foro venirem domum vidi ubi Comoediae agebantur. Datis 8 solidis intravi. Locum tandem recepi in editiore loco, ubi totam Tragoediam sero inceptam perspexi. Historia erat de Tamerlane Baiazethum sibi subjiciente. Notabile profecto erat, quam ad vivum representabantur Turcae et Tartari. Praecipue Tamerlanes ipse cum macula rubra in facie. Porro quoque mulier Maëcha in morionem mutata, equus Tamerlanis in Theatro, Baiazethi submissio, venenum Tamerlani datur." Hjärne had previously engaged in some theatricals during his studies at Uppsala University; see Dahlberg, *Komediantteatern*, 383, where the translation of the Tamerlane passage is more accurate, with respect to the character "Maëcha," than that in Brandt and Hogendoorn, *German and Dutch Theatre*, 437–438. Maacha is the equivalent of Eleazara in the Spanish original; she does indeed disguise herself as a jester or fool ("in morionem mutata") in order to rescue Bayezid. At the end of this entry, Hjärne mentions briefly a verse play in German, and he saw another play in Hamburg on June 28, 1667 (fol. 151v). The latter was identified by Bolte, "Schwedische Beiträge," 144, as another Dutch play certainly performed by the Fornenbergh troupe: Joris de Wijse, *Voorzigtige dolheit* (Amsterdam, 1650). It, too, is a translation from a Spanish play, Lope de Vega's *El cuerdo loco*; see the listings in the University of Amsterdam database ONSTAGE, at http://www.vondel.humanities.uva.nl/onstage/plays/48.

106. Quoted in Brandt and Hogendoorn, *German and Dutch Theatre*, 421 (1740 edition).

107. Albach, *Langs kermissen en hoven*, 59–61, 151–152; see also Hoppe, "English Acting Companies," 30. English actors were well known in the Spanish Netherlands; see, in addition to Albach, Schrickx, *Foreign Envoys*, esp. chap. 8; Hoppe, "English Actors at Ghent"; Brandt and Hogendoorn, *German and Dutch Theatre*, 352, 383.

108. On the Fornenbergh troupe's travels in German territories, see the summary in Albach, *Langs kermissen en hoven*, Appendix D, 151–154; Junkers, *Niederländische Schauspieler*, esp. 70–79; Brandt and Hogendoorn, *German and Dutch Theatre*, 49, 384–385; Sullivan,

Calderón, 80. On the Swedish trip, see Dahlberg, "Theatre around Queen Christina," 182–183, and her *Komediantteatern,* 135–142.

109. Brandt and Hogendoorn, *German and Dutch Theatre,* 408. Traveling companies paid their way and thus spread their repertoire by other means. For example, in 1656, when the English traveler Robert Bargrave was in Innsbruck, he encountered the English player George Jolly, who offered to give him a private performance; Bargrave declined (Tilmouth, "Music on the Travels," 157).

110. On the Fornenbergh troupe in Riga, see Albach, *Langs kermissen en hoven,* 102, 153; Junkers, *Niederländische Schauspieler,* 82. English companies in Riga are in Limon, *Gentlemen of a Company,* 91–93, from the period 1644–1648.

111. On this tour, see Scherl and Rudin, *Theater in Böhmen,* s.v. "Carl Andreas Paulsen"; Bolte, *Das Danziger Theater,* 97n1.

112. Watanabe-O'Kelly, *Court Culture in Dresden,* esp. 166–174, notes the frequent appearance of "English comedians" and their repertoire in Dresden. Sullivan, *Calderón,* 71, lays out familiar geography for theatrical travel: "The main axis was Hamburg (with nearby Altona, Lübeck, Hanover, Brunswick, Lüneburg) to Leipzig (surrounded by Halle, Dresden, Breslau and some smaller towns)."

113. Watanabe-O'Kelly, *Court Culture in Dresden,* 173. Plays associated with the Velten company are in Heine, *Johannes Velten,* chap. 2; Junkers, *Niederländische Schauspieler,* 244–246 (on p. 245 he lists a Tamerlane play of uncertain authorship in their repertoire); bibliography is in Scherl and Rudin, *Theater in Böhmen,* s.v. "Catarina Elisabeth Velten."

114. Russian examples appear, for example, in Gstach, *"Die Liebes Verzweiffelung,"* although see chapter 6 of this volume for some problems in the author's treatment.

From Tamerlane to Tamerlane and Beyond

Tamerlane and Bayezid were put through their paces again on a Russian stage in 1705, in a theater created at the order of Peter the Great. This was a different kind of theatrical experience: public, professional (although with some trainee students), and with a purpose-built stage enhanced by special machinery. This chapter tracks how the Russian court moved from Tamerlane to Tamerlane, via some familiar routes—diplomacy and court-sponsored entertainments—and how these experiences converged, as they had in the "ballets" of early 1672, in the formation of a theater. There are clear parallels to the creation of Tsar Aleksei's private court theater three decades earlier—for example, in the repertoire offered at the new venue. But the significance of this new public theater goes beyond such structural similarities, for its brief existence served as a stimulus to scholars later in the century, whose historical inquiries into Peter's theater unexpectedly revealed the scope of Tsar Aleksei's earlier enterprise. In tracing these linked performative experiences we rely again on intertheatrical networks, particularly on the concept of intertextuality, which historian Robert Henke describes as a text that "radiates in many directions," carrying "a web of resonance that can hardly be contained by binary vectors."[1] This "web of resonance" takes us backward into the repertoire of the traveling Continental players, forward into the multivalent theatrical world of eighteenth-century imperial Russia, and from there to the linked inquiries of scholars in Russia and the West who found themselves, in the early decades of the nineteenth century, sharing common academic and theatrical ground.

CONTINUING INTERESTS: DIPLOMATS ABROAD AND PERFORMANCES AT COURT

Although Tsar Fedor Alekseevich closed down his father's theater, in 1676, his diplomats continued to enjoy theatrical productions in the West. In some cases, the representatives were the same, for example Petr Potemkin, who had visited Parisian theaters in 1668 and had attended the opera in Vienna in 1674. He enjoyed similar experiences during his 1681–1682 assignment in France, Spain, and England. As in earlier missions, the trip generated a series of images: the famous full-length portrait of the ambassador, by the Spanish court painter Juan Carreño de Miranda; an engraving depicting his audience with Louis XIV in the *Almanach* for 1682; and another portrait, made in London, by Sir Godfrey Kneller (who would later paint Tsar Peter).[2] Potemkin's visits were equally rich in entertainment encounters. In Paris, he was taken to the Comédie-Française, where he saw Thomas Corneille's *L'Inconnu*, an elaborate machine play.[3] In London, Potemkin himself played an active role in procuring theatrical entertainments, for several accounts specify that at the ambassador's "particular command," he was taken to theaters. At the Dorset Garden Theatre, a large hall specially designed for musical extravaganzas, he saw *The Tempest*, a semi-opera (a genre involving spoken drama, separate musical and sung episodes, and spectacular scenic effects); this popular enhanced version of Shakespeare was originally produced in 1674 by actor-manager Thomas Betterton and playwright Thomas Shadwell. At the smaller Drury Lane Theatre, Potemkin saw part two of John Crowne's *The Destruction of Jerusalem*, another grand production that was revived several times after its 1677 premiere.[4]

Also in 1682, another of the tsar's representatives, Nikita Alekseev, was sent to Copenhagen to announce the death of Tsar Fedor and the establishment of the young co-tsars, Ivan and Peter. The party's report mentions two productions they attended there, one of which was described as a "French comedy," indicating a performance by La troupe du Roi de Danemark, which had been summoned the previous year. Shortly after Alekseev left, this troupe performed *L'Inconnu*, the work Potemkin had just seen in Paris, indicating that the ensemble could handle elaborate productions (and that Alekseev would have seen something rather impressive from them).[5] The Russian embassy sent to Spain a few years later, headed by Iakov Dolgorukii, was entertained by a "comedia" at the Retiro, in December 1687, an event reported in an avviso sent to the Medici court from Madrid.[6]

Performers on musical instruments, who had been so important for the court theater, would also have been available after Tsar Aleksei's death. Although all of the instrumentalists initially hired for the theater had departed or died by the time it was closed down, there was at least one holdover among the musical participants: the organ builder Simon Gutovskii was employed up to his death, in 1685, after which his position was taken over by his sons, and during these posttheater years, he was actively engaged in the repair of keyboard instruments at court. It is well known that Peter, as a youngster, was interested in military entertainments, but he had also been surrounded by keyboard instruments from a very young age. Gutovskii cared for the various *klevikorty*, tsynbaly, and organy belonging to the young tsarevich.[7] High-ranking families, as before, continued to own musical instruments. For example, according to the 1689 inventory of the possessions amassed by the powerful Prince Vasilii Vasil'evich Golitsyn, Regent Sofiia's close adviser, he owned organs and other keyboard instruments (klevikorty, tsynbaly), which were listed with other mechanical objects, particularly clocks; he also owned two "German flutes" and other types of instruments.[8] Even a music theoretical work such as Nikolai Diletskii's *Grammatika* (versions from the late 1670s through the early 1680s) took for granted the presence of organs as available teaching tools, and Diletskii's association with the Stroganov family meshes with ownership of such instruments by the elite.[9]

This upper-crust milieu was also influential in preserving memories of the theatrical energies of the early 1670s. V. V. Golitsyn, in addition to his musical instruments, also owned four manuscript books about the creation (or mounting) of "comedy"—this may indicate play texts or perhaps writings about theatrical presentations.[10] The play texts themselves (at least, some of them) were also accessible during this time. Johan Gabriel Sparwenfeld, a member of a visiting Swedish delegation, was in Moscow from 1684 to early 1687. He brought home many Russian texts he had collected (or had copied for him) during his stay there, including two plays from Tsar Aleksei's theater, *Joseph* and *Adam and Eve*, and also the text of Simeon Polotskii's *Prodigal Son*.[11] Sparwenfeld, a diligent book collector, cultivated a wide range of acquaintance in Moscow, in the foreign community as well as within the upper echelons of the government, especially the Golitsyn family; Prince V. V. Golitsyn, for example, helped him find a Russian-language teacher during his stay. Sparwenfeld was thus connected with many people who were in a position to have had direct knowledge, even involvement, with Tsar Aleksei's theater (he mentions Koch, "Old Dr. Blumentrost," and the son of impresario Matveev among his friends) and also people who would have known about Simeon Polotskii's plays.[12] (Simeon had been Sofiia's tutor and was thus very well known at court even after his death, in 1680.) Thus, although the court theater was closed down, all of its component parts—including the play texts themselves and the people who were familiar with or directly involved in the productions—continued to resonate in court life.

This continuing awareness forms a solid base for the events beginning in March 1697, when Tsar Peter, sole heir to the throne after the death in the previous year of his coruler, his half-brother Ivan, embarked on the life-changing trip known as the Great Embassy. This nearly eighteen-month journey, which took a large Russian party through northern and central Europe, with lengthy stops in Amsterdam, London, and Vienna, was certainly not undertaken with the goal of attending theatrical productions or hiring players. Peter was passionate about shipbuilding and its associated sciences, and the incognito status he assumed on the trip (as the soldier Petr Mikhailov) allowed him to participate in nautical vocational activities and, equally important, to avoid performing his role as head of state. As historian Jan Hennings puts it, in a chapter headed "Stage and Audience," Peter's embassy illustrates "the theatricality of diplomatic dialogue in the age of baroque culture, the way in which rulers and diplomats changed the scenery in the *theatrum praecedentiae* in order to . . . advance negotiations with other polities."[13] Granting this elaborately choreographed state-level interplay, we observe, in our focused context, that there continued to be a great deal of *actual* theater offered as part of the ceremonies: plays, concerts, operas, masquerades, and other entertainments proliferated in the major cities Peter and his suite visited, and his party participated enthusiastically. Indeed, because Peter's mission was supplied with copies of previous diplomatic reports by the Ambassadorial Chancery, they may have been primed for such experiences.[14] Peter's theatrical exposure in the West and the formation of a public theater in Moscow shortly after his return are certainly linked: the performances they encountered were a powerful and, judging by the Russian party's frequent attendance, a very enjoyable bonus of the Great Embassy, with obvious consequences.

Peter and his party, like the previous visiting Russian diplomats, were exposed to the most up-to-date entertainments the Western theatrical world had to offer. On their route from Riga to Amsterdam, their first major destination, they encountered familiar musical ornaments: fanfares sounded out along the way, and there was music at banquets and in churches, in addition to other amusements (especially fireworks).[15] In Amsterdam, they quickly sampled the city's thriving theaters. On August 17/27, 1697, they attended the Schouwburg, where they saw *De toveryen van Armida* (by Adriaen Peys) and *De gewaande advocaat* (by Peys and Pieter de Lacroix), productions noted widely in both Dutch and Russian sources. The performances were in Dutch, a language with which Peter was familiar, and they were mentioned in an elaborate engraving memorializing a spectacular fireworks display that was offered two days later.[16] The Russian account confirms the identity of one of these plays, explaining that their party saw a comedy "about the Greek goddess Cupid"—in *Armida*, there is indeed a (male) "Cupido." This Russian description offers additional detail, noting that "there were shown many battles and hellish torments and wondrous dances and other diverting things and decorations [*perspektivy*]." The visitors rewarded the performers with a monetary gift a few days later.[17] Later, during their stay in The Hague, the Russian party made two payments to "comedians," and just before their departure they paid the actor "Filip fan Gele" for his performances.[18] With these experiences under their belts, a portion of the group, including Peter, departed for England.

Shipbuilding and its related sciences were again the primary aims, but Peter managed to make time for theatrical entertainments in London on at least four occasions. On January 15, 1698, he went to the large Dorset Garden Theatre—where ambassador Potemkin had been so spectacularly entertained—and saw another semi-opera devised by the same actor-director, Thomas Betterton, who presented *The Prophetess; or, The History of Dioclesian* enhanced with music by Henry Purcell.[19] On February 8, Peter attended an unnamed theater, and on February 12, he went to another of the theaters Potemkin had visited, Drury Lane, where he saw an unidentified opera; several concerts are mentioned in English accounts around this time as well. He made a final theatrical trip on February 24, to see Nathan Lee's tragedy *The Rival Queens; or, The Death of Alexander the Great*.[20] Another member of the Russian party, the second ambassador, Fedor Alekseevich Golovin (who would be in charge of the new Moscow theater shortly thereafter), noted that he had attended two plays with the tsar after being called to London from Holland; this would have been at some point between late March and late April, suggesting still more theater visits.[21]

Extravagant entertainments continued after the party reassembled in Amsterdam and moved on to Vienna, where they arrived in mid-June 1698. The most famous event at the imperial court was the *Wirtschaft*, or masquerade, held on July 11/21, an elaborate incognito within the official incognito. In London, Peter's detachment had attended two masquerades, so this event, although very grand, would have been familiar.[22] In Vienna, there was additional entertainment overlap with the well-traveled ambassador Potemkin: both Russian parties, Potemkin's in 1674 and Peter's in 1698, saw an opera by the same composer, Antonio Draghi. Like the other large festivities Peter attended in Vienna, the opera was produced at the summer residence, the Favorita, where, on June 23 /July 3, the Russians saw *L'Arsace, fondatore dell' imperio de' Parthi* (libretto by Donato Cupeda), an event noted by other observers.[23]

Theatrical experiences continued among Russian parties abroad after Peter's embassy returned home. Indeed, even before he set out, Peter had pre-seeded some European centers with Russian students, dispatching more than thirty high-ranking attendants to study in the West in January 1697. This is how Petr Tolstoi, cited in our chapter 2, found himself in Venice studying naval sciences, which also gave him the opportunity to savor the delights of Carnival. Prince Petr Alekseevich Golitsyn was also assigned to Venice; later, traveling through Italy on his return home, in 1698, he was at the Florentine court of Grand Duke Cosimo III (another appearance!), where he recruited the young castrato singer Filippo Balatri to come to Russia with him.

The diary Balatri kept during his Russian stay, also introduced briefly in chapter 2, gives us a ground-level view of the performance opportunities we have been following. Balatri lived in Moscow with the Golitsyn family for about two years, from early 1699, and then accompanied them when they were posted to Vienna, where Golitsyn served as the first permanent Russian ambassador there, beginning in 1701.[24] Balatri's diary recalls the domestic flavor of the Foreign Quarter players drafted for Tsar Aleksei's early "ballets." In Balatri's case, although he was recruited for his impressive professional musical training, his realm in Moscow was domestic; his youth and slippery gendered identification, as a castrato, allowed him access to the terem, the secluded women's realm so little documented in other sources, Russian or foreign.[25] Balatri also frequented Moscow's Foreign Quarter, where he made music with Tsar Peter and Peter's mistress, Anna Mons, the daughter of a German merchant. Balatri described Peter himself playing dances "fairly passably" on a keyboard instrument in this environment.[26]

Balatri accompanied the Golitsyn family on their posting to Vienna early in 1701, and during his nearly two-year stay with them in that city, he observed the encounters of the ambassador's wife, Dar'ia, with theater. These accounts, too, offer a certain intimacy, for Dar'ia's visits were not rigorously ceremonious diplomatic appearances but reflected her own, tentative explorations of the city. Dar'ia attended several types of performances: Balatri mentions a Harlequin comedy (to which her Russian priest objected) and a drama on the story of Judith, which was more acceptable, apparently turning the priest into an enthusiastic theatergoer, although he initially thought that the onstage beheading was real. Dar'ia also found some comedies to be "immodest and indecent for so noble an audience," condemning "impertinent comedies" or "masquerades (those damnable occasions)." Her objections were not wholly about content but also reflected her disapproving observation of unescorted women attending such performances—and they imply multiple theater visits.[27]

THE THEATER ON RED SQUARE: REPERTORIAL LINKS TO THE MUSCOVITE PAST

As in the case of Tsar Aleksei's private court theater decades earlier, the performative exposures of the late seventeenth century, in Russia and abroad, converge in the formation of Russia's first public theater, established shortly after Peter returned from the Great Embassy. Balatri was not the only entertainer engaged to come to Russia. The Great Embassy recruited, in addition to naval experts and other specialists, a mysterious "dramaturg," who (if he indeed came to Russia) may be linked to what is apparently the first theatrical performance of the Petrine era, held at the home of Franz Lefort (on February 22 / March 4, 1699), shortly before his death.[28] Lefort was one of Peter's boon companions, their relationship solidified through Lefort's military experiences, and he accompanied Peter on the Great Embassy. The person ultimately tasked with assembling players for the planned public theater in Moscow, Johann Splawski (Splawskij), may have been another recruit from the Great Embassy. Splawski might plausibly have come into contact with the Russians abroad (possibly in Vienna, given that the Russian records list him as Hungarian). He first appeared in Russia in 1698 as a puppet master, and it was also around this time, in 1699–1700, that other such entertainers began to ply their trades there.[29] Whatever his exact route to Russia, Splawski was quickly sent back to the West to hire players, and after only one false start, he engaged a troupe headed by Johann Kunst, in Danzig, which arrived in Moscow in mid-1702.[30]

In bringing a ready-made troupe to Moscow, Splawski was following von Staden's earlier, unrealized, efforts for Matveev. Kunst's remark, in requests to the Russian planners from October 1702—"just as it is impossible to have a body without a soul, so it is impossible to have comedies without music"—forms a satisfying parallel to Rautenfels's comments about the necessity of music to accompany the "ballets" for Peter's father (dancers could no more perform without music than they could "dance without legs").[31] Peter's enterprise was meant to be public, although it closely tracked the activities of the tsar, and, like his father's theater, it ultimately lived and died according to the tsar's personal interest.[32] This second Russian theatrical experience fits into the increasingly public life Peter was promoting; this is evident, for example, in the requests for "triumphal comedies" to mark military victories and the use of theatrical matériel for the funeral observances organized in 1706 for F. A. Golovin (who, like Lefort, had accompanied Peter on the Great Embassy).[33]

The repertoire Kunst brought with his troupe—over a dozen plays—is preserved in a 1709 document that lists the transfer of theatrical materials after the closure of the Moscow theater site.[34] As in the case of the productions for Tsar Aleksei, these titles show that Kunst brought to Russia widely known theatrical subjects. Matveev's earlier Foreign Quarter writers had been, to borrow from the title of Molière's very popular work, playwrights "in spite of themselves," relying on their previous, amateur, theatrical experiences to produce something performable. In the case of Peter's theater, the repertorial ties are far more direct, for the plays Kunst brought represented the working repertoire of an active professional troupe that intended to use them as the basis of their Moscow performances.

These repertorial connections are evident in the preparations for the first two plays, which premiered in December 1702. There had been a great deal of activity over the summer and fall of that year: the Kunst troupe arrived in Moscow; Russian trainees were assembled in order to provide language-appropriate performances; and translators were engaged. (One document, from late September, describes a cumbersome process of translating the

German text into Latin and then rendering it into Russian.[35]) In October, in the midst of all this, the planners were informed that Peter wanted a victory play to mark his triumphal entry into Moscow after the successful campaign to take the northern fortress of Oreshek/Nöteborg (renamed Shlisselburg after the Russians captured it that month). Kunst and the other organizers pushed back, saying that they had insufficient knowledge of the military events and that, furthermore, "no comedian in the world" could create a new play on the spot, for immediate performance. They thus apparently modified the play(s) already in progress.[36] By mid-December two plays were ready; like the 1672 "ballets" for Aleksei's court, they were performed in a (formerly) private home that was closely associated with the ruler, in this case, the large house occupied by the recently deceased Franz Lefort, the site of the 1699 performance noted earlier. A purpose-built theater was erected on Red Square in late 1703.[37]

One of the two initial plays was on the story of Alexander the Great: *On the Fortress of Grubeton, in which the Primary Figure is Alexander of Macedon*.[38] The fortress setting reflects the requested celebration of the recent military victory, and the Alexander character could certainly refer to Peter (especially as the players were instructed to work hidden references into the text).[39] The label "Grubeton" certainly refers to the Nöteborg fortress itself: using the German spelling of the fortress that would have been familiar to the Kunst players, "Grubeton" is "Noteburg" spelled backward.

Requests for such last-minute changes would have been typical for traveling companies, but they also loosen the ties between Kunst's play as performed in Moscow and other Alexander plays. Many scholars have focused on the fact that the famous traveling Velten company included the play *Alexanders Liebessieg* in its repertoire in the late seventeenth century.[40] The subject was widely known, and the Velten play, on Alexander and his love life, has complex antecedents ranging from a version by Jean Desmarets de Saint-Sorlin that seems to have formed the basis for the performance at the Amsterdam Schouwburg (1659, translated by Barend van Velsen) and well-known settings by Cicognini (prose and verse versions, 1650s-1660s) and Racine (1665)—any or all of these might have been fodder for the Velten or other traveling companies. Alexander was also the subject of a play Peter had seen in London, by Nathan Lee.[41] The last-minute requirements of the Russian court would probably have resulted in using only the bare bones of these previous Alexander settings, which focus on amorous, not military, adventures. In this light, Kunst's ultimate product might best be characterized as "peeces and Patches" of the Alexander play tradition rather than as a setting of any specific rendition. The other play prepared for these initial performances was *On Genoveva, Countess of Trier*, also a well-worn item in the traveling companies' repertoires, although perhaps less suited for a last-minute makeover to celebrate a military victory.[42]

As in the case of the Esther play that opened Tsar Aleksei's theater, it is difficult to determine the language(s) in which these first Petrine-era offerings were given. Although contemporary accounts refer to the "German" and the "Russian" players, the two groups apparently worked together to some degree; at any rate, one of the Russian actors was given extra pay because he performed in both plays. Such a joint effort might explain why the only surviving fragments from these first performances, which are from the Alexander play, are in Russian.[43] These excerpts record comic exchanges among soldiers, and whoever performed them, they gloriously blend the Pan-European tropes we have seen throughout this study. The first fragment preserves exchanges between two "Grubitonskie" soldiers and a character named Thraso, and the second features Thraso and Parmenio—both names were common currency on Western stages, reflecting Terence's perennial comedy *The Eunuch* and known in Tsar Aleksei's theater, which also included a Thraso.[44] Yet again we see the comic character functioning as an intermediary—an observation strengthened by the appearance in Moscow, in another of the Kunst plays, of none other than Pickleherring himself, featured in the transfer lists in the play *The Incarcerated Prisoner; or, Prince Pickleherring* (also titled *On Prince Pickleherring; or, Zhodelet*).[45]

Another obvious repertorial link both to Tsar Aleksei's court theater and to widely popular European performance traditions is the play *On Baiazet and Tamerlane*, produced in Moscow in late 1704 or early 1705.[46] This was after Kunst's death (in early 1703), when the troupe was taken over by a foreigner already in Russia, the goldsmith Otto Fürst. Records show some agitation in preparing a comedy in German and Russian, again raising the question of how the two groups might have combined in performance—unfortunately, no text survives. This must have been one of the plays Kunst had brought when he came to Moscow, because the old court Tamerlane play would not have needed any translation (into Russian, at least). It was performed in the newly built theater on Red Square and required not just new and repaired costumes but also two machines (*spusknye mashiny*, "lowering machines") to create the necessary effects; we recall the Paulsen troupe's plan to bring their stage machines on their unrealized trip to Moscow earlier. Kunst's Danzig troupe would likely have been familiar with Serwouters's Tamerlane play, which was widely performed by traveling companies; although we hesitate to make definitive links, the subject, at any rate, was well established.[47]

The Tamerlane subject continued to echo in Moscow with a connection, although indirect, to another Westerner in Russia with theatrical ties: the Dutch physician Nicolaas Bidloo (d. 1735). Recruited by Peter in 1702 to come to Moscow, Bidloo shared his training and interests with those of his uncle, the poet and librettist Govert Bidloo, who was the physician to William III.[48] Given these theatrical ties, it is natural that Nicolaas was involved, at least tangentially, in Peter's theatrical endeavors; in August 1704, a translator working for Bidloo was transferred to the Moscow troupe.[49] Bidloo later supervised performances by students at his Moscow Surgical School, which opened in 1706; their offerings included panegyrical recitations as well as staged plays.[50] Peter saw one of their plays later, during the holiday season of 1722–1723. Although one witness, Friedrich Wilhelm von Bergholz, described the performance of a play about King Alexander and King Darius as quite terrible, Peter was pleased and apparently went back for a second viewing.[51]

Productions at the Surgical School may have been amateurish, but they were documented in a sketch by Bidloo himself, apparently the earliest visual image depicting a Western-style theatrical production in Russia (fig. 6.1). The unfinished painting, in watercolor, is an impressionistic, action-filled representation of swordplay by two caped actors, one of whom is detaining (or sheltering?) a swooning female character, and surrounded by bystanders reacting to the scene. The sketch is in stark contrast to a series of drawings in which Bidloo documented, in static and precise images, the beautiful gardens and house he created in Moscow. Historian Erik De Jong suggests a date of around 1730 for the garden drawings, but the theatrical image seems to be separate (in subject, medium, and technique)—given the school's theatrical activity in the mid-1720s, one wonders if it reflects performances around the time Peter attended.[52]

It was at the Surgical School much later (post-Bidloo) that another Moscow Tamerlane production took place, in 1742. Although we cannot know how, or if, it relates to the Petrine-era plays, at least we can observe that the performance evoked a similar reaction by a foreign witness. As Jacob von Stählin, who worked in a variety of literary capacities for the Russian court,

FIG. 6.1

Bidloo watercolor of a theatrical production in Russia
(Leiden University Libraries, inv. nr. BPL 2727: 21, used by permission)

remarked on seeing the production at the Surgical School: "In 1742 I saw in Moscow such a comedy, which was supposed to deal with Tamerlane; it could not have been more grotesque."[53]

UNCOVERING RUSSIA'S THEATRICAL PAST: AN EPILOGUE AND A CONCLUSION

Stählin, however, is far more important than as an exasperated witness to a mediocre performance, for in 1769, he compiled the first historical survey of the Russian theater, only one aspect of his multifaceted engagements in Russian arts and intellectual life beginning in the 1730s. Stählin's theatrical writings, although not as extensive as his works on the visual arts and music in Russia, are tantalizing because he remarks that he had intended to print some play excerpts himself—without revealing, however, just which plays he had in mind.[54] Stählin's 1769 essay, although not entirely accurate, provides an entrée into a set of works that show how knowledge of Tsar Aleksei Mikhailovich's theater gradually emerged in the writings of Russian academics.[55] These later historians were part of a prominent late eighteenth-century group actively promoting investigations into Russia's past, especially among writers centered around the publisher Nikolai Ivanovich Novikov (1744–1818).[56] It is this group that began to mine and publish the rich diplomatic and theatrical records we have relied on so heavily throughout this study.

One of the earliest of such landmark diplomatic publications appeared in the first volume of the encyclopedic source compilation *Drevniaia rossiiskaia vivliofika* (Ancient Russian library, 1773); this is where the vivid account describing the comedies witnessed by ambassador Likhachev's party in Florence in 1660 was first published.[57] Shortly thereafter, in 1778, excerpts from court records describing performances at Tsar Aleksei's theater were published, by Fedor Ivanovich Miller (Gerhard Friedrich Müller, another member of the same intellectual circle, which skewed heavily German). Miller's excerpts describe performances of the Esther and Judith plays and the involvement of Matveev's people at the fall 1674 offerings at Preobrazhenskoe (discussed in chap. 4). It is easy to trace the influence of Miller's publication, for the incorrect date he assigns these records, 1676, is repeated in several other writings.[58]

Although Stählin said nothing more about publishing plays, this task was taken up by others, with play texts issued in the much expanded second

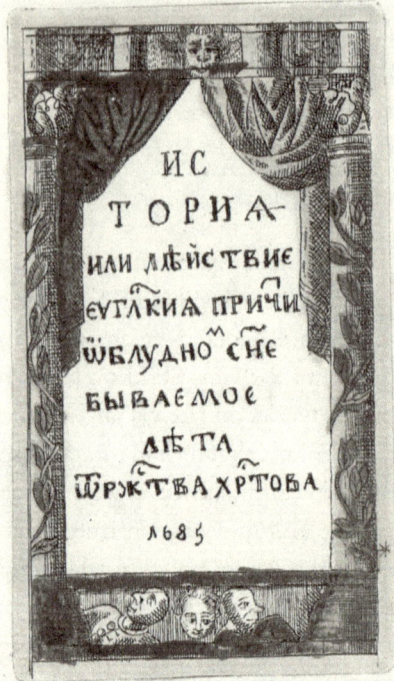 

FIG. 6.2

Simeon Polotskii, *Prodigal Son* print, dated "1685" (from Rovinskii, *Atlas*; New York Public Library Digital Collections, open access)

edition of *Drevniaia rossiiskaia vivliofika* (1788–1791). As we noted in chapter 4, this is where the first seventeenth-century play texts were printed: the court play on the Nebuchadnezzar/Judith story and Simeon Polotskii's two plays (the furnace play and *Prodigal Son*). All three were issued anonymously, with a note indicating that the texts were supplied by Miller, the very scholar who had published those first archival references to Tsar Aleksei's theater a few years earlier.[59] A different publication of Simeon's *Prodigal Son* from around this time, in the middle or late eighteenth century, reflects the newfound interest in early Russian plays and also reinforces the pervasive influences from northern Europe on Russian theatrical culture. This publication has "1685" on its title page and transmits Simeon's entire play, accompanied by illustrations showing a fully staged performance, with costumes, props, seated spectators, lighting, and so forth (fig. 6.2). The indication of the year 1685 most probably refers to a date appearing in the (textual) source on which this illustrated print was based, not to the actual year of its publication.⁶⁰ Although no specific visual sources have yet been identified, scholarly consensus has long been that these illustrations reflect Dutch influence—a logical assumption, as many Dutch artists came to the Russian court especially beginning in Peter's time, and some were directly involved in theatrical productions.⁶¹ The illustrations in this published print do not reflect Tsar Aleksei's court, for they show a Western-style audience deployed in an orderly row facing the stage, a setup that did not exist for the theatrical productions in seventeenth-century Moscow.⁶²

By the end of the eighteenth century, the academic heavy lifting on theatrical topics had passed to another of the prolific members of the Novikov circle, Aleksandr Fedorovich Malinovskii (1762–1840). Malinovskii's first essay on theater history was published in 1790, just after the three seventeenth-century plays had appeared in *Drevniaia rossiiskaia vivliofika* (1789). Malinovskii incorporates earlier work by Stählin and Miller (including the erroneous 1676 date for the Preobrazhenskoe performances) but also introduces important new research, with the first published description of the Kunst troupe and its activities. Malinovskii expands his scope in his next work, from 1808, for example, adding Anna Paulsen's theater letter and publishing the list of Kunst's plays.⁶³

Malinovskii's unpublished (and unfinished) work from 1826–1827 presents most fully his research into the history of Russian theater. This is where we see, for the first time, Rautenfels's description of Orpheus entertaining Tsar Aleksei. The quotation is unattributed in Malinovskii's work, but the source is clear (and Rautenfels is the only known published source for this information). Malinovskii summarizes the famous description as follows: "Orpheus appeared; he pronounced celebratory verses to the tsar and danced alone between two moving columns." Malinovskii knew Latin, and his formulation is close to Rautenfels's Latin text, where Orpheus dances "between two moving pyramids."⁶⁴ In this final study, Malinovskii also introduces the names (slightly garbled) of Pastor Gregorii, "Felten" (Velten), and von Staden—all familiar from our earlier chapters. Indeed, although some of the dates are slightly incorrect (and we still see the erroneous date for the Preobrazhenskoe productions), Malinovskii is clearly working through the same archival sources that form the basis of all later theatrical scholarship, published most extensively by Bogoiavlenskii in 1914.

It is likely that Malinovskii's research made its way to a non-Russian audience through the German scholarly world. As far as we have been able to determine, the first non-Russian survey of Tsar Aleksei's court theater is by Friedrich Tietz, in his 1838 book *Bunte Skizzen aus Ost und Süd*.[65] Tietz had been deeply involved in German theatrical productions and had written widely on the subject before he toured Russia from late 1832 through spring 1834. During his trip, he visited many intellectuals and academic societies in the Russian capitals.[66] Although we have so far discovered no evidence of direct contact between Malinovskii and Tietz, given the latter's long-term engagement with theater, it would seem reasonable to suppose they met at some point during Tietz's stay. It is, at any rate, apparent from Tietz's *Bunte Skizzen* that he was familiar with Malinovskii's archival work on Russian theater.[67]

If our study began with Dannenfels's troupe knocking at the door in Pskov in 1644, asking for permission to entertain there, then this proposed conduit between Malinovskii and Tietz brings us full circle. Tietz evidently acquired his knowledge of Russian theatrical history largely from Malinovskii's impressive work, either directly or indirectly, and then introduced it to Western readers in his own book.[68] The timing was fortuitous, for it was during this very period, in the early decades of the nineteenth century, that Western theater historians were beginning to explore the travels of the "English comedians" on the Continent. In this environment, references to Matveev's efforts to hire comedians and to Anna Paulsen and her Copenhagen connection would have raised—indeed, did raise—interest. Thomas Overskou, in his 1854 history of Danish theater, for example, cites Tietz by name and mentions Anna.[69]

Tsar Aleksei Mikhailovich's court theater was very short-lived, spanning the interval from the February 1672 "ballet" to the tsar's death almost exactly four years later. Nevertheless, its importance transcends this short time frame, both in its own terms, as theater, and even more broadly as an example of an energetic court-sponsored initiative into which many members of the aristocratic and bureaucratic classes were drawn and which was sustained by impressive financial and organizational support; all of this relied on long-familiar performative exposures at court. The sustained success of these productions is obvious enough, given the enormous resources devoted to them and the regularity of their productions.

The theatrical experience also tells us vividly about the court's willingness, even eagerness, to engage in such entertainments. The plays did not necessarily have the same resonance that theatrical performances, even those on the same dramatic themes, might have had at a Western court.

Nevertheless, the stories, the acting, the comedy, and the music were comprehensible from a variety of different viewpoints—that of the playwrights, the actors, and the royal family—which is, after all, precisely the point of intertheater and its multiple "intermediary norms." Indeed, the influence of these plays in Moscow extended beyond the people Matveev interacted with regularly, for example Pastor Gregorii and Georg Hüfner; they had a broader reach, certainly, at a minimum, by providing employment to carpenters, tailors, carters, local merchants, and other workers. Although we certainly do not claim that a Moscow tailor sewing a costume for Pickleherring means that he absorbed the essentials of the character, we nevertheless appreciate a deeper potential for influence. The tailors stationed at the theater over several days in January 1676 for those final plays, for example, would surely have noticed something about the productions themselves, even in the midst of the preperformance rush; the scene painters must have given some thought to context when ordered to paint large bunches of grapes for Bacchus or create beards for the giant heads.

The theater was closed down at Tsar Aleksei's death for a variety of reasons, but the experiences survived in the retention (and even distribution, for instance, to Sparwenfeld) of the actual play texts and in the official accounts of Russian diplomats, who continued to report on staged entertainments they encountered on their trips abroad.[70] The long-standing diplomatic exposure we have traced throughout this book thus not only was a catalyst spurring Tsar Aleksei's desire for a theater, as Rautenfels acknowledged in his well-known account, but also impacted Peter's choices on his Great Embassy. We are hardly the first to suggest that Peter did not emerge, fully formed, as a "modernizer" or "Westernizer"—Peter certainly did adopt many new and unconventional approaches, including his participation in the Great Embassy, but he also followed the well-worn footsteps of his own diplomatic corps. When he wanted to start a theater back home, he engaged in the same procedures his father's court had followed a generation earlier. In fact, with our realization that Matveev had tried to recruit a foreign company to come to Moscow at the very beginning of the earlier theater project, Peter's recruitment of the Kunst company as the opening act of his own theater is novel only in that it was successful. Diplomatic contacts continued to be influential in theatrical contexts, serving as catalysts much later, at the end of the eighteenth century, when Russian historians began to explore their theatrical heritage.

These observations fit comfortably within stimulating exchanges among scholars regarding the cultural directions of Russia during the late seventeenth and early eighteenth centuries. These discussions have been aimed at rethinking what has been called the Petrine divide or, as Russell Martin characterizes the traditional view in its broadest expression, the break "chiseled" in Russian history by Peter's reforms, separating the "semi-Asiatic, non-European pre-Petrine Russia" from the "enlightened, European, thoroughly westernized post-Petrine Russia." Samuel Baron and Nancy Kollmann have referred to this divide as the "bipolar way of seeing the early modern period mainly in terms of 'continuity' and 'change' (focusing on Peter I and his reforms)."[71] Taking our lead from a caution offered by Kollmann—"there were more cultural influences out there than just Orthodoxy and more cultural elites than just the nobility"—our study contributes to these ongoing discussions.[72] First, some of the important cultural influences on the Russian state drew, at least partially, from the constant diplomatic contacts throughout the seventeenth century, in our case, with the West. The reports we have examined are just as important in establishing the continuum of cultural history as they are for understanding specific political events and alliances: the "theater of diplomacy" can truly be taken both literally and figuratively. Our primary example of how such contacts framed specific actions at the Russian court, in the formation of the tsar's theater, is fairly restricted, yet it strengthens the overall cultural impact of diplomatic exchanges, as is evident in our brief survey of late sixteenth-century diplomatic contacts or the concerns of the Poteshnaia palata during Tsar Mikhail's reign.

A second area in which our study contributes to larger academic debates revolves around geographical influences on the Russian court before Peter's time. As Bushkovitch wrote: "What Peter wrought was not a turn toward Europe but a turn toward northern Europe, instead of Poland and Catholic southern Europe, which had been the hallmark of the previous generation's court culture. That earlier court culture is not just a matter of antiquarian interest, for its existence demonstrates that Russia was moving toward some sort of cultural shift before the demiurge Peter came on the scene."[73] Our detailed study of the court theater and its sources, witnesses, and participants nudges this influence firmly back into the previous generation, showing that the cultural shift to northern Europe was not just present but vigorously (and expensively) pursued during Tsar Aleksei's reign. This, in turn, might contribute to Bushkovitch's observations of the perhaps surprising acceptance of Peter's reforms—as he notes, the roots of such change (including, as he stresses, the court theater) appear already in Aleksei's reign, and this exposure may have paved the way for Peter's reforms later.[74] Our study of the theatrical period strengthens the case for such a chronological pushback.

Finally, as previously suggested, our study indicates how close examination of cultural trends and events might be integrated more fully into debates about the periodization of Russian history. Russell Martin frames the issue by quoting literary historian Margreta de Grazia, who said that periodization "works less as a historical marker than a massive value judgment, determining what matters and what does not." Martin continues by noting that, in the case of premodern Russia, "every chronological paradigm ever offered by historians ... rests on [such] assumptions," which reflect "the continuing vitality of multiple and contradictory chronological models for the early centuries of east Slavic history." It is these "multiple and contradictory" models, in the specific cultural realms we have discussed, that recall (indeed, stimulated) Nancy Kollmann's image of historical periods as "nested building blocks in a continuity occurring at many levels."[75] And this, in turn, echoes the language of intertheater, which also focuses on such "nested" moments. Such formulations, drawn from a variety of disciplines and interests, can aid in broadening the continuum of the performative and audience-building experiences we cover here to embrace a wide spectrum of opportunities, venues, and skills that included, eventually, the "ballets" and plays presented to the tsar and his family.

Our exploration of the Russian court theater also suggests productive avenues for research on Western theatrical traditions. Although we do not believe that the Moscow Tamerlane play represented a direct transfer from Marlowe's setting, its existence shows the wide influence of theatricalized versions of the Tamerlane story, including Marlowe's, which must have been part of the lived experiences of the first wave of English players on the Continent. The Russian play, with its close reliance on Du Bec's narrative, underscores the links between the foreign playwrights in Moscow and the shifting interests of contemporary historians and writers in the West. The many-layered exchanges we have followed throughout this study thus align Tsar Aleksei's theatrical dreams with those of other courts and other rulers of his time, considerably broadening the "web of resonance" of the English players and their traditions.

In his writings on intertheater, Anston Bosman proposes a borrowing from transcultural literary studies to describe the processes we have seen throughout. He quotes the scholar of comparative literature Vinay Dharwadker, who describes the circulation of texts and performances as "a montage of overlapping maps in motion."[76] The shifting networks of repertoire, desire, and performance that created and sustained the Russian theater and, more generally, the long-standing interest in performative culture at the Moscow court throughout the seventeenth century and beyond show how such a montage might be expanded and how the range of the traveling comedians' influences and entertainments might encompass much wider geographical and cultural terrains that, in turn, open new windows on the vitality and energy of the Russian court.

Or, to put it in thoroughly theatricalized terms, as it turned out, there were enough Pickleherrings to go around.

NOTES

1. Henke, introduction, 13.

2. All are widely reproduced. Carreño de Miranda's painting is in *Museo del Prado* 1:152 (No. 517); the *Almanach* image is in Hennings, *Russia*, 36–37; Sir Godfrey Kneller's portrait is in Dukelskaya and Renne, *Hermitage Catalogue* 13:91–92 (several engravings were made from this image).

3. *Mercure galant*, May 1681, pp. 306–307; Isherwood, *Music in the Service*, 302–303. *L'Inconnu* was revived several times after its premiere in 1675; the Russian party likely saw a production based on the 1679–1680 revival (see Clarke, *Guénégaud Théatre* 3:299).

4. *London Stage*, 304, which also includes contemporary comments suggesting that if curious people wanted to see the Russian ambassador, they should go to the theater, and an entry dated January 10 (before Potemkin saw *The Tempest*) implies that he had already been to the theater several times; the venues are described on pp. xxxix–xliii. On the playwrights, see Bennett, *DNB*, s.v. "Shadwell, Thomas"; Neman, *DNB*, s.v. "Crowne, John."

5. Bantysh-Kamenskii, *Obzor* 1:234. Alekseev's stateinyi spisok is in RGADA, f. 96, op. 1, kn. 110, where the comedies are described on fol. 30v ("И та комедия была издевашная, выходили шуты и иные блазные люди и играли на музыках") and fols. 34–34v ("А та была комедия французская, убраны были женской пол и мужеской в нарядные платья, а потом была комедия издевашняя," on fol. 34v). The 1683 performance of *L'Inconnu* at the Danish court is in Marker and Marker, *History*, 44.

6. Avviso dated December 8, 1687 (MAP document 25482), which was at the beginning of the trip; Spanish documents describe a performance at the end of the embassy's stay, on December 23 (Shergold and Varey, *Fuentes* 6:287; Greer and Varey, *Fuentes* 29:179–180). The trip is summarized in Bantysh-Kamenskii, *Obzor* 1:163–164; reports of the embassy's stay in Paris, in the *Mercure galant* (September 1687), refer to musical entertainments but mention no theatrical presentations.

7. *Sbornik vypisok* 1:esp. 9–13.

8. *Rozysknye dela* 4:5, 12, 18, 20, 40, 105–106, 137 (see also Roizman, *Organ*, 85). The inventory was made after Golitsyn's fall from power; see the survey in Hellie, *Economy*, chap. 24.

9. On Diletskii, see Jensen and Vorob'yov, *GMO*, s.v. "Diletsky, Nikolay"; Jensen, *Musical Cultures*, chap. 5.

10. *Rozysknye dela* 4:33 ("Четыре книги в десть, писменныя: О строении Камедии"; they were valued at one ruble).

11. On the Sparwenfeld manuscripts (held at SBV), see chapter 4 in this volume. Sparwenfeld's time in Moscow is discussed in Birgegård, *J. G. Sparwenfeld's Diary*, 15.

12. Birgegård, *J. G. Sparwenfeld's Diary*, for example 231 and 323n611 (Blumentrost and other foreigners), 229 (von Kochen), 231 and 337n736 (Matveev), 209 (the Russian teacher), and 191 and 211 (Golitsyn); book acquisitions, for example, are on 336nn727–728.

13. Hennings, *Russia*, 160.

14. *PDS* 8:699–702.

15. Payment records are in Lefort, *Sbornik materialov*, for example 369–376; an overview of the major entertainment stops is in Guzevich and Guzevich, *Velikoe posol'stvo*, 216–218.

16. The fireworks illustration is widely reproduced; the full (long) bilingual text is available at the Rijksmuseum, Amsterdam, http://hdl.handle.net/10934/RM0001.COLLECT.468457. The plays are available from the University of Amsterdam database ONSTAGE, at http://www.vondel.humanities.uva.nl/onstage/plays/470 (*Armida*) and http://www.vondel.humanities.uva.nl/onstage/plays/475 (*Advocaat*); the entry under August 27, 1697, includes contemporary comments about the performances for the Russian visitors. In the French text of the 1697 poster and in Venevitinov, *Russkie v Gollandii*, 222, the play title is given as *L'avocat imaginaire*, apparently an error, perhaps conflating it with Molière's famous *Le malade imaginaire*, which had been performed in Dutch translation at the same theater the previous year. The Dutch title given in the poster, *De gewaande advocaat*, clarifies this as a translation of Claude de La Rose's *L'advocat sans estude*.

17. The stateinyi spisok account is in *PDS* 8:917 (August 17); translation from Cross, *Peter the Great*, 21 (which includes additional reports of Peter's attendance); this description is widely cited (usually from Venevitinov, *Russkie v Gollandii*, 68). There is a laconic remark under this date in another contemporaneous Russian account of the trip: *Pokhodnyi zhurnal 1697*, 26 ("Byla komediia" [There was a comedy]); see also Lefort's undated letter in Babkin, "Pis'ma," 126, also in the context of the fireworks display. The monetary reward is in Lefort, *Sbornik materialov*, 377 (August 23).

18. Lefort, *Sbornik materialov*, 378, 399, 421 (January 22, 1698: "дано комедианту Филипу фан Геле за комедии, которых смотрели все великие и полномочные послы и дворяня и люди их").

19. The original play was by Philip Massinger and John Fletcher (Price and Laurie, *GMO*, s.v. "Betterton, Thomas"). The performance was widely observed: English accounts are in *London Stage*, 490, and Loewenson, "Some Details," 434n18 (report dated January 21), 436. *Pokhodnyi zhurnal 1698*, 4, also notes the January 15 performance.

20. The February 8 visit is in Loewenson, "Some Details," 437, referring to an entry in Luttrell, *Brief Historical Relation* 4:342. The February 12 and 24 visits are in Cross, *Peter the Great*, 21; *London Stage*, 491–492 (either at Drury Lane or Lincoln's Inn Fields; musical concerts were also offered). Other observers reported on Peter's activities; see, for example, Florentine documents in Crinò, "La visita."

21. Guzevich and Guzevich, *Velikoe posol'stvo*, 217; Cross, *Peter the Great*, 21, citing Bogoslovskii, *Petr I* 2:381.

22. The Vienna Wirtschaft is widely discussed, for example, in Hennings, *Russia*, 171–176; Dolgova, "Petr I." London masquerades are in Loewenson, "Some Details," 437–438. The Russians, in turn, gave a huge ball in Vienna on Peter's name day, June 29/July 9; Guzevich

and Guzevich, *Velikoe posol'stvo*, 217. On incognito and disguise throughout Peter's life, see Hughes, *Russia*, esp. 97–108.

23. The opera is identified in Seifert, *Die Oper*, 557, with additional newsletter accounts mentioning the tsar's presence on p. 847; see also Hennings, *Russia*, 176. On the Favorita, and Peter's time there, see Sommer-Mathis, "La Favorita," esp. 286–287n32.

24. On the diary, see Schlafly, "Filippo Balatri" and his "Muscovite *Boiarynia*"; on Balatri's early history, see Di Salvo, "Vita e viaggi," esp. 44–45, and Di Sal'vo, "Kastrat." Balatri left the Golitsyns in late 1702.

25. Schlafly, "Muscovite *Boiarynia*," focuses on the intimacy of Balatri's experiences.

26. Schlafly, "Filippo Balatri," 188–189 (Schlafly calls the instrument a harpsichord). Schlafly notes Balatri's important information about Anna Mons; according to Bushkovitch, *Peter the Great*, 178, Anna and Peter were introduced by Franz Lefort.

27. Schlafly, "Filippo Balatri," 195 (esp. n. 125); also his "Muscovite *Boiarynia*," 264–265.

28. Guzevich and Guzevich, "Bolezn'," esp. 79; they appear to identify the "dramaturg" with this 1699 performance in Guzevich and Guzevich, *Velikoe posol'stvo*, 609n663, linking him with the "gentleman" mentioned in Vanbrugh, *Short Vindication*, 21, who had "gone away with the Czar, who has made him Poet Laureat of Muscovy" (1698). Cross, *Peter the Great*, 23, considers Vanbrugh's statement to have "no substance"—the "dramaturg" thus remains murky.

29. The references from 1699 and 1700, including Splawski's arrival and possible connection with the Great Embassy, are summarized in Starikova, "Panorama," 142 (and 165n8 on his later career); see also Bogoiavlenskii, "Moskovskii teatr," 77–82. Guzevich and Guzevich, *Velikoe posol'stvo*, 269, seem to assume that Splawski was a Great Embassy recruit.

30. Bogoiavlenskii, "Moskovskii teatr," esp. 83–85, 94–96; the initial Danzig document is in Bolte, *Das Danziger Theater*, 153–154, with a partial English translation in Brandt and Hogendoorn, *German and Dutch Theatre*, 23–24. Our summary is based on Starikova's excellent studies, particularly "Russkii teatr" and "Panorama."

31. Bogoiavlenskii, "Moskovskii teatr," 92.

32. Starikova, "Russkii teatr," traces the theater from the Lefort venue to the new building, and then to its unintentional destruction.

33. Starikova, "Panorama," 152. Borrowing from the theater was appropriate because Golovin had been deeply involved in its development.

34. Starikova, "Russkii teatr," is the fundamental work on the Red Square theater and the transfer of materials to Peter's sister, Natal'ia (a later development beyond the scope of the present study). The transfer listings are preserved in two very similar documents (the ordering of the plays and their titles show small differences); we rely on the comparative presentation of these lists in Starikova, "Panorama," 145–146.

35. Discussion of translation from the German originals, from September 1702, is in *Sbornik vypisok* 2:313–314 (no titles are given, unfortunately).

36. Bogoiavlenskii, "Moskovskii teatr," 91–92; *Sbornik vypisok* 2:314–315.

37. Bruyn, *Travels* 1:40, mentions performances by both Germans and Russians at the Lefort venue over the winter. The mid-December performances are also noted in a December 20, 1702, report by Otto von Pleyer (the imperial resident in Russia), who said that "the Germans" performed "last week" and "the Russians" performed "this week" (Ustrialov, *Istoriia* 4:pt. 2, 594–595). Russian records confirm this; payment was issued on December 16 to a group of Russian players, with reference to the two plays we discuss here, on the subjects of Alexander and Geneveva (Bogoiavlenskii, "Moskovskii teatr," 99). On the theater building, see Starikova, "Russkii teatr," esp. 143.

38. Titles given in the transfer list in Starikova, "Panorama," 146: *О крепости Грубетона, в ней же первая персона Александр Македонский*; also listed as *On Alexander of Macedon* (*О Александре Македонском*).

39. Bogoiavlenskii, "Moskovskii teatr," 92, on "hidden" (*zakrytye*) names to be included. Peter's father, Tsar Aleksei, is depicted in the 1703 festivities as the Russian Philip of Macedon, another echo of the Alexander theme (Wortman, *Scenarios*, 48). The name might also acknowledge Aleksandr Menshikov, who played an important military role in the Russian victory. Menshikov was explicitly compared to Alexander the Great in a slightly later poem (1709; Grebeniuk, *Panegiricheskaia literatura*, 105–107, 204–207). Wordplay was a strong feature of late seventeenth-century Russian poetry and writing; see, for English-language descriptions, the "poetic curios" in Vroon, *DLB* 150, s.v. "Simeon Polotsky," 295, and the same author's "From Liturgy to Literature"; see also discussions in Hippisley, *Poetic Style*.

40. Heine, *Johannes Velten*, 13 (Torgau, 1690), 37–38; in the Russian context, see Tikhonravov, *Russkie dramaticheskie proizvedeniia* 1:xxxiv n. 3.

41. Schouwburg performances are available from the University of Amsterdam's database ONSTAGE, at http://www.vondel.humanities.uva.nl/onstage/plays/32; Cicognini's settings are *Le glorie e gli amori di Alessandro Magno* (a prose version, first published in 1661) and *Gli amori di Alessandro Magno* (libretto, first performed in 1651, published in 1663). Gstach, "Die Liebes Verzweiffelung," esp. 401–402, brings many of these together, including the Moscow performance, although the latter was not "am Hof" but at the Lefort house (later performances were also not at court but in the public theater on Red Square).

42. Starikova, "Panorama," 146 (*О Графине Триерской Геновеве* or *О Геновеве*); Gstach, "Die Liebes Verzweifelung," 486–488, summarizes its circulation among Western troupes.

43. Bogoiavlenskii, "Moskovskii teatr," 99; excerpts on 187–189 (the label "Grubitonskie" identifies this as the Alexander play).

44. Starikova, "Panorama," 147, suggests that the comic actor in the Kunst troupe, Johann Bendler, played Thraso—so either there were two separate casts for the Alexander play or Bendler managed to learn the role in Russian; Starikova notes that Bendler's duties included teaching Russian actors. Because the payment record in Bogoiavlenskii, "Moskovskii teatr," 99, indicates that the Russian player Roman Ammosov appeared in the Alexander play ("v persone Grubetonove"), there may be other performance permutations.

45. Pickleherring appears in the Kunst play listings as *Тюрмовой заключник или принц Пикельгяринг* or *О принце Пикельгеринге или Жоделете* (Starikova, "Panorama," 145; a substantial surviving excerpt is published in Tikhonravov, *Russkie dramaticheskie proizvedeniia* 2:105–195). Jodelet was the stage name of the French comic Julien Bedeau, for whom several plays were written; the version in Kunst's repertoire was apparently based on Thomas Corneille's *Le geôlier de soi-même, ou Jodelet prince* (1656), and there were German and Dutch renditions performed by the traveling companies and at the Schouwburg. On the latter, see the University of Amsterdam's database ONSTAGE, at http://www.vondel.humanities.uva.nl/onstage/plays/554; the German traveling repertoire is summarized in Gstach, "Die Liebes Verzweiffelung," 520–521 (although the Russian play title is inexplicably given in German), and see Karlinsky, *Russian Drama*, 47. Early scholars, for example, Tikhonravov, *Russkie dramaticheskie proizvedeniia* 1:xxxv–xxxvi, were aware of the repertorial ties between the German and Russian plays.

46. *О Баязете и Тамерлане*; title and date in Starikova, "Panorama," 146, 151. Bogoiavlenskii, "Moskovskii teatr," 127, includes records of the play's translation and preparation with documents from 1705. Starikova links the play to records from early 1705 in which musical entertainments were ordered as enhancements (thus the performance would be in the

holiday season at the end of 1704 through early 1705); after this time, over the course of 1705, the theater seems to have been in decline.

47. The Russian title in the payment records is *История явная Тамерлана, хана татарского, как победил салтана турского Баязета* (The true history of Tamerlane, Tatar khan, who vanquished the Turkish sultan Baiazet) (Bogoiavlenskii, "Moskovskii teatr," 127). This title has the same elements as the full title of Serwouters's play, although any closer identification seems risky. Morozov, *Ocherki*, 237, believes that this is the old court theater play.

48. Guzevich and Guzevich, *Velikoe posol'stvo*, 237, consider the possibility that Peter met "Gotfrid" (i.e., Govert) Bidloo in Leiden during the Great Embassy, suggesting that the later hiring of Nicolaas may support this. Additional bibliography on Bidloo's life and career is in De Jong, "Virgilian Paradise" and Dankmeijer and Röell, "Nicolaas Bidloo."

49. Bogoiavlenskii, "Moskovskii teatr," xix, 114.

50. Starikova, "Panorama," 157. Dankmeijer and Röell, "Nicolaas Bidloo," 167, specify that Peter's orders to create the hospital school were from 1706 and that the building was ready the following year.

51. The December 29, 1722, performance is in Bergholz, "Tagebuch," 20:591 (Bergholz did not attend but mentioned that the tsar was pleased); payment was issued on December 31 (*Sbornik vypisok* 2:121, which names one of the twenty-seven players involved); the January 4, 1723, encore is in Bergholz, "Tagebuch," 21:182, where he describes the play, dismissing the performance because none of the students had ever seen a "real play." A possible context for the play's subject is in Berkov, "K istorii," 390–391; on Bergholz's diary, see Sander, *Social Dancing*.

52. Bidloo's drawings (at least, the bulk of them) apparently date from between 1725 (Peter's death) and 1735 (Bidloo's death); De Jong, "Virgilian Paradise," 306, suggests a date ca. 1730, based on the growth of the gardens.

53. Stählin, "Zur Geschichte," 398; Morozov, *Ocherki*, 218.

54. Stählin's work is surveyed in Larocca, "New Perspectives"; see also Cracraft, *Petrine Revolution*, chap. 4. Stählin's theater study is "Zur Geschichte," and his remark about publishing plays is in his 1770 essay "Nachrichten von der Musik," 39. Given his specificity regarding the plays by Dmitrii Rostovskii in the 1769 theater essay, perhaps he was thinking of publishing these works.

55. The longest-lasting inaccuracy stems from Stählin, "Zur Geschichte," 397–398: "In Peter I's youth they sometimes performed spiritual plays at the Ikonospaskii [Zaikonospasskii] monastery [in Moscow], and sometimes they performed translations from French, for example *Le Médecin malgré lui*, and [also] spiritual histories. Also Princess Sofiia and her cavaliers and women from the best families performed such comedies." Although the reference to the wrong royal sister—Sofiia instead of Natal'ia—was cleared up fairly early on (for example, in Morozov, *Ocherki*, 201–206), the confusion has lingered. Stählin also omitted mention of the Kunst troupe but did know about the more recent stay in St. Petersburg of Johann Mann's actors, in 1723–1725 (on the Mann troupe, see Starikova, "Panorama," 162–163).

56. See Marker, *DLB* 150, s.v. "Nikolai Ivanovich Novikov." Coudenys, "Translation," esp. 739, characterizes Novikov's editorial approaches and contributions as both "crucial" and "haphazard."

57. Starikova, "Zapiska," 63n11, notes the connection between this Florence account and early studies of Russian theater, and in "U istokov," Starikova contextualizes the recopying of this account in the 1730s, part of the historicist impulses of a previous ruler, Empress Anna Ioannovna. The Florence account appeared in the first edition of *DRV*, in 1773 (1:fasc. 2 [February], 109–150), and was reprinted in the second edition, in 1788 (4:339–359).

58. [Miller], "Izvestie," 108–109 (records published later in *DR* 3:1131–1132). Miller's authorship is identified in Zabelin, *Opyty* 1:501; Black, *G.-F. Müller*, 181, notes Miller's many contributions to the journal in which these records were published. There are other dating errors in these eighteenth-century studies, most pertinently in the Likhachev party's account in *DRV*. The erroneous date for the Preobrazhenskoe performances is repeated in Stählin [Stelin], "Kratkoe izvestie," 4–5, a 1779 Russian translation of his German-language essay from a decade earlier; Miller's archival transcription is placed in a long footnote in this publication.

59. *DRV* 8:475 (hereafter, references are to the second edition unless otherwise noted); *RRD* 2:317; school dramas were published in volume 9 of *DRV* (see *RRD* 3). Black, *G.-F. Müller*, 181, 196, emphasizes Miller's importance in both editions of *DRV*.

60. Simeon's play was still known and accessible in court circles in the mid-1680s, after the poet's death and after the closure of the court theater, because the Swedish visitor Johan Gabriel Sparwenfeld was able to get a copy of it at this time, along with copies of plays directly associated with Tsar Aleksei's court performances, *Joseph* and *Adam and Eve*. The proposed publication date, from the mid-eighteenth century at the earliest, is discussed in *RRD* 2:esp. 315–316.

61. Rovinskii, *Russkie narodnye kartinki* 4:520–522, proposed Dutch models. Rovinskii published the entire illustrated play in *Atlas*, as No. 696. On Dutch influence, see Cracraft, *Petrine Revolution*, chap. 4, esp. p. 170 on the identity of the artist Pickaerdt (or Pikart) mentioned in Rovinskii. On pp. 169–170, Cracraft notes that in late 1703, a Russian painter was ordered to the Lefort theatrical venue to paint a backdrop depicting the newly conquered Shlisselburg for a comedy, using as a model the print by "Adr. Shonbek" (Adriaan Schoonebeck, another of the Great Embassy recruits; Pickaerdt was Schoonebeck's stepson and pupil, recruited by the latter to come to Russia in 1702). This is apparently at the time that theatrical activities were being transferred to the new building on Red Square (see Starikova, "Russkii teatr," esp. 141–144).

62. The illustrated print, unlike the *DRV* publication of Simeon's *Prodigal Son* play, does not have references to the intermedi specified between acts; in general, it transmits different stage directions, with fewer indications of musical elements. This is closer to the Sparwenfeld source, suggesting that both were based on a source also lacking such information (possibly one not used, or not intended for use, in actual performance). See *RRD* 2:313–324 on sources and text relationships.

63. The fundamental source on Malinovskii is Starikova, "Zapiska," on which our discussion is based.

64. Starikova, "Zapiska," 53. The 1687 German version of Rautenfels mentions the pyramids only in the poem ([Reutenfels], *Das Grosse und mächtige Reich*, 109–110); the 1680 Latin text includes this phrase as the setup to the poem, as cited in chapter 3. Perhaps Malinovskii did not believe that the "pyramids" were to be taken literally, thus his "moving columns" instead (and he was correct—they were in fact pyramid-shaped mountains). Other phrases indicate Malinovskii's knowledge of Rautenfels, for example, his reference to information transmitted by "our ambassadors and diplomats"; Starikova, "Zapiska," 52 and 63n11, suggests that this reflects the recent publication of Likhachev's Florence account but to our ears, it echoes Rautenfels. On Malinovskii's knowledge of Latin, see Dolgova, *SRP XVIII v.*, s.v. "Malinovskii, Aleksandr Fedorovich."

65. Tietz, *Bunte Skizzen*, esp. 191–197. A biographical sketch of Tietz (1803–1879), although with some omissions, is in Brümmer, *Allgemeine Deutsche Biographie*, s.v. "Tietz, Friedrich." Stählin's earlier German-language survey had been published in Riga; Stählin, of course, was closely associated with the Russian court.

66. These interactions are recounted in Tietz's earlier book, *Erinnerungs-Skizzen* (1836), translated into English the same year, as *St. Petersburgh*, where pp. 20–21 and 62 discuss the people and institutions he encountered).

67. For example, Tietz includes the list of Petrine-era plays that Malinovskii had published earlier, although translating the titles into German. Their presentations are not identical. Both writers, for example, describe Orpheus dancing but only Tietz correctly (à la Rautenfels) has him dancing between pyramids. Neither author gives Rautenfels's name. Tietz's reference might imply contact with Malinovskii, although he might readily have found Rautenfels's book after he returned home. Tietz also changed some information that appears in Malinovskii, for example, changing the date of the 1674 Preobrazhenskoe performances from (the erroneous) 1676 to (the equally erroneous) 1679.

68. Tietz does refer in his book to Stählin, but his primary sources appear to be the archival work published in Russian, especially Malinovskii's.

69. Bosman, "Renaissance Intertheater," 559, points to Ludwig Tieck's *Deutsches Theater* (1817) as the first to explore the "English comedians"; Overskou, *Den danske Skueplads* 1:112, cites Tietz's *Bunte Skizzen*.

70. And if we are correct in suggesting that Simeon Polotskii's two plays followed the initial group of court productions, his works would represent another example of the survival of such theatrical experiences beyond Tsar Aleksei's death.

71. Baron and Kollmann, introduction, 12; Martin, "Petrine Divide," 411. See also the discussion and many references in Waugh, "We Have Never Been Modern."

72. Kollmann, "Deeper Early Modern," 327.

73. Bushkovitch, "Change and Culture," 314.

74. Bushkovitch, "Change and Culture," esp. 312–316.

75. Kollmann, "Comment: Divides and Ends," 442; Martin, "Petrine Divide," 410.

76. Bosman, "Mobility," 514, quoting Dharwadker, "Introduction," 24.

BIBLIOGRAPHY

Note: In most cases, URL and database references are provided only for early published materials; other sources listed below are available widely online.

Ács, Pál. "Iter Persicum: In Alliance with the Safavid Dynasty against the Ottomans?" In *A Divided Hungary in Europe: Exchanges, Networks and Representations, 1541–1699*. Vol. 2, *Diplomacy, Information Flow and Cultural Exchange*, edited by Szymon Brzeziński and Áron Zarnóczki, 31–50. Newcastle upon Tyne, UK: Cambridge Scholars Publishing, 2014.

Adelung, Friedrich von. *Al'bom Meierberga: vidy i bytovye kartiny Rossii XVII veka*. St. Petersburg: A. S. Suvorin, 1903.

Aercke, Kristiaan. *Gods of Play: Baroque Festive Performances as Rhetorical Discourse*. Albany: State University of New York Press, 1994.

Akty istoricheskie, sobrannye i izdannye Arkheograficheskoi kommissiei. Vol. 4. St. Petersburg: Vtoroe otdelenie Sobstvennoi E. I. V. kantseliarii, 1842.

Albach, Ben. *Langs kermissen en hoven: Ontstaan en kroniek van een Nederlands toneelgezelschap in de 17de eeuw*. Zutphen, NLD: Walburg Pers, 1977.

Alexander, John. "The Language of the Pickelhering: A German Adaptation (1683) of Thomas Corneille's *Timocrate*." *Germanisch-Romanische Monatsschrift* 52, no. 4 (2002): 463–476.

———. "Pickleherring: An Early Modern Clown Persona and His Music." *Philologica Jassyensia* 10, no. 1 (2014): 119–133.

———. "Ridentum dicere verum (Using Laughter to Speak the Truth): Laughter and the Language of the Early Modern Clown 'Pickelhering' in German Literature of the Late Seventeenth Century (1675–1700)." In *Laughter in the Middle Ages and Early Modern Times: Epistemology of a Fundamental Human Behavior, Its Meaning, and Consequences*, edited by Albrecht Classen, 735–766. New York: Walter de Gruyter, 2010.

———. "Will Kemp, Thomas Sacheville and Pickelhering: A Consanguinity and Confluence of Three Early Modern Clown Personas." *Daphnis* 36, nos. 3–4 (2007): 463–486.

Alexander, Robert. "A Record of Twelfth Night Celebrations." *Records of Early English Drama* 16, no. 1 (1991): 12–19.

Alm, Irene. "Dances from the 'Four Corners of the Earth': Exoticism in Seventeenth-Century Venetian Opera." In *Musica Franca: Essays in Honor of Frank A. D'Accone*, edited by Irene Alm et al., 233–257. Stuyvesant, NY: Pendragon Press, 1996.

Álvarez Francés, Leonor. "The Phoenix Glides on Dutch Wings: Lope de Vega's *El amigo por fuerza* in Seventeenth-Century Amsterdam." Master's thesis, University of Amsterdam, 2013.

Amburger, Erik. "Die Mitwirkenden bei der Moskauer Aufführung des 'Artaxerxes' am 17. Oktober 1672." *Zeitschrift für slavische Philologie* 25, no. 2 (1956): 304–309.

Ardolino, Frank. "Hans and Hammon: Dekker's Use of Hans Sachs and 'Purim' in *The Shoemaker's Holiday*." *Medieval and Renaissance Drama in England* 14 (2001): 144–167.

Armstrong, William. "Shakespeare and the Acting of Edward Alleyn." *Shakespeare Survey* 7 (1954): 82–89.

Asper, Helmut. *Hanswurst. Studien zum Lustigmacher auf der Berufsschauspielerbühne in Deutschland im 17. und 18. Jahrhundert*. Emsdetten, DEU: Lechte, 1980.

Babkin, A. "Pis'ma Frantsa i Petra Lefortov o 'Velikom posol'stve.'" *Voprosy istorii*, no. 4 (1976): 120–132.

Bantysh-Kamenskii, N. N. *Obzor vneshnikh snoshenii Rossii (po 1800 god)*. 3 vols. Moscow: E. Lissner i Iu. Roman, 1894–1897.

Baron, Samuel. "Osep Nepea and the Opening of Anglo-Russian Commercial Relations." *OSP*, n.s., 11 (1978): 42–63.

Baron, Samuel, and Nancy Shields Kollmann. Introduction to *Religion and Culture in Early Modern Russia and Ukraine*, edited by Samuel Baron and Nancy Shields Kollmann, 3–16. DeKalb: Northern Illinois University Press, 1997.

Batalov, A. L. "Evropeiskie arkhitektory i voennye spetsialisty na sluzhbe Ivana IV v svete pis'mennykh istochnikov: eshche raz ob istorii Gansa Shlitte." *Muzei moskovskogo kremlia: Materialy i issledovaniia* 22 (2014): 8–32.

Baudartius, Willem. *Apophthegmata Christiana*. Deventer: Jan Evertsz Cloppenburch, 1605. Available online at https://books.google.com/books?id=ModjAAAAcAAJ.

Beliakov, A. V. "Posol'stvo Chemodanova v Venetsiiu v 1656 g." *Rossiia i mir glazami drug druga: iz istorii vzaimovospriiatiia* 8 (2017): 32–41.

———. *Sluzhashchie Posol'skogo prikaza 1645–1682 gg*. St. Petersburg: Nestor-Istoriia, 2017.

Bentley, Gerald Eades. *The Jacobean and Caroline Stage*. Vols. 1–2, *Dramatic Companies and Players*. Oxford: Clarendon Press, 1941.

Berek, Peter. "*Tamburlaine*'s Weak Sons: Imitation as Interpretation before 1593." *Renaissance Drama*, n.s., 13 (1982): 55–82.

Bergholz, Friedrich Wilhelm von. "Tagebuch." *Magazin für die neue Historie und Geographie*, edited by A. F. Büsching, vol. 20 (1786): 331–592; vol. 21 (1787): 178–360.

Berkov, P. N. "Iz istorii russkoi teatral'noi terminologii XVII–XVIII vekov ('Komediia,' 'intermediia,' 'dialog,' 'igrishche' i dr.)." *TODRL* 11 (1955): 280–299.

———. "K istorii russkogo teatra 1720-kh godov ('Dialog o Gofrede, pobedivshem saratsiny')." *TODRL* 10 (1954): 389–407.

Berry, Lloyd, ed. *The English Works of Giles Fletcher, the Elder*. Madison: University of Wisconsin Press, 1964.

Berry, Lloyd, and Robert Crummey, eds. *Rude and Barbarous Kingdom: Russia in the Accounts of Sixteenth-Century English Voyagers*. Madison: University of Wisconsin Press, 1968.

Bessonov, P. A. "Zapisnoi raskhodnyi stolbets prikazu Galitskie cheti. 182 goda." *Vremennik Imperatorskogo moskovskogo obshchestva istorii i drevnostei rossiiskikh* 24 (1856): pt. 2, 1–44.

Bevilacqua, Alexander, and Helen Pfeifer. "Turquerie: Culture in Motion, 1650–1750." *Past and Present* 221 (2013): 75–118.

Biblioteka literatury drevnei Rusi. Vol. 6, *XIV–seredina XV veka*. St. Petersburg: Nauka, 1999.

Birgegård, Ulla, ed. *J. G. Sparwenfeld's Diary of a Journey to Russia 1684–87*. Slavica Suecana, Series A: Publications, vol. 1. Stockholm: Kungl. Vitterhets Historie och Antikvitets Akademien, 2002.

Blaak, Jeroen. *Literacy in Everyday Life: Reading and Writing in Early Modern Dutch Diaries.* Leiden: Brill, 2009.
Black, J. L. *G.-F. Müller and the Imperial Russian Academy.* Kingston: McGill-Queen's University Press, 1986.
Bogoiavlenskii, S. K. "Moskovskii teatr pri Tsariakh Aleksee i Petre." *ChOIDR* 2 (1914): pt. 1, iii–xxi, 1–192.
——. *Nauchnoe nasledie o Moskve XVII veka.* Moscow: Nauka, 1980.
Bogoslovskii, M. M. *Petr I: Materialy dlia biografii.* Vol. 2, *Pervoe zagranichnoe puteshestvie.* 1941. Reprint, Slavistic Printings and Reprintings, vol. 2, no. 205. Series editor, C. H. van Schooneveld. The Hague: Mouton, 1969.
Bolte, Johannes. *Das Danziger Theater im 16. und 17. Jahrhundert.* Hamburg: Leopold Voss, 1895.
——. "Schwedische Beiträge zu unserer älteren Theatergeschichte." *Archiv für das Studium der neueren Sprachen und Literaturen* 131, n.s., 31 (1913): 144–145.
Bond, Edward, ed. "Russia at the Close of the sixteenth century, Comprising the Treatise 'Of the Russe Common Wealth,' by Dr. Giles Fletcher; and the Travels of Sir Jerome Horsey, Knt." *Hakluyt Society* 20 (1856; entire volume).
Borg, Dagmar. "En komedi om Adam och Eva." Licentiate thesis, Uppsala University, 1947.
Bosman, Anston. "History between Theaters." In *From Performance to Print in Shakespeare's England,* edited by Peter Holland and Stephen Orgel, 191–207. Basingstoke, UK: Palgrave Macmillan, 2006.
——. "Mobility." In *Early Modern Theatricality,* edited by Henry Turner, 493–515. Oxford: Oxford University Press, 2013.
——. "Renaissance Intertheater and the Staging of Nobody." *ELH* 71, no. 3 (2004): 559–585.
Boterbloem, Kees. *Moderniser of Russia: Andrei Vinius, 1641–1716.* Houndmills, UK: Palgrave Macmillan, 2013.
Bouterse, Jan. "The Van Bolhuis Auction (1764)." *Fellowship of Makers and Researchers of Historical Instruments Quarterly* 89 (1997): 20–22.
Bowers, Fredson, ed. *The Dramatic Works of Thomas Dekker.* Vol. 1. Cambridge: Cambridge University Press, 1953.
Bowers, Rick. "*Tamburlaine* in Ludlow." *Notes and Queries* 45, no. 3 (1998): 361–363.
Bowles, Edmund. "The Impact of Turkish Military Bands on European Court Festivals in the 17th and 18th centuries." *Early Music* 34, no. 4 (2006): 533–559.
Brand, Peter, and Bärbel Rudin. "Der englische Komödiant Robert Browne (1563–ca. 1621)." *Daphnis* 39, nos. 1–2 (2010): 1–134.
Brandt, George, and Wiebe Hogendoorn, comps. *German and Dutch Theatre, 1600–1848.* Theatre in Europe: A Documentary History. Cambridge: Cambridge University Press, 1993.
Bredekamp, Horst. "*Kunstkammer*, Play-Palace, Shadow Theatre: Three Thought Loci by Gottfried Wilhelm Leibniz." In *Collection, Laboratory, Theater: Scenes of Knowledge in the 17th Century,* edited by Helmar Schramm et al., 266–282. Berlin: Walter de Gruyter, 2005.
Brennan, Michael, ed. *The Origins of the Grand Tour: The Travels of Robert Montagu, Lord Mandeville (1649–1654), William Hammond (1655–1658), Banaster Maynard (1660–1663).* London: Hakluyt Society, 2004.
Brikner, A. G. "Lavrentii Ringuber." Review of *Relation du voyage en Russie fait en 1684 par Laurent Rinhuber,* by Laurent Rinhuber. *ZhMNP* 231 (February 1884): 396–421.
——. "Russkie diplomaty-turisty v Italii v XVII stoletii." *Russkii vestnik* 128 (March 1877): 5–44.
Brown, John Russell. "Marlowe and the Actors." *Tulane Drama Review* 8, no. 4 (1964): 155–173.
Brown, Peter. "How Muscovy Governed: Seventeenth-Century Russian Central Administration." *Russian History* 36, no. 4 (2009): 459–529.

———. "Muscovite Government Bureaus." *Russian History* 10, no. 3 (1983): 269–330.
Brown, William Edward. *A History of Seventeenth-Century Russian Literature*. Ann Arbor, MI: Ardis, 1980.
Brümmer, Franz. "Tietz, Friedrich." In *Allgemeine Deutsche Biographie*, 38:292–293. Leipzig: Duncker & Humblot, 1894.
Bruyn, Cornelis de. *Travels into Muscovy, Persia, and Part of the East-Indies*. Vol. 1. London: Printed for A. Bettesworth et al., 1737.
Bubnov, N. Iu., and N. S. Demkova. "Vnov' naidennoe poslanie iz Moskvy v Pustozersk 'Vozveshchenie ot syna dukhovnago ko ottsu dukhovnomu' i otvet protopopa Avvakuma (1676 g.)." *TODRL* 36 (1981): 127–150.
Bulgakov, A. S. "Komediia o Tamerlane i Baiazete ('Temir-Aksakovo deistvo')." In *Starinnyi spektakl' v Rossii*, 317–357. Leningrad: Academia, 1928.
Burnett, Stephen. *Christian Hebraism in the Reformation Era (1500–1660)*. Leiden: Brill, 2012.
Bushkovitch, Paul. "Change and Culture in Early Modern Russia." *Kritika: Explorations in Russian and Eurasian History*, n.s., 16, no. 2 (2015): 291–316.
———. "Cultural Change among the Russian Boyars 1650–1680: New Sources and Old Problems." *Forschungen zur osteuropäischen Geschichte* 56 (2000): 91–111.
———. "The Epiphany Ceremony of the Russian Court in the Sixteenth and Seventeenth Centuries." *Russian Review* 49, no. 1 (1990): 1–17.
———. *Peter the Great: The Struggle for Power, 1671–1725*. Cambridge: Cambridge University Press, 2001.
———. *Religion and Society in Russia: The Sixteenth and Seventeenth Centuries*. New York: Oxford University Press, 1992.
Bussow, Conrad. *The Disturbed State of the Russian Realm*. Translated and edited by G. Edward Orchard. Montreal: McGill-Queen's University Press, 1994.
Buturlin, M. D. *Documenti che si conservano nel R. Archivio di Stato in Firenze, Sezione Medicea, riguardanti l'antica Moscovia (Russia) / Bumagi florentinskogo tsentral'nogo arkhiva kasaiushchiiasia do Rossii*. Moscow: Grachev, 1871.
Calendar of State Papers and Manuscripts, Relating to English Affairs, Existing in the Archives and Collections of Venice. Vol. 33, 1661–1664. Edited by Allen B. Hinds. London: His Majesty's Stationery Office, 1932.
Catalogue of the Museum of the Worshipful Company of Clockmakers of London. 2nd ed. London: Blades, East and Blades, 1902.
Cavalli, Francesco. *Artemisia: Dramma per musica by Nicolò Minato*. Edited by H. Schulze and S. E. Stangalino. Kassel: Bärenreiter, 2013.
Cerasano, S. P. "Edward Alleyn, the New Model Actor, and the Rise of the Celebrity in the 1590s." *Medieval and Renaissance Drama in England* 18 (2005): 47–58.
Chambers, E. K. *The Elizabethan Stage*. 4 vols. Oxford: Clarendon Press, 1923.
Charykov, N. V. *Posol'stvo v Rim i sluzhba v Moskve Pavla Meneziia (1637–1694)*. St. Petersburg: A. S. Suvorin, 1906.
Chertkov, A. D. "Opisanie posol'stva, otpravlennogo v 1659 godu ot Tsaria Alekseia Mikhailovicha k Ferdinandu II-mu, Velikomu Gertsogu Toskanskomu." *Russkii istoricheskii sbornik* 3 (1840): pt. 4, 311–369.
Chew, Samuel. *The Crescent and the Rose: Islam and England during the Renaissance*. New York: Oxford University Press, 1937.
Chistiakova, E. V., ed. *"Oko vsei velikoi Rossii": Ob istorii russkoi diplomaticheskoi sluzhby XVI–XVII vekov*. Moscow: "Mezhdunarodnye otnosheniia," 1989.
Clarke, Jan. *The Guénégaud Theatre in Paris (1673–1680)*. 3 vols. Lewiston, NY: Edwin Mellen Press, 1998–2007.

Cohn, Albert. *Shakespeare in Germany in the Sixteenth and Seventeenth Centuries*. 1865. Reprint, New York: Haskell House, 1971.

[Collins, Samuel]. *The Present State of Russia, In a Letter to a Friend at London; Written by an Eminent Person Residing at the Great Czars Court at Mosco for the Space of Nine Years*. London: Printed by John Winter, 1671. Available online at EEBO.

[Coryate, Thomas]. *Coryat's Crudities; Reprinted from the Edition of 1611*. Vol. 2. London: Printed for William Cater, 1776. Available at Eighteenth-Century Collections Online, Gale Cengage Learning, document number CW3301549261.

Coudenys, Wim. "Translation and the Emergence of History as an Academic Discipline in 18th-Century Russia." *Kritika: Explorations in Russian and Eurasian History*, n.s., 17, no. 4 (2016): 721–752.

[Coyett, Balthasar]. *Posol'stvo Kunraada fan-Klenka k tsariam Alekseiu Mikhailovichu i Feodoru Alekseevichu / Historisch verhael, of Beschryving van de Voyagie, Gedaen onder de suite van den Heere Koenraad van Klenk*. Translated by A. M. Loviagin. St. Petersburg: Glavnoe upravlenie udelov, 1900.

Cracraft, James. *The Petrine Revolution in Russian Imagery*. Chicago: University of Chicago Press, 1997.

Crewdson, Richard. *Apollo's Swan and Lyre: Five Hundred Years of the Musicians' Company*. Rochester, NY: Boydell Press, 2000.

Crinò, Anna Maria. "Rapporti culturali, diplomatici e commerciali degli Zar di Russia con i Granduchi di Toscana e Venezia nel Seicento." *Annali della facoltà di Economia e Commercio in Verona*, series 2, vol. 1 (1965–1966): 235–278.

———. "La visita di Pietro il Grande in Inghilterra dalle lettere di Thomas Platt ad Apollonio Bassetti." *Nuova rivista storica* 37, nos. 5–6 (1953): 439–449.

Croskey, Robert. "The Composition of Sir Jerome Horsey's 'Travels.'" *JGO*, n.s., 26, no. 3 (1978): 362–375.

Cross, Anthony. *Peter the Great through British Eyes: Perceptions and Representations of the Tsar since 1698*. Cambridge: Cambridge University Press, 2000.

Crummey, Robert O. *Aristocrats and Servitors: The Boyar Elite in Russia, 1613–1689*. Princeton, NJ: Princeton University Press, 1983.

———. "Court Spectacles in Seventeenth-Century Russia: Illusion and Reality." In *Essays in Honor of A. A. Zimin*, edited by Daniel Clarke Waugh, 130–146. Columbus, OH: Slavica, 1985.

Curtis, A. Ross. *Crispien Ier: La Vie et l'œuvre de Raymond Poisson comédien-poète du XVIIe siècle*. Toronto: University of Toronto Press, 1972.

———. "The Theatre of an Actor-Playwright: Raymond Poisson." *Australian Journal of French Studies* 4, no. 2 (1967): 225–243.

Dahl, Staffan. *Codex AD 10 der Västeråser Gymnasial-Bibliothek*. Publications de l'institut slave d'Upsal 2. Uppsala: Almqvist & Wiksell, 1949.

Dahlberg, Gunilla. *Komediantteatern i 1600-talets Stockholm*. Stockholmsmonografier utgivna av Stockholms stad 106. Stockholm: Komittén för stockholmsforskning, 1992.

———. "The Theatre around Queen Christina." *Renaissance Studies* 23, no. 2 (2009): 161–185.

Dal', V. I. *Tolkovyi slovar' zhivogo velikorusskogo iazyka*. 4 vols. 1880–1882. Reprint, from 1955 ed., Moscow: "Russkii iazyk," 1981.

Dankmeijer, J., and T. Röell. "Nicolaas Bidloo and the Institution of Medical Education in Moscow." In *Boerhaave and His Time. Papers Read at the International Symposium in Commemoration of the Tercentenary of Boerhaave's Birth*, edited by Gerrit Arie Lindeboom, 165–169. Leiden: Brill, 1970.

De Jong, Erik. "Virgilian Paradise: A Dutch Garden near Moscow in the Early 18th Century." *Journal of Garden History* 1, no. 4 (1981): 305–344.

Demidova, N. F. *Sluzhilaia biurokratiia v Rossii XVII v. i ee rol' v formirovanii absoliutizma.* Moscow: Nauka, 1987.

———. *Sluzhilaia biurokratiia v Rossii XVII veka (1625–1700): Biograficheskii spravochnik.* Moscow: Pamiatniki istoricheskoi mysli, 2011.

Denny, Walter. "Images of Turks and the European Imagination." In *Court and Conquest: Ottoman Origins and the Design for Handel's "Tamerlano" at the Glimmerglass Opera,* edited by Walter Denny et al., 3–17. Kent: Kent State University Museum, 1998.

Derzhavina, O. A. "U istokov russkogo teatra (Bibleiskaia istoriia ob Adame i Eve na zapadnoevropeiskoi i russkoi stsene XVII veka)." In *Russkaia literatura na rubezhe dvukh epokh: XVII–nachalo XVIII v.,* 84–104. Moscow: Nauka, 1971.

Dharwadker, Vinay. "Introduction: Cosmopolitanism in Its Time and Place." In *Cosmopolitan Geographies: New Locations in Literature and Culture,* edited by Vinay Dharwadker, 1–14. New York: Routledge, 2001.

"Diary of the Journey of Philip Julius, Duke of Stettin-Pomerania, through England in the Year 1602." Edited by Gottfried von Bülow. *Transactions of the Royal Historical Society* 6 (1892): 1–67.

Dimmock, Matthew. *New Turkes: Dramatizing Islam and the Ottomans in Early Modern England.* Aldershot, UK: Ashgate, 2005.

Di Salvo [Sal'vo], M. "Kastrat Petra Velikogo: Filippo Balatri v Moskovii (1699–1701)." In *Inozemtsy v Rossii v XV–XVII vekakh: Sbornik materialov konferentsii 2002–2004 gg.,* 430–439. Moscow: Drevlekhranilishche, 2006.

Di Salvo, Maria. "La missione di I. Čemodanov a Venezia (1656–1657): osservazioni e nuovi materiali." In *Italia, Russia e mondo slavo: studi filologici e letterari,* edited by Maria Di Salvo and Alberto Alberti, 97–116. Biblioteca di studi slavistici 17. Florence: Firenze University Press, 2011.

———. "*Vita e viaggi* di Filippo Balatri (Preliminari all'edizione del testo)." *Russica romana* 6 (1999): 37–57.

Dmitrieva, Olga, and Natalya Abramova, eds. *Britannia and Muscovy: English Silver at the Court of the Tsars.* New Haven: Yale University Press, 2006.

Dneval'nye zapiski prikaza Tainykh del 7165–7183 gg. Edited by S. A. Belokurov. Moscow: Izdanie Imperatorskogo obshchestva istorii i drevnostei rossiiskikh pri Moskovskom universitete, 1908.

Dnevnik Mariny Mnishek. Edited by D. M. Bulanin. Translated by V. N. Kosliakov. St. Petersburg: Dmitrii Bulanin, 1995.

Dolgova, S. R. "Petr I na maskarade v Vene." In *Petrovskoe vremia v litsakh—2013: Materialy nauchnoi konferentsii,* edited by V. V. Meshcheriakov and I. V. Saverkina, 148–152. St. Petersburg: Izdatel'stvo Gosudarstvennogo Ermitazha, 2013.

Droste, Heiko, and Ingrid Maier. "Christoff Koch (1637–1711): Sweden's Man in Moscow." In *Travelling Chronicles: News and Newspapers from the Early Modern Period to the Eighteenth Century,* edited by Siv Gøril Brandtzæg et al., 119–139. Leiden: Brill, 2018.

Du Bec, Iean. *Historie van t'leven ende de daden van den Grooten Tamerlanes.* Translated by I. L. B. Rotterdam: Ian Leendersz[oon] Berewout, 1613. Available online at https://play.google.com/books/reader?id=5FJkAAAAcAAJ; 1638 edition available online at https://play.google.com/books/reader?id=nUMPd1Mo2R4C; 1647 edition available online at https://play.google.com/books/reader?id=lA5pAAAAcAAJ.

Du Bec, Jean. *Histoire du grand empereur Tamerlanes.* Rouen: Chez Richard l'Allemant, 1595. Available online at https://books.google.com/books?id=hBBJAAAAcAAJ.

———. *The Historie of the Great Emperour Tamerlan.* Translated by H. M. London: Printed for William Ponsonby, 1597. Available online at EEBO.

Dubrovskii, I. V. "Novye dokumenty po istorii otnoshenii Rossii i Italii pri Ivane Groznom." *Russkii sbornik: Issledovaniia po istorii Rossii*, no. 14 (2013): 7–72.

Dukelskaya, Larissa, and Elizaveta Renne. *The Hermitage Catalogue of Western European Painting*. Vol. 13, *British Painting: Sixteenth to Nineteenth Centuries*. Florence: Giunti, 1990.

Dukes, Paul. "Paul Menzies and his Mission from Muscovy to Rome, 1672–1674." *Innes Review* 35, no. 2 (1984): 88–95.

Dumschat, Sabine. *Ausländische Mediziner im Moskauer Rußland. Quellen und Studien zur Geschichte des östlichen Europa* 67. Stuttgart: Steiner, 2006.

———. "Coster (Köster) von Rosenburg, Johann(es)." In *Biographisches Lexikon für Schleswig-Holstein und Lübeck* 13, 112–116. Neumünster, DEU: Wachholtz, 2011.

Dunning, Chester. "Lost Chapters of John Milton's *Moscovia*." *Canadian-American Slavic Studies* 45, no. 2 (2011): 133–161.

———. *Russia's First Civil War: The Time of Troubles and the Founding of the Romanov Dynasty*. University Park: Pennsylvania State University Press, 2001.

[Du Verdier, Antoine]. *Het tweede deel Petri Messiae, dat is De verscheyden lessen Antony du Verdier, heere van Vauprivas, vervolgende die van Pieter Messias*. Translated by I. L. B. Rotterdam: Ian Leendersz[oon] Berewout, 1613. Available online at https://play.google.com/books/reader?id=dA0UAAAAQAAJ.

Dzhensen [Jensen], K., and I. Maier. *Pridvornyi teatr v Rossii XVII veka*. Moscow: Indrik, 2016.

Ekaterininskaia, A. A. "Pridvornyi teatr Alekseia Mikhailovicha: organizatsionnye osnovy deiatel'nosti." Avtoreferat, Sanktpeterburgskaia gosudarstvennaia akademiia teatral'nogo iskusstva, 2012.

Elgenstierna, Gustaf. *Den introducerade svenska adelns ättartavlor: Med tillägg och rättelser*. 9 vols. Stockholm: Norstedt, 1925–1936.

Ellersieck, Heinz. "Russia under Aleksei Mikhailovich and Feodor Alekseevich, 1645–1682: The Scandinavian Sources." PhD diss., University of California, Los Angeles, 1955.

Ellis-Fermor, U. M., ed. *Tamburlaine the Great*. London: Methuen, 1930.

Evans, N. E. "The Meeting of the Russian and Scottish Ambassadors in London in 1601." *SEER* 55, no. 4 (1977): 517–528.

Fabris, Dinko. "Italian Soundscapes: Souvenirs from the Grand Tour." In *Passaggio in Italia: Music on the Grand Tour in the Seventeenth Century*, edited by Dinko Fabris and Margaret Murata, 23–32. Utrecht: Brepols, 2015.

Findeizen, N. F. *Ocherki po istorii muzyki v Rossii*. 2 vols. Moscow: Gosudarstvennoe izdatel'stvo Muzsektor, 1928.

Fitzmyer, Joseph. *A Christological Catechism: New Testament Answers*. New York: Paulist Press, 1982.

Flemming, Willi. "Deutsches Barockdrama als Beginn des Moskauer Hoftheaters (1672)." *Maske und Kothurn* 2/3 (1958): 97–124.

Floria, B. N. *Russkoe gosudarstvo i ego zapadnye sosedi (1655–1661 gg.)*. Moscow: Indrik, 2010.

———. *Vneshnepoliticheskaia programma A. L. Ordina-Nashchokina i popytki ee osushchestvleniia*. Moscow: Indrik, 2013.

Forsten, G. V. "Datskie diplomaty pri moskovskom dvore vo vtoroi polovine XVII veka." *ZhMNP* 355, no. 9 (September 1904): 110–181.

Frost, Robert. *The Northern Wars: War, State, and Society in Northeastern Europe, 1558–1721*. New York: Longman, 2000.

Fürstenau, Moritz. *Zur Geschichte der Musik und des Theaters am Hofe zu Dresden*. Vol. 1. Dresden: Rudolf Kuntze, 1861.

Garvin, Wilhelma. *The Development of the Comic Figure in the German Drama from the Reformation to the Thirty Years' War*. Philadelphia: Westbrook Publishing, 1923.

Gill, Roma. "'Such Conceits as Clownage Keeps in Pay': Comedy and *Dr. Faustus*." In *The Fool and the Trickster: Studies in Honour of Enid Welsford*, edited by P. V. A. Williams, 55–63. Cambridge: D. S. Brewer, 1979.

Glixon, Beth, and Jonathan Glixon. *Inventing the Business of Opera: The Impresario and His World in Seventeenth-Century Venice*. Oxford: Oxford University Press, 2006.

Glixon, Jonathan, and Beth Glixon. "Oil and Opera Don't Mix: The Biography of S. Aponal, a Seventeenth-Century Venetian Opera Theater." In *Music in the Theater, Church, and Villa: Essays in Honor of Robert Lamar Weaver and Norma Wright Weaver*, edited by Susan Parisi, 131–144. Warren, MI: Harmonie Park Press, 2000.

Göllner, Carl. *Turcica: die europäischen Türkendrucke des XVI. Jahrhunderts*. 3 vols. Bucharest: Editura Academiei Republicii Socialiste România, 1961–1978.

Goloubeva, Maria. *The Glorification of Emperor Leopold I in Image, Spectacle and Text*. Mainz: Verlag Philipp von Zabern, 2000.

Golubtsov, A. P. "Pamiatniki Prenii o vere, voznikshikh po delu korolevicha Val'demara i tsarevny Iriny Mikhailovny." *ChOIDR* 2 (1892): pt. 2, i–xxvi, 1–305.

Gorbatov, E. N. "Novye materialy po delu arkhiepiskopa Iosifa (Kurtsevicha) 1643 g." *Vestnik tserkovnoi istorii*, nos. 1/2 (2017): 5–45.

Gorbatov, E. N., T. A. Oparina, and S. M. Shamin. "Biografii inozemnykh poteshnikov tsaria Mikhaila Fedorovicha: Feska Tsymbal'nikov/Fedor Zaval'skii." In *Vspomogatel'nye istoricheskie distsipliny v sovremennom nauchnom znanii. Materialy XXIX Mezhdunarodnoi nauchnoi konferentsii*, 107–109. Moscow: Institut vseobshchei istorii RAN, 2017.

Goudriaan, Elisa. "The Cultural Importance of Florentine Patricians. Cultural Exchange, Brokerage Networks, and Social Representation in Early Modern Florence and Rome (1600–1660)." PhD diss., Leiden University, 2015.

Gravers, Sven. "Johan Henrik von Kochen." In *Svenskt biografiskt lexikon*, 21:439–445. Stockholm: Norstedt, 1975–1977.

Grebeniuk, V. P., ed. *Panegiricheskaia literatura petrovskogo vremeni*. Moscow: Nauka, 1979.

Greenhill, Rima. "From Russia with Love: A Case of *Love's Labour's Lost*." *Oxfordian* 9 (2006): 9–32.

Greer, Margaret Rich, and J. E. Varey. *Fuentes para la historia del teatro en España*. Vol. 29, *El teatro palaciego en Madrid: 1586–1707. Estudio y documentos*. Madrid: Támesis, 1997.

Griffin, Clare. "The Production and Consumption of Medical Knowledge in Seventeenth-Century Russia: The Apothecary Chancery." PhD diss., University College London, 2012.

Griffith, Eva. *A Jacobean Company and Its Playhouse: The Queen's Servants at the Red Bull Theatre (c. 1605–1619)*. Cambridge: Cambridge University Press, 2013.

Gruber, Isaiah. "The Muscovite Embassy of 1599 to Emperor Rudolf II of Habsburg." Master's thesis, McGill University, 1999.

Gstach, Ruth. *"Die Liebes Verzweiffelung" des Laurentius von Schnüffis: Eine bisher unbekannte Tragikomödie der frühen Wanderbühne*. Berlin: Walter de Gruyter, 2017.

Günther, Kurt. "Das Moskauer Judithdrama von Johann Gottfried Georgii." *Studien zur Geschichte der russischen Literatur des 18. Jahrhunderts* 4 (1970): 41–208.

———. "Neue deutsche Quellen zum ersten russischen Theater." *Zeitschrift für Slawistik* 8, no. 5 (1963): 664–675.

———. "Das Weimarer Bruchstück des ersten russischen Dramas 'Artaxerxovo dejstvo' (1672)." *Studien zur Geschichte der russischen Literatur des 18. Jahrhunderts* 3 (1968): 120–178.

Gurliand, I. Ia. *Ivan Gebdon: Kommissarius i rezident (Materialy po istorii administratsii Moskovskogo gosudarstva vtoroi poloviny XVII veka)*. Iaroslavl': Tipografiia gubernskogo pravleniia, 1903.

Gurr, Andrew. "The Great Divide of 1594." In *Words That Count: Essays on Early Modern Authorship in Honor of MacDonald P. Jackson*, edited by Brian Boyd, 29–48. Newark: University of Delaware Press, 2004.

———. *The Shakespearean Playing Companies*. Oxford: Clarendon Press, 1996.

———. *Shakespeare's Opposites: The Admiral's Company 1594–1625*. Cambridge: Cambridge University Press, 2009.

———. "Who Strutted and Bellowed?" *Shakespeare Survey* 16 (1963): 95–102.

Gus'kov, A. G. "Dumnyi d'iak E. I. Ukraintsev: problema obespechennosti istochnikami istorii zhizni prikaznogo sluzhashchego vtoroi poloviny XVII v." In *Srednevekovaia lichnost' v pis'mennykh i arkheologicheskikh istochnikakh*, edited by L. A. Beliaev et al., 83–88. Moscow: Institut rossiiskoi istorii RAN, 2016.

Guzevich, D. Iu., and I. D. Guzevich. *Velikoe posol'stvo: rubezh epokh, ili nachalo puti: 1697–1698*. St. Petersburg: Dmitrii Bulanin, 2008.

Guzevich, I. D., and D. Iu. Guzevich. "Bolezn' i smert' Fransua Leforta." In *Petrovskoe vremia v litsakh—2004: Materialy nauchnoi konferentsii*, edited by G. Vilinbakhov, 63–106. St. Petersburg: Izdatel'stvo Gosudarstvennogo Ermitazha, 2004.

Haekel, Ralf. *Die Englischen Komödianten in Deutschland. Eine Einführung in die Ursprünge des deutschen Berufsschauspiels*. Heidelberg: Winter, 2004.

Hakluyt, Richard. *Hakluyt's Collection of the Early Voyages, Travels, and Discoveries, of the English Nation*. Vol. 1. New edition, with additions. London: Printed for R. H. Evans, 1809.

Hansen, Günther. *Formen der Commedia dell'Arte in Deutschland*. Edited by Helmut G. Asper. Emsdetten, DEU: Lechte, 1984.

Harder-Gersdorff, Elisabeth. "Lübeck, die Kompagnie der Novgorodfahrer und der Rußlandhandel vor der Gründung St. Petersburgs. Eine Untersuchung zum 17. Jahrhundert." *Hansische Geschichtsblätter* 120 (2002): 97–147.

Harris, F. R. *The Life of Edward Mountagu, K.G., First Earl of Sandwich (1625–1672)*. Vol. 2. London: John Murray, 1912.

Heiberg, Steffen. "v. Ehrenschild, Conrad Biermann." In *Dansk biografisk lexikon*, 4:128–130. Copenhagen: Gyldendal, 1980.

Heine, Carl. *Johannes Velten. Ein Beitrag zur Geschichte des deutschen Theaters im XVII. Jahrhundert. Inaugural-Dissertation zur Erlangung der Doctorwürde [...] Halle-Wittenberg*. Halle: Ehrhardt Karras, 1887.

Hellie, Richard. *The Economy and Material Culture of Russia: 1600–1725*. Chicago: University of Chicago Press, 1999.

Helmers, Helmer. "Public Diplomacy in Early Modern Europe: Towards a New History of News." *Media History* 22, nos. 3–4 (2016): 401–420.

Henke, Robert. Introduction to *Transnational Exchange in Early Modern Theater*, edited by Robert Henke and Eric Nicholson, 1–15. Aldershot, UK: Ashgate, 2008.

Hennings, Jan. *Russia and Courtly Europe: Ritual and the Culture of Diplomacy, 1648–1725*. Cambridge: Cambridge University Press, 2016.

[Henslowe, Philip]. *Henslowe's Diary*. Edited by R. A. Foakes and R. T. Rickert. Cambridge: Cambridge University Press, 1961.

Hilton, Julian. "Pickelhering, Pickleherring and What You Will." In *Elizabethan and Modern Studies: Presented to Professor Willem Schrickx on the Occasion of His Retirement*, edited by J. P. Vander Motten, 131–142. Ghent: Seminarie voor Engelse en Amerikaanse Literatuur, 1985.

Hippisley, Anthony. *The Poetic Style of Simeon Polotsky*. Birmingham Slavonic Monographs 16. Birmingham: Department of Russian Language and Literature, University of Birmingham, 1985.

Hirsch, Ferdinand, ed. "Brandenburg und Rußland 1673–1679." *Urkunden und Actenstücke zur Geschichte des Kurfürsten Friedrich Wilhelm von Brandenburg*. Vol. 19, *Politische Verhandlungen* 12, pt. 2, 247–330. Berlin: Georg Reimer, 1906.

Holmes, William. *Opera Observed: Views of a Florentine Impresario in the Early Eighteenth Century*. Chicago: University of Chicago Press, 1993.

Hoppe, Harry. "English Acting Companies at the Court of Brussels in the Seventeenth Century." *Review of English Studies*, n.s. 6, no. 21 (1955): 26–33.

———. "English Actors at Ghent in the Seventeenth Century." *Review of English Studies* 25, no. 100 (1949): 305–321.

Hotson, Leslie. *The First Night of "Twelfth Night."* New York: Macmillan, 1954.

Houts, Consuelo. "Two Sources for Racine's *Bajazet*." Master's thesis, University of Washington, 1937.

Hughes, Lindsey. "The Moscow Armoury and Innovations in Seventeenth-Century Muscovite Art." *Canadian-American Slavic Studies* 13, nos. 1–2 (1979): 204–223.

———. *Russia in the Age of Peter the Great*. New Haven: Yale University Press, 1998.

———. *Sophia, Regent of Russia: 1657–1704*. New Haven: Yale University Press, 1990.

Hunt, Mary Leland. *Thomas Dekker: A Study*. New York: Columbia University Press, 1911.

Hutchings, Mark. "The 'Turk Phenomenon' and the Repertory of the late Elizabethan Playhouse." *Early Modern Literary Studies* 13, no. 2 (2007; also as special issue 16).

Ingram, Anders. *Writing the Ottomans: Turkish History in Early Modern England*. New York: Palgrave Macmillan, 2015.

Interpreter's Dictionary of the Bible: An Illustrated Encyclopedia Identifying and Explaining All Proper Names and Significant Terms and Subjects in the Holy Scriptures, Including the Apocrypha. 4 vols. Edited by George Arthur Buttrick. New York: Abingdon Press, 1962.

Irvine, Verity. "The 'Oriental' Ambassador in 17th Century French Comedy." PhD diss., University of Kent at Canterbury, 2004.

Isherwood, Robert. *Music in the Service of the King: France in the Seventeenth Century*. Ithaca, NY: Cornell University Press, 1973.

[Istomin, Karion]. *Bukvar' sostavlen Karionom Istominym gravirovan Leontiem Buninym otpechatan v 1694 godu v Moskve*. Edited by V. I. Luk'ianenko and M. A. Alekseeva. Leningrad: Avrora, 1981.

Iurkin, I. N. *Andrei Andreevich Vinius 1641–1716*. Moscow: Nauka, 2007.

Janetzkius Redivivus. Oder: Der neubelebte weltberuffene lustige Janetzkii. N.p.: [ca. 1689–1700].

Jensen, Claudia. *Musical Cultures in Seventeenth-Century Russia*. Bloomington: Indiana University Press, 2009.

Jensen, Claudia, and Ingrid Maier. "Orpheus and Pickleherring in the Kremlin: The 'Ballet' for the Tsar of February 1672." *Scando-Slavica* 59, no. 2 (2013): 145–184.

———. "Pickleherring Returns to the Kremlin: More New Sources on the Pre-History of the Russian Court Theatre." *Scando-Slavica* 61, no. 1 (2015): 7–56.

Jensen, Claudia, and John Powell. "'A Mess of Russians Left Us but of Late': Diplomatic Blunder, Literary Satire, and the Muscovite Ambassador's 1668 Visit to Paris Theatres." *Theatre Research International* 24, no. 2 (1999): 131–144.

"Journal du Sieur de Catheux." In *Une ambassade russe à la cour de Louis XIV*, edited by A. P. Galitzin, i–vi, 1–32. Bibliothèque russe, n.s., 3. Paris: Librarie A. Franck, 1860.

Junkers, Herbert. *Niederländische Schauspieler und niederländisches Schauspiel im 17. und 18. Jahrhundert in Deutschland*. The Hague: Martinus Nijhoff, 1936.

[Kalachev, N.]. "Materialy ob ustroistve teatral'nykh predstavlenii v Moskve i Preobrazhenskom v 1672-m i 1673-m godakh." *Arkhiv istoricheskikh i prakticheskikh svedenii, otnosiashchikhsia do Rossii* 6 (1869): pt. 2, 16–26.

Kaplan, Joel. "Middleton's Tamburlaine." *English Language Notes* 13, no. 4 (1976): 258–260.
Kaplun, M. V. "Personazhi-shuty v 'Iudifi' I. G. Gregori v kontekste repertuara 'angliiskikh komediantov.'" *Vestnik Sankt-Peterburgskogo gosudarstvennogo universiteta kul'tury i iskusstv*, no. 3 (March 2015): 61–65.
———. "Rekonstruktsiia intermedii 'Artakserksova deistva' Ioganna Gotfrida Gregori." *Germenevtika drevnerusskoi literatury* 19 (2020): 135–156.
Karlinsky, Simon. *Russian Drama from Its Beginnings to the Age of Pushkin*. Berkeley: University of California Press, 1985.
Karpiak, Robert. "Researching Early Keyboards in Russia." *Continuo* 20, no. 1 (1996): 2–6.
Katri(t)zky, Peg [M. A. Katritzky]. "Pickelhering and Hamlet in Dutch Art: The English Comedians of Robert Browne, John Green, and Robert Reynolds." *Shakespeare Yearbook* 15 (2004): 113–140.
Katritzky, M. A. "'A Plague o'These Pickle Herring': From London Drinkers to European Stage Clown." In *Renaissance Shakespeare/Shakespeare Renaissances*, edited by M. Procházka et al., 159–168. Newark: University of Delaware Press, 2014.
———. *Women, Medicine and Theatre, 1500–1750: Literary Mountebanks and Performing Quacks*. Aldershot, UK: Ashgate, 2007.
Kazakova, N. A. "A. A. Vinius i stateinyi spisok ego posol'stva v Angliiu, Frantsiiu i Ispaniiu v 1672–1674 gg." *TODRL* 39 (1985): 348–364.
———. "Stateinye spiski russkikh poslov v Italiiu kak pamiatniki literatury puteshestvii (seredina XVII v.)." *TODRL* 41 (1988): 268–288.
Kholodov, E. G. *Teatr i zriteli: Stranitsy istorii russkoi teatral'noi publiki*. Moscow: Gosudarstvennyi institut iskusstvoznaniia, 2000.
Khoroshkevich, A. L., ed. *Martin Gruneveg (otets Ventseslav): dukhovnik Mariny Mnishek. Zapiski o torgovoi poezdke v Moskvu v 1584–1585 gg*. Moscow: Pamiatniki istoricheskoi mysli, 2013.
Kiefer, Frederick. "Lost and Found: William Boyle's *Jugurth*." *Medieval and Renaissance Drama in England* 28 (2015): 17–29.
Kirkendale, Warren. *The Court Musicians in Florence during the Principate of the Medici*. Florence: Leo S. Olschki, 1993.
Kitching, Laurence. *Europe's Itinerant Players and the Advent of German-Language Theatre in Reval, Estonia: Unpublished Petitions of the Swedish Era, 1630–1692, in the Reval City Archives*. Frankfurt: Peter Lang, 1996.
Klarwill, Victor, ed. *Fugger-Zeitungen: ungedruckte Briefe an das Haus Fugger aus den Jahren 1568–1605*. Vienna: Rikola, 1923.
Klautova, O. Iu. "Zapadnoevropeiskoe iskusstvo glazami russkikh puteshestvennikov XV–XVII vv." *TODRL* 49 (1996): 427–439.
Kleimola, Ann. "Hunting for Dogs in 17th-Century Muscovy." *Kritika: Explorations in Russian and Eurasian History*, n.s., 11, no. 3 (2010): 467–488.
Knolles, Richard. *The Generall Historie of the Turkes*. London: Printed by Adam Islip, 1603. Available online at EEBO.
Knutson, Roslyn. "*Henslowe's Diary* and the Economics of Play Revision for Revival, 1592–1603." *Theatre Research International* 10, no. 1 (1985): 1–18.
Koch, Ernst. "Die Sachsenkirche in Moskau und das erste Theater in Rußland." *Neues Archiv für Sächsische Geschichte und Altertumskunde* 32 (1911): 270–316.
Kochegarov, K. A. "K istorii prebyvaniia v Rossii getmana P. D. Doroshenko v 1677–1685 godakh." *Slavianovedenie*, no. 2 (2013): 17–33.
Köhne, Bernhard. "Poroschin in Berlin. 1654." *Schriften des Vereins für die Geschichte der Stadt Berlin* 20 (1882): 1–8.

Kollmann, Nancy S. "Comment: Divides and Ends—The Problem of Periodization." *Slavic Review* 69, no. 2 (2010): 439–447.

———. "A Deeper Early Modern: A Response to Paul Bushkovitch." *Kritika: Explorations in Russian and Eurasian History*, n.s., 16, no. 2 (2015): 317–329.

Konovalov, Sergey. "England and Russia: Three Embassies, 1662–5." *OSP* 10 (1962): 60–85.

———. "Patrick Gordon's Dispatches from Russia, 1667." *OSP* 11 (1964): 8–16.

Kotoshikhin, Grigorii. *O Rossii v carstvovanie Alekseja Mixajloviča*. Edited by Anne Pennington. Oxford: Clarendon Press, 1980.

Kozlovskii, I. P. *Pervye pochty i pervye pochtmeistery v moskovskom gosudarstve*. 2 vols. Warsaw: Tipografiia Varshavskogo uchebnogo okruga, 1913.

Krol', P., A. V. Malov, and S. M. Shamin. "Pol'skii triumf v Varshave v 1661 g. po sluchaiu pobed pol'sko-litovskikh voisk predydushchego 'schastlivogo goda': Moskovskii perevod spetsial'nogo vypuska pervoi pol'skoi gazety *Merkuriusz Polski* iz arkhiva Tainogo prikaza." *Slověne: International Journal of Slavic Studies* 8, no. 2 (2019): 350–376.

Kröll, Katrin. "Theatrum Mundi versus Mundus Theatri: A Study of the History of Fairground Arts in Early Modern Times." *Nordic Theatre Studies* 2/3 (1989): 55–90.

Kudriavtsev, I. M., ed. *"Artakserksovo deistvo"—Pervaia p'esa russkogo teatra XVII v.* Moscow: Izdatel'stvo Akademii nauk SSSR, 1957.

Lahana, Martha. "Novaia Nemetskaia Sloboda: Seventeenth Century Moscow's Foreign Suburb." PhD diss., University of North Carolina at Chapel Hill, 1983.

Lande, Joel B. *Persistence of Folly: On the Origins of German Dramatic Literature*. Ithaca, NY: Cornell University Press, 2018.

Larin, B. A. *Tri inostrannykh istochnika po razgovornoi rechi Moskovskoi Rusi XVI–XVII vekov*. St. Petersburg: Izdatel'stvo S.-Peterburgskogo universiteta, 2002.

Larocca, Giuseppina. "New Perspectives on Jacob von Stählin: Towards an Intellectual Biography." *Slavonica* 23, no. 1 (2018): 42–52. DOI 10.1080/13617427.2018.1471807.

Larson, Orville. "Giacomo Torelli, Sir Philip Skippon, and Stage Machinery for the Venetian Opera." *Theatre Journal* 32, no. 4 (1980): 448–457.

Lavrent'ev, A. V. *Tsarevich-Tsar'-Tsesar'. Lzhedmitrii I, ego gosudarstvennye pechati, nagradnye znaki i medali 1604–1606 gg*. St. Petersburg: Dmitrii Bulanin, 2001.

Lefeber-Morsman, Marieke. "Augsburger Instrumentenbauer und ein Augsburger Spinett in St. Petersburg." *Das mechanische Musikinstrument* 36, no. 108 (2010): 7–14.

Lefort, Frants. *Sbornik materialov i dokumentov / Recueil de documents*. Edited by E. E. Lykova. Compiled by T. A. Lapteva and T. B. Solov'eva. Moscow: Drevlekhranilishche, 2006.

Leichtentritt, Hugo. "Mechanical Music in Olden Times." *Musical Quarterly* 20, no. 1 (1934): 15–26.

Leitsch, Walter. *Das Leben am Hof König Sigismunds III. von Polen*. Vols. 2 and 3. Vienna: Verlag der Österreichischen Akademie der Wissenschaften, 2009.

Lenhoff, Gail. "The Tale of Tamerlane in the *Royal Book of Degrees*." In *Mesto Rossii v Evrazii / The Place of Russia in Eurasia*, edited by Gyula Szvák, 121–129. Budapest: Magyar Ruszisztikai Intézet, 2001.

———. "Temir Aksak's Dream of the Virgin as Protectress of Muscovy." *Die Welt der Slaven* 49, no. 1 (2004): 39–64.

Leunclavius, Johannes. *Annales sultanorum Othmanidarum*. Frankfurt: Claude de Marne and Johann Aubry, 1588. VD16 L 1364; available online at https://play.google.com/books/reader?id=AzoVAAAAQAAJ&printsec=frontcover&output=reader&hl=en&pg=GBS.PP5.

Leve, James. "Humor and Intrigue: A Comparative Study of Comic Opera in Florence and Rome during the Late Seventeenth Century." PhD diss., Yale University, 1998.

Levin, Richard. "The Contemporary Perception of Marlowe's Tamburlaine." *Medieval and Renaissance Drama in England* 1 (1984): 51–70.

Lewenklaw, Johannes. *Neuwe Chronica Türckischer Nation*. Frankfurt: Claude de Marne and Johann Aubry, 1595. VD16 L 1367; available online at https://play.google.com/books/reader?id=1Z9aW_JqbwsC&printsec=frontcover&output=reader&hl=en&pg=GBS.PP5.

Likhachev, D. S. *Poeziia sadov: K semantike sadovo-parkovykh stilei. Sad kak tekst*. 2nd ed., corrected and expanded. St. Petersburg: Nauka, 1991.

———, main ed. *Puteshestviia russkikh poslov XVI–XVII vv.: Stateinye spiski*. Moscow: AN SSSR, 1954.

Likhachev, D. S., A. M. Panchenko, and N. V. Ponyrko. *Smekh v drevnei Rusi*. Leningrad: Nauka, 1984.

Limon, Jerzy. *Gentlemen of a Company: English Players in Central and Eastern Europe, 1590–1660*. Cambridge: Cambridge University Press, 1985.

Lindell, Robert. "Music and Patronage at the Court of Rudolf II." In *Music in the German Renaissance: Sources, Styles, and Context*, edited by John Kmetz, 254–271. Cambridge: Cambridge University Press, 1994.

———. "New Findings on Music at the Court of Maximilian II." In *Kaiser Maximilian II: Kultur und Politik im 16. Jahrhundert*, edited by Friedrich Edelmayer and Alfred Kohler, 231–245. Wiener Beiträge zur Geschichte der Neuzeit 19. Vienna: Verlag für Geschichte und Politik, 1992.

Liseitsev, D. V. *Posol'skii prikaz v epokhu Smuty*. Moscow: Institut rossiiskoi istorii RAN, 2003.

Liseitsev, D. V., N. M. Rogozhin, and Iu. M. Eskin. *Prikazy Moskovskogo gosudarstva XVI–XVII vv. Slovar'-spravochnik*. Moscow: Tsentr gumanitarnykh initsiativ, 2015.

Litavrin, G. G., main ed. *Osmanskaia imperiia i strany tsentral'noi, vostochnoi i iugo-vostochnoi Evropy v XVII v*. Vol. 2. Moscow: "Pamiatniki istoricheskoi mysli," 2001.

Litsevoi letopisnyi svod XVI veka. Rus' (1400–1410 gg. ot V.Kh.). Vol. 11. Moscow: Transneft', 2013–2014.

Lodyzhenskii, A. "Russkoe posol'stvo v Angliiu v 1662 g." *Istoricheskii vestnik* 1, no. 3 (September–December 1880): 433–453.

Loewenson, Leo. "Some Details of Peter the Great's Stay in England in 1698: Neglected English Material." *SEER* 40, no. 95 (1962): 431–443.

London Stage 1600–1800. Part 1, 1660–1700. Edited by William Van Lennep. Carbondale: Southern Illinois University Press, 1965.

Longworth, Philip. *Alexis: Tsar of All the Russias*. New York: Franklin Watts, 1984.

———. "Russian-Venetian Relations in the Reign of Tsar Aleksey Mikhailovich." *SEER* 64, no. 3 (1986): 380–400.

Lonicer, Philipp. *Chronicorum Turcicorum ... tomus primus*. Frankfurt: Georg Rab [et al.], 1578. VD16 L 2463; available online at https://play.google.com/books/reader?id=AxBHAAAAcAAJ&printsec=frontcover&output=reader&hl=en&pg=GBS.PP5.

Louria, Yvette, trans. "The Comedy of Artaxerxes (1672)." *Bulletin of the New York Public Library* 72, no. 3 (1968): 139–210.

Lukichev, M. P. "S. F. Chizhinskii—perevodchik i diplomat XVII v." In *Rossiia v IX–XX vekakh: Problemy istorii, istoriografii i istochnikovedeniia*, 250–253. Moscow: Russkii mir, 1999.

Luttrell, Narcissus. *A Brief Historical Relation of State Affairs from September 1678 to April 1714*. Vol. 4. Oxford: Oxford University Press, 1857.

Lyseck, Adolphus. *Relatio eorum, quae circa Sac. Caesareae Maiest. ad Magnum Moscorum Czarum Ablegatos Annibalem Franciscum de Bottoni*. Salzburg: J. B. Mayr, 1676. Available online at https://books.google.com/books/about/Relatio_Eorum_Quae_circa_Sac_Caesareae_M.html?id=6KpKAAAAcAAJ.

[Lyseck, Adolphus]. "Skazanie Adol'fa Lizeka o posol'stve ot imperatora rimskogo Leopol'da k velikomu tsariu moskovskomu Aleksiiu Mikhailovichu, v 1675 godu." Translated by I. Tarnava-Borichevskii. *ZhMNP* 16, no. 10 (October 1837): 327–394.

Machyn, Henry. *A London Provisioner's Chronicle, 1550–1563*. Edited by Richard W. Bailey, Marilyn Miller, and Colette Moore. Electronic edition at https://quod.lib.umich.edu/m/machyn/.

Maggs, Barbara. "Firework Art and Literature: Eighteenth-Century Pyrotechnical Tradition in Russia and Western Europe." *SEER* 54, no. 1 (1976): 24–40.

Magli, Tatiana. "Nuovi materiali sull'ambasceria russa del 1659–1660 a Ferdinando II di Toscana." *Russica romana* 6 (1999): 209–225.

Maier, Ingrid. "Habent sua fata litterae. Två ryska 'utbytesstudenters' brev från Lübeck hem till Moskva under tsar Boris Godunovs tid (1604)." *Kungl. Humanistiska Vetenskaps-Samfundet i Uppsala 2008* (2009): 91–108.

Maier, Ingrid, and Winfried Schumacher. "Eine Straßburger Artistenfamilie auf Europatournee: Zum Werdegang des Seiltänzers Simon Dannenfels in der ersten Hälfte des 17. Jahrhunderts." *Zeitschrift für Geschichte des Oberrheins* 164 (2016): 245–256.

Maier, Ingrid, and S. M. Shamin. "Pskovskoe teatral'noe leto 1644 goda: Afisha stranstvuiushchikh nemetskikh komediantov." *Rodina*, no. 8 (2013): 64–67.

———. "Straßburger Mummenschanz im russischen Pleskau im Jahre 1644? Eine deutsche Schaustellertruppe versucht ihr Glück im Zarenreich." *JGO* 64, no. 1 (2016): 1–25.

Mamone, Sara. *Serenissimi fratelli principi impresari: Notizie di spettacolo nei carteggi medicei; Carteggi di Giovan Carlo de' Medici e di Desiderio Montemagni suo segretario (1628–1664)*. Florence: Le lettere, 2003.

Marker, Frederick, and Lise-Lone Marker. *A History of Scandinavian Theatre*. Cambridge: Cambridge University Press, 1996.

Marsh, Christopher. *Music and Society in Early Modern England*. Cambridge: Cambridge University Press, 2010.

Martens, Anke. *Hamburger Kaufleute im vorpetrinischen Moskau*. Hamburger Beiträge zur Geschichte der Deutschen im europäischen Osten 6. Lüneburg: Institut Nordostdeutsches Kulturwerk, 1999.

Martin, Russell. "Choreographing the 'Tsar's Happy Occasion': Tradition, Change, and Dynastic Legitimacy in the Weddings of Tsar Mikhail Romanov." *Slavic Review* 63, no. 4 (2004): 794–817.

———. "Dynastic Marriage in Muscovy, 1500–1729." PhD diss., Harvard University, 1996.

———. "Muscovite Esther: Bride Shows, Queenship, and Power in *The Comedy of Artaxerxes*." In *The New Muscovite Cultural History: A Collection in Honor of Daniel B. Rowland*, edited by Valerie Kivelson et al., 21–42. Bloomington: Slavica, 2009.

———. "The Petrine Divide and the Periodization of Early Modern Russian History." *Slavic Review* 69, no. 2 (2010): 410–425.

Massa, Isaac. *A Short History of the Beginnings and Origins of These Present Wars in Moscow under the Reign of Various Sovereigns Down to the Year 1610*. Translated and with an introduction by G. Edward Orchard. Toronto: University of Toronto Press, 1982.

Massar, Phyllis. "Costume Drawings by Stefano della Bella for the Florentine Theater." *Master Drawings* 8, no. 3 (1970): 243–266, 297–317.

Maurice, Klaus, and Otto Mayr, eds. *The Clockwork Universe: German Clocks and Automata 1550–1650*. New York: Neale Watson Academic Publications, 1980.

Mazon, A. [André] A. "'Artakserksovo deistvo' i repertuar pastora Gregori." *TODRL* 14 (1958): 355–363.

Mazon, André, and Frédéric Cocron, eds. *"La Comédie d'Artaxerxès"* (*Artakserksovo deistvo*) *présentée en 1672 au Tsar Alexis par Gregorii le Pasteur*. Paris: Institut d'Études slaves de l'Université de Paris, 1954.

McJannet, Linda. *The Sultan Speaks: Dialogue in English Plays and Histories about the Ottoman Turks*. New York: Palgrave Macmillan, 2006.

Megale, Teresa. "Fiorillo, Giovan Battista." In *Dizionario Biografico degli Italiani*. Electronic edition at https://www.treccani.it/enciclopedia/giovan-battista-fiorillo_(Dizionario-Biografico)/.

Melnikoff, Kirk. "Jones's Pen and Marlowe's Socks: Richard Jones, Print Culture, and the Beginnings of English Dramatic Literature." *Studies in Philology* 102, no. 2 (2005): 184–209.

[Mexía, Pedro]. *De Verscheyden lessen Petri Messiae*. Leiden: Jan Claesz van Dorp, 1607. Available online at https://play.google.com/books/reader?id=o5blIRe4JyIC.

Michelassi, Nicola. "Il Teatro del Cocomero di Firenze: uno stanzone per tre accademie (1651–1665)." *Studi secenteschi* 40 (1999): 149–186.

Michelassi, Nicola, and Salomé Vuelta Garcia. "Il teatro spagnolo della scena fiorentina del seicento." *Studi secenteschi* 45 (2004): 67–137.

[Miege, Guy]. *A Relation of Three Embassies from His Sacred Majestie Charles II to the Great Duke of Muscovie, the King of Sweden, and the King of Denmark. Performed by the Right Ho-ble the Earle of Carlisle in the years 1663 and 1664*. London: Printed for John Starkey, 1669. Available online at EEBO.

Mikulin, N. B. "Kommentarii k naznacheniiu rossiiskogo poslannika v Angliiu Grigoriia Ivanovicha Mikulina i ego prebyvaniiu v Londone v 1600–1601 gg." *Vspomogatel'nye istoricheskie distsipliny* 27 (2000): 32–38.

[Miller, G. F.]. "Izvestie o nachale Preobrazhenskogo i Semenovskogo polkov Gvardii." *Opyt trudov vol'nogo rossiiskogo sobraniia pri Imperatorskom Moskovskom Universitete* pt. 4 (1778): 107–144.

Milwright, Marcus. "So Despicable a Vessel: Representations of Tamerlane in Printed Books of the Sixteenth and Seventeenth Centuries." *Muqarnas* 23 (2006): 317–344.

Milwright, Marcus, and Evanthia Baboula. "Bayezid's Cage: A Re-examination of a Venerable Academic Controversy." *Journal of the Royal Asiatic Society* 21, no. 3 (2011): 239–260.

Møller, Vilhelm. "Københavns første Teater." *Tilskueren: maanedsskrift for litteratur samfundsspørgsmaal og almenfattelige videnskabelige skildringer* (1902): 617–634.

Mordison, G. Z. *Istoriia teatral'nogo dela v Rossii: Osnovanie i razvitie gosudarstvennogo teatra v Rossii (XVI–XVIII veka)*. Pt. 1. St. Petersburg: Sankt-Peterburgskaia gosudarstvennaia Akademiia teatral'nogo iskusstva, 1994.

Morozov, P. O. *Ocherki iz istorii russkoi dramy XVII-XVIII stoletii*. St. Petersburg: V. S. Balashev, 1888.

Morsman, Marieke. "Quicquid rarum, occultum et subtile: Augsburg Musical Automata around 1600." Master's thesis, Utrecht University, 2006.

Moskovskaia tragediia ili rasskaz o zhizni i smerti Dimitriia. Translated by A. Braudo and I. Rostsius. St. Petersburg: V. S. Balashev, 1901.

Murad, Orlene. *The English Comedians at the Habsburg Court in Graz, 1607–1608*. Elizabethan and Renaissance Studies 81. Salzburg: Institut für englische Sprache und Literatur, 1978.

Murata, Margaret. "Musical Encounters Public and Private." In *Passaggio in Italia: Music on the Grand Tour in the Seventeenth Century*, edited by Dinko Fabris and Margaret Murata, 35–51. Utrecht: Brepols, 2015.

Murdoch, Tessa. *Exhibiting the Renaissance: Treasures of the Royal Courts. Tudors, Stuarts and the Russian Tsars, Victoria and Albert Museum, 9th March to 14th July 2013*. Berlin: Humboldt-Universität, 2015. DOI 10.18452/7692.

Museo del Prado: Inventario general de pinturas. Vol. 1, La colección real. Madrid: Museo del Prado, 1990.

Musvik, Victoria. "'And the King of Barbary's Envoy Had to Stand in the Yard': The Perception of Elizabethan Court Festivals in Russia at the Beginning of the Seventeenth Century." In Court Festivals of the European Renaissance: Art, Politics and Performance, edited by J. R. Mulryne and Elizabeth Goldring, 225–240. Aldershot, UK: Ashgate, 2002.

Nehring, Wladislaus. "Eine unbekannte Episode aus dem Leben J. Veltens." Zeitschrift für vergleichende Litteraturgeschichte, n.s. 6 (1893): 1–4.

Nicolae, Florentina. "Foreign Names in Dimitrie Cantemir's Historical Works." Humanistica Lovaniensia 56 (2007): 343–347.

Nikolaenko, O. N. "K voprosu o stanovlenii zhanra traveloga v literature XVI–XVII vv.: Sub"ektivnoe nachalo v 'stateinykh spiskakh' D. Likhacheva." Vestnik Tomskogo gosudarstvennogo universiteta, no. 379 (2014): 24–27.

Nikolaev, S. I. "Russkie intermedii XVII v.: Novye materialy." TODRL 55 (2004): 423–426.

Noe, Alfred. Nicolò Minato Werkverzeichnis. Vienna: Verlag der Österreichischen Akademie der Wissenschaften, 2004.

Nystrøm, Eiler. Den danske Komedies Oprindelse. Copenhagen: Gyldendal, 1918.

Ocasar Ariza, José Luis. "The Genetic Edition of Classical Texts with Multiple Variants." Variants, no. 5 (2006): 161–180.

Olearius, Adam. The Travels of Olearius in Seventeenth-Century Russia. Translated and edited by Samuel Baron. Stanford: Stanford University Press, 1967.

———. Vermehrte Newe Beschreibung Der Muscowitischen vnd Persischen Reyse (Schleswig 1656). Edited by Dieter Lohmeier. Tübingen: Max Niemeyer, 1971.

Oparina, T. A., and S. M. Shamin. "Biografii inozemnykh poteshnikov tsaria Mikhaila Fedorovicha: Iurii Proskurovskii i Ivan Ermis." Vspomogatel'nye istoricheskie distsipliny v sovremennom nauchnom znanii. Materialy XXVIII Mezhdunarodnoi nauchnoi konferentsii, 400–402. Moscow: Akvilon, 2016.

"Opis' i prodazha s publichnogo torga [...] Mikhaily Tatishcheva." Vremennik Imperatorskogo moskovskogo obshchestva istorii i drevnostei rossiiskikh 8 (1850): pt. 3, 1–33.

Orrell, John. "A New Witness of the Restoration Stage, 1660–1669." Theatre Research International 2, no. 1 (1976): 16–28.

Overskou, Thomas. Den danske Skueplads, i dens Historie, fra de første Spor af danske Skuespil indtil vor Tid. Vol. 1. Copenhagen: Thieles bogtrykkeri, 1854.

Oxford annotated Bible, with the Apocrypha. Edited by H. G. May and B. M. Metzger. Oxford: Oxford University Press, 1965.

Panchenko, A. M. "Deklamatsiia Sil'vestra Medvedeva na temu strastei Khristovykh." In Rukopisnoe nasledie drevnei Rusi po materialam Pushkinskogo doma, 115–135. Leningrad: Nauka, 1972.

Parfaict, Claude, and François Parfaict. Histoire du théâtre françois: Depuis son origine jusqu'à présent. Vol. 10. Paris: P. G. Le Mercier, 1747.

Parfenov, A. T. "K voprosu o pervoistochnikakh 'Temir-Aksakova deistva.'" Vestnik Moskovskogo universiteta, series 10 (Filologiia), no. 2 (1969): 16–30.

Parfent'ev, N. P. Professional'nye muzykanty Rossiiskogo gosudarstva XVI–XVII vekov. Cheliabinsk: Izdatel'stvo Cheliabinskogo poligraficheskogo ob"edineniia "Kniga," 1991.

Pass, Walter. Musik und Musiker am Hof Maximilians II. Wiener Veröffentlichungen zur Musikwissenschaft 20. Tutzing: Hans Schneider, 1980.

Perepisnaia kniga goroda Moskvy 1638 goda. Moscow: M. P. Shchepkin, 1881.

Perondinus, Petrus. Magni Tamerlanis Scytharum Imperatoris Vita. Florence: n.p., 1553. Available online at https://books.google.com/books?id=8-9YAAAAcAAJ.

Pettegree, Andrew. *The Invention of News: How the World Came to Know about Itself*. New Haven: Yale University Press, 2014.

Pierling, Paul. *Saxe et Moscou: Un médecin diplomate; Laurent Rinhuber de Reinufer*. Paris: Émile Bouillon, 1893.

Pivovarova, N. S., main ed. *Istoriia russkogo dramaticheskogo teatra ot ego istokov do serediny XX veka: Uchebnik*. 5th ed., corrected. Moscow: Rossiiskii institut teatral'nogo iskusstva–GITIS, 2019.

Platonov, S. F. *Lektsii po russkoi istorii*. 6th ed., with corrections and additions. Edited by I. Blinov. St. Petersburg: Senatskaia tipografiia, 1909.

Pletneva, A. A. "*Skomorokh i skomoroshestvo*: K istorii slov i poniatii." In *Evoliutsiia poniatii v svete istorii russkoi kul'tury*, edited by V. M. Zhivov and Iu. V. Kagarlitskii, 93–108. Moscow: Iazyki slavianskikh kul'tur, 2012.

Pokhodnyi zhurnal 1695–1703 goda. St. Petersburg: n.p., 1853.

Polnische königliche Hochzeit. Augsburg: Samuel Dilbaum, 1606. Available online at https://play.google.com/books/reader?id=kyRXAAAAcAAJ.

Pontoppidan-Sjövall, Karin. "En Josef-komedi i Codex Sparfwenfeldtianus." Licentiate thesis, Uppsala University, 1946.

Posol'stvo P. I. Potemkina v Ispaniiu v 1667–1668 godakh. Dokumenty i materialy. Compiled by V. A. Vediushkin and E. E. Rychalovskii. Moscow: Indrik, 2018.

Powell, John. *Music and Theatre in France, 1600–1680*. Oxford: Clarendon Press, 2000.

Preobrazhenskii, A. A. *Ural i Zapadnaia Sibir' v kontse XVI–nachale XVIII veka*. Moscow: Nauka, 1972.

Protopopov, V. V. "Notnaia biblioteka tsaria Fedora Alekseevicha." *PKNO 1976* (1977): 119–133.

Prudovskii, P. I., comp. *Rossiia i Prussiia v seredine XVII veke*. Vol. 1. Moscow: Drevlekhranilishche, 2013.

Przybyszewska-Jarmińska, Barbara. "*Dramma per musica* at the Court of the Polish Vasa Kings in the Accounts of Foreign Visitors." In *Italian Opera in Central Europe*. Vol. 3, *Opera Subjects and European Relationships*, edited by N. Dubowy et al., 205–217. Berlin: Berliner Wissenschafts-Verlag, 2007.

———. "Habsburg Queens of Poland and Music at the Polish Royal Court at the End of [the] 16th and in the 17th Centuries." *Arti musices: Hrvatski muzikološki zbornik* 47, nos. 1–2 (2017): 7–25.

Radziwiłł, Albrycht Stanisław. *Memoriale rerum gestarum in Polonia: 1632–1656*. Edited by Adam Przyboś and Roman Żelewski. 5 vols. Wrocław: Polska akademia nauk, 1968–1975.

———. *Pamiętnik o dziejach w Polsce*. Edited by Adam Przyboś and Roman Żelewski. 3 vols. Warsaw: Państwowy Instytut Wydawniczy, 1980.

Rambaud, Alfred. *Recueil des instructions données aux ambassadeurs et ministres de France depuis les traités de Westphalie jusqu'à la Révolution française. VIII, Russie*. Vol. 1, *Des origines jusqu'à 1748*. Paris: F. Alcan, 1890.

Rangström, Lena. "Certamen Equestre: The Carousel for the Accession of Karl XI in 1672." In *Europa Triumphans: Court and Civic Festivals in Early Modern Europe*, edited by J. R. Mulryne et al., 2:292–323. Aldershot, UK: Ashgate, 2004.

[Rautenfels, Jacob]. "Skazaniia svetleishemu gertsogu toskanskomu Koz'me tret'emu o Moskovii." In *Utverzhdenie dinastii*, compiled by A. Liberman, translated by A. Stankevich, 231–406. Istoriia Rossii i doma Romanovykh v memuarakh sovremennikov XVII–XX vv. Moscow: Fond Sergeia Dubova, 1997.

"Reporte of a Bloudie and Terrible Massacre in the Citty of Mosco." In *The False Dmitri: A Russian Romance and Tragedy Described by British Eye-Witnesses, 1604–1612*, edited by Sonia E. Howe, 27–62. 1916. Reprint, Oriental Research Partners. Cambridge: Biddles, 1972.

[Reutenfels, Jacobus]. *Das Grosse und mächtige Reich Moscovien.* Nürnberg: Johann Christoph Lochner, 1687. Available online at https://books.google.com/books?id=n_JgAAAAcAAJ.

Reutenfels, Jacobus. *De Rebus Moschoviticis ad Serenissimum Magnum Hetruriae Ducem Cosmum Tertium.* Padua: Frambotti, 1680. Available online at https://books.google.com/books?id=3g8jmgEACAAJ.

Riewald, J. G. "New Light on the English Actors in the Netherlands, c. 1590–c. 1600." *English Studies* 41, no. 2 (1960): 65–92.

Rinhuber, Laurent. *Relation du voyage en Russie fait en 1684.* Berlin: Albert Cohn, 1883.

Robinson, A. N. "Pervyi russkii teatr kak iavlenie evropeiskoi kul'tury." In *Novye cherty v russkoi literature i iskusstve (XVII–nachalo XVIII v.)*, edited by A. N. Robinson, 8–27. Moscow: Nauka, 1976.

Rogozhin, N. M. *Posol'skii prikaz: Kolybel' rossiiskoi diplomatii.* Moscow: Mezhdunarodnye otnosheniia, 2003.

Roizman, L. I. "Iz istorii organnoi kul'tury v Rossii (vtoraia polovina XVII veka)." *Voprosy muzykoznaniia* 3 (1960): 565–597.

———. *Organ v istorii russkoi muzykal'noi kul'tury.* Moscow: Muzyka, 1979.

Rosand, Ellen. *Opera in Seventeenth-Century Venice: The Creation of a Genre.* Berkeley: University of California Press, 1991.

"Rospis' vsiakim veshcham, den'gam i zapasam, chto ostalos' po smerti boiarina Nikity Ivanovicha Romanova i dachi po nem na pomin dushi." Compiled by E. V. Barsov. *ChOIDR* 3 (1887): pt. 1, 1–128.

Rouillard, Clarence. *The Turk in French History, Thought, and Literature (1520–1660).* Part 4. Études de littérature étrangère et comparée 13. Paris: Boivin, 1941.

Rovinskii, D. A. *Russkie narodnye kartinki.* 5 vols. St. Petersburg: Imperatorskaia Akademiia nauk, 1881.

———. *Russkie narodnye kartinki: Atlas.* Vol. 1. St. Petersburg: Ekspeditsiia zagotovleniia gosudarstvennykh bumag, 1881.

Rozysknye dela o Fedore Shaklovitom i ego soobshchnikakh. 4 vols. St. Petersburg: Obshchestvennaia pol'za, 1884–1893.

Rye, William B. *England as Seen by Foreigners in the Days of Elizabeth and James the First.* London: John Russell Smith, 1865.

Sander, Elizabeth. *Social Dancing in Peter the Great's Russia.* Hildesheim: Georg Olms, 2007.

Satkowski, Leon. "The Palazzo Pitti: Planning and Use in the Grand-Ducal Era." *Journal of the Society of Architectural Historians* 42, no. 4 (1983): 336–349.

Savel'eva, E. A. *Knigi iz sobraniia Andreia Andreevicha Viniusa.* St. Petersburg: Biblioteka Rossiiskoi Akademii nauk, 2008.

Sazonova, L. I. *Literaturnaia kul'tura Rossii. Rannee Novoe vremia.* Moscow: Iazyki slavianskikh kul'tur, 2006.

———. "Pravoslavnaia liturgiia v poeticheskom tvorchestve Simeona Polotskogo." In *Simiaon Polatski: svetapohliad, hramadska-palitychnaia i literaturnaia dzeinasts'*, 173–195. Polotsk: Natsyianal'ny polatski historyka-kul'turny muzei-zapavednik, 2010.

———. "Teatral'naia programma XVII v. 'Aleksei chelovek bozhii.'" *PKNO 1978* (1979): 131–149.

Sbornik vypisok iz arkhivnykh bumag o Petre Velikom. Edited by G. V. Esipov. 2 vols. Moscow: Universitetskaia tipografiia, 1872.

Schade, Richard E. *Studies in Early German Comedy 1500–1650.* Columbia, SC: Camden House, 1988.

Scherl, Adolf, and Bärbel Rudin. "Carl Andreas Paulsen" and "Catarina Elisabeth Velten." In *Theater in Böhmen, Mähren und Schlesien. Von den Anfängen bis zum Ausgang des 18.*

Jahrhunderts. Ein Lexikon, edited by Alena Jakubcová and Matthias J. Pernerstorfer, 503–505, 714–717. Theatergeschichte Österreichs 10, no. 6. Vienna: Österreichische Akademie der Wissenschaften, 2013.

Schlafly, Daniel L. "Filippo Balatri in Peter the Great's Russia." *JGO* 45, no. 2 (1997): 181–198.

———. "A Muscovite *Boiarynia* Faces Peter the Great's Reforms: Dar'ia Golitsyna between Two Worlds." *Canadian-American Slavic Studies* 31, no. 3 (1997): 249–268.

Schlueter, June. "English Actors in Kassel, Germany, during Shakespeare's Time." *Medieval and Renaissance Drama in England* 10 (1998): 238–261.

———. "New Light on Dekker's *Fortunati*." *Medieval and Renaissance Drama in England* 26 (2013): 120–135.

Schrickx, Willem. "English Actors at the Courts of Wolfenbüttel, Brussels and Graz during the Lifetime of Shakespeare." *Shakespeare Survey* 33 (1980): 153–168.

———. *Foreign Envoys and Travelling Players in the Age of Shakespeare and Jonson*. Wetteren, BEL: Universa, 1986.

Schwarcz, Iskra. "'Iter persicum' Tectanders und sein Rußlandbild." In *Rußland, Polen und Österreich in der Frühen Neuzeit: Festschrift für Walter Leitsch zum 75. Geburtstag*, edited by Christoph Augustynowicz et al., 191–210. Vienna: Böhlau, 2003.

Schwartz, Rudolf. *Esther im deutschen und neulateinischen Drama des Reformationszeitalters: Eine litterarhistorische Untersuchung*. 2nd ed. Oldenburg, DEU: Schulzesche Hof-Buchhandlung und Hof-Buchdruckerei, 1898.

Scott, Virginia. *The Commedia dell'Arte in Paris, 1644–1697*. Charlottesville: University Press of Virginia, 1990.

Seaton, Ethel. "Fresh Sources for Marlowe." *Review of English Studies* 5, no. 20 (1929): 385–401.

Seifert, Herbert. "The Institution of the Imperial Court Chapel from Maximilian I to Charles VI." In *The Royal Chapel in the Time of the Habsburgs: Music and Ceremony in the Early Modern European Court*, edited by J. J. Carreras López et al., 40–47. Woodbridge, UK: Boydell Press, 2005.

———. *Die Oper am Wiener Kaiserhof im 17. Jahrhundert*. Wiener Veröffentlichungen zur Musikgeschichte 25. Tutzing, DEU: Hans Schneider, 1985.

Shamin, S. M. *Kuranty XVII stoletiia: Evropeiskaia pressa v Rossii i vozniknovenie russkoi periodicheskoi pechati*. St. Petersburg: Al'ians-Arkheo, 2011.

———. "Nakry kak odin iz atributov gosudarevoi vlasti: ot Ivana IV do Petra I (k voprosu o tsarskom trubnichem chine)." *Kapterevskie chteniia* 13 (2015): 322–337.

———. "O nesushchestvovavshikh teatral'nykh postanovkakh v Rossii XVII stoletiia: Istoricheskii fakt mezhdu literaturnym sochineniem i dokumentom." In *Vspomogatel'nye istoricheskie distsipliny: Materialy XXVII Mezhdunarodnoi nauchnoi konferentsii*, 476–477. Moscow: RGGU, 2015.

———. "Slovo 'kuranty' v russkom iazyke XVII–nachala XVIII v." *Russkii iazyk v nauchnom osveshchenii* 13, no. 1 (2007): 119–152.

———. "Tsirk tsarevicha Alekseia Mikhailovicha." *Studia Slavica et Balcanica Petropolitana*, no. 2 (July–December 2016): 136–151.

Shamin, S. M., and K. Dzhensen [Jensen]. "Inozemnye poteshniki pri dvore pervykh moskovskikh tsarei." *Rossiiskaia istoriia*, no. 1 (January–February 2018): 32–46.

Sharkova, I. S. "Posol'stvo I. I. Chemodanova i otkliki na nego v Italii." In *Problemy istorii mezhdunarodnykh otnoshenii: Sbornik statei pamiati akademika E. V. Tarle*, 207–223. Leningrad: Nauka, 1972.

Shcherbachev, Iu. N. "Iz donesenii pervogo datskogo rezidenta v Moskve (1672–1676 gg.)." *ChOIDR* 2 (1917): pt. 2, 32–42.

Shergold, N. D. *A History of the Spanish Stage from Medieval Times until the End of the Seventeenth Century*. Oxford: Clarendon Press, 1967.

Shergold, N. D., and J. E. Varey, eds. *Fuentes para la historia del teatro en España*. Vol. 6, *Teatros y comedias en Madrid: 1687–1699. Estudio y documentos*. London: Tamesis Books Ltd., 1979.

Shmurlo, E. F. "Posol'stvo Chemodanova i Rimskaia kuriia." *Zapiski russkogo nauchnogo instituta v Belgrade* 7 (1932): 1–25.

Simonov, R. A., and O. R. Khromov. "'Chasy na krugu'—naibolee rannee tochno datiruemoe 1663 godom listovoe izdanie moskovskogo pechatnogo dvora." *Drevniaia Rus'. Voprosy medievistiki* no. 3 (25) (2006): 19–34.

Skrzhinskaia, E. Ch. *Rus', Italiia i Vizantiia v Srednevekov'e*. St. Petersburg: Aleteiia, 2000.

Slovar' knizhnikov i knizhnosti Drevnei Rusi. Vyp. 3, *XVII v*. 4 vols. St. Petersburg: Dmitrii Bulanin, 1992–2004.

Slovar' russkikh ikonopistsev XI–XVII vekov. Edited and compiled by I. A. Kochetkov. 2nd ed. Moscow: Indrik, 2009.

Slovar' russkogo iazyka XI–XVII vv. Moscow: Nauka, 1975–.

Smirnova, E. S. "Simon Ushakov—'Historicism' and 'Byzantinism': On the Interpretation of Russian Painting from the second half of the Seventeenth Century." In *Religion and Culture in Early Modern Russia and Ukraine*, edited by Samuel H. Baron and Nancy Shields Kollmann, 169–183. DeKalb: Northern Illinois University Press, 1997.

Sobranie gosudarstvennykh gramot i dogovorov, khraniashchikhsia v Gosudarstvennoi kollegii inostrannykh del. Vol. 4. Moscow: S. Selivanovskii, 1828.

Solov'ev, S. M. *Istoriia Rossii s drevneishikh vremen*. Vol. 5 of *Sochineniia*. Books 9–10. Moscow: Mysl', 1990.

Sommer-Mathis, Andrea. "*La Favorita festeggiante*: The Imperial Summer Residence of the Habsburgs as Festive Venue." In *Architectures of Festival in Early Modern Europe: Fashioning and Re-Fashioning Urban and Courtly Space*, edited by J. R. Mulryne et al., 275–298. European Festival Studies 4. Abingdon, UK: Routledge, 2018.

Sowerby, Tracey. "Material Culture and the Politics of Space in Diplomacy at the Tudor Court." In *Beyond Scylla and Charybdis: European Courts and Court Residences outside Habsburg and Valois/Bourbon Territories 1500–1700*, edited by Birgitte Bøggild Johannsen and Konrad Ottenheym, 47–55. Copenhagen: University Press of Southern Denmark, 2015.

Spencer, Forrest, and Rudolph Schevill. *The Dramatic Works of Luis Vélez de Guevara: Their Plots, Sources, and Bibliography*. University of California Publications in Modern Philology 19. Berkeley: University of California Press, 1937.

Spieltexte der Wanderbühne. Vol. 1, *Engelische Comedien und Tragedien*. Edited by Manfred Brauneck. Berlin: De Gruyter, 1970.

Stählin [Stelin], Jakob von. "Kratkoe izvestie o teatral'nykh predstavleniiakh v Rossii." 1779. Reprinted in *Muzykal'naia starina*, no. 3 (1907): 4–25.

———. "Nachrichten von der Musik in Rußland." In *M. Johann Joseph Haigold's Beylagen zum neuveränderten Rußland*, part 2, 37–192. Riga: J. F. Hartknoch, 1770.

———. "Zur Geschichte des Theaters in Rußland." In *M. Johann Joseph Haigold's Beylagen zum neuveränderten Rußland*, part 1, 397–432. Riga: J. F. Hartknoch, 1769.

Starikova, L. M. "K istorii domashnikh krepostnykh teatrov i orkestrov v Rossii kontsa XVII–XVIII vv." *PKNO* 1991 (1997): 53–65.

———. "Panorama teatral'no-zrelishchnoi zhizni russkikh stolits v petrovskuiu epokhu." *Voprosy teatra: Proscaenium*, nos. 3–4 (2017): 141–169.

———. "Russkii teatr petrovskogo vremeni, komedial'naia khramina i domashnie komedii tsarevny Natal'i Alekseevny." *PKNO* 1990 (1992): 137–156.

———. "U istokov istorii russkogo teatra." In *Sumarokovskie chteniia. Materialy Vserossiiskoi nauchno-prakticheskoi konferentsii*, 20–25. St. Petersburg: Sankt-Peterburgskii gosudarstvennyi institut teatra, muzyki i kinematografii, 1993.

———. "'Zapiska o vozniknovenii i razvitii teatral'nogo iskusstva v Moskve so vremeni Alekseia Mikhailovicha po 19 vek' A. F. Malinovskogo." *PKNO 1993* (1994): 51–64.
Stein, Louise K. "Opera and the Spanish Political Agenda." *Acta Musicologica* 63, fasc. 2 (1991): 125–167.
———. *Songs of Mortals, Dialogues of the Gods: Music and Theatre in Seventeenth-Century Spain.* Oxford: Clarendon Press, 1993.
Stennikova, P. A. "Tserkovno-teatralizovannye deistva v Rossii XVI–XVII vv. (na primere "Peshchnogo deistva" i "Shestviia na osliati" v Verbnoe voskresen'e)." Diss., Iuzhno-Ural'skii gosudarstvennyi universitet, Cheliabinsk, 2006.
Stensen, Niels [Steno, Nicolaus]. *Nicolai Stenonis epistolae et epistolae ad eum datae.* Vol. 1. Edited by Gustav Scherz. Copenhagen: Nyt Nordisk, 1952.
Stone, Gerald, ed. *A Dictionarie of the Vulgar Russe Tongue: Attributed to Mark Ridley.* Bausteine zur slavischen Philologie und Kulturgeschichte, series B, n.s., 8. Cologne: Böhlau, 1996.
Stone, John A. "The Pastor and the Tzar: A Comment on *The Comedy of Artaxerxes.*" *Bulletin of the New York Public Library* 72, no. 4 (1968): 215–251.
Stříbrný, Zdeněk. *Shakespeare and Eastern Europe.* Oxford: Oxford University Press, 2000.
Stronks, Els. "No Home Grown Products: Illustrated Biblical Poems in the Dutch Republic." In *Illustrated Religious Texts in the North of Europe, 1500–1800*, edited by Feike Dietz et al., 221–236. Farnham, UK: Ashgate, 2014.
Sullivan, Henry. *Calderón in the German Lands and the Low Countries: His Reception and Influence, 1654–1980.* Cambridge: Cambridge University Press, 1983.
Sverdrup Lunden, Siri. *The Trondheim Russian-German MS Vocabulary: A Contribution to 17th-Century Russian Lexicography.* Oslo: Universitetsforlaget, 1972.
Swoboda, Marina. "The Old Testament 'Apocrypha' in Early Russian Drama." In *The Old Testament Apocrypha in the Slavonic Tradition: Continuity and Diversity*, edited by Lorenzo DiTommaso and Christfried Böttrich, 429–451. Texts and Studies in Ancient Judaism 140. Tübingen: Mohr Siebeck, 2011.
Szweykowska, Anna. "Widowiska baletowe na dworze Zygmunta III." *Muzyka* 11, no. 1 (1966): 27–36.
Testaverde, Anna Maria. "Le 'riusate carte': Un inedito repertorio di scenari del secolo XVII e l'ombra di Molière." *Medioevo e Rinascimento: Annuario del Dipartimento di studi sul Medioevo e il Rinascimento dell'Università di Firenze* 11 (1997): 417–446.
Theiner, Augustin, ed. *Monuments historiques relatifs aux règnes d'Alexis Michaélowitch, Féodor III et Pierre le Grand, czars de Russie, extraits des Archives du Vatican et de Naples.* Rome: Imprimerie du Vatican, 1859.
Thomas, Vivien, and William Tydeman, eds. *Christopher Marlowe: The Plays and Their Sources.* London: Routledge, 1994.
Tieck, Ludwig. *Deutsches Theater.* 2 vols. Berlin: Realschulbuchhandlung, 1817.
Tietz, Friedrich. *Bunte Skizzen aus Ost und Süd: Entworfen und gesammelt in Preußen, Rußland, der Türkei, Griechenland, auf den ionischen Inseln und in Italien.* Leipzig: Brockhaus, 1838.
———. *Erinnerungs-Skizzen aus Rußland, der Türkei und Griechenland: Entworfen während des Aufenthalts in jenen Ländern in den Jahren 1833 und 1834.* 2 vols. Coburg: Sinner, 1836.
———. *St. Petersburgh, Constantinople, and Napoli di Romania, in 1833 and 1834.* London: A. Richter, 1836.
Tikhonravov, N. S. *Russkie dramaticheskie proizvedeniia 1672–1725 godov.* 2 vols. St. Petersburg: Izdanie D. E. Kozhanchikova, 1874.
Tilmouth, Michael. "Music on the Travels of an English Merchant: Robert Bargrave (1628–61)." *Music and Letters* 53, no. 2 (1972): 143–159.

[Tolstoi, P. A.]. *Puteshestvie stol'nika P. A. Tolstogo po Evrope 1697–1699*. Edited by L. A. Ol'shevskaia and S. N. Travnikov. Moscow: Nauka, 1992.

———. *The Travel Diary of Peter Tolstoi: A Muscovite in Early Modern Europe*. Translated by Max J. Okenfuss. DeKalb: Northern Illinois University Press, 1987.

Topolski, Jerzy. "Periodization and the Creation of the Narrative Wholes." *Storia della Storiografia* 37 (2000): 11–16.

Topychkanov, A. V. *Povsednevnaia zhizn' dvortsovogo sela Izmailova v dokumentakh prikaznoi izby poslednei chetverti XVII veka*. Moscow: OAO "Moskovskie uchebniki i Kartolitografiia," 2004.

Topyčkanov, A. V. "Die Musik in den ländlichen Zarenresidenzen der zweiten Hälfte des 17. Jahrhunderts." In *Musik am russischen Hof. Vor, während und nach Peter dem Großen (1650–1750)*, edited by Lorenz Erren, 44–54. Berlin: Walter de Gruyter, 2017.

Tsvetaev, D. V. "Pamiatniki k istorii Protestantstva v Rossii." *ChOIDR* 3 (1883): pt. 1, i–xxi, 1–150.

Uspensky, B. A. "The Schism and Cultural Conflict in the Seventeenth Century." In *Seeking God: The Recovery of Religious Identity in Orthodox Russia, Ukraine, and Georgia*, edited by Stephen Batalden, 106–143. DeKalb: Northern Illinois University Press, 1993.

Ustrialov, N. G. *Istoriia tsarstvovaniia Petra Velikogo*. Vol. 4, pt. 2. St. Petersburg: Vtoroe otdelenie Sobstvennoi E. I. V. kantseliarii, 1863.

Vanbrugh, John. *A Short Vindication of The Relapse and The Provok'd Wife from Immorality and Prophaneness*. London: Printed for H. Walwyn, 1698. Available online at EEBO.

Vander Motten, J. P. "Jacob Hall and Other Rope Dancers on the Continent, 1678–1682." *Theatre Notebook* 73, no. 1 (2019): 45–59.

Velimirović, Miloš. "The First Organ Builder in Russia." In *Literary and Musical Notes: A Festschrift for Wm. A. Little*, edited by Geoffrey Orth, 219–228. Bern: Peter Lang, 1995.

———. "Liturgical Drama in Byzantium and Russia." *Dumbarton Oaks Papers* 16 (1962): 351–385.

Venevitinov, M. A. *Russkie v Gollandii: Velikoe posol'stvo 1697–1698 g*. Moscow: O. O. Gerbek, 1897.

Verweij, Michiel. "The *Terentius Christianus* at Work: Cornelius Schonaeus as a Playwright." In *The Early Modern Cultures of Neo-Latin Drama*, edited by Philip Ford and Andrew Taylor, 95–105. Leuven: Leuven University Press, 2013.

Veselovskii, A. N. *Zapadnoe vliianie v novoi russkoi literature*. 2nd ed. Moscow: "Russkoe tovarishchestvo pechatnogo i izdatel'skogo dela," 1896.

Veselovskii, S. B. *D'iaki i pod'iachie XV–XVII vv*. Moscow: Nauka, 1975.

Vesti-Kuranty II: *Vesti-Kuranty: 1642–1644 gg*. Edited by N. I. Tarabasova et al. Moscow: Nauka, 1976.

Vesti-Kuranty III: *Vesti-Kuranty: 1645–1646, 1648 gg*. Edited by N. I. Tarabasova et al. Moscow: Nauka, 1980.

Vesti-Kuranty IV: *Vesti-Kuranty: 1648–1650 gg*. Edited by V. G. Dem'ianov et al. Moscow: Nauka, 1983.

Vesti-Kuranty VI: *Vesti-Kuranty: 1656 g., 1660–1662 gg., 1664–1670 gg*. Part 1, *Russkie teksty*. Edited by A. M. Moldovan and Ingrid Maier. Moscow: Rukopisnye pamiatniki drevnei Rusi, 2009.

Vesti-Kuranty VII: *Vesti-Kuranty: 1671–1672 gg*. Edited by V. B. Krys'ko and Ingrid Maier. Moscow: Azbukovnik, 2017.

Viktorov, A. E. *Opisanie zapisnykh knig i bumag starinnykh dvortsovykh prikazov 1584–1725 g*. 2 vols. Moscow: S. P. Arkhipov, 1877–1883.

Villani, Stefano. "Ambasciatori russi a Livorno e rapporti tra Moscovia e Toscana nel XVII secolo." *Nuovi studi livornesi* 14 (2008): 37–95.

———. "A 'Republican' Englishman in Leghorn: Charles Longland." In *European Contexts for English Republicanism*, edited by Gaby Mahlberg and Dirk Wiemann, 163–177. Farnham, UK: Ashgate, 2013.

———. "Una finestra mediterranea sull'Europa: i 'nordici' nella Livorno della prima età moderna." In *Livorno 1606–1806: Luogo di incontro tra popoli e culture*, edited by Adriano Prosperi, 158–177. Livorno: Allemandi, 2009.

Vinogradoff, Igor. "Russian Missions to London, 1569–1687: Seven Accounts by the Masters of the Ceremonies." *OSP*, n.s., 14 (1981): 36–72.

Vitsen [Witsen], N. *Puteshestvie v Moskoviiu 1664–1665, Dnevnik*. Translated by V. G. Trisman. St. Petersburg: Symposium, 1996.

Vorob'ev, E. E. "Kliuch razumeniia." In *Pravoslavnaia entsiklopediia*, 36:62–64. Moscow: "Pravoslavnaia entsiklopediia," 2014.

Vroon, Ronald. "From Liturgy to Literature: Prayer and Play in the Early Russian Baroque." In *Culture and Authority in the Baroque*, edited by Massimo Ciavolella and Patrick Coleman, 122–137. Toronto: University of Toronto Press, 2005.

Vykhody gosudarei tsarei i velikikh kniazei, Mikhaila Feodorovicha, Aleksiia Mikhailovicha, Feodora Aleksievicha, vseia Rusii samoderzhtsev (s 1632 po 1682 god). Moscow: Avgust Semen, 1844.

Wade, Mara. *Triumphus Nuptialis Danicus: German Court Culture and Denmark, the Great Wedding of 1634*. Wolfenbütteler Arbeiten zur Barockforschung 27. Wiesbaden: Harrassowitz, 1996.

Watanabe-O'Kelly, Helen. *Court Culture in Dresden: From Renaissance to Baroque*. Houndmills, UK: Palgrave, 2002.

———. "The Early Modern Period (1450–1720)." In *The Cambridge History of German Literature*, edited by Helen Watanabe-O'Kelly, 92–146. Cambridge: Cambridge University Press, 1997. DOI 10.1017/CHOL9780521434171.

Watson, Christine. "*Žalobnaja komedija*: En tidig rysk pjäs och dess historia." Thesis, Uppsala University, 2005.

Waugh, Daniel Clarke. "The Best-Connected Man in Muscovy? Patrick Gordon's Evidence Regarding News and Communication in Muscovy in the Seventeenth Century." *Journal of Irish and Scottish Studies* 7, no. 2 (Spring 2014): 61–124.

———. *The Great Turkes Defiance: On the History of the Apocryphal Correspondence of the Ottoman Sultan in Its Muscovite and Russian Variants*. Columbus, OH: Slavica, 1978.

———. "Ioannikii Galiatovs'kyi's Polemics against Islam and Their Muscovite Translations." *Harvard Ukrainian Studies* 3/4, part 2 (1979–1980): 908–919.

———. "The Library of Aleksei Mikhailovich." *Forschungen zur osteuropäischen Geschichte* 38 (1986): 299–324.

———. "We Have Never Been Modern: Approaches to the Study of Russia in the Age of Peter the Great." *JGO* 49, no. 3 (2001): 321–345.

———. "What Was News and How Was It Communicated in Pre-Modern Russia?" In *Information and Empire: Mechanisms of Communication in Russia, 1600–1850*, edited by Simon Franklin and Katherine Bowers, 213–252. Cambridge: Open Book Publishers, 2017.

Waugh, Daniel Clarke, and Ingrid Maier. "Muscovy and the European Information Revolution: Creating the Mechanisms for Obtaining Foreign News." In *Information and Empire: Mechanisms of Communication in Russia, 1600–1850*, edited by Simon Franklin and Katherine Bowers, 77–112. Cambridge: Open Book Publishers, 2017.

Weaver, Robert Lamar. "Florentine Comic Operas of the Seventeenth Century." PhD diss., University of North Carolina, 1958.

Weaver, Robert Lamar, and Norma Wright Weaver. *A Chronology of Music in the Florentine Theater 1590–1750*. Detroit Studies in Music Bibliography 38. Detroit: Information Coordinators, 1978.

Weiner, Jack. "The Death of Philip IV of Spain and the Early Russian Theatrical Repertoire." *Theatre Research / Recherches théâtrales* 10, no. 3 (1970): 179–185.

Wesselofsky, Alexis. *Deutsche Einflüsse auf das alte russische Theater von 1672–1756*. Prague: W. Nagel, 1876.

West, William. "Intertheatricality." In *Early Modern Theatricality*, edited by Henry Turner, 151–172. Oxford: Oxford University Press, 2013.

Willan, Thomas. *The Early History of the Russia Company, 1553–1603*. Manchester: Manchester University Press, 1956.

Williams, Simon. *Shakespeare on the German Stage*. Vol. 1, *1586–1914*. Cambridge: Cambridge University Press, 1990.

Wortman, Richard. *Scenarios of Power: Myth and Ceremony in Russian Monarchy*. Vol. 1, *From Peter the Great to the Death of Nicholas I*. Princeton, NJ: Princeton University Press, 1995.

Zabelin, I. E. *Domashnii byt russkogo naroda v XVI i XVII st.* Vol. 1, pt. 1, *Domashnii byt russkikh tsarei v XVI i XVII st.* 3rd ed. with additions. Moscow: A. N. Mamontov, 1895.

———. *Domashnii byt russkogo naroda v XVI i XVII st.* Vol. 1, pt. 2, *Domashnii byt russkikh tsarei v XVI i XVII st.* Posthumous ed. Moscow: Sinodal'naia tipografiia, 1915.

———. *Domashnii byt russkogo naroda v XVI i XVII st.* Vol. 2, *Domashnii byt russkikh tsarits v XVI i XVII st.* 3rd ed. with additions. Moscow: A. N. Mamontov, 1901.

———. "Dopolneniia k dvortsovym razriadam." *ChOIDR* 1 (1882): pt. 2, i–xv, 1–288; *ChOIDR* 3 (1882): pt. 1, 289–640.

———. *Opyty izucheniia russkikh drevnostei i istorii*. 2 vols. Moscow: Grachev, 1872–1873.

Zagorodniaia, I. "Chasy v diplomaticheskikh podarkakh." *Rodina*, no. 11 (2004): 73–78.

Zamyslovskii, E. E. *Tsarstvovanie Fedora Alekseevicha*. St. Petersburg: Zamyslovskii i Bobylev, 1871.

Zguta, Russell. *Russian Minstrels: A History of the Skomorokhi*. [Philadelphia]: University of Pennsylvania Press, 1978.

Zhatkin, D. N., and A. A. Riabova. "Osmyslenie khudozhestvennogo svoeobraziia dramaturgicheskogo tvorchestva Kristofera Marlo v literaturovedcheskikh issledovaniiakh A. T. Parfenova." *Izvestiia vysshikh uchebnykh zavedenii: Povolzhskii region. Gumanitarnye nauki*, no. 1 (2014): 150–161.

Żórawska-Witkowska, Alina. "*Dramma per musica* at the Court of Ladislaus IV Vasa (1627–1648)." In *Italian Opera in Central Europe*. Vol. 1, *Institutions and Ceremonies*, edited by M. Bucciarelli et al., 21–49. Berlin: Berliner Wissenschafts-Verlag, 2006.

Zvereva, S. G. "Gosudarevy pevchie d'iaki posle 'Smuty' (1613–1649 gg.)." *Germenevtika drevnerusskoi literatury* 2 (1989): 355–382.

INDEX

Page numbers in italics refer to figures.

academies (Florence). *See* Florence, performance venues and academies
acrobats (Russia), 32, 35
Admiral's Men, 213–220
Alekseev, Nikita, 236
Aleksei Alekseevich (tsarevich, son of Tsar Aleksei), 93, 102n116, 119
Aleksei, Man of God (*Aleksei chelovek bozhii*), 155, 158, 181n54, 186n118
Aleksei Mikhailovich (tsar of Russia), 7, 11, 15–16, 42–44, 57–60, 83, 92, 104–105, 119; attendance at theatrical productions, 143, 146–148, 150, 152, 154–158, 166–167, 188, 226n8; death of, 116, 166–167, 169, 174. *See also* "ballets" for the Russian court: sources describing
Alleyn, Edward, 214–215, 216–217, 231n85
Amsterdam, 74, 83, 115, 147; performance venues, 221, 239, 243. *See also* Great Embassy; operas and staged performances associated with Russian diplomats; Peter the Great
Andrusovo, Treaty of, 86, 88, 89, 92
Anglesi, Domenico, 78, 99n85
animals as entertainment and gifts, 35–36, 84, 101n104, 101n111, 107–108, 110, 113, 152, 154
Arkhangel'sk, 21, 63, 70, 75, 76, 85, 89, 177n5, 185n99
Armano, Giuseppe, 63, 64, 96n25

Avramii (bishop of Suzdal'), 20
Avvakum (archpriest) and Old Believers, 169–170, 171

Baiazet (character in Russian play). *See* Russian court theater, *Tamerlane*
Balatri, Filippo, 74, 240–241
"ballets" for the Russian court: calendrical associations, 107–108, 113, 119 (*see also* Russian court theater, calendrical associations); dance and music, 106–107, 109, 112, 113, 115, 128, 144; February 1672 production, 105, 107–117, 120–123, 128, 144, 165, 169; May 1672 production, 113–115, 120–122, 144, 146; productions after formation of court theater, 149, 150, 152, 155–158, 171–172; sources describing, 106–115, *111*, 119–123 (*see also* Greflinger, Georg; Rautenfels, Jacob); venue, 109–110, 114, 121–122, 135n12, 149
"ballets" for the Russian court, characters and participants: Foreign Quarter residents, 105, 115–117, 121, 123 (*see also* "ballets" for the Russian court: sources describing); Hasenkroeg, Dirck, 110, 115, 118, 120, 136nn24–25, 224; Orpheus, *see* mythological characters in Russian "ballets" and theater; Pickleherring, *see* Pickleherring: in "ballets" for the Russian court

INDEX

Bargrave, Robert, 72, 74, 98n55, 234n109
Baudartius, Willem, 203, 207, 211
Bayezid I (Ottoman sultan), 188, 194, *195*, 206, 221, 222
Berewout, I. L., 204, 228n35
Bergholz, Friedrich Wilhelm von, 245, 258n51
biblical sources, 11–12, 13, 14, 45, 47n4, 55n119, 74, 143, 175. *See also* liturgical drama; Russian court theater, plays and themes
Bidloo, Nicolaas, 245, 246, 258n52
Bogoiavlenskii, S. K., 104, 160, 167, 179n36, 184n92, 185n101, 249
Boisrobert, F., 90
Boreel, Jacob, 207
Bosman, Anston, 7–8, 118, 119, 212, 218, 254
Bottoni, H. F. von, 161, 163–164
Brandenburg, 22, 124, 156
brass and wind instruments (excluding theater, Russia and abroad), 27, 32, 77, 82, 84; association with *skomorokhi*, 52n83, 56n125; *surny* (shawms), 25, 48n22, 181n55; *truby* (horns, trumpets, cornetts) and performers, 25–27, 37, 48n22, 75, 77, 181n55. *See also* fanfare and processional music; Russian court theater, participants: instrumentalists and dancers; weddings: Russian
Browne, Robert, 119, 215–216, 220
Bulgakov, A. S., 193, 208–214
Bushkovitch, Paul, 8, 167, 252–253

Carlisle. *See* Charles Howard, First Earl of Carlisle
Carnival, 70–71, 73–74, 77–78, 119, 240. *See also* "ballets" for the Russian court: calendrical associations; Russian court theater, calendrical associations
Catheux, Sieur de, 90–91
Cavalli, Francesco, 71, 80, 97n48
chanceries and departments: Ambassadorial Chancery, 4, 24, 92, 132, 160, 161, 162, 163, 168, 207, 238; Apothecary Chancery, 154, 168 (*see also* Russian court theater: venues); Armory, 37, 60; Chancery of the Great Court, 36, 44–45; Galitskaia Department, 160, 162; Privy Chancery, 99n69; Siberian Chancery, 151, 154, 168; Smolensk Chancery, 161; Tsaritsa's Craftsmen Chancery, 36, 37; Vladimirskaia Department, 142, 152, 160, 168. *See also Poteshnaia palata*
Charles Howard, First Earl of Carlisle, 84–86, 88, 102n114
Charles II (king of England), 83
Chemodanov, I. I., 61–63, *62*, 95n14; in Florence, 63–70, 73, 78, 82, 95n20, 96n34; in Venice, 70–75, 82
Christian IV (king of Denmark), 5
chronicles (Russian), 193–194, *195*, 198–199, 212
clocks and clockmakers, 38, 39–40, 41, 53n88, 53nn90–91, 237
Cohn, Albert, 8, 13
Collins, Samuel, 59
commedia dell'arte, 90–91, 100n87. *See also* Fiorillo commedia troupe; Napolioni, Marco
Copenhagen, 6, 86, 129, 131, 139n60, 140n61, 147, 177n3, 236, 250
Correr, Angelo, 73–74
Cosimo de' Medici (grand duke of Tuscany), 66–67, 68, 116–117, 240. *See also* Florence and Livorno, Russian missions to
Courland, Duchy of, 92–93, 94, 124–126. *See also* Rautenfels, Jacob
Coyett, Balthazar, 138nn46–47, 166–167, 185nn99–100
Cracow, 30–31, 32
Cracraft, James, 13, 259n61

Dance and dancing (abroad, excluding theatrical), 24–25, 30, 31, 51n61, 64–65, 67–68, 76–77, 78, 96n34
Dance and dancing (Russia, excluding theatrical), 24, 30–33, 34, 85. *See also* "ballets" for the Russian court; Russian court theater, participants: instrumentalists and dancers
Dannenfels, Simon, 1–7, *3*, 46, 223, 250
Danzig, 6, 34, 127, 229n46, 242, 245
declamations and recitations, 12, 18n21, 174–175, 186n120. *See also* Simeon Polotskii: declamations and recitations
Dekker, Thomas, 218–220
Denmark, relations with, 5, 55n113, 131, 147. *See also* Copenhagen; Gjøe, Mogens; Waldemar Christian

Denmark, Russian missions to, 55n113, 236; Ukraintsev mission, 131, 147
Diletskii, Nikolai, 137n38, 237
diplomatic missions to Russia. *See individual states and cities*
diplomatic reports. *See stateinye spiski; and individual states and cities*
Dmitrii (pretender, tsar), 29, 30–33
Dolgorukii, Iakov, 236
domra and *domra* players, 36, 38, 51n73
Dorpat (Tartu), 2, 6
Dresden, 145, 219, 224, 234n112
Drevniaia rossiiskaia vivliofika (Ancient Russian library), 175, 247–249
Du Bec, Jean, 193–209, 211, 253; Dutch translation as source for Russian play, 200–205, 224, 228n30
Dutch Republic, missions to Russia, 207; van Klenk mission, 138nn46–47, 166–167, 185nn99–100
Dutch Republic, Russian missions to, 75, 83, 147, 207–208. *See also* Amsterdam; Great Embassy; Peter the Great
Dutch theatrical companies and traditions, 113, 171, 223. *See also* Fornenbergh, Jan Baptist van; Serwouters, Johann
Du Verdier, Antoine, 204, 205, 211, 228n34, 230n58

Eberschildt, Adolph, 152, 180n43
Elizabeth I (queen of England), 24–25, 26–27, 30
Engelische Comedien und Tragedien, 118, 144, 185n112, 213, 219. *See also* "English" comedians; Pickleherring
Engels, Peter, 93, 103n144, 142, 150, 176n3, 179n31. *See also* Russian court theater, participants: actors and artists
England, missions to Russia, 23–24, 27–28, 48n18, 84–86; Charles Howard, First Earl of Carlisle mission, 84–86, 88, 102n114; Fletcher mission, 35; Horsey mission, 27–28, 29, 32–33, 35, 40, 49nn39–40. *See also* Collins, Samuel; Ridley, Mark
England, Russian missions to, 22, 23–24; Mikulin mission, 21, 26–27, 94n3; Nepea mission, 19, 20, 22–23, 35, 49n38; Pisemskii mission, 24–25, 33; Potemkin mission, 236, 239, 254n4; Prozorovskii mission, 83–84; Vinius mission, 147, 178n24, 207–208. *See also* fanfare and processional music; Great Embassy; Hebdon, John; London, performance venues and ensembles; Peter the Great
"English" comedians: and comic style, 4, 7–8, 117–119, 133, 144, 170–171; and traveling companies on the Continent, 3, 6, 16, 118–119, 170–171, 189, 212–225, 230n64, 250, 253. *See also* intertheater; Pickleherring; *and names of individual acting troupes*
Ermis, 42–43, 45, 46, 54n105, 55n110
Ernst I (duke of Saxe-Gotha), 145, 178n18
Esther. *See* Russian court theater, plays and themes
Evdokiia Streshneva (tsaritsa, second wife of Tsar Mikhail), 38, 42
Evelyn, John, 84, 101n104

Faceted Palace (Granovitaia palata), 38, 52n79
falcons and falconry, 42, 54n100
False Dmitrii. *See* Dmitrii (pretender, tsar)
fanfare and processional music: in diplomatic ceremony abroad, 22–23, 26, 27, 70, 84, 90, 101n104, 102n128, 239; in Russia, 23, 43, 85, 88. *See also* weddings: Russian
Fedor Alekseevich (tsar of Russia), 93, 98n69, 169, 236
Fedor Ivanovich (tsar of Russia), 25, 27, 29, 35
Felipe Prospero (prince, Spain), 79–80, 82
Ferdinand II de' Medici (grand duke of Tuscany), 17, 65–68, 77, 79, 82. *See also* Florence and Livorno, Russian missions to; Florence, performance venues and academies
Ferrara, 49n30, 70
Ferrara-Florence, Council of, 19–20, 47n2
Filimonatus, Justus. *See* Grelle, Laurentius
Fiorillo commedia troupe, 69, 90–91, 97n41
fireworks, 89, 239; in Russia, 107–108, 110, 122, 138n46. *See also* "ballets" for the Russian court: sources describing; Waldemar Christian
Fletcher, Giles, 35, 51n68

Florence and Livorno, Russian missions to, 61–63, 84, 88; Chemodanov mission, 63–70, 66, 73, 78, 82, 95n20, 96n34; Likhachev mission, 17, 76–82, 247 (see also *stateinye spiski*: for Likhachev mission to Florence). *See also* Florence, performance venues and academies; Hebdon, John

Florence, performance venues and academies, 67–70, 77–81, 91, 99n81. *See also* operas and staged performances associated with Russian diplomats

Fomin, Ivan, 76

Foreign Quarter (*Nemetskaia sloboda*, Moscow), 10–11, 16, 141, 145, 171, 175, 200, 207–208, 222, 224, 240–241. *See also* "ballets" for the Russian court, characters and participants; Gregorii, Johann; Russian court theater, participants

Fornenbergh, Jan Baptist van, 6, 222–224, 234n110

France, Russian missions to, 58–59, 65, 69, 89, 147; Potemkin mission, 90–92, 158, 236. *See also* Paris, performance venues and ensembles

Frankfurt, 170, 215–216, 217

Gabel, Frederik, 107
Giovan Carlo (cardinal, Medici prince), 65, 68, 77–78
Gjøe, Mogens, 148, 150, 155, 166–167
Golitsyn, P. A. and family, 74, 240–241
Golitsyn, V. V., 237
Golovin, F. A., 239, 242
Gordon, Patrick, 88
Gransbarra, Urbano, 71, 73
Great Embassy, 11, 238–241, 243, 251. *See also* Peter the Great; *and individual states and cities*
Greflinger, Georg, 108–110, 112, 119, 128, 134n9
Gregorii, Johann, 172, 177n10, 224, 249; and Russian court theater, 123, 141–146, 148, 150, 152–153, 159–160, 168, 191–192
Grelle, Laurentius, 5–6, 10 (as "Filimonatus"), 17n6
Grundel-Helmfelt, Simon, 106–108, 111, 147
Gruneweg, Martin, 34, 51n61
gusli and *gusli* players, 38, 54n98

Gutovskii, Simon, 53n88, 59, 168, 177n5, 180n49, 237. *See also* organs and keyboard instruments; Russian court theater, participants: instrumentalists and dancers

Hamburg, 115, 116, 136n24, 177n3, 222–224. *See also* Greflinger, Georg
Hammond, William, 82, 100n96
Hasenkroeg, Dirck (Dietrich Hasenkrug): and "ballets" for the Russian court, 110, 115, 118, 120, 136nn24–25, 224; and Russian court theater, 128, 142, 149, 156, 165, 168, 177n5
Hebdon, John, 63, 64, 76, 98n65, 101n103; commissions for Russian court, 75, 83, 100n99, 132
Hennings, Jan, 9, 238
Henslowe, Philip, 214, 216–217, 219–220
Hesse, Hermann Dietrich, 156, 182n60
Hjärne, Urban, 223, 233n105
Holy Roman Empire, missions to Russia, 40, 87, 256n37; Bottoni mission, 161, 163–164
Holy Roman Empire, Russian missions to, 27, 50n45, 58–59, 88, 94n4; Golitsyn mission, 74, 240–241; Potemkin mission, 158, 240; Vel'iaminov mission, 25–26; Vlas'ev mission, 25–26, 30. *See also* fanfare and processional music: in diplomatic ceremony abroad; Great Embassy; Kakasch, Stephan; Peter the Great; Vienna
Horn, Bengt, 108, 121
Horsey, Jerome, 27–28, 29, 32–33, 35, 40, 49nn39–40
hymns, Protestant, 14, 162. *See also* intertheater; Luther, Martin and Lutheranism; Russian court theater, plays and themes: Adam and Eve

Innsbruck, 2, 56n123, 234n109
intertheater, 7–8, 11, 13, 118–119, 123, 212, 218, 225, 253; as relating to Russian theatrical productions, 15–16, 105, 118–119, 143, 162, 170, 251. *See also* "English" comedians; Pickleherring
Ioasaf (patriarch), 108–109, 112, 113

Irina Fedorovna (tsaritsa, wife of Tsar Fedor
    Ivanovich), 28
Irina Mikhailovna (daughter of Tsar
    Mikhail Fedorovich), 5
Italian states, missions to Russia.
    See individual cities
Italian states, Russian missions to.
    See Ferrara-Florence, Council of; *and
    individual cities*
Ivan Mikhailovich (tsarevich, brother of
    Tsar Aleksei), 43–44, 46
Ivan III (grand prince of Russia), 20
Ivan IV (the Terrible, tsar of Russia), 22, 27,
    29, 48n18, 50n45
Ivan V (co-tsar, with Peter), 236, 238
Izmailovo, 93, 103n144, 186n120

Jacob (duke of Courland). *See* Courland,
    Duchy of
Janetzky, Christian, 132, 133, 140n65. *See also*
    Paulsen and Velten acting troupe
Johann Georg II (elector, Saxony), 145

Kakasch, Stephan, 29, 37
kant, 14, 162
keyboard instruments. *See* organs and
    keyboard instruments
Kholmogory, 28, 49n42
Kholodov, E. G., 147–148, 182n62
Khovralev, Neudacha, 24–25
Kiev and Kievan Academy, 155, 165
Klenk, Koenraad van, 138nn46–47, 166–167,
    185nn99–100
Koch, Christoff, 106–108, 110, *111*, 113, 116,
    134n3, 147, 156, 164, 182n70, 238
Kollmann, Nancy Shields, 8, 252, 253
Königsberg, 6, 130, 139n59
kontsert. *See* Russian Orthodox church,
    Orthodoxy: singers and sacred singing
Kotoshikhin, Grigorii, 24, 48n21
Krutsevich, Iosif (bishop, archbishop),
    37, 41
Kunst, Johann, 242–245, 249, 251, 257n44
kuranty. *See* news and information
    gathering: *kuranty*

Ladislaw (Władysław) Vasa (king of
    Poland), 44, 55n120
Lefort, Franz, 241, 242, 243

Leopold (Medici prince), 65, 67–68
Leopold I (Holy Roman emperor), 88, 158
Leunclavius (Lewenklaw), Joannes, 203, 211,
    228nn31–32
Likhachev, V. B., 17, 76–82, 247. *See also
    stateinye spiski*: for Likhachev mission to
    Florence
liturgical drama, 11–12, 20, 51n59, 101n112,
    174–175, 181n58, 186n121
Livonia, 1, 115, 156
Livorno. *See* Florence and Livorno, Russian
    missions to
Lodygin, Ivan, 42–44, 45, 46
London, performance venues and
    ensembles, 27, 49n35, 147, 178n24, 236, 239,
    254n4; Rose Theater, 214, 216, 219–220.
    See also Great Embassy; England,
    Russian missions to; operas and staged
    performances associated with Russian
    diplomats; Peter the Great
Longland, Charles, 63–64, 76
Lonicer, Philip, 222, 228n40
Loon, Hans and Melchior, 38–41, 52n79,
    52n84, 54n98. *See also* organs and
    keyboard instruments
Louis XIV (king of France), 89, 236
Luhn. *See* Loon, Hans and Melchior
Luther, Martin and Lutheranism, 143, 145–146,
    152, 162, 177n10, 180n42, 208. *See also*
    Gregorii, Johann; hymns, Protestant;
    intertheater; Rinhuber, Laurentius;
    Russian court theater, plays and themes
L'vov, A. M., 36, 44–45, 55n113, 55n116
Lyseck, Adolphus, 163–164

Machyn, Henry, 22–23
Madrid: theatrical venues and entertainers,
    89–90, 100n93, 102nn123–124
Magliabechi, Antonio, 117, 136n28
Malinovskii, A. F., 249–250, 259n64
Marais (theatrical troupe), 90, 103n139
Mariia Dolgorukova (tsaritsa, first wife of
    Tsar Mikhail), 37
Mariia Miloslavskaia (tsaritsa, first wife of
    Tsar Aleksei), 93. *See also* "ballets" for the
    Russian court: venue; Miloslavskii family
    and residence
Marina Mniszek (tsaritsa, wife of Dmitrii),
    30–33, 40

290   INDEX

Marlowe, Christopher: *Tamburlaine the Great*, 16, 193–194, 209–220, 222, 225, 230n52, 231n73, 231n78, 253. *See also* Admiral's Men; London, performance venues and ensembles: Rose Theater; Russian court theater, *Tamerlane*

Martin, Russell, 252, 253

Martinez, Gabriello, 65, 66

Marvell, Andrew, 84, 102n114

Mary (queen of England), 22–23

masks and masquerade, 31–33, 73–74, 240, 241

maslenitsa (Shrovetide), 70, 108, 119. *See also* "ballets" for the Russian court: calendrical associations; Carnival; Russian court theater, calendrical associations

Massar, Phyllis, 80–82

Matveev, A. S., 11, 92–94, 107, 134n4, 178n21; as "ballet" organizer, 112, 113–114, 116–117, 121, 175; as theatrical organizer, 125–128, 131–132, 141–143, 146–152, 154, 156–158, 160, 164–165, 171, 192; fall of, 167–170. *See also* Aleksei Mikhailovich; Natal'ia Naryshkina

Maximilian II (Holy Roman emperor), 27

Mayerberg, Augustin von, 87

McJannet, Linda, 200–201, 227nn23–24, 229n42

mechanical objects and self-playing instruments, 39–40, 53nn90–91, 75, 82, 83. *See also* clocks and clockmakers; Hebdon, John: commissions for Russian court; organs and keyboard instruments

Medici family. *See* Florence and Livorno, Russian missions to

Menzies, Paul, 145–147, 164

Meshchanskaia Quarter, 151. *See also* Russian court theater, participants: actors and artists

Mexía, Pedro, 203–204, 205, 207

Miege, Guy, 84–86

Mikhail Fedorovich (tsar of Russia), 5, 14–15, 33–34, 37, 40, 252

Mikulin, Grigorii, 21, 26–27, 48n29, 94n3

Miller (Müller), F. I., 247, 248, 249

Miloslavskii family and residence, 93, 109–110, 114, 121–122, 149

Mitau (Jelgava), 92, 126

Molière, 69, 90–91

Molvianinov, Iakov, 44

Morozov, P. O., 20, 170, 186n115, 258n47

Moryson, Fynes, 170, 216, 227n20

musical instruments. *See* "ballets" for the Russian court: dance and music; fanfare and processional music; *Poteshnaia palata*; Russian court theater, participants: instrumentalists and dancers; *skomorokhi*; Time of Troubles; weddings; *and individual instrument families*

mythological characters in Russian "ballets" and theater, 110, 113–114, 119–121, 137n38, 164–166, 184n94, 189; Orpheus, 110, 112–114, 116, 119–120, 123, 137n38, 165, 249. *See also* Simeon Polotskii

Napolioni, Marco, 69, 97n41

Narva, 106, 108, 113, 147

Natal'ia Alekseevna (tsarevna, sister of Peter the Great), 256n34, 258n55

Natal'ia Naryshkina (tsaritsa, second wife of Tsar Aleksei), 93, 104, 107, 116, 134n4, 143, 167. *See also* Aleksei Mikhailovich: attendance at theatrical productions; "ballets" for the Russian court: sources describing

Nemetskaia sloboda (Foreign Quarter). *See* Foreign Quarter (*Nemetskaia sloboda*, Moscow)

Nepea, Osip, 19, 20, 22–23, 35, 48n29, 49n38

news and information gathering, 5, 10, 58, 98n65, 106, 124, 129–130, 139n59; *kuranty* (news summaries), 10, 46, 56n123, 88, 207. *See also* Grelle, Laurentius; Hebdon, John; Koch, Christoff; *stateinye spiski* (diplomatic reports); *and individual diplomatic missions*

Nikon (patriarch), 60

Nordischer Mercurius. *See* Greflinger, Georg

Novgorod, 113, 124, 134n3, 155

Novikov, N. I., 247, 249

Olearius, Adam, 39, 53n95, 84

operas and staged performances associated with Russian diplomats (named works only): *Amphitryon* (Molière, Paris), 90–91; *L'Arsace, fondatore dell' imperio de' Parthi* (Draghi, Vienna), 240; *Artemisia* (Cavalli, Venice), 71, 72, 97n48, 98n55; *Il*

Convitato di pietra (commedia dell'arte performance, Florence, Paris), 68–69, 91; *Les Coups de la fortune* (Boisrobert, performed by Marais troupe, Paris), 90; *The Destruction of Jerusalem* (Crowne, London), 236; *Les Faux Moscovites* (Poisson, Paris), 91–92, 103n136; *Le Fortune di Rodope e Damira* (Ziani, Venice), 71; *Il Fuoco eterno* (Draghi, Vienna), 158; *De Gewaande advocaat* (Peys and de Lacroix, Amsterdam), 239, 255n16; *Giuditta* (opera, Warsaw), 44; *L'Inconnu* (Corneille, Paris), 236; *Ipermestra* (Cavalli, Florence), 80–82, 81, 100n96; *Narciso transformato* (favola pastorale, Warsaw), 45–46; *The Prophetess; or, The History of Dioclesian* (Betterton, London), 239; *The Rival Queens; or, The Death of Alexander the Great* (Lee, London), 239, 243; *La Serva nobile* (Anglesi, Florence), 78, 79; *The Tempest* (Betterton and Shadwell, London), 236; *De Toveryen van Armida* (Peys, Amsterdam), 239. *See also* individual states and cities

Ordin-Nashchokin, Afanasii, 58, 92–94, 103n140

organs and keyboard instruments (in Russia, excluding theater): definitions of (including non-keyboard meaning), 27–29, 36, 39, 49n41, 50n43, 50n46, 51n70, 53n86, 53n91; as diplomatic gifts, 27–28, 40, 177n5; images of and imagery relating to, 47n4, 49n38, 52n74; organs and organists, 20, 37, 38–42, 47n3, 48n18, 50n45, 52n84, 54n98, 59, 237; ownership of, 29–30, 33, 37, 39, 41, 53n95, 237; at *Poteshnaia palata* and elsewhere, 36–38, 52n79, 181n55; *stramenty/strementy*, 39, 53n85, 53nn87–88; *tsymbaly* and *tsymbaly* players, 29, 36–38, 40–41, 237. *See also* clocks and clockmakers; Gutovskii, Simon; Hasenkroeg, Dirck; Loon, Hans and Melchior; mechanical objects and self-playing instruments; *Poteshnaia palata*; Russian court theater, participants: instrumentalists and dancers

Orpheus. *See* mythological characters in Russian "ballets" and theater

Ottoman Empire, 59, 78, 131–132, 145, 148, 155, 188–189, 207. *See also* Turks, as theme and images

papal cities. *See individual cities*
Parfenov, A. T., 189, 193–196, 198, 205, 209–210, 212, 226n12
Paris, performance venues and ensembles, 69, 90–91, 236. *See also* France, Russian missions to; operas and staged performances associated with Russian diplomats
Paulsen and Velten acting troupe, 128–132, 130, 133, 139n56, 139n58, 140n61, 141, 147, 224, 243–245, 249, 250
Paulsen, Carl and Anna. *See* Paulsen and Velten acting troupe
percussion instruments, 43–44, 181n55. *See also* fanfare and processional music, weddings
periodization of Russian history, 8, 252
Perondinus, Petrus, 205, 206, 212, 228n40
Persia, 29, 35, 177n5, 226n5, 229n50
Peter the Great (tsar of Russia), 8, 11, 16, 236, 237, 238–243, 245, 251. *See also* Great Embassy; operas and staged performances associated with Russian diplomats; *and individual states and cities*
Philip IV (king of Spain), 89
Pickleherring, 16, 132, 133, 170, 244; in "ballets" for the Russian court, 108–110, 113–114, 117–119, 120–121, 142; in *Tamerlane*, 190, 208–209. *See also* "English" comedians; intertheater; Russian public theaters (early eighteenth century), repertoire: Pickleherring theme
Pisemskii, Fedor, 24–25, 26, 33, 48n29
Play of the Furnace (*Peshchnoe deistvo*). *See* liturgical drama
Poisson, Raymond, 91–92
Poland-Lithuania, missions to Russia, 53n90, 86–88
Poland-Lithuania, relations with, 58, 86, 92. *See also* Andrusovo, Treaty of
Poland-Lithuania, Russian missions to, 62; L'vov mission, 44–45, 55n116; Proestev mission, 44–46; Vlas'ev mission, 30–33, 40. *See also* Warsaw

Polotsk, 58, 59–60, 95n12
Poroshin, F. F., 58
Posnikov, A. 61, 63, 65, 68
Posol'skii prikaz. *See* chanceries and departments: Ambassadorial Chancery
postal networks. *See* news and information gathering
Potemkin, P. I., 88–92, 102n122, 158, 236, 239, 240, 254n4
Poteshnaia palata (Entertainment Hall), 34–37, 181n55, 252; entertainers and employees associated with, 36–37, 38, 40–41, 44; other entertainment venues, 35, 37, 38, 44, 55n111. *See also* organs and keyboard instruments; Russian court entertainment and entertainers
poteshnik (entertainer), 5, 37, 38, 42, 54n98. *See also* Russian court entertainment and entertainers
Proestev, S. M., 44–46
Proskurovskii, Iurii, 37, 38, 41
Prozorovskii, P., 83–84
Pskov, 1–6, 124–127, 134n3

Radziwiłł, Albrycht Stanisław, 44, 55n116, 55n121
Rautenfels, Jacob, 9, 52n79, 66–67, 134n2, 136nn28–30, 242, 249, 251, 259n64, 260n67; and "ballets" and theater for Russian court, 106–107, 112–113, 116–117, 122, 171
recitations. *See* declamations and recitations; Simeon Polotskii
Repskii, Vasilii, 93–94, 142, 160, 168, 187n127
Reutenfels, Jacob. *See* Rautenfels, Jacob
Reval (Tallinn), 2, 6, 106, 138n46
Riccoboni, Louis, 171, 223
Ridley, Mark, 28–29
Riga, 5, 6–7, 86, 124–126, 128–132, 139n58, 140n61, 140n63, 224, 234n110
Rinhuber, Laurentius, 144–146, 160, 161, 163, 172, 178n11, 178n16, 178n20, 183n78
Robinet, Charles, 91–92, 103n139
Roizman, L. I., 39, 49n41, 51n64, 53n88, 177n5
Romanov, N. I., 39, 40, 41, 53n95, 168
Rome, Russian missions to, 20, 49n30, 145–147, 178n20

ropewalkers, 2, 4, 43–44, 54n105. *See also* Dannenfels, Simon; Russian court entertainment and entertainers
Rudolph II (Holy Roman emperor), 25, 29, 40
Rumiantsev, S., 89, 90
Russia, cultural influences on: from Belarus and Ukraine, 11–13, 93 (*see also* Simeon Polotskii); from northern Europe, 10–11, 93, 104–105, 170, 248–249, 251–253, 259n61. *See also* "ballets" for the Russian court; Russian court theater, plays and themes; Russian court theater, *Tamerlane*
Russian court entertainment and entertainers (excluding music), 35–36, 42–43, 46, 51n68, 65, 123–124, 163–164, 167, 181n55, 185n99; concept of privacy, 28, 30–31, 33, 36, 49n40, 105; for royal children, 39, 42, 43–44, 53n91, 59. *See also Poteshnaia palata; and under individual instrument families*
Russian court theater, antecedents, 11–12, 18n21, 83, 105; audience formation, 11–12, 123–124, 176. *See also* "ballets" for the Russian court; declamations and recitations; liturgical drama; Simeon Polotskii
Russian court theater, calendrical associations, 150, 153, 156, 157, 159, 165, 181n58. *See also* "ballets" for the Russian court: calendrical associations
Russian court theater, participants: actors and artists, 141–146, 148–152, 154–157, 159–166, 171, 181n52, 183n79, 191–193, 251 (*see also* Engels, Peter; Staden, Nicolaus von); Gregorii, Johann, 141–146, 148, 150, 152–153, 159–160, 168, 191–192; Hasenkroeg, Dirck, 128, 142, 149, 156, 165, 168, 177n5; instrumentalists and dancers, 59, 125–128, 131, 142, 146–147, 149–151, 154–159, 164, 168, 171, 174, 178n12, 192 (*see also* Gutovskii, Simon; Repskii, Vasilii); languages associated with plays, performances, 143–144, 145–146, 152, 177n10; teachers and organizers, 148, 152, 163, 165, 171, 174, 179n31, 180n46, 191–192 (*see also* Matveev, A. S.: as theatrical organizer; Rinhuber, Laurentius; Staden,

INDEX

Nicolaus von). *See also* chanceries and departments; Foreign Quarter (*Nemetskaia sloboda*, Moscow)
Russian court theater, plays and themes (excluding *Tamerlane*): Adam and Eve, 160, 162–163, 169, 174, 237; *Artakserksovo deistvo* (The Play of Ahasuerus, also as Esther), 106, 116, 142–150, 152, 155–157, 159–161, 170, 172–173, 177n11, 188, 244; Bacchus and Venus, 164–167, 174, 188; David and Goliath, 164–167, 174; Esther, see *Artakserksovo deistvo*; Joseph, 160, 161–162, 174, 193, 237; Judith, 151–157, 159, 161, 165, 170, 172–176, 180n51, 181n52, 186nn114–115, 191, 208, 248; St. George (Georgii, Eorgii), 159, 161–162, 166, 193; Tobit, 151–153, 155, 160, 172, 174. *See also* mythological characters in Russian "ballets" and theater
Russian court theater, *Tamerlane*, 16, 151, 159, 161, 188–193, 226n8; comic characters, 170, 172–174, 189–190, 208–209; contexts in Western theatrical settings, 218–225, 253 (*see also* Marlowe, Christopher); literary sources, 193–209, 211, 212, 224; musical elements, 189–190, 208, 210–211, 213. *See also* Russian court theater, participants; Russian court theater, venues
Russian court theater, venues: Apothecary (*Apteka*), 148–150, 153–154, 159, 168; Posol'skii dvor, 94, 160–161, 165, 193; Preobrazhenskoe selo, 141–142, 146, 147–151, 152, 154–160, 163, 247, 249. *See also* "ballets" for the Russian court: venue; Russian public theaters (early eighteenth century): venues
Russian Orthodox church, Orthodoxy, 5, 20, 24, 31, 56n125, 60, 73–74, 123, 138n47, 146, 163; singers and sacred singing, 13, 14, 23–24, 27, 37, 43, 48n18, 60, 65, 67 (see also *kant*). *See also* Avvakum (archpriest) and Old Believers; dance and dancing (Russia, excluding theatrical); masks and masquerade; *skomorokhi*
Russian public theaters (early eighteenth century), 16–17, 235, 241–247, 246; as stimulus for early research, 16–17, 247–250 (see also *Drevniaia rossiiskaia vivliofika*);

venues, 241–247, 256n37, 259n61. *See also* Kunst, Johann
Russian public theaters (early eighteenth century), repertoire, 242; Alexander theme, 243–244, 245, 257n39; comic elements, 244, 257n44; Pickleherring theme, 244, 257n45; Tamerlane theme, 244–247, 257n46, 258n47
Russian theatrical terminology. *See* theatrical terminology (Russian sources, Russian productions)

Sauvage, Jean, 28–29, 48n22, 50n42
Savin, A. G., 22
self-playing instruments. *See* mechanical objects and self-playing instruments
Serristori, Antonio, 61, 63–65, 67
Serwouters, Johann: *Den grooten Tamerlan*, 220–223, 221, 224, 225, 233n102, 245, 258n47
Shakespeare, William, 26, 186n116, 216, 218, 236
Shevrigin, Istoma, 49n30
Sigismund III Vasa (king of Poland), 31, 32
Simeon Polotskii, 12, 14, 93, 119, 143, 169, 184n94; declamations and recitations, 12, 60, 105, 123, 138n48, 176; plays, 12, 174–176, 187n127, 237–238, 248–249, 248, 259n60, 259n62, 260n70. *See also* declamations and recitations
singing, secular (Russian court), 13–14, 35, 123. *See also* "ballets" for the Russian court: dance and music; Russian court theater, plays and themes; Russian court theater, *Tamerlane*
skomorokhi (secular itinerant entertainers), 14, 31, 32–33, 35, 38, 43, 51n64, 52n83, 56n125
Smolensk, 58, 59, 95n6, 127, 165
Sofiia Alekseevna (tsarevna, regent), 237, 238, 258n55
Spafarii, Nikolai (Nicolae Milescu), 119, 137n38
Spain, Russian missions to, 147, 236; Potemkin mission, 88–90, 102n122, 236
Sparwenfeld, J. G., 182n72, 187n123, 237–238, 251, 259n60
Splawski, Johann, 241–242

Staden, Nicolaus von, 92–93, 145, 149, 249; theatrical recruiting trips, 114, 124–132, 130, 139n52, 140n63, 141–143, 224, 242

Stählin, Jacob von, 245–247, 249, 258nn54–55

stateinye spiski (diplomatic reports), 9, 20–21, 24, 63–64, 65–66, 74–75, 91, 98n69, 158, 238; for Likhachev mission to Florence, 76, 95n20, 98n68, 258n57, 259n58. See also individual states and cities

Stockholm, 2, 6, 7, 86, 106, 113, 126–127

storytellers, 35, 51n73

stringed instruments (in Russia, excluding theater), 32, 38, 85–86. See also *domra* and *domra* players; *gusli* and *gusli* players

Surgical School (Moscow), 245–247

Sweden, relations with, 9, 58, 92, 105, 106, 152. See also "ballets" for the Russian court: sources describing; Grundel-Helmfelt, Simon; Koch, Christoff; Sparwenfeld, J. G.

Tallinn. See Reval

Tamburlaine the Great. See Marlowe, Christopher; Russian court theater, *Tamerlane*

Tamerlane (historical figure), 188; images of in West, 189, 194–196, 200, 204–205, 206, 221, 222, 225. See also chronicles (Russian)

Tamerlane (Russian court play). See Russian court theater, *Tamerlane*

Tamerlane (theatrical subject). See "English" comedians: and traveling companies on the Continent; Marlowe, Christopher; Russian court theater, *Tamerlane*; Russian public theaters (early eighteenth century), repertoire: Tamerlane theme; Serwouters, Johann

Tartu. See Dorpat

Tatishchev, Mikhail, 29, 33, 37, 50n46

Theater on Red Square (Moscow). See Russian public theaters (early eighteenth century): venues

theatrical terminology (Russian sources, Russian productions): *balet/balety*, 56n123, 135n19, 149, 152; *komediia*, 45–46, 56n123, 75, 79, 83, 101n102, 136n22, 143, 158, 169, 177n6; *perspektivy*, 93, 103n144, 120, 142, 150, 239. See also "ballets" for the Russian court: sources describing; Engels, Peter

Thirty Years' War, 6

Tietz, Friedrich, 249–250, 260n67

tightrope and tightrope walkers. See ropewalkers

Time of Troubles, 29–33

Titov, Vasilii, 14

Tolstoi, Petr, 74, 240

Topolski, Jerzy, 8

traveling theatrical companies. See "English" comedians: and traveling companies on the Continent; *and names of individual acting troupes*

Trondheim vocabulary, 39, 48n22, 53n86

Trubetskoi, I. P., 155, 158, 181n54

tsymbaly. See organs and keyboard instruments

Turks, as theme and images, 16, 58, 64, 78, 99n84. See also Gjøe, Mogens; Ottoman Empire; Staden, Nicolaus von: theatrical recruiting trips; Ukraintsev, E. I.; Vinius, A. A.

Ukraintsev, E. I., 131–132, 147, 229n47

Ushakov, Simon, 12–13, 14, 18n24

Veiger, Matvei, 1, 5

Vel'iaminov, M. I., 25–26

Velten, Johannes. See Paulsen and Velten acting troupe

Venetian Republic, missions to Russia, 59; Vimina, Alberto, 59, 61, 95n6

Venetian Republic, Russian missions to, 20, 61–63, 70–75, 84, 88, 145, 240; Chemodanov mission, 70–75, 82, 95n20. See also Hebdon, John; Tolstoi, Petr

Venice, performance venues, 70–72, 73. See also operas and staged performances associated with Russian diplomats

veselyi (merrymaker). See *poteshnik*

Vicenza: Teatro Olimpico, 44

Vienna, 58–59, 88, 91, 146, 158, 240–241. See also Balatri, Filippo; Great Embassy; Holy Roman Empire, Russian missions to; operas and staged performances associated with Russian diplomats; Peter the Great

Vilnius. See Wilno

Vimina, Alberto, 59, 61, 70, 95n6

Vinhagen, Philip, 113

Vinius, A. A., 207–208, 229n43, 229n46; in England, 147, 178n24, 207–208; in France and Spain, 147

Vlas'ev, A. I., 25–26, 30–33, 40, 50n48, 50n56

Voin-Brant, Iurii, 42–43

Vologda, 85–86, 101n112, 186n121

Waldemar Christian (son of King Christian IV), 5–6, 46, 56n125

Warsaw, 44–46; Royal Theater, 44, 55n120. *See also* operas and staged performances associated with Russian diplomats

weddings, 6, 30–33, 194–196; Russian, 31, 37–38, 41. *See also* Waldemar Christian

West, William, 7, 61

Wilno, 58, 59, 64, 67, 116

wind instruments. *See* brass and wind instruments

Witsen, Nicolaas, 207, 229n44

Zaval'skii, Fedor, 41, 52n83, 54n97

Zheliabuzhskii, I. A., 84, 88

Zoe (Sofiia) Paleologue (wife of Ivan III), 20

CLAUDIA JENSEN is Affiliate Instructor at the Department of Slavic Languages and Literatures, University of Washington. She is author of *Musical Cultures in Seventeenth-Century Russia* (2009) and editor (with Miloš Velimirović) of Nikolai Findeizen's *History of Music in Russia from Antiquity to 1800*, volumes 1 and 2 (2008).

INGRID MAIER is Professor Emerita of Russian at the Department of Modern Languages, Uppsala University. She has published several monographs on modern and historical Russian linguistics, Russian cultural history, and Russian translations of seventeenth-century newspapers, including editions of these translations (*Vesti-Kuranty*).

STEPAN SHAMIN is Senior Researcher at the Institute of Russian History, Russian Academy of Sciences. He is author (in Russian) of *Foreign "Pamphlets" and "Curiosities" in Russia from the 16th to the Beginning of the 18th Centuries* (2020) and *Seventeenth-Century Kuranty* (2011).

DANIEL C. WAUGH is Professor Emeritus of History, International Studies, and Slavic Languages and Literatures at the University of Washington. He is author of *The Great Turkes Defiance* (1978) and (in Russian) *History of a Book: Viatka and "Non-modernity" in Russian Culture in the Era of Peter the Great* (2003).

www.ingramcontent.com/pod-product-compliance
Lightning Source LLC
Chambersburg PA
CBHW030118240426
43673CB00041B/1322